THE TRIALS OF
MADAME RESTELL

ALSO BY NICHOLAS L. SYRETT

An Open Secret: The Family Story of Robert and John Gregg Allerton
American Child Bride: A History of Minors and Marriage in the United States
The Company He Keeps: A History of White College Fraternities
Age in America: The Colonial Era to the Present (co-editor)

THE TRIALS
OF MADAME
RESTELL

*Nineteenth-Century America's
Most Infamous Female Physician
and the Campaign to Make
Abortion a Crime*

NICHOLAS L. SYRETT

THE
NEW
PRESS

NEW YORK
LONDON

© 2023 by Nicholas L. Syrett

Requests for permission to reproduce selections from this book should be made through our
website: https://thenewpress.com/contact.

Published in the United States by The New Press, New York, 2023
Distributed by Two Rivers Distribution

ISBN 978-1-62097-745-3 (hc)
ISBN 978-1-62097-809-2 (ebook)
CIP data is available

The New Press publishes books that promote and enrich public discussion and understanding of the issues vital to our
democracy and to a more equitable world. These books are made possible by the enthusiasm of our readers; the support of
a committed group of donors, large and small; the collaboration of our many partners in the independent media and the
not-for-profit sector; booksellers, who often hand-sell New Press books; librarians; and above all by our authors.

www.thenewpress.com

Composition by Westchester Publishing Services
This book was set in Garamond Premier Pro and Trajon Pro

Printed in the United States of America

10 9 8 7 6 5 4 3 2 1

To Angela and Tim, Alex and Zach

*and to all those working
to keep abortion legal and accessible*

CONTENTS

SPRING ST.

BROOME ST.

ELIZABETH ST.

BROOME ST.

❻

BOWERY

CANAL ST.

CANAL ST.

BAXTER ST.

WEST ST.

WASHINGTON ST.

GREENWICH ST.

HUDSON ST.

❺

W. BROADWAY

CHRUCH ST.

BROADWAY

CENTRE ST.

❼

BAYARD ST.

HENRY ST.

MADISON ST.

FRANKLIN ST.

OLIVER ST.

❹

❷ CHAMBERS ST.

THE
PARK

PARK ROW

Hudson River

BARCLAY ST.

FULTON ST.

NASSAU ST.

LIBERTY ST.

PEARL ST.

SOUTH ST.

East River

❶

RECTOR ST.

WALL ST.

MORRIS ST.

BROAD ST.

WHITEHALL ST.

BATTERY PL.

MADAME
RESTELL'S
NEW YORK

THE BATTERY

❶ MADAME RESTELL'S FIRST HOME AND
OFFICE, 148 GREENWICH STREET

❷ MADAME RESTELL'S SECOND HOME
AND OFFICE, 162 CHAMBERS STREET

❸ MADAME RESTELL'S THIRD HOME AND
OFFICE, 657 FIFTH AVENUE

❹ MRS. BIRD'S HOME AND OFFICE, 18
OLIVER STREET

❺ MADAME COSTELLO'S HOME AND
OFFICE, 34 LISPENARD STREET

❻ HOME OF ANN MARIA PURDY, 341
BROOME STREET

❼ THE TOMBS, 101 CENTRE STREET

55TH ST.

53RD ST.

5TH AVE.

❸

PARK AVE

52ND ST.

50TH ST.

Map by Elisabeth McCalden.

THE TRIALS OF
MADAME RESTELL

INTRODUCTION

The *New York Express* told the story this way: In the middle of March in 1855, a forty-three-year-old English immigrant named Ann Trow Lohman, a resident of Lower Manhattan, set out on an errand. Lohman had a large order of linens that she needed to be repaired. She took her carriage, or perhaps an omnibus, up Broadway to the headquarters of the Shirt-Sewers' and Seamstresses' Union, located at 1 Astor Place, about one and a half miles north of Lohman's sizable residence at 162 Chambers Street.[1]

Later that week, when the Shirt-Sewers' and Seamstresses' Union delivery girl returned part of Lohman's order to her home, she was surprised to see the name "Madame Restell" on the door. That was not the name on the order. This name she knew, for it was notorious throughout New York and indeed the better part of the United States. Madame Restell was no ordinary client; she was the "female abortionist," a "professor of infanticide," a "child murderess," the "wretched creature who builds her fortune upon the misfortunes of her sex, caring no more for their sufferings of mind or body than does the butcher for the lives of the animals which it is his business to take." Or at least that's how newspapermen described her. It would have been difficult to live in New York City in the year 1855 and not be aware of Madame Restell, who had been advertising her services in newspapers there and elsewhere since 1839. By 1855, she had been arrested multiple times, tried twice, and already spent a year as a prisoner on Blackwell's Island (now

Roosevelt Island). Publishers released cheap transcripts for sale on the city streets in the wake of these trials. Even when her own advertisements did not appear in the papers, her name was invoked as the symbol of abortion in antebellum New York; "Restellism" was by that point a synonym for the termination of a pregnancy.[2]

Rushing back uptown, the delivery girl reported to her supervisor just whose linens the Union of Seamstresses had been mending. After consultation, the board of managers "bundled up her linen, and promptly returned it to her," along with a note, which explained that "although in need of work, they should never be poor enough to accept patronage from a woman of her character." It is unlikely that the women employed at the Shirt-Sewers' and Seamstresses' Union—that is, the actual seamstresses—were ever consulted before Lohman's business was refused. The ladies who sat on the board of managers prided themselves on their reputation as upstanding members of society. This was part of the reason they served, voluntarily, on the board of this charity in the first place. They were in a position to refuse good work in the name of virtue; not so the women who actually worked, day in and day out, at the union, assembling and repairing the clothing of New Yorkers as well as of the garment manufacturers who profited from their labor.[3]

The union was essentially a cooperative of, at any given time, between seventy and one hundred seamstresses, who worked out of "a spacious and comfortable work-room," according to the *New York Times*. Run by a board of lady managers, the union had been established to provide work for the "suffering needle-women of our City," "many of whom are vainly endeavoring to support life from a pittance of $2 a week." Patrons brought their linens to the union for construction or repair, and the women who worked there could be ensured a decent wage. In an industry where women might spend much of their days seeking out work, moving from sweatshop to factory trying to sell their labor, the union was designed to provide steady employment.[4]

The Friday of the following week, March 16, the *New York Express* published a short article recounting the entire incident under the title "Madame Restell Repudiated." Compared with the coverage Restell had already garnered in the papers of New York, the article, which was only thirteen lines long, was insignificant. But that the paper had chosen to print it at all signals that its editors found the incident noteworthy. The *New York Tribune* thought so as well, reprinting the article on the same day, as did other papers in Upstate New York. This reporting led to coverage in the *New York Atlas* two days later, wherein the editor claimed it was "in bad taste, to repudiate the small charity which Madame Restell, in all seeming honesty, made."[5]

The *Atlas* also reprinted Madame Restell's own response to the original story, which she claimed was "false in every particular." She clarified that no "assumed name" was given, rather "the work given to them [the Union] was for the person whose name was given," that is, Ann Lohman, her legal name. She explained further that no large order was placed last week, rather, "the women of the 'Union' had been working for [her] for the last six months, and the last work sent was in their possession for at least six weeks." She claimed that there was no note refusing her business and that no sign announced her name at 162 Chambers Street: "There is not now, and never was Madame Restell's name, either on the door, or anywhere else in the mansion." She told the story from her perspective: she had long taken her sewing to the Shirt-Sewers' and Seamstresses' Union "as a matter of charity and benevolence to extend them a helping hand." On this particular occasion, she explained, she had delivered some sewing to the union on behalf of "a lady in the country," "believing, that in thus contributing to give them employment, [she] was committing no grievous wrong, but assisting them in the only way they deserved assistance, viz: by furnishing them with work."[6]

Because, in some way or another, the board of managers of the Shirt-Sewers' Union had indeed divulged this story to the press, even if not in quite the fashion the newspaper reported, Restell then excoriated both the union and the *Express*. She asked rhetorically if it was "an offense to help the needy who loudly call for help?" She criticized the "women who reap the fruits of the hard earnings of the poor sewing girls in their

PORTRAIT OF MADAME RESTELL,
[TAKEN BY STRYPE, THE ARTIST.]

This drawing of Madame Restell by Frederick C. Strype dates from 1847, eight years prior to the incident with the Shirt-Sewers' and Seamstresses' Union, and is a relatively sympathetic depiction of her. Reprinted from the *Wonderful Trial of Madame Restell*, November 16, 1847.

employ," accusing the lady managers of profiting from the labor of the seamstresses. She attacked the lady managers for revealing her name in the first place: "They could not submit to hide their light or their super-lative virtue under a bushel. They must proclaim both the one and the other in the market places and in the highways. They must *advertise* their excessive purity in the newspapers." She accused the union of using her name to drum up business, claiming that any article about her would serve as advertisement for "their shirt concern." Near the end of her dia-tribe, Restell made a series of suggestions: Perhaps it would not be amiss for them to "notify the public" by a placard or a sign "that all persons bringing shirts to be made are required to bring reference from the last place where they had shirts made." And "that all such persons applying to have shirts made or mended, must be church members of six or seven years' standing," or to post up "moral shirts made here." With that, she signed off.[7]

The incident was typical. Newspapers regularly reported on Restell, and the coverage ranged from the newsworthy to the mundane. Only a year later, the *New York Police Gazette* ran a story reporting on the fact that Madame Restell and her husband did not have any friends: "When they drive through Broadway they are shunned by the crowd, like a pair of lepers. They are as isolated in a city of three quarters of a million of inhabitants as they would be on the most desolate spot on God's earth." This story was reprinted as far away as Wheeling, West Virginia, and Milwaukee, Wisconsin, a testament to Restell's national fame.[8] While Restell could not possibly keep up with this much coverage, on many occasions she took it on herself to write back to newspapers to set the record straight. She was unafraid to publicly assert her right to guard her reputation and to operate her business in New York. That alone upset many people.

For some New Yorkers, Madame Restell was emblematic of all that was wrong with the growing city, and by extension with a changing sexual and moral culture in the United States writ large. Her sins were legion: by terminating *or* delivering the pregnancies of single women, she contributed to immorality because she helped those women—and their seducers—hide the fruits of their sins. When she secretly found new homes for their illegitimate children, she helped hide the shame that the sinners should rightfully have been bearing. She terminated the pregnancies of white, middle-class, married women at a moment when newly arrived immigrants had large families, which some nativists feared was the end of American civilization as they knew it. She called herself a "female physician," but she had no medical degree and no formal training; the growing number of educated MDs wanted her out of business. She was a successful businesswoman when business was meant to be a man's domain. She had a husband, but his own occupation was largely eclipsed by her fame, almost entirely inverting what was seen as the proper gendered order of a marriage. On top of all this, her profits were sizable, and she was not afraid to show them off. She dressed in fine clothing, paraded about town in a carriage pulled by matching horses, and lived in a large home—indeed, she would soon move to an enormous mansion on Fifth Avenue, which her detractors would refer to as a "palace of death."

All of this was true.

Also true was that she could not have had this success without skill and demand for her services. No client ever died in her care, which is not something many other female—or male—physicians could say. And despite the clamor of voices who decried her practice, a stream of clients—eventually a river—quietly and steadily came to her door. The voices speaking out against her were loud and plentiful; few and far between were those who spoke in her defense. So she did it herself.

Madame Restell, the pseudonym of Ann Trow Summers Lohman, was in business in New York City from 1839 to 1878. She ran what was called a lying-in hospital, a place where women could stay during their pregnancies and be delivered of their babies. She sold contraception to prevent pregnancy, as well as emmenagogues, herbal remedies to restore menstruation. She also terminated pregnancies, either by manually bringing on miscarriage or via an abortifacient, an herbal concoction designed to stimulate labor. It was the abortions that made her famous, though people objected to most of her services at one time or another. While her detractors called her an abortionist, she used the term "female physician," because abortion was not her only skill. She saw to all of women's reproductive needs. She was a female practitioner who saw women patients, like midwives had been doing for centuries.

Restell had the skill, the good fortune, and, paradoxically, the horrible luck to go into business at precisely the moment monumental changes were underway in how Americans lived, loved, and worked. In the mid-nineteenth century, more and more Americans moved to cities. They worked for wages in the open market, they consolidated their finances, and they had smaller families. As a consequence of these changes, American thinking about sex and gender and children also changed, all of which would have an enormous impact on how Americans thought about abortion. Some Americans, mainly women, found abortion newly necessary, while a vocal minority, mostly men, condemned it as child murder. No figures are available, but there is no doubt that during this era the number of women who chose to terminate a pregnancy, sometimes multiple pregnancies, increased dramatically. Large numbers of single and married women began to regulate their reproductive lives by means that earlier generations of women had utilized far less frequently. Abortion was not the only way of doing so—contraception, abstinence, prolonged lactation, and delayed first marriage, not to mention the rise of commercialized sex as an outlet for men, also played a role in the declining birth rate—but abortion was the most controversial and freighted of these changes.

When Restell began practicing in 1839, early-term abortions had been criminalized for only a decade, but the laws were rarely enforced, and the crime was a misdemeanor. In earlier centuries in America, abortion had been largely unregulated, and there is evidence that Indigenous, African American, and Euro-American women were aware of herbal remedies, native to North America, that brought on miscarriage. Over the course of Restell's career, a once unremarkable procedure became increasingly criminalized across the country. By 1872 in New York State, abortion at any stage was a felony, and both the abortion provider and the woman who had undergone the procedure could be charged, though they faced different punishments. Almost anyone who had assisted a woman in obtaining an abortion—via medicine or surgery—was also liable to prosecution. These laws were passed by legislators, urged on by male doctors, to put people like Madame Restell out of business and, at least in the doctors' telling, to protect women. And yet the women kept coming, not just to Restell's office but to the offices of countless other female physicians.

Madame Restell herself was sui generis. No other female physician of her era was so vilified. No other became so wealthy. She became the living symbol of all her contemporaries, who, like her, continued to break the law that was meant to punish them and to regulate women's reproductive autonomy. No one answered back like she did either. In an era when the dialogue about abortion and contraception was so overwhelmingly one sided, so misogynist and condemnatory of women's ability to make choices about their own bodies, Restell was often a lone voice speaking publicly for women. She was self-interested, to be sure—a trait rarely condemned in men—and she could be vague and pedantic in defending her practice, but that was precisely because to be explicit was to admit to breaking the law, which she could not do if she wanted to stay in business.

While Restell was unique, certainly the services she provided were not. Female physicians were in operation throughout the nineteenth century, not just in New York but across the developing nation. And while lawmakers often spoke out about Restell, in particular, the laws they passed targeted specific practices—abortion and contraception—that were administered and sold by thousands of practitioners nationwide and demanded by countless clients. The life of Madame Restell provides a window into the decades-long process whereby American lawmakers—urged on by doctors and so-called vice crusaders—slowly but surely limited American women's bodily autonomy, criminalizing not just the termination of pregnancy but also any attempt to prevent it in the first place via contraception. Restell's life also serves as a prism for understanding the steady decline in respect for women's understanding about their own bodies, as the purview of male doctors slowly but surely usurped a domain that had once been occupied by women and midwives. The eventual downfall of Madame Restell was only the most famous example of sacrifices made in the nineteenth-century quest to purge American culture of sexual sin and to limit the reproductive freedom of American women.

The 1855 incident with the Shirt-Sewers' and Seamstresses' Union, illustrative as it might be of her peculiar notoriety as well as of her character and backbone, was the most minor of distractions in Madame Restell's ascent to a place of prominence in New York's illicit market in reproductive services. In the years that followed, her fame and fortune would only increase, and she would, time and again, outwit the doctors, the lawmakers, the police, and the vice crusaders who saw her as a threat to the morality not just of people in New York City but of those throughout the United States. Until, at last, she no longer could. And at that moment Madame Restell would exit this life in a manner as shocking and as singular as her career itself was. This is her story.

1

ANN TROW SUMMERS LOHMAN

The first advertisement she placed was small and unobtrusive. It appeared in the *New York Sun* in late March of 1839 and was the first instance in which Ann Trow Summers Lohman was transformed into Madame Restell, though in this advertisement she opted for the more unassuming "Mrs. Restell." She addressed married women readers and asked them: "Is it not but too well known that the families of the married often increase beyond the happiness of those who give birth would dictate?" She then described scenarios in which a woman might want to limit her childbearing years. "Is it desirable, then, is it moral for parents to increase their families, regardless of the consequences to themselves, or the well being of their offspring, when a simple, easy, healthy, and certain remedy is within our control?" Clearly Restell thought not. She then announced that she had opened an office "where married females can obtain the desired information" at 160 Greenwich Street, near Cortland. It would be open between the hours of 10:00 a.m. and 9:00 p.m.[1]

Madame Restell was officially in business.

At first Restell was vague about what, precisely, she was selling. Just information? Medicine? Medical services? Over time, it became clear that Restell offered what midwives had offered for centuries. She sold emmenagogues to revive a woman's menstrual flow, which could be disrupted for a variety of reasons, including low body weight, hormonal imbalances, or stress. She delivered babies. She terminated pregnancies, either through medicine (abortifacients) or through manual intervention (by bringing on miscarriages). Sometimes she sold contraceptives. Most of these practices had been uncontroversial—indeed unregulated—in the United States and its earlier colonies. But times were changing. Madame Restell lived and worked in what had become the biggest city in the country, at a time when more and more Americans—including immigrants like herself—were moving to urban areas. She ran her own business, selling goods and services as the economy itself was expanding and as increasing numbers of Americans, especially those in cities, were purchasing what they needed to survive rather than producing it in their own households. All of these factors worked in her favor. More controversial was what she was selling and that she was doing it on an open market out of her home, rather than relying on local networks of families, neighbors, and friends, through which midwives had traditionally found their clients. Madame Restell had melded a traditional woman's role, that of midwife, with the urban market economy at precisely the moment when gender roles and traditional conventions of marriage and sexual propriety were also undergoing seismic shifts, especially in cities like New York. Madame Restell had announced her arrival, but was New York ready for her?

* * * *

Very little in the story of Madame Restell's origins would have suggested a rise to fame as a notorious female physician in New York City, more than three thousand miles and an entire ocean away from the place of her birth. Ann Trow, as she was first named, was born in the village of Painswick in the county of Gloucestershire, in the western part of England, not far from its border with Wales. At the time of her birth on May 5, 1811, Painswick had fewer than five thousand residents and was largely sustained by the cloth weaving trade, which relied on the many streams that flowed through Painswick and the mills built to power the looms that spun wool into textiles. Ann was the daughter of John Trow and his wife, Anne Biddle Trow. She was baptized in the Church of England a month after her birth, on June 9,

1811. Her parents had been married for almost ten years at the time of her birth, and her father is listed in various records as a "labourer," likely in one of the textile mills or perhaps in agriculture. In 1802, both of her parents signed the marriage register with an *X*, meaning they were very likely illiterate.[2]

Ann was her parents' fourth child, after three brothers. Anne Biddle Trow would give birth to five more children, four sons and a daughter, following daughter Ann. All were baptized in the Church of England in their local parish of Stroud. Given the gaps between their births, it is possible that some of Ann's siblings died soon after birth and were not baptized. A family of eleven, the Trows lived in Painswick in a cottage called Combe House.[3]

Like many women of her era, the next time Ann Trow appears in historical records is at the moment of her marriage. On March 26, 1829, Ann Trow married twenty-six-year-old Henry Summers in the village of Wootton Bassett, a little under thirty miles southeast of Painswick, in the county of Wiltshire. How they met is uncertain, though it is clear that Henry, who is listed in some records as a tailor, was himself born and raised in Wootton Bassett. Ann Trow was seventeen years old at the time of her marriage. This was younger than the average age of first marriage for women at the time, but it was perfectly legal and would not have been regarded as especially unusual. Ann and Henry posted banns (announcements of their intent to marry) three Sundays in a row before their marriage. Ann did not give birth until eleven months later, so it does not appear that pregnancy brought them to the altar, but it also cannot be ruled out: an initial pregnancy could have ended in miscarriage.[4]

Ann and Henry Summers remained in Wootton Bassett following their marriage. Their daughter, Caroline Summers, was born there the following year and baptized on February 21, 1830. She would be their only child. The next step in their lives together was both the most consequential and the one for which there is the least documentation: they emigrated from England to the United States. We do not know precisely when they chose to do so, or on which ship they voyaged;

many of these early records were destroyed by fire in the late nineteenth century. It is certain that they had arrived in New York by the late summer of 1831, when they first appear in records there. Sometime in that eighteen-month period they made the choice to leave behind the lives they knew in England in the hopes of a fresh start in the United States. Immigration to the United States in the early part of the nineteenth century was nothing like the deluge it became by the late 1800s. Just over 23,000 people immigrated to the United States in the year 1830, for example. During the whole decade of the 1830s, only about 600,000 people did so. This pales in comparison with the millions who arrived beginning in the 1880s. Most arrivals in this earlier era came from Ireland, Germany, England, and France. English emigrants like the Summerses were essentially economic migrants. They left not because of the religious persecution that had pushed some early English settlers to colonial New England but because they, like many immigrants today, believed they could do better in the United States than they could do at home.[5]

Ann, Henry, and their infant daughter, Caroline, likely embarked on their journey from the Port of Liverpool, which is where most English emigrants departed. The cost of tickets on ships—especially packet ships, which carried both mail and people—remained relatively low during the 1820s and 1830s, which meant that even those who were poor enough to be attracted to economic opportunities in the United States were also able to afford the ticket to get there. While the voyage's price included food, passengers needed to cook it themselves. They were also responsible for bringing their own bedding. If they were sailing in the lower-cost steerage section, which most did, they were crowded in among their fellow passengers. Sanitation on board was often poor, which made the ships dirty and smelly; rats and insects were common. The only entrance to the steerage section on a freighter was through a hole in the deck, which meant there was almost no ventilation. In 1830, when the Summerses likely made their way from England to New York, the sailing time was over two weeks. Many found the voyage monotonous, while others suffered from seasickness and found it quite the opposite. Still others succumbed to diseases like cholera and typhus and died. Ann and Henry Summers made the trip with Caroline, whom Ann had to care for throughout the voyage. The Summerses would have been enormously relieved when they arrived in New York Harbor.[6]

Long before the opening of the immigrant processing stations at Castle Garden (in 1855) and Ellis Island (in 1892), those arriving in New York City from abroad would have disembarked at the lower tip of Manhattan, either on the east side, at what is now South Street Seaport, or on the west side via the Hudson River. Some captains anchored off the coast of Long Island or New Jersey and sent smaller boats with their human cargo to Manhattan. Under the New York State Passenger Act of 1824, each ship captain arriving in New York was required to provide a manifest of his passengers that included their names, ages, prior places of settlement, and occupations. The shippers then had to attest that they would be financially responsible for the cost of an immigrant should he or she fall into sickness or poverty within two years of arrival.[7]

No sooner had immigrants arrived in Lower Manhattan than a series of "runners" boarded the ships trying to convince newly arrived passengers to purchase a steamboat ticket to another destination upstate or farther west or to entrust them with his or her belongings and come with the runner to a boardinghouse located near the seaport. At the time the Summerses arrived in Manhattan, there was very little immigration control, and inspectors were primarily interested in whether passengers were healthy and appeared to be capable of supporting themselves. The modern immigration system of passports and visas as we know it today did not yet exist. Instead, immigration to New York was effectively a municipal affair and was really only for those who arrived by ship. Countless immigrants entered the city and state from other states and from Canada without ever registering. Once the Summerses had arrived, they were able to disembark and, provided they were healthy, they were effectively on their own. There were emigrant aid societies in the city, but most of them were organized around specific nationalities and none catered specifically to the English.[8]

In 1830, New York City had approximately two hundred thousand residents, which made it the largest city in the United States. Of those, just under eighteen thousand were foreign born. The remainder of the residents were native-born people of English, Irish, Dutch, and Huguenot ancestry. A sizable minority of Black New Yorkers—just under fourteen thousand, all of whom were free after 1827—and a small minority of Native peoples lived in the city. New York had achieved its status as the country's largest city in part through the very process that Ann, Henry, and Caroline Summers had recently undertaken themselves: immigration. More immigrants arrived in New York Harbor than at any other port of arrival. New York also dominated the manufacturing economy, meaning that it was a destination not just for immigrants from other countries but, more significantly, for migrants from rural areas of the United States, especially for people who were no longer able to make a living as farmers or in farming families. New Yorkers worked in the shipping, brewing, sugar, publishing, and garment manufacturing trades, among many others. New York also grew when it became a trade destination for importers, especially after the opening of the Erie Canal in 1825, which connected New York with the Great Lakes via the Hudson River.[9]

In 1830, New York effectively meant Manhattan, and really only Lower Manhattan at that. The towns of Brooklyn, Bushwick, and Williamsburg existed independently and were not incorporated into the city of New York until 1898. In 1830, the vast majority of New Yorkers lived below Fourteenth Street, though beginning in the 1820s, some wealthier residents had already begun to move uptown, the domain of the grand estates that Alexis de Tocqueville referred to as "country houses," complete with lawns and orchards, some of which were visible from the East River. Homes like these were the province of only the very wealthiest. The more moderately wealthy left Lower Manhattan for Hudson Square and for newly developed neighborhoods on Bond and Bleecker Streets. Broadway was the commercial hub of the island, home to genteel residences and churches like Trinity and St. Paul's as well as storefronts, hotels, restaurants, and theaters. Pedestrians strolled along the avenue, the high and the low mixing indiscriminately. The occasional pig also joined them. As the city expanded, former private residences along lower Broadway were subdivided into boardinghouses and occupied by clerks and other laborers. As the wealthy moved uptown, Lower Manhattan became even more densely commercialized, and parts of it—especially farther east in the Five Points neighborhood—became poorer, largely home to newly arrived immigrants.[10]

In many Lower Manhattan neighborhoods where laboring people and immigrants lived, workplaces and residences intermingled. Indeed, many people's homes served also as their workplaces. Greenwich Village was home to the building trades, Corlears Hook, located along the East River, to the shipping industry. Five Points was home to any number of businesses, including tailors, breweries, and tobacco manufactories. In poorer neighborhoods, two- and three-story homes that had originally been designed for one family were often packed with multiple families, who sometimes lived crowded together in one room, reliant on chamber pots and sometimes a privy in the backyard. Some of the most crowded of buildings housed more than one hundred people. Many households kept livestock, pigs in particular, that often wandered around the neighborhoods scavenging for food. The poorest of neighborhoods, like Five Points, were squalid with waste, odor, and disease.[11]

When the Summers family first arrived in New York City, it is likely that Henry found work as a tailor, the occupation listed for him at least once in English records. Though the Summerses do not appear in city directories in the 1830s, for which one would have had to pay a fee, one later account has them living on William Street, two blocks east of Broadway. Ann Summers worked as a seamstress, a skill she might have learned from Henry or perhaps from her mother. It was among the very most common occupations for women in New York during this era, and it paid badly. It was the kind of work that could supplement the income for a couple or for parents whose daughter still lived with them. Women, especially those with young children, could usually take in piecework, a form of work where laborers were paid by the piece instead of by the hour. They could do this work at home, which allowed them to manage a household and care for its residents at the same time that they sewed. As a longtime friend of Madame Restell's, named Phoebe Parry, would attest many years later: "She was a Mrs. Somers [then], and she was a seam stress; she worked for a shop in Broadway, making pantaloons; that was her business." Ann Summers may have worked in the shop on Broadway or may have assembled pantaloons for the shop out of her own home. Either way, by combining their earnings, Ann and Henry Summers managed to survive.[12]

This state of affairs, however tenuous, did not last long. On August 1, 1831, Henry Summers died of a bilious fever, a catchall term that referred to any kind of fever thought to originate in disorders related to bile. It is impossible to say with any certainty precisely what caused Henry Summers's death. Certainly disease—typhoid, typhus, malaria, tuberculosis, yellow fever, and outbreaks of cholera—was rampant in the tenements into which immigrants crowded in Lower Manhattan at the time. The underlying cause of his bilious fever could well have been one of those diseases. The record for Henry's death noted that he was twenty-seven years, three months, and twenty-eight days old. The Summerses had not been in New York for even a whole year.[13]

Ann Summers was now the single mother of a daughter who was not yet two years old. Ann had one skill, sewing, but it was unlikely to pay enough to fully support herself and her daughter. Her employment options were relatively limited. The best-paying jobs for a woman at the time were as a domestic servant or as a sex worker. Both were largely unsuitable for a woman with a child. Live-in domestic servants, the most common female occupation at the time, were unmarried women without families of their own to support; most employers would not have welcomed a servant and her infant daughter. There was a thriving sex trade in antebellum New York, both brothels and streetwalkers located in among the wealthiest and the poorest of neighborhoods. Sex work paid, far and away, better than any other occupation available for women at the time, but it could be dangerous and unpleasant work, and Ann was similarly unlikely to find a brothel that would want to take in her child as well as herself, though it was not impossible. The extant evidence suggests that in the interim, Summers continued to support herself as a seamstress.[14]

Observers at the time noted that one of the reasons wages were so low for seamstresses was that there was too much competition, too many women in search of these jobs, which drove wages down. There were also seasonal fluctuations for work—large orders were generally geared toward the winter and summer seasons—that made off-season work harder to find, especially for those women who worked out of their own homes. These women might waste precious time searching for work, time that they could have spent sewing. Women's wages were also lower simply because they were being paid to women, who were assumed to be primarily dependent on men—husbands or fathers—who could support them. Even though many of New York's working women during this period were heads of household, the sole wage earners in their families, employers took advantage of the assumptions about family life to pay women less than men, even when they did similar work. Historian Christine Stansell has estimated that wages for a seamstress in New York between 1820 and 1860 averaged between 75¢ and $1.50 per week, increasing in the later 1850s. That is between $21 and $43 per week in today's dollars. It was for reasons like these that wealthy and charitable ladies would eventually establish the Shirt-Sewers' and Seamstresses' Union, to which Ann Lohman would later take her linens.[15]

To care for her infant daughter and support both of them, Ann Summers either worked from home by taking in piecework or found a neighbor or friend with whom she could leave Caroline during the day, perhaps in exchange for a portion of her wages. Neighborhood networks in early New York could be dense with camaraderie, as well as with conflict. In the crowded tenements in which New York's immigrant women made their homes, there was little sense of privacy; neighbors were perpetually in one another's business. While this living on top of one another often led to arguments, sometimes even physical fights, many women also came to the aid of one another. Though Summers left behind no trace of what her years of single motherhood were like, it is possible that those around her aided the young widow, not yet twenty years old and newly arrived from England.[16]

Summers remained single for two years. On September 30, 1833, the *New York Spectator* printed a tiny notice of her remarriage: "On Sunday, 11th ult., by the Rev. Mr. Geissenhainer, Jun., CHARLES LOHMAN, of St. Petersburg, Russia, to ANN SUMMERS, of Bristol, England." While the paper was incorrect about Summers's place of birth, Bristol was not too far from Painswick, and the paper was correct in other details of the announcement. Reverend Joseph Geissenhainer Jr. was the assistant pastor of St. Matthew's Lutheran Church from 1827 to 1840 and married countless immigrant couples, primarily those from Germany, who made up the bulk of his congregants at St. Matthew's.[17]

The groom, Charles Lohman, was born in St. Petersburg, Russia, on August 8, 1809. Nineteenth-century St. Petersburg was home to a large population of ethnic Germans, as well as to twenty-two periodicals printed in German, which may be where Lohman learned his trade. At the time of their marriage, he was twenty-four years old to Ann Summers's twenty-two years. It is unclear when Lohman left Russia for the United States; his earliest appearance in available records comes at the time of his marriage to Summers. Lohman worked in publishing, one of the fastest-growing industries in antebellum New York. By 1834, he was publishing books and magazines, at first issuing "a weekly quarto magazine of some fifteen or sixteen pages, handsomely printed, and to contain—price six-pence—authentic American history." It was called the *American Library*. In 1838, he released the two-volume *Retrospect of Western Travel* by the English social theorist and novelist Harriet Martineau. In 1837, he published an edition of *The Addresses and Messages of the Presidents of the United States to Congress*, a one-volume compendium of all the inaugural, annual, special, and farewell addresses of all former presidents. Just one year earlier, in the Marine Court of the City of New York, Lohman had sworn his allegiance to that same nation that was now his home, renouncing "forever all Allegiance and Fidelity to any foreign Prince, Potentate, State or Sovereignty, whatever; and particularly to the Empire of Russia, of whom I am now a subject." Charles Lohman was on his way to becoming an American.[18]

From 1833 to 1838, we know little of how Ann Lohman occupied her time. She could have continued her work as a seamstress, helping to supplement the household income. She might have remained at home, caring for her daughter, Caroline. In 1838, twenty-five-year-old Ann and eight-year-old Caroline sailed for England, presumably to visit the Trow family. Charles did not accompany them. They returned to New York on the *Ontario* on October 25, 1838. The Lohmans' ability to afford a trip home for Ann and Caroline indicates that their finances were in good order. This trip occurred less than six months before Madame Restell would first appear in a newspaper advertising her services.[19]

At some point, likely during the early years of their marriage if we are to judge by her appearance, Charles commissioned a portrait of his new bride. The portrait was tiny—under two inches by two inches—and mounted on a yellow gold brooch, surrounded by forty-six white chrysolites, glittering crystal-like gemstones. The oil and tempera portrait shows Ann seated in a red armchair and wearing a dark blue dress that reveals her white shoulders. Her brown eyes gaze slightly to the left of the viewer and her hair lies flat against her head, beginning to curl at her ears, where it then descends behind her head and in front of her ears. In the portrait, which is undated, she looks young and demure, though the bare shoulders lend an air of eroticism to the likeness. Etched on the back of the brooch are the words "Wife of Ch's R. Lohman. New York." Ann's own name does not appear. The portrait appears amateurish to the untrained eye, but it could have been quite an investment. It served as a symbol both of their ability to procure such a portrait, for which Ann would have had to sit some length of time, and of their union together. The brooch also raises questions: Who was its intended wearer? Surely not Ann herself. Miniatures like these were generally given as keepsakes, as ways for people to re-

Miniature of Ann Lohman, circa 1836 or later. Inscribed on the back are the words "Wife of Ch's R. Lohman. New York." Courtesy of the Museum of Contraception and Abortion, Vienna.

member the person pictured, often during courtship. Perhaps it was originally a gift from Ann to her daughter, Caroline. Or it could have been commissioned by Charles in the months prior to his wife's journey home, as a way to remember her when she was absent. It is the only image of Ann that survives unrelated to her later appearances in court. The portrait depicts Ann Lohman, not Madame Restell.[20]

During the period she likely sat for this portrait, Ann Trow Summers Lohman transformed herself into the female physician named Madame Restell. Her work in medicine built on traditions dating back millennia. For most of human history, women had assisted one another in birth. In the United States and its earlier colonies, some select women—Black, white, Native, and Latina, enslaved and free—emerged as particularly skilled at midwifery. They were not formally schooled in medicine. Instead, they trained with older women who were already skilled midwives. While almost all women in early America assisted in the ritual of birth at one time or another—as friends, relatives, and helping neighbors—a woman in labor and her family called on a skilled midwife to oversee a birth. The midwife stayed with a parturient woman until she gave birth, directing the other women in attendance on how to aid her. Women called on midwives for other medical needs, especially those related to obstetrics and gynecology, as well as for help with ailments particular to children. Some midwives were also relied on by their communities as healers who prescribed various combinations of herbal remedies for a wide variety of ailments. These remedies included emmenagogues. Because some midwives gained reputations as healers, they were sometimes suspected of otherworldly powers, which could lead to accusations of witchcraft. Depending on the era in which they practiced, midwives could be paid in cash or through a barter system, whereby a woman and her husband remunerated the midwife in goods or services. Midwifery was seen both as a calling—in that certain women more than others seemed to possess the skills needed to be successful—and as a career, for thousands of years the only one to which women had any access. Fundamentally, people trusted midwives not just because they demonstrated their skill but also because everyone was aware that they had been trained by the midwives who had come before them.[21]

In the 1830s, when Lohman trained in midwifery, the field of medicine was at a crossroads. In earlier eras, male doctors assumed medical legitimacy not via attending medical school but by training alongside practicing doctors, in ways not at all dissimilar from how midwives trained. The first medical school in the United States, the College of Philadelphia, was not founded until 1765. By the early nineteenth century, however, increasing numbers of young men were formally training as doctors by attending medical colleges and earning degrees. Even the courses taught at medical colleges were relatively rudimentary, however, and doctors-in-training combined apprenticeship with two years of courses, which themselves were a repetition of one another to make the lessons stick. For years, and despite the growing number of formally trained doctors, women's reproductive services continued to remain within the purview of midwives. That began to change, first in the United Kingdom and France, when male doctors developed the medical fields of obstetrics and gynecology and began to argue that male or "man midwifery" was superior to that of midwifery practiced by women. The male doctors relied on their formal scientific training to make this argument. At the same time, they also introduced a number of instruments into the birthing room—primarily the forceps but also various medications—to justify both their presence and the superior level of their skill. Historians have demonstrated that infant mortality actually increased as a result of some of these innovations, which could result in injury and infection. By the early nineteenth century, obstetrics courses were being offered in American medical colleges, which did not admit women. Regardless, first in Europe and the United Kingdom and by the later eighteenth century in the United States, formally trained male doctors were making inroads into what had formerly been the domain of more informally trained midwives. By 1839, when Ann Lohman first went into business, the stage had been set in the United States for a showdown between male obstetricians and the midwives they were slowly but surely replacing.[22]

Within a year of advertising her services, Madame Restell began to refer to herself as a "female physician." She did not have an MD. The first woman in the United States to receive formal medical training, Elizabeth Blackwell, did not earn her degree until 1849. In using the term "physician," Restell was not actually attempting to deceive. She and other New Yorkers would have understood a physician to be a practitioner of medicine, distinct from a surgeon, who was capable of operating on people and was without question male. No medical doctor was licensed at the time. With a handful of short-lived exceptions, states simply did not issue licenses until later in the nineteenth century. Not until 1889 would the Supreme Court rule that states were within their rights to do so. Thus, no unsuspecting patient would have believed

that a female physician was formally trained. For Restell, the phrase
meant that she was a woman who provided medical services to other
women, medical services that were almost exclusively related to that
which made women distinct from men: their capacity for pregnancy.
Restell was hardly the only woman to call herself a female physician, or
even just a physician. *Longworth's* 1838–39 and 1839–40 city directories list an Elizabeth Mott, female physician, residing at 119 Spring
Street. Others in the trade, including Mrs. Bird and Mrs. Sarah Anne
Welch, one-time competitors of Restell's, used the same language,
both in city directories and in advertisements. There is no question
that by the later 1840s, "female physician" became synonymous with
"abortion" in the minds of many, but that should not detract from
what those who used the phrase might have meant by it. In employing
this language, Restell and others like her were not simply describing
their trade; implicitly they were also asserting their claim on this term
at a moment when medicine was changing and women were losing
ground in a domain that had largely been theirs for centuries, if not
millennia.[23]

The evidence, and it is circumstantial, suggests that Ann Lohman
learned the practice of midwifery from a male doctor named William
Evans. For a time, the Lohmans lived on Catherine Street, near Dr. Evans's office, which may be how they came to know him. Evans had
been advertising at least since 1837 and operated out of an office at
100 Chatham Street, which ran along the east side of City Hall Park in
Lower Manhattan (now renamed Park Row). His advertisements included medications for his "celebrated CAMOMILE and APERI-
ENT ANTI-BILIOUS PILLS," which he claimed would alleviate any
number of health problems. Another advertisement explained that
Evans would be helpful to "those afflicted with Delicate Diseases, in
all their various forms, gonorrhoea, gleets [urethral discharge], stric-
tures, suppression of urine, inflammation of the testis; likewise the de-
structive stages of lucs, sore throat, nodes, phagadenic ulcers [skin
lesions], and mercurial eruptions." This advertisement explained also
there would be "the most perfect secrecy observed," likely because many

of these ailments were the symptoms of sexually transmitted infections. Evans claimed to be a member of the Royal College of London and to be a "regular" physician, that is a fully trained MD, though it is challenging to verify either claim. That he made a point of reiterating them casts doubt on their veracity. In style and substance, the advertisements are not dissimilar from the ones Madame Restell would begin to place in 1839, though Evans focused more on medical ailments particular to men, but not to the exclusion of women altogether. In another advertisement, he explained: "One of the most dangerous epochs to females is at the change of life and it is then they require a medicine, which will so invigorate their circulations, and thus strengthen their constitutions as may enable them to withstand shock." Here he was likely nodding to women who had ceased menstruation at menopause. In yet another, however, he explained that he was proficient in the "diseases of married and unmarried females," perhaps those that might result from intercourse.[24]

The eventual form of Ann Lohman's business would hew much more closely to that of a traditional midwife's than Evans's did. But in her first instantiation, her advertisements focused primarily on medicine, on compounds she could sell to female customers who either wanted to avoid becoming pregnant or wished no longer to be so. Evans also specialized in selling medicines. Lohman and her husband could easily have learned the trade from Evans. They could also have bought the medicines from a third party and simply sold them.

None of this, however, tells us why Lohman might have *wanted* to be a midwife or why she entered into the trade of selling emmenagogues and abortifacients. Recall that Ann was the fourth of at least nine children. She had witnessed the toll this would have taken on her mother, who had given birth to these children—and perhaps others—over the course of more than two decades. Indeed, it is quite possible that a youthful Ann Trow attended her mother in childbirth more than once. Like many women of her era, Anne Biddle Trow had little to no control over her reproductive life. Pregnancy itself remained dangerous, many women died during childbirth, and raising nine children was sure to have been exhausting, one baby having stopped nursing only for Anne to discover she was pregnant with the next. Ann Lohman chose a different route. She and Charles never had children. While he may have been sterile, it is also possible that from the beginning of their marriage, they had made a conscious decision not to have children, taking advantage of the very sort of medication they both would later sell. Her advertisements, from the very outset, were grounded not in hype and medical jargon but in the language of one woman talking to another about why a wife and mother might want to limit the number of children she had. Madame Restell was speaking from the experience of her own mother and herself. Of course, like other midwives and druggists, Lohman likely also chose to pursue this line of work because it could be lucrative. She had seen Dr. Evans's practice, so she must have had some idea of how he was able to support himself.

Businesses like Dr. Evans's and Madame Restell's, which sold medicines designed to cure various ailments, prevent pregnancy or end it, alleviate sexually transmitted infections, and reduce aches and pains through quick-fix medicines, were regarded by many as quackery, pure and simple. Advertisements usually included an address—sometimes multiple locations—at which customers might purchase the remedies. They also encouraged readers to write away for treatment. Many of the products were likely harmless; worse, their vendors probably knew they would have no demonstrable effect on those who took them. But this was not universally the case. Some abortifacients and emmenagogues were quite effective. Abortifacients, which had been used for centuries, worked in two different ways, depending on their ingredients. Many of them functioned by simply making the women who took them ill, so ill that one consequence, if they were effective, was the termination of the pregnancy. Abortifacients were typically made up of some combination of tansy, rue, turpentine, black cohosh, hellebore, and pennyroyal, plants that once grew wild across North America, or in the case of turpentine, a resin that is distilled from trees. Other abortifacients could contain prostaglandins, including a form of ergot, a fungus found on rye and other grains. Prostaglandins are hormones, and one of their effects is to stimulate labor, when a pregnancy is not at full term, by contracting the uterus, which would terminate a pregnancy if the contractions persisted. (Misoprostol, a synthetic prostaglandin, is used to induce miscarriage today, often alongside mifepristone.) The evidence indicates that Restell sold different drugs depending on how far along a woman was in her pregnancy, meaning that she had an understanding of the different properties of the abortifacients she sold.[25]

Abortifacients could be deadly, however, if taken in the wrong dosage or if administered by someone without training. In August 1839, for instance, New York's coroner held an inquest at a brothel at 117 Walker Street "on the body of a negro wench named Sarah Tuttle, a servant in that seminary for young ladies." She had "procured an ounce of oil of tanzy [sic], which she attempted to administer to herself, for the purpose of producing abortion." Upon taking half the medication, "she was immediately thrown into the most dreadful paroxysms, and though medical aid was called in, and every remedy adopted for her relief, she survived less than one hour." The coroner's jury ruled that the oil of tansy had caused her death. A skilled midwife or physician advised her patients on how and when to take an abortifacient to achieve the desired outcome.[26]

Surgical abortion could also be dangerous when managed by an unskilled practitioner. In March 1840, New York newspapers reported on the case of Susan Skaats, who died after one doctor, Charles H. Jackson of 209 Bowery, terminated her pregnancy. At first, the details were unclear, but it later emerged that Skaats and Jackson had both boarded at the same home when Skaats had first arrived in New York and were likely involved with each other sexually. Following the abortion, Skaats left the home on the Bowery to recuperate at a boarding-house on Houston Street. When she began to complain of illness, the landlord called none other than Dr. Jackson, who treated Skaats without admitting that he knew her. He was later charged with manslaughter in her death. Both pregnancy and surgery could be risky in this era, and it is possible that Jackson used surgical instruments to terminate the pregnancy that increased the risk to Skaats, rather than simply attempting to induce a miscarriage.[27]

The differences between Evans's practice and Restell's practice primarily had to do with their clientele. In addition to selling medication related to preventing or terminating a pregnancy, Restell also attended to women during their confinements and delivered their babies. She was running what was called a lying-in hospital, really no more than a room or two in her own home in which pregnant women could stay during their confinements, the last weeks or months of a pregnancy. She was also capable of bringing on a miscarriage manually by inserting her hand or an instrument into the uterus, inducing contractions. Eventually her practice would expand to include helping women find homes for the children they could not, or did not want, to care for themselves, essentially acting as an adoption broker. In time, all of these parts of her practice—even the delivery of children—would get her in trouble, but at least initially the controversy was related to selling medication that could terminate a pregnancy, which had been made illegal in New York less than a decade earlier.

For most of American history, abortion early in a pregnancy was both legal and unregulated. Native tribes, enslaved Africans, and Euro-American colonists had knowledge of, and access to, the herbs that made up abortifacients. In 1668 in Middlesex County, Massachusetts, for instance, when Elizabeth Wells's mistress noticed signs of her pregnancy and threatened to send her to a doctor to confirm it, Wells broke down and confessed that she was no longer pregnant because she had already ingested an herbal abortifacient called savin boiled in beer. In one instance from mid-eighteenth-century Connecticut, a group of young people referred to administering an abortifacient as "taking the trade," a practice common enough that it had acquired a slang equivalent. No state passed a law regulating abortion until Connecticut did so in 1821; until that time English common law regulated that which was unenumerated by statutory law. Under common law, abortion was perfectly legal so long as it occurred before quickening, the moment when a woman felt the fetus move within her, usually sometime around the fourth or fifth month of pregnancy, though it varied by the woman. Any action a person took to end a pregnancy was not a crime if it occurred before quickening. This was partially a practical matter: there was no reliable way to confirm that a woman was pregnant *until* the moment of quickening, the cessation of menstruation being explicable by other factors. The quickening doctrine also had philosophical or theological roots: some believed this was when the fetus became "ensouled," the moment the fetus crossed the boundary from being a mass of cells to becoming a potential human being. Under common law, even an abortion post-quickening was considered a misdemeanor, a quick fetus not yet being a full person.[28]

Such was the law of the land until 1821, when first Connecticut and later nine other states and one federal territory during the 1820s and 1830s enacted statutes criminalizing certain kinds of abortion. Most of these legal changes came either as the result of sensationalized cases of abortion gone awry or as an effort to protect women from medicine that could be poisonous. The Connecticut law, for instance, was passed after a bizarre incident in which a preacher forced the girl he had impregnated to take an abortifacient, and then kidnapped her and her sister. The early statutes did not fully depart from common law, however, in that most maintained a distinction between abortion pre- and post-quickening, even if the statutes also newly criminalized the former. Many of the statutes were explicitly focused on abortifacients alongside other poisons that might be sold or administered to women who sought to terminate their pregnancies. In the words of historian James C. Mohr, many of these laws were essentially "a poison control measure." The same medicine that might effect the termination of a pregnancy, if taken in sufficient dosage, could also poison the woman who took it, as in the case of Sarah Tuttle in New York in 1839. The Connecticut law did not in any way change the common law; it simply reinforced it, with a specific focus on abortifacients.[29]

Following the lead of Connecticut and a handful of other states, New York legislators passed a law in 1829 that went into effect beginning in 1830, the law under which Madame Restell was operating when she began her business nine years later. The law was part of an entire rewriting of New York's statutes, which meant that this law was never voted on, on its own, by New York's legislators. Instead, a committee drafted it, and the legislature voted on an enormous compendium of laws that also happened to include this one. The legislature dealt with abortion in three clauses of the *Revised Statutes*. In volume 2, among the various definitions of what constituted manslaughter, were the following:

> Section 9. Every person who shall administer to any woman pregnant with a quick child, any medicine, drug or substance whatever, or shall use or employ any instrument or other means with intent thereby to destroy such child, unless the same shall have been necessary to preserve the life of such mother, or shall have been advised by two physicians to be necessary for such purpose, shall be deemed guilty of manslaughter in the second degree.

Unlike Connecticut's law, this one jointly covered both abortifacients and surgical abortion. The only new introduction into the law was the punishment: abortion of a quick child would now be considered manslaughter instead of a misdemeanor. Punishment for second-degree manslaughter was set at between four and ten years in a state prison, a marked difference from when abortion post-quickening was only a misdemeanor.[30]

Another statute, almost thirty pages later, augments the above statutes in a way that does not include an exception for a pregnancy that was not yet quick. Section 21 of title VI "Offenses Punishable by Imprisonment in a County Jail, and by Fines," reads:

> Every person who shall willfully administer to any pregnant woman, any medicine, drug, substance or thing whatever, or shall use or employ any instrument or other means whatever, with intent thereby to procure the miscarriage of any such woman, unless the same shall have been necessary to preserve the life of such woman, or shall have

been advised by two physicians to be necessary for that purpose; shall, upon conviction, be punished by imprisonment in a county jail not more than one year, or by a fine not exceeding five hundred dollars, or by both such fine and punishment.

Now even early-stage abortions were criminalized, though clearly the punishment—for a misdemeanor instead of for a felony—indicated that lawmakers saw this as a lesser crime. This statute was the first in the United States to criminalize early-term abortions and the first to make explicit the "therapeutic exception"—the ability of a doctor to approve an exception—though the latter had been available in practice earlier.[31]

Lawmakers worked on section 21 at the same time that they were debating a number of other statutes meant to regulate doctors. Sections 22 and 23 were meant to punish doctors who prescribed medication while intoxicated and druggists who sold harmful medications without clearly marking them as poisonous, respectively. In other words, the legislators were far less concerned with protecting the fetus than they were with controlling doctors and protecting the lives of women. Indeed, in considering another statute (that the legislature declined to pass) that regulated a variety of medical surgeries, the legislators who drafted it included this explanation: "The rashness of many young practitioners in performing the most important surgical operations for the mere purpose of distinguishing themselves, has been a subject of much complaint, and we are advised by old and experienced surgeons, that the loss of life occasioned by the practice, is alarming." In these legislators' view, some newly trained doctors were operating on patients in ways that endangered the patients' lives, not unlike the doctors who used forceps to deliver babies when many midwives thought them unnecessary. This was partially how formally trained doctors distinguished and professionalized themselves: by using treatments unavailable to those who were not trained. Regardless of the motivations, by 1830, abortion in any form was criminalized in New York State, albeit with different punishments, depending on when in the pregnancy the procedure was performed.[32]

The law, however, was virtually unenforceable. Authorities primarily acted on it when a woman died as the result of an abortion, and in those cases the primary crime was the woman's death. Otherwise, the vast majority of women who terminated their pregnancies, if successful, had no interest in implicating the person who had aided them. More significantly, even if they could locate both a formerly pregnant woman and the person who had administered an abortifacient, it was almost impossible for authorities to determine whether the woman's pregnancy had quickened. Unless a woman's pregnancy had been showing—itself more difficult to assess in an era when clothes were much more concealing than they are today—only she knew whether she had felt the telltale flutter in her womb. Because emmenagogues remained perfectly legal, it was very easy for both a woman and her doctor to insist that the medication she had taken was simply for the purpose of restoring her courses, not for terminating her pregnancy. And who could prove otherwise?

Though Madame Restell's advertisements were never particularly forthright, she did sell both abortifacients and emmenagogues, along with medication that she advertised as contraceptive. A medication sold as an emmenagogue could well act as an abortifacient. Physicians like Restell and Evans played on this uncertainty when they placed their advertisements, representing their products as being emmenagogues when, depending on who took them, they might also work to terminate a pregnancy. In practice, Restell did attempt to discern among women who were pregnant, women who had ceased menstruating for reasons unknown, and women who wanted to prevent pregnancy. But in order to stay in business, she always played on the blurriness between the three categories as well as on women's acknowledgment of that gray area. In fact, women's own knowledge of their bodies, as well as the experiential knowledge of female physicians like Madame Restell, would become central to the struggles over the regulation of pregnancy and abortion.

* * * *

In 1839 when Ann Trow Summers Lohman placed her first advertisement, she had moved to a new home at 160 Greenwich Street, in between Cortland and Liberty Streets. The Lohmans had left the east side of Manhattan, closer to City Hall, for a house on the west side, only two blocks from the Hudson River. They were moving up in the world. The U.S. census, taken just a year later, enumerates Charles as the head of household but gives no names for other residents, as was customary in 1840. Included in the entry for the Lohman residence are two men between the ages of thirty and forty—Charles and likely a servant—one girl under the age of ten (Caroline), and three women between the ages of twenty and thirty: Ann and two others, probably servants. In 1839, Ann Lohman had been in New York for eight years, and her first husband had been dead almost as long. She had been married to Charles Lohman for six years, and her daughter, Caroline, was now nine years old. She herself was only twenty-seven. When the ad first ran in the *New York Sun*, she must have wondered if anyone would come. She was ready to serve them, but would anyone knock on her door? Certainly she could not have anticipated the life before her, the notoriety that awaited her. Unbeknownst to her, in placing that first advertisement, Ann Lohman had taken the first step toward becoming the most famous woman in New York.[33]

2

A LETTER TO MARRIED WOMEN

On Sunday, July 21, 1839, the district attorney for New York City, James R. Whiting, woke up to an attention-grabbing account of one "Mrs. Restell, alias, Mrs. Loman [*sic*]," printed in the *Sunday Morning News*. "This notorious pander to the profligate," the article began, "perseveres in her nefarious traffic, notwithstanding the expositions which we have made respecting her character, and that of her compounds." "There is a statute against creating abortion, founded in wisdom and in a knowledge of the human constitution, and for a woman to virtually overthrow that law by her daily practices, is not to be borne by this community. The time will soon come when Mrs. Restell will learn this, and lest she may think we speak thoughtlessly, we now, for the last time, solemnly advise her to give up the business in which she is engaged. If she do not, we will not be answerable for the consequences which it is certain must ensue."[1]

As it turned out, editors and reporters at more papers than just the *Sunday Morning News* would be well occupied with warning Madame Restell against continuing her business for years to come. Their reporting, which made note of New York's rarely enforced 1829 statute that made administering abortifacients or surgically terminating a pregnancy a crime, was but one rivulet in a wave of coverage that swelled in 1839, the year Restell founded her business. In part what reporters found noteworthy was just how open Restell was in pursuing her trade.

While abortion had been available and legal to the point of quickening from the colonial era onward, it was rarely discussed openly because it was generally thought to be the remedy for those who had had sex out of wedlock. Acknowledging abortion was admitting to earlier sins. Restell was now advertising both her services and her products quite regularly and doing so in a manner that ran counter to New York state law, which had newly criminalized abortion both before and after quickening in 1830. The language of the coverage is also telling: newspapermen took great umbrage not just at how brazen Restell was but at the fact that even after they condemned her business and her advertising, she blithely continued on, uncowed by their warnings. She was defiant.[2]

Advertisements for abortion and contraceptives had been appearing in newspapers since the early 1830s, in part thanks to the advent of the penny press, the cheap tabloids sold by the copy (instead of by subscription), that began publishing in New York in 1833 and that were directed toward a much larger audience. These papers partially made up for their low prices by running many advertisements. "Widow Welch's Pills," for instance, first appeared in New York's *Evening Post* in 1833, and by 1837, W. Labausn, MD, was selling the pills "particularly adapted to disorders incident to the FEMALE SEX" out of an office on Broad Street. In 1837, Mrs. Margaret Bird, who would become one of Madame Restell's chief competitors by the 1840s, also began advertising her services as a midwife, "having been duly qualified, in a lying in hospital in Europe." She also sold various medicines that were effective for indigestion and other stomach ailments. By early 1838, she claimed to be the only source in New York for "Dr. Vandenburgh's Female Renovating Pills, From Germany," which were an "effectual remedy for suppression, irregularity, and all cases where nature does not have her regular and proper course." While there were a number of reasons that nature might not be running her proper course in a woman, pregnancy was certainly noteworthy among them.[3]

Some very early advertisements did include language that made explicit their purpose, disguised as a warning to women of the supposedly harmful "side effects" of pills administrated for other purposes. An ad for "Dr. Van Humbert's Female Renovating Pills," for example, cautioned that "they must not be taken during pregnancy, as they would produce abortion." Two years later, Dr. Van Humbert's ads had modified their wording: "They must not be taken during p*******y, as they would produce a******n." While the message remained clear, this advertiser was likely trying to evade unwanted legal attention.[4]

Madame Restell employed a similar word game briefly in 1839, the first year she advertised, but soon thereafter switched to using euphemistic language that skirted the line but that nevertheless made it clear what was on offer. Her formula for many years was to run two advertisements on the same page, spaced apart, but whose messages reinforced each other. The first ad purveyed the actual products and services: "Madame Restell, Female Physician, has had ample evidence to satisfy her that many of the complaints to which females are subject, have been principally, if not wholly, owing to the absence, heretofore, of any proper, safe, efficient and certain medicine in cases of suppression, irregularity and stoppage of those functions of nature upon which the health and even the life of every female depends." Restell then touted the benefits of being able to discuss these matters with a member of one's own sex, a female physician, and informed readers that her (wholly fictitious) grandmother, the original Madame Restell, had developed these Female Regulating Pills in Europe thirty years ago. "The most obstinate and long seated cases of irregularity, suppression, &c. have been removed by the Female Regulating Pills." Only enhancing their appeal, Restell cagily explained that "it is necessary for the married to abstain from their use," for reasons that would be explained in the full directions accompanying the pills. For $1, a box could be purchased from Restell herself at her new office at 148 Greenwich Street, just down the street from her previous residence at number 160.[5]

The second advertisement, one column to the left and half a page down, was styled as a letter "To Married Women," in which she "begs leave to call attention of the married to a subject of the most vital im-

portance, connected not only with their well-being, health and happiness, but often their very existence." The "letter" continued at some
length, using language that struggled to be as vague as possible but that
nevertheless conveyed Restell's main message: pregnancy was dangerous, and she had the means to prevent it. "Much of the suffering, misery, wretchedness and vice existing around us," she warned, "can be
attributable to our ignorance of the capacity granted to us for a wise
end to control, in no small degree, our own destinies; but for this many
who pine in poverty, toiling but to live, and living but to toil, may, in a
few years, acquire a comfortable competence, and extend to their offspring those advantages of education and acquirements, of which their
present pecuniary circumstances deprive them of bestowing." And
then her missive took a darker turn: "But for this, many a mother,
scarce in the meridian of life, would be spared the anguish and suffering of old age; but for this, many an affectionate wife and fond mother
would be snatched from the jaws of an early and premature grave; but
for this, many a now bereft husband would have still been blessed with
the endearing companionship of the partner of his joys and sorrows."
"Are we not bound by every obligation, human and divine," she then
asked her readers, "by our duty to ourselves, to our husbands, and more
especially to our children, to preserve, to guard, to protect our health,
nay our life, that we may rear and watch over those to whom we are
allied by ties the most sacred and binding?"[6]

In essence, Restell was playing on women's very real fears of mortality that attended every pregnancy during the nineteenth century.
While we do not have particularly accurate maternal mortality rates
for that era, some have estimated that even as late as the early twentieth century at least one mother died for every 154 live births. In other
words, pregnancy could be very dangerous for women, most of whom
knew someone who had died as a result of childbirth. Restell acknowledged this legitimate fear, and just for good measure, she framed it as a
concern about being able to ensure the welfare of one's husband and
children. No deceased wife or mother could care for her family, after
all. Without ever using the words "abortion," "sex," or "pregnancy,"

Restell had crafted an advertisement that, in addressing women directly, empowered them to save themselves from the dangers of unwanted pregnancy. For a price, of course. Those interested could visit Restell on Greenwich Street or send away for a circular that would explain her products and services in more detail. Restell posted somewhat more extensive leaflets at street corners, public docks, and wharves. She would also mail longer versions of these leaflets to anyone who wrote asking for more information. Advertisements ran not just in New York papers but in other cities on the Eastern Seaboard as well. In 1839, the advertisements explained that her products could be purchased at branch offices in Philadelphia, at 39½ South Eighth Street, near Chestnut, and in 1840, in Boston at 7 Essex Street, near Washington. There is no evidence that Restell operated either of these other offices personally. She must have either employed someone to sell the products or sold them to some sort of middleman who ran the offices.[7]

It was these ads, which ran exceedingly regularly from 1839 through the 1840s, that may have most irked her fellow New Yorkers, not only because they appeared frequently but also because they were forthright. Restell sought to persuade readers of the benefits of family limitation in language that was relatively frank. While Restell was rarely explicit about what she was offering, she wrote at length about why it was justified, about why women might be interested in this product. These also were not modest advertisements tucked away in a corner of the paper. She unapologetically took up inches of space alongside ads for real estate and auction sales, the shipping news, and updates from the stock market. She presumed her services to be legitimate. And she addressed her ads to married women directly. Never mind that family limitation was often in the best interests of both father and mother, Restell was proposing to give wives the tools to regulate birth, a kind of sexual autonomy, without their husbands' knowledge or consent. It was also the case that even though Restell concerned herself with married women, most would have understood that she was not going to turn away single women who sought out her services. This was perceived by many as an invitation to licentiousness, as a way for single women to have sex without consequence, to subvert decency and morality in service of their own lust.

There was a good deal of commentary in the press about the shamelessness of the advertisements themselves, let alone the services Restell was selling. In March of 1839, for instance, the *Herald* printed an editorial called "Morals of the Rising Generation" that explained what worried at least some New Yorkers about Madame Restell and her colleagues:

> Within the last two years, owing to the laxity of the public authorities, matters and things of the most deleterious tendency have been openly advocated in print—doctrines which are enough to make our ancestors rise from their graves to witness the desecration of the altars they spent so much time, labor and intellect to rear. . . . But now we have arrived at a new era in philosophy and morals, for we find that "the New View" is not merely inculcated, but that professors have appeared in the field, who unblushingly advertise their "certain remedy," which is first to demoralize our daughters and sisters, and then bring them to an early grave. We ask again, will the guardians of our city's honor permit this plague to sweep over the land? . . . We say, without fear of contradiction, that venal as the presses of London and Paris avowedly are, no newspaper there would have dared to publish such a filthy libel as the advertisement of Mrs. Restell, which appeared in the "Sun" of the 18th inst.

This commentator, who may have been writing satirically, seemed to care little for whether Restell was breaking the law or not; the problem was her offense to morality. In providing abortion, Restell was also aiding those intent on illicit sex.[8]

* * * *

It was in this context of rising indignation and anger that district attorney James Whiting read the July 1839 article in the *Sunday Morning*

News about the "notorious pander" Restell. He took out ink and paper and began to write a letter to accompany the story in the *News*: "I send the enclosed to the Grand Jury that if they deem it a matter of importance they may examine into it. I can credibly inform that several cases of abortion have been effected under her advice and medicines." "My view of the conduct of this woman *may* not meet with your approbation. . . . If it does the Grand Jury shall have all my best efforts to put down a practice so horrible in itself and frightful to the best interests of the human race."[9]

In an era before the advent of a paid police force whose role it was to investigate crimes and bring them to the attention of prosecutors, Whiting was relying on his authority to prod the grand jury to investigate Madame Restell. If the grand jury found charges credible, it could issue a "true bill," or an indictment. Next, Whiting helpfully provided the name of a contact who might strengthen their case. "The Grand Jury will be able to procure much information and the names of the necessary witnesses from Samuel Jenks Smith, Editor of the Sunday Morning News." He clearly believed that Smith, an editor who had publicly refused to print Restell's advertisements, had information about possible witnesses who could be used to indict her.[10]

Grand juries, which were rooted in English common law, partially acted to screen out baseless accusations so that the courts were not clogged with vengeful complainants and so that only those allegations that could be supported by evidence were brought to trial. A sitting body appointed by the county and city of New York composed of no fewer than twelve, no more than twenty-four members—all men—a grand jury had the power to call witnesses to testify about alleged crimes. Testimony could take the form of a deposition or of a series of questions and answers. Grand jury proceedings were conducted behind closed doors, so while the results of grand jury investigations—in the form of indictments and presentments—were public, and while newspapers reported on them if the accused or the alleged crime were noteworthy, the substance of witness interviews was not accessible to the general public. The secrecy had numerous justifications: to prevent suspects from fleeing or tampering with evidence if they knew they were accused and to protect the reputations of those who were accused but might never be indicted.[11]

Within a month, the grand jury had begun investigating Madame Restell. On August 20, 1839, New York City's grand jury summoned Pamela Palmer and her friend Hester Wells to testify. In the case of both Palmer and Wells, what survives in the archives are sworn depositions summarizing their testimony and signed by each in front of a witness. Palmer, who lived at 90 Reade Street with her husband, Daniel, a broker, claimed that she had consulted Madame Restell because she believed that she might be pregnant: "I hadn't been regular, but I did not know from any new feelings that it was so," meaning that she had felt no signs of the pregnancy. All she knew was that she had missed her period. "I saw Mrs. Restell at her office or place of business," Palmer continued, "and informed her that I did not know whether I was in the family way or not and I wanted her to give me something by which I could tell whether it was so or not. She gave me this phial and said I would find out by that. She told me to call again and let her know whether it had any affect [*sic*] on me. I was to take two drops night and morning until I took it all up." Palmer's friend Wells, however, who lived with her husband on Thomas Street, about two blocks away from Palmer, claimed that she believed Palmer had gone to Madame Restell's to procure medicine to terminate the pregnancy, not just to determine whether it existed. In Wells's more believable telling, Palmer was there for an abortifacient.[12]

According to Palmer, Restell had informed her that if she was *not* pregnant, the medicine would make her regular, a clever way of describing the medicine's effect that omitted mentioning what it might do if she *were* pregnant. Because there was no reliable way to know whether a woman in the early stages of parturition was pregnant or simply "blocked" for some other reason, Restell skirted the law by prescribing medicine to restore menstrual regularity even as the drug's intended purpose likely would have been clear. She was, in essence, disguising an abortifacient as an emmenagogue.

In her testimony, Palmer explained that she had taken the full dose of the medicine, which she said smelled of turpentine, and waited to see if the medicine could tell her if she was pregnant. By Palmer's account, nothing happened immediately, but "about three weeks after I quit taking the medicine I miscarried. I had felt no life before—I had been hard at work, and having a great deal of care on my mind I think it was the hard work + care on my mind that produced it." Palmer seems to have been cognizant that connecting the medicine to the miscarriage would be problematic for Restell, so she blamed the miscarriage on labor and stress. She may even have believed that she herself could be charged with abortion, though that was not (yet) the case under New York state law. Her friend Wells confirmed: "In 4 or 5 weeks after getting the medicine Mrs. Palmer sent for me at night. I went there between 8 + 9 o'clock a dr. then had been with her. When I arrived there she told me she had miscarried. She was very ill." Wells also deposed that Palmer had told her she was unsure whether the hard work or the medicine had produced the miscarriage.[13]

No record of an indictment stemming from these depositions survives in the archives. This was likely because Palmer's testimony deliberately questioned the efficacy of the medicine Restell had sold her and also misrepresented the reason for her visit to Restell in the first place. Without a witness who could testify that Restell had sold Palmer medication for the express purpose of terminating a pregnancy, there was no case. Wells, who believed that had been the reason for the visit to Restell, had not seen or heard the crucial conversation, Restell and Palmer having withdrawn to another room for a consultation. The secrecy around sex and abortion worked in the legal favor of abortionists: those who sought abortions were exceedingly unlikely to be interested in testifying about their experience of terminating a pregnancy. Single women desperately wanted to keep their sexual activity a secret, and married women hesitated to be criticized for turning their back on what was assumed to be their primary duty in life, motherhood. And no woman wanted to see her name in the newspapers having anything to do with sex. Appearing as a witness would almost certainly lead to publicity. While Palmer's and Wells's testimony appears to have become mired in a legal dead end, officials in New York may also have chosen not to pursue the case because they had come upon another, much more promising, witness.

Despite the reasonable fears of publicity that surrounded testifying about prior sexual experience, on August 6, 1839, a woman named Anna Dall swore out a deposition to Robert Taylor, special justice for the city and county of New York. Dall, who was eighteen and single, explained that she had realized she was pregnant in mid-July of that year and had gone to Moses Cohen, the father of her child and a second-hand dealer, who lived at 247 Hudson Street, to inform him of her condition. She explained that she was afraid, especially of what her mother would do if she found out. Cohen advised her to go to a woman he had heard about who lived on Greenwich Street: Madame Restell. Upon arriving, Dall stated the reason for her call, and Restell asked her how long she had been pregnant. "Two months," Dall replied. Restell gave her a box of pills and told her to take two or three pills, twice per day, until they were all gone and that the pills should relieve her of her pregnancy. The deposition continued, explaining that Restell had told her that if the pills did not work, she should return for a different medicine when she was further along in her pregnancy.[14] The court would later learn that in this case, the pills were composed of ergot, a prostaglandin that could have brought on uterine contractions, and "cautharides," likely cantharidin, essentially Spanish fly, which would have made Dall ill enough to bring on miscarriage.[15]

Dall left Restell's office with the box of pills, for which she had paid $1. But she feared the result of taking them, perhaps especially because even Restell herself did not seem entirely confident that they would be effective. Dall opted not to terminate her pregnancy, though she did keep the pills, which she still had when she was deposed on August 6. The records do not indicate how the special justice found Dall or why she chose to speak to him about her experience some three weeks after she obtained the abortifacient. It does not appear that Dall herself was particularly interested in prosecuting Madame Restell, or she might have approached an official in the days after she first bought the medicine. Rather, it seems more likely that, via word of mouth, Taylor found out about her case and persuaded her to give a deposition.

Ten days later, on August 16, that deposition led to an indictment. The grand jury had found that Restell "willfully, maliciously, and unlawfully did administer to, and cause to be administered to, and taken by one Anna Dall, single woman, divers large quantities, of a certain medicine, drug, substance, or thing, that is to say thirty pills composed of cautharides and ergot ... with intent thereby to cause and procure the miscarriage of the said Anna Dall." The indictment is something of a reach. Given that Dall did not even take the abortifacient, Restell was essentially being charged with having sold it to her. While the indictment was careful to explain that Dall was not pregnant with "a quick child," which would have been a more serious crime, the grand jurors did go out of their way to describe Restell as being "of a wicked and evil disposition of a corrupt and depraved mind." The indictment was signed by James R. Whiting, District Attorney.[16]

On August 17, the New York County Court of General Sessions issued a bench warrant for the arrest of Madame Restell. Gil Hays, an officer of the court, was tasked with collecting Restell from her home. He brought her before the court, however unwilling she may have been, where she was joined by her lawyer, Mr. M.D. Crafts. There she heard the indictment read and entered her plea. Then Crafts, the district attorney, and the recorder (the technical name for the judge) discussed the matter of bail. The district attorney initially asked for bail to be set at $2,000. Crafts countered at $1,000, and the recorder compromised at $1,500, about $43,000 in today's dollars. Following the indictment, Crafts rose and told the court that he was ready to go to trial immediately, to which the recorder explained that the court was nearly concluded with its labors for the term and would not be able to hear the case so swiftly. As the court offices had closed for the day and no one had come forward to post bail, Restell was imprisoned in the city's jail, known popularly as the Tombs.[17]

Located just on the edge of Five Points, New York's notorious slum, the Tombs was a complex of buildings—including the court itself—enclosed in a high granite wall, impressive in its grandeur. The imposing front entrance, on Centre Street, was raised above street level and flanked by four huge columns crowned with palm leaves. A stay in the Tombs was temporary; those who were convicted would be sent to the prisons at Blackwell's Island or Sing Sing, depending on the severity of the crime. Women were housed apart from men, and women of means were accommodated separately on the second floor of what had originally been a debtors' prison. Poorer women from the nearby slums were housed on the first floor, where they slept on raised planks, and were regularly put to labor cleaning the prison. Later that night, Restell's husband and her former neighbor, Dr. William Evans, returned to the Tombs. Evans stood as Restell's bail, and she was released in the early hours of Sunday morning. Because of the brevity of her stay, it is unlikely that Restell interacted much with her fellow prisoners, though she would have plenty of opportunity to do so in the years to come.[18]

Though Restell was now free on bail, her ordeal was far from over. Later that week, the *Herald* returned to the story, predicting that the trial of this "philosopher in petticoats" will "give rise to some of the most remarkable developments ever seen in a court of law." The *Herald* also provided one of the first descriptions of Restell we have. "The youth, beauty, black eyes, raven hair, and singular physiognomy of the accused," the reporter enthused, combined with the legal acumen of her counsel, "would be, in themselves, enough to attract half the city to the Halls of Justice." The *Herald* predicted many clashing views on Restell's operation, including the "experience of Mrs. Restell's patients and proselytes." The editor also hinted at one of the reasons abortion might be particularly noxious to some New Yorkers: Restell was "endeavoring to set a limit to population here, at a time when Americans are inviting the poor and the rich, the young and the old, the lame, the halt, and the blind to come and take up their abode in this land of promise." In other words, Restell's clientele, some of whom were presumed to be middle- and upper-class married ladies, were terminating pregnancies even as Catholic immigrants were continuing to have large families that swelled the population. There were, it seemed, multiple reasons to object to the practice of abortion. This nativist outcry would become even more fierce in the years to come. Finally, the *Herald* explained that if Restell were convicted, she would be fined $500 and could spend as much as a year in the city prison on Blackwell's Island.[19]

The trial seemed to be perpetually delayed. It is possible that because Dall never actually took the medication, she made less than an ideal witness. Restell would later say that the language barrier between the two—Dall was an immigrant and native German speaker—had made it difficult for Dall to fully understand that Restell was telling her *not* to take the medication during pregnancy. If this disingenuous explanation was to be believed by the jury, a favorable verdict might not be secured. While the *Herald* looked forward to Restell's case being heard in October by the court of general sessions, by November the newspaper was noting that business had picked up considerably at Restell's office on Greenwich Street and that there was still no trial. She continued to place regular advertisements in the *Herald* through the end of 1839 and on into 1840.[20]

On December 17, 1839, four months after giving her testimony to the grand jury, Dall was admitted to the New York City Almshouse at Bellevue, the destination of last resort for the impoverished and the only public option for an unmarried pregnant woman at the time. Charitable institutions that served as lying-in hospitals insisted that clients prove marriage, which Dall could not do. Dall gave birth to twins two months later. On March 13, 1840, she died in obscurity at Bellevue of puerperal fever, a bacterial infection commonly contracted following childbirth.[21]

It took an additional eight months for the DA to finally drop the case. On November 18, 1840, the deputy clerk of the court of general sessions recorded the case as nolle prosequi, or "Nol. Pros." Six days later, Restell took out ads in the *Herald* and the *Sun* telling her side of the story, including her claim that language differences led Dall to misunderstand the purposes of the medication she had sold her. Over the course of her career, Restell regularly addressed New Yorkers via the press. She was not the only public figure to do so and the back-and-forth that was sometimes featured in New York newspapers was entertaining for readers and also served as a venue for public figures to present their side of an argument. It was, however, highly unusual for a woman to do so under her own name. That "Madame Restell" was itself a pseudonym may have served as some cover initially, but it was not long before everyone knew her true identity. "The flimsiness and injustice of the prosecution," she argued, "covered the investigation with ridicule and shame, and resulted, after a procrastination of sixteen months, as every person of the least common sense, would have predicted."[22]

But Restell was not content simply to acknowledge her legal victory. For two more paragraphs she elaborated on why her preventive powders were, in fact, beneficial for women. "For married ladies whose health imperatively forbids a too rapid increase of family, is not the discovery of Madame Restell's specific one of the greatest blessings? And is it not in the highest degree unjust to intimate that wives, sisters, and mothers want but the opportunity to be vicious. Shame on him who can entertain such a sentiment." Restell continued to make the case that what she offered was only meant for married women who needed it for reasons of health. All those who intimated otherwise were casting aspersions on the virtue of the women of New York. Always the saleswoman, she directed any interested parties to her office—148 Greenwich Street in New York—and to satellite locations at 7 Essex Street in Boston and 8 South Seventh in Philadelphia. She signed off, "So much for persecution."[23]

* * * *

All this public attention, combined with Restell's steadfast refusal to admit that she was doing anything wrong—indeed her championing her service as a veritable boon to women's health—caught the notice of a young newspaperman named George Washington Dixon, who for

James C. Platt, portrait of George Washington Dixon, 1846. Newspaper editor George Washington Dixon waged war on Restell in the 1840s, primarily through his publication *Dixon's Polyanthos*. Courtesy of the National Portrait Gallery, Smithsonian Institution.

good or ill, can be credited with bringing much more scrutiny to Restell and her practices. At the beginning of 1841, Dixon launched an all-out campaign to see Restell arrested, tried, and imprisoned.

Born in Virginia, likely in 1801, Dixon rose to fame as a singer in the Italian "buffo" tradition, performing up and down the East Coast, making regular stops in New York. Rumored to be of mixed race, he was also a blackface minstrel, singing music he wrote himself. His most famous tune was "Ole' Zip Coon." By the 1830s he had also turned to journalism, first in Boston, where he continued to perform, and later in New York, where he moved in 1838 and gave up singing for a spell. In that year he began a newspaper with a colleague and friend named William J. Snelling that they initially called the *Polyanthos and Fire Department Album*, later shortened to *Polyanthos* or *Dixon's Polyanthos*. Dixon was himself in and out of courts on various libel trials in the late 1830s, eventually pleading guilty in one of them and spending six months doing hard labor on Blackwell's Island for accusing a New York minister of various sexual improprieties.[24]

In 1840, Dixon returned to the *Polyanthos* and parted ways with Snelling. During this era, the paper typically featured theater reviews, advertisements, gossip, and commentary on New York life and generally lauded itself on policing the morals of New York women. It particularly reveled in stories of sexual indiscretion and political corruption, published in the guise of moral outrage. This was a way both to sell papers and to have a defense at the ready if accused of pandering to immorality. It is not hard to see how Restell might enter Dixon's crosshairs. In February of 1841, just a few months after Restell's indictment in the case of Anna Dall had finally been dismissed, perhaps triggered by her escape from the law, Dixon set his sights on bringing her down.[25]

In the February 16 issue of the paper, Dixon printed a full-page story on Restell, dissecting her advertising at length, in which he accused her of allowing married women to evade their duties as mothers and of encouraging vice among single women. He also vowed to reprint the story every week until she was indicted. He claimed that in the course of one year, Restell had "procured several hundred abortions, she has committed several hundred crimes, punishable by the laws of man, and condemned by the law of God. We do not say so. She says it herself. Preventive Powders! There is no such thing in nature. There is but one preventive, which is but abstinence."[26]

No one, it seemed, could escape the snare of her viciousness. He warned seamen, who traveled for long periods of time, that Restell would allow their wives to have affairs with impunity. He warned young men in search of brides that they could no longer expect their future wives to be virginal. He warned fathers: "Madame Restell tells your daughter how she may defile her body and debase her mind without fear or hesitation. Say she is virtuous; can she remain so when she is thus

A.E. Baker, "Mad^{me} Rastille's Practice," 1840. This illustration made fun not only of the women who sought out Restell's treatment, but also of Restell herself, who is shown here advising a man in a bonnet that warm ice cream and hair powder "will reduce it." The women in the satirical illustration are all far advanced in their pregnancies, not the kind of client Restell would have seen, at least not for an abortion. Courtesy of the American Antiquarian Society.

openly encouraged and invited to sin?" He then spoke to unmarried women, explaining that Restell could teach them how to "impose upon your husband or deceive your lover. Your unborn infant need not be presented at the font or blessed by the priest; Madame Restell can prevent its eyes from ever opening and throw its mangled body into the dock." And Dixon was just getting started. The story continued on for many hundreds of words, always returning to Restell's standard advertisements, which he quoted in full only to tear apart.[27]

It is hard to know whether Dixon's sense of moral insult was genuine or if he was feigning horror. There is no question that much of the writing in the paper postures outrage about moral wrongs only to regale its readers with endless details about various scandals. But that does not mean he was not angered by the autonomy Restell offered to women, the ability to control their own reproduction independent of men and the opportunities this presented for possibly deceiving them. Dixon was no moralist. The *Polyanthos* regularly covered the careers of celebrated prostitutes and other figures of the urban demimonde with admiration, and he later enjoyed a career in the sporting culture of the "flash" papers that catered to gentlemen slumming about town. But he could certainly object to Restell and abortion on misogynist grounds.[28]

True to his word, Dixon continued to publish the same full-page attack on Restell in subsequent issues of the *Polyanthos*, as well as other coverage of Restell and some of her fellow female physicians. On March 6, he advocated against waiting for a complaining witness to indict her for her crimes—because one was unlikely to present herself—and argued to prosecute Restell for her ads themselves, which all but stated the purpose of her business. He also attacked her qualifications, saying "there is no doubt that she has enjoyed extensive opportunities to become acquainted with all the functions of the organs on which she professes to operate as far as experience goes, and every harlot of the Five Points is alike qualified."[29]

On March 17, 1841, the grand jury made a presentment of both Madame Restell and one of her competitors, Madame Costello, for being a "public nuisance." The grand jury was not charging either of the women with committing an abortion; instead this was about their advertisements. The *Polyanthos* crowed victory under the headline "Restell Caught at Last." Dixon claimed that the men of the grand jury could not "look on calmly while the young and inexperienced females of our city were loudly advertised that they could sin with impunity; that the way to vice was made easy; and that the road to ruin had been cushioned and covered with flowers for the edification of delicate young ladies." Dixon also took a good deal of the credit, claiming that it was the fact that the *Polyanthos* had continued to run his diatribe that had led the presentment against Mesdames Restell and Costello.[30]

The grand jurors made clear that they believed they had a duty to morals. They emphasized, in particular, that the availability of abortion and contraception enables "the vile seducer . . . to present his victim that which removed the last fear that remains, after surmounting all obstacles." In other words, the grand jury depicted unmarried sex as being more likely to occur when a man could convince an unwilling woman that there would be no serious consequences to their actions. The grand jurors conceived of single women's virtue as bound up in their lack of sexual desire; seducers could pressure women into sex, thus stealing their virtue, if contraception and abortion were available. Whatever the moral crimes committed here might be, however, the grand jury seemed to recognize that its presentment rested on shaky legal ground. "We earnest[ly] pray," they closed, "that if there is no law that will reach this, which we present as a PUBLIC NUISANCE, the court will take measures for the procuring the passage of such a law."[31]

Two days after the presentment, Restell herself responded in the *New York Herald* in an address to "Mr. John D. Keese (Druggist) and other Gentlemen of the Grand Jury." Restell began by insinuating that Keese might have had a pecuniary motive to put her out of business and that this was one cause for the presentment being filed in the first place. Then Restell launched into a lengthy rebuttal of the terms of the presentment itself, essentially impugning the grand jurors' estimation of New York's women, their own wives and daughters. "I cannot conceive how men who are husbands, brothers, or fathers, can give utterance to an idea so intrinsically base and infamous," she wrote, "that their wives, their sisters, or their daughters, want but the opportunities and 'facilities' to be vicious; and if they are not so, it is not from an innate principle of virtue, but from fear." "What! is female virtue, then," she argued, "a mere thing of circumstance and occasion? Is there but the difference of opportunity between it and prostitution? Would your wives, and your sisters, and your daughters, if once absolved from fear, all become prostitutes?—all sell their embraces for gold, and descend to a level with the most degraded? Such abhorrent, detestable, and disgusting estimate of female virtue, it is but hoped may be confined within the narrowest possible bounds."[32]

In her defense, Restell went on to explain that her preventive powders were designed for married women and might also encourage early marriage among young people who could wed and have legitimate sexual relations without the fear of pregnancies they could not yet afford. She also pointed out, as she regularly did in her advertisements and circulars, that there were women for whom it was dangerous to give birth, who put themselves at greater risk than the average woman by becoming pregnant. "Many weakly wives have been saved from a premature grave, to be a succor and a blessing to those near and dear to them." She signed off by affirming her respect for the institution of the grand jury but also hoping that it would eschew "hasty, inconsiderate, and injudicious conduct" so as to avoid "bringing the body and the institution into just ridicule or rebuke." Restell was unlikely to have convinced members of the grand jury to change their minds, but she was making a public case for the legitimacy of birth control, and implicitly abortion, a case that also served, fortuitously, as an advertisement for her services. The grand jury's presentment was never to be tested, however, as Restell would soon find herself embroiled in an even more significant legal battle.[33]

3

In the Family Way

In May of 1839, Ann Maria Purdy found herself "in the family way." She was twenty-one years old and had been married for three years, as of the previous November. She had a ten-month-old son and "was concerned about her having to stop nursing the infant at so young an age" when the next child was born. On one fateful day in July of 1839, Purdy expressed worries about her situation to a washerwoman named Rebecca, who sometimes worked for Purdy. Rebecca asked her if she had ever heard of "Madam Restell"; Purdy claimed she had not. Rebecca reminded Purdy of the newspaper ads placed by Restell and eventually brought her one from the *Sun*. Purdy explained that she did not understand the meaning of the ads, so Rebecca had to spell it out for her. Rebecca further explained that she knew a woman on Mulberry Street (Purdy then lived only one block east, on Mott Street) who had been to see Restell and "had received relief from her."[1]

Now very excited by this information, the next evening Purdy left her house "on a pretended errand," so that her husband would not know what she was doing, and made her way to Restell's office at 148 Greenwich Street. When she arrived, there were two women in a waiting room. Madame Restell appeared from behind a curtain and asked if she could help Purdy. Once Purdy had recounted the reason for her visit, Restell told her to come back the next day with $1 and she would be able to provide her with something to relieve her. When she returned, Restell sold Purdy a "phial containing liquid of a yellowish color" for $1 and told her to take fifteen drops of the liquid "in dry sugar" three times per day, "which would cause her to miscarry."[2]

Purdy took a dose that evening and one or two the next day, but almost immediately she had "become afraid of it," and so she sent for Rebecca. Rebecca told her not to be afraid and also gave her the name and address of the woman she knew on Mulberry Street who had been relieved by Restell. The woman, being called on by a stranger who was asking about her use of an illegal abortifacient, understandably claimed she did not recollect any medication and was unable to provide Purdy any further information. Purdy's mind was made up: she did not want to take any more of the medicine until she found out what was in it. She decided to send it to her doctor to have him determine its contents and advise her. Because she did not want to admit to him that she had taken any of it, however, she sent "a small girl in [her] employment to Dr. Marvin with the phial and contents, telling the girl to say to the Dr. that a young lady of her acquaintance had that and was going to take it and that she would be obliged to the Dr. if he would send her word what it was." The doctor gave the girl a note explaining that the liquid was oil of tansy and spirit of turpentine, "one of the most dangerous preparations that could be taken by a female." Purdy took no more of the medicine.[3]

On July 19, just over two weeks after the initial visit to Restell, Rebecca, who was African American and whose last name never appears in the court records, was once again at the home of Purdy, commiserating with her about her situation, when she "again advised . . . her to call again on Madam Restell." Rebecca volunteered to look after her son while Purdy went to see Restell again. When she arrived at Restell's office, Purdy explained that she had ceased taking the medicine because it had done nothing for her, and she wondered if Restell could do anything else to bring her relief. Restell answered in the affirmative, saying she could cause her to miscarry "without causing her any pain or to be sick for a single day" and that she would not ever have to wean the son she was currently nursing. Asked about the price, Restell informed Purdy that she usually charged $40 or $50 and sometimes as much as

$100; what could Purdy afford? When Purdy explained that she was poor, Restell said she could perform the procedure for $20. But even that was too high for Purdy. She did, however, have a pawn ticket for a gold watch and chain and two rings. Would Restell accept that as a guarantee until Purdy could come up with the $20? Restell went behind the curtain to consult with someone—likely her husband, Charles Lohman—and returned, telling Purdy that if she promised it was "a sure ticket," that she could accept that along with $5. Purdy assured her that it was valid, and Restell told her to come the next day, when another woman would perform the procedure. Restell was essentially operating on a sliding scale, charging one price to those women who could most afford it and bargaining with women like Purdy, who would be paying for the procedure on an installment plan.[4]

The next evening, Purdy returned to Greenwich Street at eight o'clock. She waited in "the store" for some time, and eventually Restell invited her behind the curtain, where she saw a man. This was almost certainly Restell's husband, Charles. The presence of a man "very much alarmed" Purdy, in part because she was under the impression that she was in a "'bad house' and that the man had some ill design upon her person and that Madam Restell had entrapped her there for that purpose." Both the man and Restell told her that there was no need to be alarmed, and then the man put "his hand upon her breast and saying to Madam Restell, 'She is only about three months gone.'" Restell placed a small box and a blanket on the floor and asked Purdy to re-move her hat and lie down. Purdy became even more anxious that the man was going to "attempt to have carnal knowledge of her," but both Restell and the man assured her that they intended no harm and per-suaded her "to lie down upon the blanket with her head upon the box." Upon Purdy lying down, the man "stooped down and raised her clothes and . . . put his hand or his hand and an instrument both into her person for some considerable distance, and from the extension and pressure of the parts, [she was] under the impression that it was his hand, which was kept there about two minutes, at which time the parts within appeared to be separating and caused a good deal of pain."

Restell consulted with the man, who assured her he had been success-ful and then told Purdy that she would likely be sick in two or three days, that she might need to employ a physician, and that she would need to find someone to look after her son at that time. Restell then informed Purdy that she must not tell "what had taken place to any one as it was a states prison act and it would go worse with [Purdy] than it would with her, Madam Restell." Purdy replied that she would tell no one. She also recounted that she had left Restell with the pawn ticket and $1, not having the full $5 that Restell had asked for the pre-vious day. Despite Purdy's inability to pay, Restell and the mysterious man had still done their part.[5]

While there were multiple methods for terminating a pregnancy, the one employed by "the man" and also the one Restell consistently practiced, was to irritate the cervix or perhaps the uterine wall, which would lead to contractions and the expulsion of the fetus. She and Lohman may also have burst the amniotic sac, which would deprive the fetus of what it needed to survive. Restell and Lohman may have used instruments like a curette (to scrape the interior of the uterus) or a bougie (to stimulate or irritate the cervix), or they may simply have used their hands. In most cases, Restell did not perform full abortions, especially when dealing with pregnancies of four months' gestation or earlier. Abortions in the second trimester or later would have required more specialized equipment, like forceps, and would also have man-dated a greater dilation of the cervix. While this type of abortion was performed by doctors in the interest of women's health, and while Restell could well have possessed the equipment and the knowledge to do so, Restell was in the business of bringing on miscarriages rather than of performing full terminations.[6]

There were a number of advantages to this method, not the least of which is that patients did not have to deliver in Restell's office. Rather, most women left the office still pregnant and returned home, where they would miscarry the fetus in a way that, generally speaking, would be indistinguishable from a spontaneous miscarriage that occurred without any interference at all. As with a miscarriage, however, and as

Restell advised Purdy, a woman might need the care of a doctor to ensure that she also passed the placenta, or afterbirth, which could become infected if it remained within the womb. Just as with a normal miscarriage, some women required medical care, as did Ann Maria Purdy. Others did not, especially when the pregnancy was not advanced. Contrary to myths about abortion during the nineteenth century, when done correctly by a skilled professional like Madame Restell, it was not a dangerous procedure. It could, of course, be painful, but likely not any more than a naturally occurring miscarriage of a fetus of a few months' gestation.

Madame Restell misrepresented the law in New York when telling Purdy that the penalty for abortion would be worse for Purdy than for Restell herself. In fact, in 1839 and until the New York state legislature changed its abortion statute in 1845 (in part in response to this very case), women who received abortions were not criminally liable; only the abortionist herself or himself was. Anyone who administered an abortion on a woman pregnant with a "quick child" could be found guilty of manslaughter and held in state prison for between four and seven years. An abortion terminating a pregnancy not yet quick—likely the case for Purdy if she was only three months pregnant—was a misdemeanor, and the punishment was a fine of up to $500 or up to a year in county jail or both. But one can imagine why Restell might warn Purdy not to reveal her identity or what she had done, because the results for Restell herself could be dire. Especially with a client like Purdy, whom Restell did not know and who, by her own telling, seemed to have so little knowledge of what Restell was actually doing for her, one could not be too careful in warning Purdy not to speak about the procedure she had received in Greenwich Street.[7]

Purdy claimed that Restell was anxious to have her leave following the operation, so Purdy put her hat back on and departed, heading along Cortland Street to Broadway, where she caught an omnibus toward her home at Mott and Grand. She was by that point quite weak and considered asking another passenger for help. Instead, she managed to alight at Grand Street. Fearing what might happen in the night, she told her landlady that she thought she might be miscarrying, owing to having done some heavy labor the day before, and then spent the night in "the most excruciating and distressing pain." The next day, Sunday, she sent for Dr. Marvin (the same doctor who had identified the abortifacient as tansy and turpentine) to attend her when she became feverish. On Tuesday she delivered the fetus; the afterbirth did not come until Friday, which was not abnormal. Marvin suspected what Mrs. Purdy had done and asked her if she had not used "improper means." Purdy confessed but begged him not to tell her husband. Marvin acquiesced, which is telling in itself. While he may have disapproved of what Purdy had done, he did not come forward to lodge a complaint against Madame Restell or the mysterious man who had performed the abortion. Instead, he tended to Purdy's needs and kept her secret for the time being. Even as some doctors began lining up publicly in opposition to abortion and its practitioners, there were still some medical school–trained physicians who were willing to look the other way, especially if that is what their patients wanted.[8]

Purdy kept silent about her abortion for almost two years, telling only a few close friends. But in March of 1841, she found herself so unwell that she consulted a doctor, who confirmed that she was suffering from tuberculosis, that she was unlikely to recover, and that indeed her death was imminent. About to meet "her Maker," Purdy chose this moment to confess to her husband, William, that unbeknownst to him she had procured an abortion two years previously at the hands of Madame Restell. William Purdy then approached justice of the police court, Henry W. Merritt, who along with the clerk of the police, took a deposition from Mrs. Purdy at her home at 341 Broome Street, at the corner of the Bowery (she had moved in the intervening two years). Madame Restell was almost immediately arrested, and what followed was her first protracted interaction with the law, one that would not be fully resolved for a year and a half. If Restell had primarily been tried in the court of public opinion in 1840, 1841 would see her tried in a court of law.[9]

When Restell arrived at the police court, she was informed of the nature of the charge and told she had a right to counsel. Her husband, who was with her at the time, said he would go get her counsel, John Morrell. About five minutes after Lohman left, Merritt asked Restell if she would accompany him to Purdy's residence, so that Purdy, who he explained was ill, might identify Restell. Restell acquiesced, and Merritt accompanied her to a boardinghouse at the corner of Bowery and Broome, where Purdy now resided, just three blocks from her former residence. There he read Purdy's deposition out loud and asked Purdy if she could identify the woman from whom she had purchased the phial of medicine and who was present in Greenwich Street when the man performed the abortion. Purdy identified Restell as that woman and signed a deposition to that effect. Restell was permitted to ask Purdy any questions she liked, but according to Merritt, "Restell put a number of questions to Mrs. Purdy, which Mrs. Purdy answered, but neither the questions nor answers were put down, because [Merritt] did not think it material to put them down." The officer who accompanied Restell and Merritt to the Purdy residence claimed they could not have been inside for more than twenty or thirty minutes, not enough time for Restell to be joined by her counsel.[10]

On the strength of this deposition, Restell was taken into custody and imprisoned once again in the Tombs. As in her previous brief stay there two years earlier, Restell would have been confined on the second floor of the women's division of the prison, away from the more common criminals drawn from nearby Five Points. She remained imprisoned for two days, after which she was examined by police magistrates, who pressed her on her real name. It was early enough in her career that there still remained some confusion about the difference between her actual name, Ann Lohman, and her pseudonym, Madame Caroline Restell. She declined to answer and repeated her innocence. She remained imprisoned and on March 26, Justice Merritt set her bail at $5,000. On April 1, Restell was committed to trial in the court of general sessions, amid a throng of onlookers, some of whom had come to support her, others of whom were simply curious about this mysterious persona. The next day, Judge Ingliss reduced bail to $3,000, which he stipulated would need to be guaranteed by two sureties, one for $2,000 and another for $1,000.[11]

Three days later, Purdy's husband, William, appealed to the court for permission to remove his wife from the city and to take her to New Jersey, where she would be more comfortable. The court ordered that Purdy's testimony could be taken de bene esse at her home, meaning that this deposition would be allowed to stand in for her testimony both before the grand jury and at trial if she did not live to attend either. While Restell and her counsel were offered the chance to cross-examine Purdy during this process, they declined, protesting that taking the deposition in this way ran counter to the law and the rights accorded to the defendant to be able to cross-examine her accuser in a court of law. Purdy, "her skin of the purest white, and a slight hectic flush, the emblem of consumption on her cheeks," according to the *Evening Post*, affirmed her testimony on April 5 at her home, Restell and her attorneys present. Her husband then removed her to Newark, New Jersey, where she died of tuberculosis on the 28th of April.[12]

In the meantime, *Polyanthos* editor George Washington Dixon was ecstatic, claiming victory over Restell and excoriating his fellow newspapermen for not condemning Restell sooner: "We entered the battlefield alone. Like St. Paul before Nero, no one stood by us. . . . The work

In this cartoon, Ann Maria Purdy is depicted sacrificing her child—the fetus in the jar—to Madame Restell, while Mrs. Bird and Death look on. Reprinted from *Dixon's Polyanthos*, March 27, 1841, page 90.

which we have begun, we intend to finish, until all these lieutenants of Satan are driven, howling, from the society of the innocent and the virtuous." The story on Restell was on the front page of the March 27 edition of the *Polyanthos*, accompanied by a gruesome cartoon of a skeleton approaching two female figures. Restell appears in the foreground with a skull and crossbones on her dress; in the background, on a platform in front of a cemetery, is a contemporary of Restell's, Mrs. Bird, who is depicted with a bird's head. Kneeling before Restell is a young woman with a fetus in a jar, likely meant to be Purdy sacrificing her child to Restell. In this cartoon, Bird and Restell are agents of death.[13]

The article that accompanied it from the same issue details a long list of Restell's supposed crimes, some of them either exaggerated or of questionable veracity. Dixon replayed many of his objections to Restell's practice in the accompanying article and delivered a detailed account of Purdy's affidavit. Among the story's most dramatic claims is the following: "Restell has taken the alarm; she is stirred up, like an adder that had long been lurking in security among the reeds, but feeling the end of a sharp stick upon his back, raises his poison head, and darts forth his tongue, while his red eyes blaze with fury, and he resolves to do all the mischief he can to his assailants." While no other paper devoted so much space to coverage of Restell and her contemporaries— at least during 1841—others certainly echoed Dixon's condemnation of Restell and of the newspapers that allowed her business to grow. Horace Greeley, the editor of the *Tribune*, which adhered to higherbrow standards, chimed in:

At last, when the woman had made a fortune, and her newspaper accomplices large sums by their mutual iniquity, a deluded creature is nearly murdered, through the joint influences of publications in The Sun and the practices of Madame R and behold, Justice *almost* aroused! He opens one eye, reaches out his arm and grasps one of the culprits, leaving the other untouched! Is that right? Ought they who for base lucre have willfully abetted beforehand the crimes of this wretch to escape wholly unpunished? The public must answer.

Greeley, who gave little credence to Dixon's stand against Restell, describing the *Tribune* as the sole paper to condemn her, also indicted his competitors the *Sun* and *Herald*, who profited by her advertisements. This was a long-standing complaint made not just by newspaper editors who pointed out the hypocrisy of the *Sun* and *Herald* decrying Restell's crimes as they featured her advertisements but also by lawmakers and other officials.[14]

Newspaper coverage of this particular trial also contributed to the growing discourse about abortion in antebellum America, sometimes despite itself. Unlike the archetypal patients of abortionists who were depicted in newspapers either as fallen women hoping to avoid revealing their secrets or as wealthy married women selfishly limiting their families so they could enjoy lives of luxury, Purdy was married and a mother and claimed she sought to terminate her pregnancy for the good of her existing family. She also was not a rich woman. She was one among many of Restell's clients who confounded the typical representations in the antebellum press of those who sought abortion. Abortion's foes knew that it was more effective to paint abortionists' clients as either wealthy and selfish or seduced and wronged; desperate married women were much more sympathetic. And Purdy was exactly that, a married mother who worried about having to wean her son if she should have another child too soon. While newspapers acknowledged all of these facts about Purdy, their other coverage of abortion and the women who sought it effectively portrayed Purdy as an exception to the rule.

Some of the blame for the abortion, both in the press and in Purdy's own deposition, also centered on Rebecca, the washerwoman who guided Purdy to Restell's door. In Purdy's testimony, the African American Rebecca is cast both in the role of Restell's booster and as a font of sexual knowledge not possessed by the white Purdy. It is not hard to believe that Purdy might have employed a Black woman to clean or launder for her, but the fact that Rebecca occupies so central a role in this tale—alongside Restell, of course—deflects the attention away from the choices Purdy herself made in terminating her pregnancy. Purdy remains an innocent naïf, the swarthy and knowing Rebecca urging her on toward danger and sin. The central role of Rebecca might have been Purdy's own way of absolving herself of responsibility, or it could be that Justice Merritt asked questions that led Purdy toward those answers. Either way, newspapers also focused on this aspect of the story, the *Morning Courier and New-York Enquirer,* for instance, claiming that Purdy had "consulted an old negress" to ascertain what to do, with the *Herald* explaining Purdy had "talked with a negro wench on the subject." While there is no evidence to suggest that Restell ever had an African American clientele—Black women likely consulting Black midwives in their own community—the overall effect of the coverage was to implicate African American culture in illicit and illegal sexual knowledge.[15]

Dixon's coverage, as well as that of some other newspapers, also delighted in detailing the difficulty Restell had in finding sureties to post bail on her behalf; that is, men who owned property of sufficient value and who would commit that value to the court as a surety against Restell disappearing before her trial. If she disappeared, they would forfeit their property. This was a tough ask in good circumstances, but Restell's reputation made it much harder. The *New York Spectator* claimed that while a number of men initially volunteered, they withdrew their offers upon learning that their names would be publicized as supporters of Restell.

On April 22, the grand jury indicted Restell on four charges: the first two were for "unlawfully, wickedly, wilfully [*sic*] and maliciously" administering a noxious medicine to Purdy (the phial of tansy that she had stopped taking); the other two were for using "certain instruments, to wit, one piece of wire, and one pair of pliers with the intent thereby then and there to procure the miscarriage of the said Ann Maria Purdy." Because Purdy was not pregnant with a quick child, the alleged crimes were all misdemeanors and any fines or punishment would be spent in the city jail on Blackwell's Island, not in state prison. For now, Restell remained imprisoned in the Tombs.[16]

Restell was not without visitors during her time at the Tombs. In addition to her lawyers and her husband, the *New-York Atlas* reported cheekily that "a number of ladies who have received great service at the hands of Madame Restell in the hour of their trouble, have called at 'The Tombs' to see if they can be serviceable to her in her *confinement*," also a synonym for pregnancy. She was also visited on two occasions by members of the American Female Moral Reform Society (AFMRS), a group of women dedicated to eliminating the sexual double standard. They made it a practice of visiting women confined in jail as well as in houses of prostitution, where they hoped to convert them to proper Christian living. While they opposed everything for which Madame Restell stood, even she was not fully beyond redemption. At the very least, visiting her made for good reading in the *Advocate for Moral Reform*. While the first visit had not been received well, they visited the "mistress of abominations" a second time, during which they gave her a religious tract. In their words, "She rejected the tract, saying she had plenty of good reading, pointing at the same time to a lot of novels with which she was supplied; and turning her back in anger, said, 'I will hear nothing from you—I fear neither God nor man, nor care for heaven or hell!'"[17]

Restell's lawyers, Ambrose Jordan and John Morrell, were, of course, working to make sure Restell could be liberated as soon as possible. In late April they moved to quash the indictment against Restell on the grounds that the testimony of Ann Maria Purdy should be inadmissible, taken as it was de bene esse. Her counsels argued, in essence, that Purdy, who had still been alive when the grand jury met, should have appeared before them to give her testimony instead of having her statement presented in lieu of that testimony. They were met with forceful rejoinders from the district attorney, and in early May, Judge Inglis ruled against Restell, stating that there was nothing faulty about the indictment and that it was likely based on more than simply the testimony of Purdy. Restell was thus arraigned and the indictment was read. She pleaded not guilty and was remanded back to jail for trial, which would have taken place a week later but was postponed because the prosecutor was otherwise engaged in another trial.[18]

In the interim, Restell once again addressed New Yorkers and newspapermen by writing to them in the *Herald* on May 3. One newspaper has

> charged me with "manslaughter" and even "murder," knowing at the same time that the charge is misdemeanor, and has also attempted to create an impression I caused the death of the woman on whose affidavit I have been detained, when it is notorious that for eighteen months after her alleged treatment, (in June, 1839,) she had enjoyed sufficient good health to enable her to attend balls, parties, &c., with late hours, and exposures incident to such indulgences. But even if it were otherwise, is there any justification for the uncalled for comments indulged in by the Courier & Enquirer and others, before the party accused is put on the defence. Justice and common sense requires that no party shall be adjudged guilty merely on a charge, as charges are easily made, and may, on trial, prove unfounded, false, or malicious.

On the one hand, Restell was correct that she had not been charged with a felony, in large part because there was no real connection between Purdy's death from tuberculosis and the abortion she alleged Restell performed almost two years earlier. Simply performing an abortion was still a misdemeanor under New York state law if it was performed before the moment of quickening, and no one was alleging that this abortion was performed post-quickening. On the other hand, however, Restell had been running advertisements in major newspapers for two years that hinted at the very crime she was accused of committing, if not on this particular person. That newspapermen took her at her word and believed she indeed had performed an abortion and had sold an abortifacient could hardly have surprised her. Her insistence that she was only selling "preventive," rather than abortive, powders was less than fully believable.[19]

Ten days after publishing this letter, Restell was finally able to find someone wealthy enough to serve as her surety. Newspaper accounts vary, but it appears that both her husband and a man named Selden Braynard served as her sureties. Each could demonstrate to the court that they possessed at least $6,000. Restell paid Braynard for his services, as newspapers noted that he had "transacted a pretty large business in the bailing line," meaning he worked as an early version of a bail bondsman. He is listed as a "broker" in the 1841 city directory. Restell was free, having spent almost two months in the Tombs. She again commenced advertising her services.[20]

Madame Restell's trial began on Wednesday, July 14, 1841, in the court of general sessions once a jury had been selected and sworn. Ten men admitted that they had read or talked too much about the case and were already prejudiced against Restell; they were dismissed. In addition to the twelve members of the jury, this court also included the recorder, Frederick Tallmadge, who was the senior judge, as well as two additional judges and two aldermen. The misdemeanor counts of the indictment were for administering medicines designed to produce miscarriage on June 2, 1839, and for surgically producing miscarriage on July 20, 1839. No matter what happened, the maximum Restell would spend in prison was a year. Restell continued to be represented by attorneys Jordan and Morrell; District Attorney Whiting and Associate Attorney LaForge took the case on behalf of the prosecution. Restell entered the courtroom "attired in the most elegant manner, in a black satin walking dress, white satin bonnet of the cottage pattern, and a very elegant white veil of Brussels lace." This description comes from George Washington Dixon of the *Polyanthos*, meaning that if even he could concede she looked elegant, she must have cut quite a figure.[21]

The first witness called was William Purdy. The DA asked a series of questions that allowed Purdy to attest to his relationship with his late wife, Ann Maria, and to having witnessed her sign the deposition on which the case largely rested. Jordan, Restell's attorney, then asked questions that were clearly designed to cast doubt on the virtue of the late Ann Maria, in part by insinuating that she was in the habit of venturing out on the Bowery on her own or in the company of a young man named Mowbray. After a final two questions about whether William was currently sleeping with a woman to whom he was not married—again designed to sully his character and to which the DA objected—Purdy was excused. His testimony did not amount to much, largely having confirmed what his wife had included in her deposition.[22]

The next witness was police magistrate Henry W. Merritt, who had taken Ann Maria Purdy's deposition on March 22 and who had also brought Restell to be identified by Purdy on the same day. At issue here for both sides, established by a long series of questions and answers, was whether Merritt had followed proper procedure in interviewing Purdy and in taking Restell to Purdy's home to be identified without benefit of counsel. Jordan was beginning to build the foundation for overturning the case against Restell. The trial adjourned for the day at the end of Merritt's testimony.[23]

On Monday, July 19, the trial resumed with the recorder presenting his justification for why Purdy's deposition was admissible as evidence in the proceedings. Following a lengthy exploration of case law and English common law—the basis for the legal system in the United States—and despite much objection from Restell's attorneys, Tallmadge explained, "I am, therefore, of the opinion, that the deposition is admissible."[24]

The trial proceeded with the calling of additional witnesses, the next of whom was Gilbert F. Hays, the officer who had arrested Restell on March 22 and had seen her interactions with police magistrate Merritt at the police office and at the Purdy residence on Broome Street. Hays was sworn as a witness for the defense with the purpose of trying to establish that Merritt had told Restell that the only purpose in going to Purdy's house was to be identified by Purdy, instead of also to cross-examine her. Hays could not confirm this, as Restell's attorneys wanted him to do. Instead, he claimed that Restell had affirmed her willingness to go to Purdy's without her counsel (who her husband was simultaneously trying to locate) and that she had had an opportunity to question Purdy. Merritt was recalled for further examination, confirming much of his earlier testimony. The DA then proceeded to read out loud the depositions of Ann Maria Purdy, with which many in the courtroom were now familiar.[25]

It is striking the degree to which most of the trial to this point had been procedural. So much hinged on Ann Maria Purdy's testimony, and thus all of the questioning of her husband, Hays, and Merritt was necessary to establish that these were her words and that those words were admissible. The next witness, Lucinda Van Buskirk, was surely of more interest to those assembled in the courtroom and to those who would read about the trial in the papers, if only because she could add to the story instead of reconfirming the basic outlines. Van Buskirk testified that she was a married woman and had been friends with Ann Maria Purdy. She had gone with Purdy to Madame Restell's office in July 1839, after Purdy had miscarried, for the purpose of retrieving the watch, chain, and rings that Purdy had pawned to pay for the abortion. According to Van Buskirk, Restell quite logically told Purdy that she could not return the jewelry until Purdy had paid the remainder of the $20 fee, saying, "We have done it very low, much lower than we are in the habit of doing it, and I have given $5 of the $6 to the doctor," presumably meaning the man who had actually performed the abortion. "She said 'if you had gone your full time, it would have cost you a good deal more.'" Purdy replied that she would be obliged to tell her husband, likely because he would notice that the jewelry was missing, and Restell again told her not to do this because abortion was "a State Prison offence for you as well as for me." Restell did not return the jewelry at that time but asked Purdy the address of her boardinghouse so that she might call on her another time for the money.[26]

Upon cross-examination by one of Restell's attorneys, Van Buskirk also admitted that she had accompanied Purdy "to gratify an idle curiosity in seeing Madame Restell, of whom she had heard so much." She also recounted that she saw a number of other customers there, one she believed was a married woman. Two men also came in, and a third "gentleman" came in and "purchased some medicine of accused and gave her $5 for it." She also admitted that she had not heard half the conversation between Purdy and Restell because it had taken place out of her earshot. In the end, there was little new information here, just more confirmation that Purdy had paid Restell—in one form or another—and that someone else could attest to this.[27]

The final witness called by the prosecution was Purdy's physician, Dr. David D. Marvin, who testified that he had attended her from the 21st to the 29th of July, when she was "laboring under severe pains," and that it took one or two days for her to deliver the fetus. "He was inclined to believe from her previous good health and the suddenness of her delivery that it was premature." Because the fetus was obviously premature in terms of its growth, he seems to have meant that she had done something to effect the premature delivery. Multiple papers then reported that Marvin said, "Mrs. P was a woman of ordinary intellect, of fickle disposition, not illiterate for her station, but easily influenced. She was in the habit of visiting her neighbors considerably." He confirmed the earlier testimony of William Purdy that Ann Maria had been seen repeatedly in the company of a Mr. Mowbray. Finally, and perhaps most oddly, he related that he had accompanied Ann Maria to the pawn shop to recover the watch, chain, and gold rings, which he then held in safekeeping for her. The watch was accidentally destroyed when it came into contact with quicksilver (mercury), but Marvin later returned the chain and rings to Mrs. Purdy. When asked, he also testified that he had no knowledge of Purdy ever going to Restell's with the watch, and he had certainly not been to Madame Restell's office himself. Finally, he recounted that Purdy had been up and about until the winter of 1840 and that her condition was pulmonary consumption, or tuberculosis. Her death could not be attributed to the abortion. Indeed, if prosecutors had believed that Restell was responsible for her death, they would have increased the charges considerably, which they did do when women died following illegal abortions. At the end of Marvin's testimony, the prosecution rested its case.[28]

It was now the moment for Restell's attorneys to mount a defense. Morrell's first witness was Barrow A. Cohen, who worked at the shop where Purdy pawned the jewelry. Though he could not specifically remember Purdy or Marvin picking up the jewelry, he did have a sworn affidavit from Purdy attesting that the pawn ticket had been lost, an affidavit he had taken as proof of her ownership of the jewelry. The purpose of the testimony was to cast doubt on the testimony of other witnesses that the jewelry had been used as collateral for procuring the abortion.[29]

Morrell then recalled two prior witnesses, Dr. Marvin and William Purdy. Marvin confirmed that he believed that the affidavit presented by Cohen was indeed the one Purdy had brought to the pawnbrokers. Purdy's testimony was more complicated, but much of it amounted to the defense lawyer attempting to portray William Purdy as vengeful, implying that the prosecution of Restell occurred only after Purdy tried to extort money from her, presumably at a moment prior to his enlisting the help of the police in prosecuting the crime. This was a risky strategy, in that establishing a link between William Purdy and Restell as much as conceded that there was a prior connection between Ann Maria Purdy and Restell. The blackmail plot worked only if one were to believe that the entire scenario was cooked up by William Purdy on his wife's deathbed as a moneymaking scheme, which was something of a stretch.[30]

The final witness, Huron Betts, does not appear in the printed pamphlet of the trial that Dixon, of the *Polyanthos*, published. This may have been because his testimony, while it did not necessarily cast doubt on Restell's guilt, did serve to question William Purdy's motivations in coming forward in the first place. Restell's lawyer had just asked Purdy if he had tried to blackmail Restell by offering to withhold his testimony against her and additionally whether he had asked Betts to go with him to Restell's to make that offer. He replied in the negative. Betts testified, however, that three or four weeks ago, Purdy had asked him to approach Restell with the offer of his silence and the silence of other witnesses. Betts claimed that he "went into the house of Madame Restell and saw a woman." The *New York Herald* reported that Betts had seen Restell and delivered his message. On cross-examination for the prosecution, Betts reiterated that Purdy had approached him about doing this and that Purdy had told him that he had gotten the indictment against Restell. Betts explained that he had known Purdy for at least "three or four months" and had seen him around occasionally. And Betts's testimony, if it were to be believed, did not actually negate the possibility that Restell had performed the abortion; it just made Purdy look shady and opportunistic.[31]

With testimony concluded, all four attorneys—Jordan and Morrell for the defense, LaForge and Whiting for the people—gave closing arguments. The defense then asked Recorder Tallmadge to instruct the jury that in order to find Restell guilty on the count of the indictment related to the surgical abortion, they must determine that she employed an instrument in performing the operation. Tallmadge demurred, explaining that the statute itself was unclear about whether perhaps a hand might qualify as an instrument. With that and some pro forma instructions, the jury was dismissed to begin deliberations.[32]

Most newspapers reported that the jury took only five minutes to declare Restell guilty of the two misdemeanors of administering an abortifacient and terminating a pregnancy with an instrument. Restell's attorney immediately moved for an arrest of judgment to give him time to prepare his case to appeal to the Supreme Court of the State of New York. The court granted Jordan time till the first day of the next term. In the meantime, newspapers like the *Polyanthos* and many others broadcast their victory, with Dixon taking a good part of the credit for the pursuit of Restell in the first place. The *Brooklyn Evening Star* explained of Restell, "She is a woman, without a woman's nature, who aimed to make herself wealthy by foul and unnatural practices upon the weak and credulous. . . . When Madame Restell is punished, we hope no other of her race may arise to outrage morality, and pander to vice." While many celebrated Restell's conviction, the case was far from over, her counsel having raised many questions about the validity of Purdy's deposition, questions which they were now documenting in a bill of exceptions that would be presented to the high court.[33]

Two days later, Restell herself took out an advertisement in the *New York Tribune*:

To the Public.—The testimony elicited on the trial of the under-signed, and the verdict of a jury upon that testimony, is before the public, and she has no objections, if correctly reported, that they should stand side by side, for the judgement of the public. That the undersigned is willing, unshrinkingly so, to abide the issue, was in evidence on the trial; that all overtures and proposals made to her to compound with the witnesses for the prosecution to induce them to absent themselves, &c., were spurned; and the public, perhaps, may be aware, that important principles of evidence and law are involved, to be adjudicated upon by the highest tribunals of the country, which may completely reverse the aspect in the premises. She indulges the hope that, as the whole matter will be carried up before another and higher court, the public will await the decision of the courts of appeal.

MADAME RESTELL

148 Greenwich st.

While the bulk of this letter is essentially asking the public to wait and see what the court of appeals says about her case, perhaps the most important point here is that Restell specifically claims that she "spurned" all "overtures and proposals" made by witnesses for the prosecution to "absent themselves." Here she is referring to the possibility that the entire case, factual though it might have been, was brought only because William Purdy, realizing that his wife was on death's door, attempted to extort money from Restell once he found out about Ann Maria's abortion two years earlier. This allegation had no real bearing on the veracity of the claims made by the Purdys. The point for Restell was to induce the public to wait for the final outcome of the legal machinations.[34]

In the interim, however, fear and intrigue about an unrelated incident gripped the city of New York. Just four days after Restell's conviction, Mary Rogers, a twenty-one-year-old cigar store employee—known about town as the "beautiful cigar girl"—went missing after she told her fiancé she would be visiting some family members. Rogers had disappeared once before, in the summer of 1838, and it had been publicized in newspapers. Three days after this second disappearance, however, her corpse was found floating in the Hudson River near Hoboken, New Jersey. Some speculated that she had been abducted, raped, and murdered by a gang, others that she had died at the hands of an abortionist, either in New Jersey or in New York. As the tragedy of Rogers's inquest unfolded in New York throughout the fall of 1841, receiving attention across the country, Restell's case awaited its appeal. Sentiment against Restell grew, especially if she might also be responsible for the mysterious death of the beautiful cigar girl. As Dixon's *Polyanthos* speculated in October of that year, "Mary Rogers was last seen in the direction of Madame Restell's house—the dreadfully lacerated body at Weehawken bluff bore the marks of no ordinary violation." This theory gained greater traction when Edgar Allan Poe published a short story in three installments (in 1842 and 1843) called "The Mystery of Marie Rogêt," based loosely on the case, that insinuated that a botched abortion was to blame. To this day, the murder has not been solved, though historians think it likely that Rogers was procuring an abortion during both of her disappearances.[35]

Dixon's *Polyanthos* folded in November of 1841 with no definitive resolution in the Restell case, though Dixon would move on to a number of "flash" newspapers that catered to young men on the make about town. By this point most other newspapers were covering Restell and her business, in part goaded on by Dixon and his 1841 campaign against her, as well as by the trial and its appeal. The appeal was heard in late May of 1842, when the Supreme Court of the State of New York was in session in Manhattan, with James Whiting continuing to represent the people, and with Restell, who had remained free pending appeal, retaining Ambrose Jordan. The bill of exceptions, or appeal, focused almost exclusively on the inadmissibility of the testimony of Ann Maria Purdy. The supreme court found these arguments compelling, with associate justice Greene Bronson finding that the prosecutor should not have taken depositions de bene esse in a criminal case and used them in evidence without the consent of the defendant, especially so because Restell had not yet been indicted at the time of the examination, only arrested. "Dying declarations," like the kind taken from Purdy, Bronson explained, were to be utilized only in trials pertaining to the death of the person dying, not to her abortion years earlier. Bronson noted that witnesses must generally appear in court and be examined by the accused party, and that in the case of this deposition, the accused should have been present for the first round of inquiry. "The Court of General Sessions acted without authority in ordering the examination of Mrs. Purdy, and the depositions taken before the recorder were, therefore, extrajudicial and void." Bronson was not making a ruling on the evidence or on Restell's guilt or innocence; instead, his job was simply to evaluate the trial itself and whether the district attorney had followed proper procedure. Finding that he had not, Bronson granted Restell a new trial. However, given that the majority of the evidence had been ruled inadmissible, the consequence was that Restell's conviction was overturned. The district attorney did not seek a retrial. In July of 1842, one year after it had begun, and three years after the alleged crime, *People v. Madame Restell* finally concluded.[36]

The next month, Restell took the opportunity once again to address New Yorkers by having the entire supreme court opinion reprinted in the *New-York Tribune* and the *New York Herald*, prefaced by a long letter from her. She began by focusing on the newspaper coverage of her that had begun months earlier, questioning why reporters had condemned her so unanimously. "Was it that the object of it [Restell] was tried and convicted, on proper and legal testimony, of some unheard of and most horrid atrocity!—Of murder, of manslaughter, of arson, or some other heinous felony! No, not so. *Worse than all this.* She was *charged* with the commission of a *misdemeanor!* It was this charge, unsustained (as the Supreme Court declare) by a particle of legal testimony, which caused this mighty newspaper volcano to burst upon her devoted head." She went on to explain that a reading public whose

minds were so poisoned by this kind of newspaper coverage was unlikely to be able to acquit her once some of its members found themselves in the jury tasked with evaluating her supposed crimes. While
she did not believe that the court of general sessions "acted from other
than correct motives," she did find it rather curious that the supreme
court had found that its officials had abandoned common law, precedent, and statute in conducting the trial. This, too, she blamed on
a press that "exaggerated, perverted, misrepresented, magnified" the
crime of which she was accused.[37]

Because she predicted that no newspaper would actually report that
her conviction had been overturned, she wanted to make sure New
Yorkers were aware it had occurred and why Justice Bronson had seen
fit to do so. She first declared Ann Maria Purdy's testimony on the
matter of the pawn ticket to be inconsistent, in that she swore in the
key affidavit that she had given it to Restell, but in an earlier affidavit
produced at the pawn shop that she had lost it. Both statements cannot
be true, and Restell herself was never proved to have been in possession
of the pawn ticket, at least not independently of Purdy's testimony.
Restell also explained that Huron Betts's testimony contradicted William Purdy's assertion that he had never visited Restell in an attempt to
blackmail her, allowing her to buy his silence. "The immateriality of
this Purdy's testimony upon the main question at issue [the abortion]
was all that saved him from an indictment for perjury." Here Restell
argued that because Purdy's testimony did not bear on the central question of whether Restell had performed the abortion itself, he was not
charged with perjury, but she clearly felt he should have been and that
all of his testimony was tainted by the evidence given by Betts.[38]

Finally, and here she skirted dangerously close to admitting she actually had performed the abortion, she vehemently denied that there
had ever been a man present "on that special occasion." Purdy's testimony had been clear that it was a man who had brought on her miscarriage, but Restell alleged that this claim was made only to shock
people with the specter of the intermingling of the sexes. In essence,
she declared the introduction of a man as surgeon in the affidavit

"a production intended to be startlingly horrid." Instead, Restell explained,

> In no case do I engage a "man" or physician, for the simple and all-abundant reason that, whatever I undertake, I feel myself competent, as well by study, experience, and practice, to carry through properly; and, so far from requiring a physician in my practice it is not unusual for me to be called for in preference to a "doctor" in confinements, where a proper delicacy forbids the presence of a male practitioner, and also in such other cases in which it is more fitting and proper, and more in consonance with our ideas of propriety, that a lady, provided always she is skillful, should attend in preference to a gentleman.

She closed by noting that all of the exceptions taken by her lawyer were sustained by the supreme court, and she thanked Ambrose Jordan for the "faithful, able and fearless manner in which he had conducted himself throughout." She signed herself "MADAME RESTELL, Female Physician, 148 Greenwich-street, N.Y." The full opinion of the supreme court followed.[39]

Whether Charles Lohman or another man brought on Ann Maria Purdy's miscarriage or Madame Restell did, we will never know. That no one ever seems to have considered charging him or some other man with the crime certainly points to the possibility that Restell might have done it herself. It is also possible that Purdy found herself unable to identify the man, but she could recall the face of the woman present. Or perhaps the district attorney became so wrapped up in prosecuting the public face of the operation that he was less concerned with who, physically, had terminated the pregnancy. Had Purdy lived to testify at trial, we might have learned more about the identity of this unnamed man. Instead, even though Restell all but admitted to her trade in this letter, she did so quite clearly to assert that she was a competent and skilled female physician who could provide to women what they could not get from a male physician: delicacy, understanding, propriety. This letter, like others she published in newspapers, served as much as an advertisement (note her address at the end) as an absolution. She wanted possible customers to know that they would be seen by a skilled female physician, not by a man.

Madame Restell emerged from the trial relatively unscathed. She had also been free during the appeals process, unlike during the two months after her initial arrest. While it is quite clear that she had indeed sold Ann Maria Purdy an abortifacient and that she or a male associate had also brought on her miscarriage, she went free because the police magistrate bungled the evidence collection and the court of general sessions, in its zeal to prosecute Restell, accepted this faulty testimony. There were more wide-ranging consequences. As we shall see, the uproar over Restell's release and the death of Mary Rogers at the close of Restell's first trial did eventually lead New York City lawmakers to institute a permanent police force to investigate crimes like murder and misdemeanors like abortion. And these events likely also contributed to New York state lawmakers passing much stricter legislation to regulate abortion. But in the immediate wake of her prosecution, Restell had also gained enormous amounts of publicity. It was unlikely that any New Yorker—indeed anyone in the whole of the Northeast—did not now know who might be able to help in the event of an unwanted pregnancy. But just in case, she had been advertising her services the entire time.

4

MADAME RESTELL'S COMPETITION

Madame Restell's rise to prominence was hardly ensured from the outset. When she began practicing in the late 1830s, she was not alone, and her competition only increased as New York itself grew in population. Other irregular physicians like Restell were setting up shop to meet the needs of a city that had reached five hundred thousand inhabitants by 1850 and would add another three hundred thousand in the following decade alone. Advertisements for female monthly pills and preventive powders appeared in newspapers, urging readers to consult any number of other druggists and doctors, some of whom, like Restell, also advertised pseudonymously. Other female physicians also listed themselves in New York's city directories; in all likelihood, they also offered contraception and abortion. During the 1840s, Restell's chief competition came in the form of two other women: Mrs. Bird and Madame Costello. Indeed, by the mid-1840s, a newspaper-reading New Yorker would likely have lumped all three together, neither having achieved a reputation that surpassed the others, though these three certainly achieved greater notoriety than did some of their minor competitors. In part because of their advertisements, which often ran alongside one another in newspapers, Bird, Costello, and Restell were sometimes targeted together by the police magistrates and the grand jury. Recall the joint indictment of Costello and Restell by the grand jury in 1841, their advertisements supposedly constituting a public nuisance. Despite the fact that there must have been plenty of customers to go around, the three women were also fiercely competitive, and sometimes in under-handed ways. All of this played out in the newspapers, not only because reporters covered their exploits religiously but also because the women themselves occasionally took to the papers to speak to their clients or make accusations against one another. Getting to know Mrs. Bird and Madame Costello helps to understand the antebellum New York mar-ket in contraception, abortion, and midwifery and also throws into re-lief why Restell emerged from the decade of the 1840s the premier provider of all three.

* * * *

Mrs. Bird had been in business the longest. Her real name was Marga-ret Dawson, and she had been advertising her services as a midwife since 1837. She claimed to have been "duly qualified, in a lying-in hospi-tal in Europe, as may be seen by her testimonials and certificates." Her actual origins are the murkiest of the three practitioners, though she was likely a German immigrant, the surname Dawson perhaps coming from a husband she had married in New York. In city directories she listed herself variously as "Margaret Bird, physician," and "Margaret Dawson, widow." She also had two children, both of whom immigrated from Germany in the 1840s. They may have been twins, the product of Daw-son's first marriage.[1]

In her work as a physician, Mrs. Bird sold "soothing syrup for children cutting teeth," "Mrs. Bird's Nipple Salve" for sore nipples, and various pills meant for indigestion. By early 1838, she was offering "Dr. Vandenburgh's Female Renovating Pills From Germany." Like Restell, Bird was also a midwife and delivered babies in her residence. She moved around with some frequency, likely an indication that busi-ness was not steady and that she was unable to properly support herself. When she first started advertising, she was living at 7 Division Street, just at the edge of Five Points. In May 1838, she announced a move uptown to 322 Bowery, "one door above Bleecker street, where ladies can be accommodated with board, pleasant furnished rooms, and the best of attendance during their confinement. Mrs. Bird continues to be consulted on all diseases incidental to females. Advice gratis." By 1840, however, Bird was listed in the city directory as a physician at 18 Oliver Street. She had returned downtown, again living just outside of Five Points proper. While it might not have been quite the lying-in hospital that she occupied on the Bowery, it was a two-story home with bedrooms to accommodate women in their confinements. Two years later, she was at 83 Duane Street and the next year had returned to Oliver Street.[2]

Like Madame Restell, Mrs. Bird began to garner more attention in 1841. In late March of that year, just as Restell herself was arrested for Ann Maria Purdy's abortion, newspapers announced that Bird was in custody, charged with "being accessory by mismanagement to the death of one Maria E. Shaw, who died in her house after giving birth to a child." This newspaper, the *Log Cabin*, noted Bird's reputation as one who afforded "accommodations, concealment, and medical aid to women about to become mothers without being wives." Private lying-in hospitals like the ones run by Bird and Restell were generally no more than the homes of those women, with perhaps a room or two (depending on the size of the home) set aside for a pregnant woman to rest in the weeks leading up to labor and birth. They were not hospitals, as such. But in an era when most women still gave birth at home, some single women may not have been able to do so, especially if they wanted to keep their pregnancies a secret. Private lying-in hospitals provided one means of doing so, but precisely because of this they came in for censure by the same people who suspected that Bird and Restell were selling contraceptives to single women or were helping them to terminate their pregnancies. While we have no data about the marital status of their clientele, Bird's and Restell's lying-in patients were more likely to be single than married, if only because married women had other options for giving birth. Those with money could hire a midwife or a doctor to attend them at home, and those without could be accommodated at the New York Asylum for Lying-In Women, which took only married women. Private lying-in hospitals catered to single women, but ones who had enough money to be able to avoid the almshouse.

Some of these women may have been poor, but their lovers or seducers were willing to pay for their stay at a private lying-in hospital so as to conceal their pregnancies. In other cases, some of the growing number of wage-earning women might have been able to scrape together enough of their earnings to afford a month's confinement at a private lying-in hospital, or their parents might have done so to protect their reputations.[3]

In the case of twenty-year-old Maria E. Shaw, "to avoid the exposure consequent on being confined at home, . . . [she] was taken by her mother to the house of Mrs. Bird, (alias Mrs. Margaret Dawson, No. 18 Oliver street, female midwife) about 8 weeks since, to be boarded, taken care of and confined." One newspaper reported that Shaw had been seduced by a man named Rodgers, but additional details were not given. At the inquest, Shaw's mother, Eliza Hill, explained that "she was always a delicate person . . . she was very feeble before her confinement." According to the *New York Evening Express*, at Mrs. Hill's insistence, Mrs. Bird called in a Dr. James Wright, who lived on the same street, to examine her. He advised that a doctor, himself or someone else, be called when Shaw went into labor. On Sunday, March 21, Shaw gave birth to a baby girl, but there was no doctor in attendance. According to Bird, "The labor was not difficult or protracted. There was no instrument or other means used to facilitate. I never use instruments upon my own responsibility," explaining why she believed her own actions did not cause Shaw's death. Following the birth, Shaw was doing poorly, and Bird called on Dr. Wright again, who administered stimulants. Nevertheless, Shaw died about three and a half hours later. Shaw's mother, to avoid the "exposure of a public burial," conspired with Bird to have Shaw's body secretly taken by a carman to the home of the undertaker, who had arranged to have Shaw buried in the cemetery at the corner of East Broadway and Catherine Street. The carman, however, grew suspicious about why the coroner was not involved, as he normally would be, and told his employer, who immediately summoned a police magistrate and eventually the coroner, who ordered a postmortem examination and called for an inquest. The jury at that inquest found that Shaw had been "in a very precarious state of health and much debilitated, when she came to the house of Mrs. Bird." Therefore, while it was "highly improper" of Bird not to have heeded Dr. Wright's initial advice, nevertheless, Shaw "died in child bed" and Mrs. Bird was released.[4]

The actions of Shaw and her mother demonstrate the real need that women like Mrs. Bird served in a growing city like New York, where sex outside of marriage was increasingly common but where the older remedies for it—pressuring the couple to marry—no longer worked. The shame of an illegitimate pregnancy had brought them to Mrs. Bird, where Shaw could spend the final weeks of her confinement away from the eyes of those who would see her growing belly. Even after her tragic death, Eliza Hill wanted to shield her daughter and herself from the infamy that attended a pregnancy out of wedlock. As Bird herself explained of the unorthodox burial, "The reason for having the dead interred privately was for fear of having the disgrace of having [an] illegitimate child. . . . I have never had anyone buried from my house in a similar way before." Despite the fact that Shaw died of natural causes—indeed, would likely have died no matter where she gave birth— George Washington Dixon of the *Polyanthos* pounced on the incident, running repeated stories about Mrs. Bird alongside his coverage of Madame Restell and her arrest in the Purdy trial.[5]

In an article on March 27, Dixon railed against the secrecy of the planned burial, claiming that Bird sought to hide her crimes, rather than also acknowledging that Hill was partially trying to shield her daughter and herself from the stigma of illegitimacy. He claimed that Bird was unqualified to treat patients, especially one like Shaw, who was both ill and pregnant, and called on *regular physicians* of our city—those who have received the necessary qualifications for the practice of medicine—to come forward in the defense of legitimate practice." While some individual doctors had certainly turned against the practice in the 1830s and 1840s as more of their clients sought abortions from them, Dixon was among the first to stage the abortion debate as one between female lay practitioners and male doctors, even if he was doing it for the publicity alone. As he put it of the former, "When these woman fiends send their victim post-haste to the bar of God, they box her up and send her off in the night—for fear of the disgrace attendant on having an illegitimate child!!!!"[6]

On the next page, Dixon printed a full-page, three-column-wide anonymous letter that he quite likely wrote himself. It was a letter of outrage over Bird's practices that also congratulated Dixon for all the work he had already done to "expose the character of Mrs. Bird, Madame Restell, and others, and to bring public opinion upon their odious and wicked vocation." While Bird was currently in hot water for her role in helping Shaw give birth to a child, who was still alive, the letter focused as much on Bird's role as an abortion provider. "What is the service that Mrs. Bird engages to perform? *Unequivocally it is to produce abortion—to kill the embryo in the womb.*" He then claimed that terminating a pregnancy was actually too risky even for doctors with formal medical training. This was false. Doctors had long relied on abortion when women's lives were endangered by pregnancy. Medical textbooks explained in some detail the various means of terminating a pregnancy. Based on this falsehood, however, Dixon asked rhetorically, "But is it at all likely that a female should be in possession of experience altogether denied to the veteran of the medical fraternity?" Among Dixon's many arguments about abortion, however, was his belief that women were simply unfit for practicing medicine, of any kind. Later in the letter, blatantly contradicting himself, Dixon wrote, "If any one asks if Mrs. Bird has ever succeeded in producing abortion, I answer, Yes, she has—for I have interested myself in this matter, and acquainted myself with the particulars." His caveat to this strange admission was that no matter her success at terminating pregnancies, Bird always inflicted great pain, and some of her clients did not survive.[7]

Dixon then alleged that Bird charged varied amounts to different clients, which he depicted as a system of extortion but was just a sliding scale. Those who could afford more were charged more. Those who could not were still not turned away. Some, he explained, worked in

"The Case of Madame Restell." This cartoon of both Madame Restell (*center*) and Mrs. Bird (*right*) supposedly documented all of the ways female physicians murdered fetuses, children, and their mothers. Reprinted from *Dixon's Polyanthos*, April 3, 1841, page 97.

Bird's home in exchange for her services, though he put it this way: "It is not uncommon to have one or more girls slaving reluctantly under her despotic eye." In other words, those young women who could not afford to pay at all could exchange household labor—cleaning, cooking, and needlework—for Bird's services. What Dixon staged as exploitation can better be seen as Bird's willingness to serve even the poorest clientele. Dixon's letter continued at some length, employing convoluted logic in accusing Bird of creating the very problem—illegitimate pregnancy—she was hired to eliminate. "Victims are actually created by her pretensions, and lured within her influence by the most iniquitous motives, when her machinations are crowned by perfidy and robbery." Dixon had put the cart before the horse, ignoring the fact that practitioners like Bird came into existence because of demand, not the other way around.[8]

Dixon believed that Maria Shaw's death was the beginning of the end for Mrs. Bird: "This filthy pimp—this sordid cormorant shall no longer prey with impunity upon the vitals of our city. The domestic sanctuary shall be sentineled—innocence and virgin purity shall not be deflowered unwarned—outraged and filched guardians shall be befriended—the poison disseminated through all our arteries, shall meet with a panacea." He then claimed that her home would be filled with spies in an effort to bring her down. It was not to be, at least not in the short term.[9]

The next issue of the *Polyanthos* featured another cartoon on its front page. The headline was "The Case of Madame Restell," her arrest for the abortion of Ann Maria Purdy having occurred only a week prior. In this cartoon, however, Mrs. Bird also makes an appearance. She is pictured on the right, her head that of a bird, standing above a plank noted with her address, 18 Oliver Street. Madame Restell, center, is pictured in a dress with small coffins running around the hem. Death, in the form of the tall skeleton, oversees many other skeletons, most of them babies but also an adult woman, who is depicted with twin fetuses, all having died at the hands of an abortionist. Finally, a young woman approaches Restell, holding the corpse of an infant in a bottle. Accompanying the cartoon were five stanzas of a poem, each numerically linked with one of the figures in the cartoon. Perhaps the most noteworthy are the words spoken by the three deceased fetuses on the left of the cartoon:

> *I only lived to sigh and weep,*
> *Then in an ash-box went to sleep*
> *I drew on breath with grief and pain,*
> *And then I sank to rest again.*
> *We three ne'er saw the lovely earth;*
> *We three ne'er knew a living birth;*
> *But killed by powders in the womb,*
> *The river served us for a tomb.*

The deceased woman also speaks:

I was once a maiden fair,
But, caught in the seducer's stare
Two twins to me by God were given,
And Restell sent us all to heaven.

The cartoons and the coverage of Bird, Restell, and, later, Costello, despite acknowledging the differences between the three, indicted them all with the same charges: they were incompetent, they were murderers, and they encouraged vice and licentiousness.[10]

Depicting the skeletons of the fetuses as being akin to fully grown infants, even if just for the sake of an arresting drawing, also blurred the lines between a fetus terminated by an abortifacient—which might have been no larger than a bean—and a fully developed baby. While some historians have dated the emergence of the anti-choice fixation on the fetus to the later nineteenth century, writing and artwork like this, even if its purpose was primarily to sell newspapers, shows that by the early 1840s abortion's foes were quite comfortable likening a fetus to a baby.

*   *   *   *

On the same day the *Polyanthos* announced that Mrs. Bird had "absconded" in the wake of the Maria Shaw allegations (in an article titled "Flight of a Bird," accompanied by a picture of a bird, of course), Madame Costello made an appearance in the *Polyanthos*, also in the form of a poem:

Costello, Bird, and Restell
Say, shall these fiends go on from day to day—
Still drug and poison, purge and puke and slay,
Till this fair island be with graves o'erspread
One vast, continuous city of the dead;
And all in steeples, in default of stones,
Be, to each towering apex, built of bones.

This poem likened all three in its accusation that they were all working to turn New York into a "vast, continuous city of the dead." Dixon was not one to shrink from hyperbole.[11]

In including Costello along with Bird and Restell, Dixon was acknowledging Costello's central role as female physician in the growing reproductive services sector in antebellum New York. Madame Costello was actually named Catharine Maxwell. Born in 1795 in Boston as Catharine Cashdollar (sometimes spelled Kerstaller), her first husband was Jacob Weatherwax. Jacob died by suicide in 1831, leaving Catharine with at least three daughters, Anna, Maria, and Margaret. At some point Catharine remarried, to a man named Daniel Ames, and then again to William Maxwell, upon the death of Ames. She relocated to New York around 1840, where she lived at 34 Lispenard Street, just one block below the corner of Church and Canal, in what is now called Tribeca. Her home was next door to a station on the underground railroad at 36 Lispenard, where abolitionist David Ruggles operated a printing press and established the headquarters of the New York Vigilance Committee, and where Frederick Douglass spent time at the home there in 1838 during his escape from bondage. City directories list Madame Costello as "Catharine Costello, widow of Daniel," though the census indicates that her husband, William, lived with her until her death in 1876. Costello began advertising her services in early 1840. Like Restell, she offered "female monthly pills," "acknowledged by the first Physicians in the United States as the very best medicine that ladies laboring under a suppression of their natural illness can take." She also ran a lying-in hospital for those who wished to avoid "attention at their residence" that might come from people observing their pregnancies. Board and the "best of nursing" were available at her residence. Dixon thought Costello "a humble imitation of Madame Restell without her genius, and also without her wickedness." Dixon also believed that Costello was more apt to traffic in remedies with no medicinal content whatsoever. The *New York Sporting Whip* believed, by contrast, that Costello was more cautious than Restell, "and it is not generally known that she is an abortionist," this in 1843.

Nevertheless, Costello clearly was also in the business of terminating pregnancies at 34 Lispenard Street. She also had far more run-ins with the law than did Restell.[12]

Restell and Costello directly competed with each other in their advertisements. In response to Costello's advertisements, Restell placed ads in 1841 that called all female monthly pills other than her own counterfeit. Costello countered by referring to her own pills as "genuine." Restell answered back with a longer advertisement:

> CAUTION TO FEMALES. SO VARIOUS and desperate are the expedients resorted to by ignorant, though impudent pretenders, with the object of imposing upon females, that Madame Restell deems herself called upon to put them on their guard. . . . Females, therefore, need not be deceived by those who, though too ignorant and unskillful to discover and introduce a valuable medicine, are yet despicable and dishonest enough to palm off upon the unsuspecting or simple, miserable counterfeits and imitations of the genuine.

Whether there was any actual need for so much competition among female physicians remains unclear. There seems to have been no shortage of women in need of their services. More than anything, Costello and Restell appear to have been competing in matters of reputation. Restell, in particular, wanted to distinguish her practice from what she saw as the subpar services provided by Costello. She wanted to be known as a true female physician, not a quack.[13]

The pseudonyms employed by all three served a number of functions. In the case of the Mesdames Costello and Restell, their use of "Madame" and European surnames connoted a certain allure and authority, and in Restell's case, at least, her pseudonym linked to the backstory of her fictional Parisian grandmother. All three also claimed that they had trained in the kind of hospital to which American women of the era would not have had access, thus making them seem more qualified. Using a pseudonym may also have allowed multiple female employees to act the part of "Madame Restell" or "Mrs. Bird"

when seeing to the needs of a client, the name standing in for the services available at their homes rather than for one person in particular.
And finally, a pseudonym could also serve to shield one from the law—
Restell sometimes claiming in court that she was really Ann Lohman,
for instance. It should be noted, however, that it did not take all that
long for newspapers and law enforcement to recognize the real names
behind the pseudonyms. Official trial records for Restell usually used
both her names. The one disadvantage to the pseudonyms was that
they did not allow the women to take full ownership of their work in
meeting the needs of thousands of women. Using a pseudonym partially admitted that what they were doing was not just criminal but
shameful.

Costello and Bird both regularly found themselves in trouble with
the law, Costello more so than Bird because her career lasted much
longer. Furthermore, neither Costello nor Bird seemed to have been as
talented as Restell, both in the practice of medicine and in the man-
agement of their businesses. Three major trials between 1843 and
1846 led to jail time for both Bird and Costello. While conviction on
charges of abortion was unusual because of the secrecy surrounding the
practice, the circumstances that led to these three abortions were not
at all out of the ordinary.

The first case concerned Costello. On Saturday, March 2, 1843, she
was arrested for terminating the pregnancy of a young Frenchwoman
named Zulma Marache. Also arrested were Marache's fiancé, Napoleon Lareux, and Marache's upstairs neighbor, Catherine Guetal, both
of whom were charged as accessories. What was unusual about the case
was that Marache published a long explanation of the events from her
point of view in the *Herald*, which allows us a window on the abortion.
In Marache's telling, she had consented to sex with Lareux under
promise of marriage, and when she became pregnant, he told her he
was unable to marry her and insisted that she take an abortifacient,
which he procured from a doctor on Reade Street. After multiple attempts to terminate the pregnancy via different abortifacients, super-

vised by Guetal, all of which failed, Lareux told Marache he wanted her to go to Madame Costello's at 34 Lispenard Street, where Costello "would displace the child." Lareux threatened to poison Marache if she refused. It is difficult to know how truthful Marache was being when she claimed that Guetal and Lareux forced her, in a variety of ways, to terminate the pregnancy. While it is plausible, it was also the case that proclaiming she had no interest in an abortion was one way to partially redeem her own reputation. It also fit nicely into the narrative of an innocent young woman who was seduced under promise of marriage and then forced to abort her child, the very narrative that newspapermen and others relied on when they indicted abortionists for corrupting the youth of New York.[14]

On February 14, 1843, Marache visited Madame Costello, who brought on a miscarriage, with Marache later delivering the fetus in her own home. In the wake of the pregnancy and abortion, Lareux broke off his engagement with Marache, which prompted Marache to bring a civil suit against Lareux for breach of promise. That suit included allegations about the abortion, which prompted New York district attorney James Whiting to question Marache and to bring charges against Costello, Lareux, and Guetal in December of 1843. All three were arrested and released on bail swiftly thereafter.[15]

The trial of Costello, Guetal, and Lareux did not occur until late March of 1844. Costello's defense amounted to a series of alibi witnesses who placed her in Newton, Massachusetts, on February 14. Her daughter, son-in-law, and a livery stable keeper all said they saw her in Newton over the weekend of February 12–14, and her cook claimed she was absent from New York on the day in question. On March 23, DA Whiting addressed the jurors and, at great length, defended the conduct of Marache and impugned the testimony of all of Costello's alibi witnesses. The jury deliberated for thirty minutes and found all three of the accused guilty. Soon thereafter, Costello published a letter in the *Herald* defending herself, noting also that her attorney was filing an appeal to the New York State Supreme Court alleging that the court of general sessions had erred procedurally and that the "verdict is contrary to law." She wanted all readers to know "for the information of the public generally, and of such as are at present unacquainted with her, that she continues to practice her profession as usual." Ten days later, Lareux was sentenced to two months in county jail and fined $250, and Guetal, about whom the jurors urged the court to act with mercy, was fined only $25. Costello remained out on bail pending the outcome of her appeal. In May of 1845, New York's supreme court rejected one of Costello's lawyer's exceptions but affirmed that the trial court had erred procedurally. The supreme court ordered that Costello be granted a new trial, though a change in district attorneys seems to have meant that never happened. Madame Costello had evaded imprisonment. At least this time.[16]

In the midst of Costello's legal wrangling, Mrs. Bird and Madame Restell both found themselves once again the subject of investigation. On April 15, 1844, a young woman named Eliza Munson died at the residence of Mrs. Bird following an abortion. Like Marache, Munson's story was one of seduction and abandonment, though the choice to terminate the pregnancy was her own. A native of New Haven, Connecticut, she had been seduced by a man named James Frazee, a silver plater from Plainfield, New Jersey, now living in Newark. Upon realizing she was pregnant, in December of 1843, Munson traveled to New York City to visit Madame Restell, having seen her advertisements in newspapers. The link between Restell and Bird was at first vague, newspapers reporting that following the procedure at Restell's, "[Munson] did not, however, recover, but continued to languish until a few weeks since, when she placed herself under the treatment of Mrs. Bird." It was now April of 1844, approximately four months after the alleged abortion at Restell's. Fearing that Munson was dying, Bird called in a Dr. James Sweeney, who confirmed the end was near and informed police, who sent the coroner to perform an antemortem examination of Munson. Based on that examination and Munson's testimony, Restell was arrested and brought before the victim, who identified Restell as her abortionist, explaining *"that is the woman* who performed the operation." Restell was taken to the Tombs, and Munson died at four o'clock on the morning of the 15th of April.[17]

There was one glaring problem with Munson's declaration: it was a lie. In all likelihood, Mrs. Bird persuaded Munson to accuse Restell, rather than Bird herself, of performing the abortion, even if the facts of the case made the lie less than fully believable. Munson claimed that she had visited Restell in December, after all, and it was now April. If Munson died from complications related to a surgical abortion, it was much more likely that the operation had taken place closer to the time of her death, not four months earlier. For the time being, however, it was Restell who remained imprisoned in the Tombs as New York's newspapers covered the developing case. Restell was likely enraged that Bird had implicated her—and her reputation—in the death of Munson.

On April 16, the coroner resumed his investigation of Munson's death, calling a number of witnesses who were acquainted with the victim. A landlady and a friend both testified that they had seen Munson earlier that year and that she had not seemed to be ill. Next to testify was Sweeney, who had attended Munson at her death. Sweeney confirmed that the cause of death, which had by then been verified by a postmortem examination, was inflammation of the wounded uterus, exacerbated by the placenta remaining in the womb. As he explained, "I have been 22 years practicing midwifery, and I never saw a case of abortion terminating fatally before." When asked by jurors about the timing of the abortion, Sweeney explained that he did not think it possible that the placenta delivered in April could possibly have been related to a pregnancy terminated in December. "The anxiety evinced on the part of Mrs. Bird to make me believe that Madame Restell had committed the abortion that led to the state of disease in the body of deceased, induced me to think that Mrs. Bird might have produced the abortion herself."[18]

By April 18, the *New York Herald* explained that "the testimony shows conclusively that the abortion was produced at that house [18 Oliver Street] by Mrs. Bird, who has been allowed to escape, while the Coroner, his assistants, and officers of justice, were devoting their energies to secure the arrest of Madame Restell, who, it appears from the testimony, had nothing to do with the cause of the death of deceased." Testimony on the afternoon of April 17 had only served to further confirm what the prior day's evidence had begun to make clear. Randolph L. Primrose, a friend of the deceased and a cousin of James Frazee (the purported father), testified that Munson had confided in him the purpose of her visit to Mrs. Bird. Primrose had visited Munson at 18 Oliver Street, both before and after Bird had performed the operation.[19]

Primrose also testified that Munson was to pay Mrs. Bird $30 for the abortion and for boarding at her home and that she would be employed in sewing at Mrs. Bird's "so that nobody would notice her." Primrose painted a sad picture of Munson's last days alive. She was afraid of both Mrs. Bird and her son, who lived with her. Even in the days before Mrs. Bird fled, neither the son nor Bird attended to Munson, even as she still had not recovered from the procedure.[20]

The following day, the next witness was called: Gershom Frazee, brother of James Frazee. When Gershom first met Munson five or six weeks previously,

> she told me she was pregnant by my brother . . . she said she had had a child four years before, which had lived until it was seven months old; . . . she then said she was in that way and she was determined to get rid of it; she wanted me to go with her to Mrs. Bird's to have an abortion procured, or to see that she got there; I told her that I should not do it, as I believed it was a state prison act to go to a house of that kind; she said she had lost her character three or four years ago by having a child, and she would rather die than be caught in that situation again; she had been tempted to make way with herself at that time.

Munson was just one among many women who, with greater social freedoms but without much in the way of reliable contraception, found themselves in horrible situations. Some reports claimed that James Frazee had promised to marry her and then reneged on that pledge. Gershom disputed this claim but admitted that James had told him he was the father of Munson's child. Having already given birth to an illegitimate child, not to mention losing that child, Munson was unwilling to go through that experience again. She would do anything to terminate the pregnancy.[21]

The final witness at the coroner's inquiry was Dr. John C. Peters, who had conducted the postmortem examination. He concluded that Munson had been pregnant within the last four weeks and that the injuries could not be a result of terminating a pregnancy in December of the prior year. He found her uterus to be wholly intact, if enlarged to twice its normal size. He made clear that, when performed correctly, abortion "would leave no marks of violence upon the uterus." Such was the case for Munson. Her problem, however, and the cause of death, was excessive bleeding related to peritonitis. At that point it hardly mattered, for most agreed that the bulk of the evidence indicated that Mrs. Bird had performed an abortion on the body of Eliza Ann Munson. The coroner's jury retired for an hour and a half and came back with the following verdict:

> That Eliza Ann Munson's illness was caused by injuries arising from an abortion produced by violent means upon her person, by Margaret Dawson, alias Mrs. Bird, and by subsequent neglect, to which Francis Kowing [Mrs. Bird's son] was accessory after the fact at least, and that during the investigation, the said Eliza Ann Munson died thereof.

This was only the finding of the coroner's inquest, of course. A criminal trial would still have to be conducted in order to prosecute Bird. Warrants were thus issued for Bird and her son and daughter, Francis and Albertina Kowing, both of whom were arrested. By virtue of the findings of the coroner's jury, Madame Restell was also released from the Tombs. Mrs. Bird, however, was in the wind.[22]

On Friday, May 17, Mrs. Bird finally surrendered herself to authorities and was admitted to bail. Her children had already been released on bail. The trial began on Friday, September 13, 1844. The principal witnesses were the same as those who appeared before the coroner, and their testimony mostly remained consistent. On the second day of testimony, the defense entered into the record the testimony of Eliza Ann Munson that had been taken in extremis prior to her death, and then spent most of its time calling witnesses who attested to the fact that Madame Restell had also been charged with the same crime, even though that charge was largely based on Mrs. Bird's own claims dating from March. Finally, the defense called a doctor in an effort to discredit the earlier medical testimony, but, as the *Herald* explained it, "he however, only clinched it, by saying that from the testimony of the physicians he was convinced that the delivery must have been of very recent date." With that, the defense counsel spoke on behalf of Mrs. Bird, the recorder charged the jury with their instructions, and they retired to deliberate. The jury quite promptly returned a guilty verdict, and the sentence was suspended to allow the defense time to assemble a list of exceptions. It is unclear whether Bird declined to file an appeal or if it was swiftly denied by the supreme court; either way, Mrs. Bird was sentenced one month after her conviction, in mid-October. She was fined $250 and sentenced to city prison—on Blackwell's Island—for six months. Most accounts of the sentencing made it clear that the court had been lenient "in consequence of the advanced age of the prisoner (she is 70 years old,) but that they were determined in these cases to inflict the full penalty of the law." It is unclear whether her daughter and son were found guilty or were sentenced.[23]

By early 1845, the year of Mrs. Bird's imprisonment, it was the rare week that passed without some abortion-related incident in the news. Costello, Restell, and others also regularly placed advertisements in the press, the female physicians battling it out to establish their reputations. By that year, Mrs. Bird had been jailed once and both Costello and Restell had been charged, tried, and convicted and had their convictions overturned. Recall also that Mary Rogers, whose disappearance and death in 1841 coincided with Restell's trial, had by 1845 come to be associated with abortion in the minds of many New Yorkers, in part thanks to Edgar Allan Poe's serialized short story "The Mystery of Marie Rogêt," which intimated that Restell had been responsible for her death via a botched abortion. Newspapermen and some doctors also continued to call on New York's legislators to pass harsher laws to punish abortion, despite the fact that neither Costello nor Restell had gone free because the laws were ineffective but rather because their trials had been marred by procedural errors.[24]

New York was not the only state changing its laws related to abortion at this time. In January of 1845, Massachusetts passed a bill that made even *attempted* abortion a misdemeanor punishable by one to seven years in jail and a fine of up to $2,000. If a woman died by an abortion, the crime was upgraded to a felony. In passing these more stringent laws, Massachusetts legislators were sending a message that such activity would no longer be tolerated.[25]

New York followed suit only a few months later. On May 13, 1845, New York's governor signed into law a revision of the 1829 statute, which the new law also repealed. The act went to the legislature's medical committee before it passed to the judiciary committee, which would normally have had complete supervisory power over any act related to crime, demonstrating that New York's regular physicians had a real hand in shaping the legislation. Long before the American Medical Association strategized to outlaw abortion, medical men were organizing to ban the practice. An Act to Punish the Procurement of Abortion, and for Other Purposes departed from its predecessor in two important ways. The first section essentially reiterated the 1829 statute that declared it to be second-degree manslaughter to administer an abortion, either surgical or medicinal, on a woman pregnant with a quick child. The second section, however, was aimed at pharmacists and made the sale of abortifacients a crime punishable by between three months and one year in a county jail. Importantly, this section did not specify whether the pregnancy needed to be quick to qualify for conviction. The first section applied to quickened pregnancies, the second to any pregnancy. Since it was almost impossible to evaluate whether a woman was pregnant in the very earliest stages and because she could always claim that she was taking an emmenagogue to "relieve a blockage," not to terminate a pregnancy, this section of the statute would prove difficult to enforce. The third section was perhaps the most novel. It criminalized the act of receiving an abortion for the woman herself, whether by surgical means or by taking an abortifacient. The punishment was a fine not exceeding $1,000 and between three and twelve months in county jail. As historian James Mohr has pointed out, legislators were admitting here that to stop abortion from taking place, it was no longer enough to criminalize the act of providing an abortion, they also needed to try to deter women from seeking out the service by making it a crime for the women themselves. While newspapers had long portrayed abortionists as preying on pregnant women, sometimes in league with the men who seduced them, criminalizing the act of *obtaining* an abortion was an acknowledgment that many women wanted to terminate their pregnancies. While couched in the language of safety, the statute tacitly recognized two new truths: that married women were seeking to limit the size of their families and that their single sisters were having sex outside of wedlock. Legislators had decided that punishment might serve as a deterrent to both. The 1845 statute had both broadened the scope of what constituted the crime of abortion to include the women who obtained them and increased various forms of punishment.[26]

Among the very first people to be tried following the passage of the new legislation was none other than Madame Costello. While investigating the alleged disposal and sale of a body by Costello's husband, William Maxwell—supposedly the result of death either during an abortion or labor—a police officer named A.M.C. Smith had stumbled on another case, that of Emily Dobson. The *New York Evening Post* alleged that in April of 1844, seventeen-year-old Dobson had gone to work as an assistant in the dry goods store of one Charles Mason, on Avenue D. She also worked in the home of Mason's family, assisting his wife and three children by cooking and cleaning. She began to spend more time with the family and eventually "the beauty of the girl created desires in the man, which her innocence did not allay." Mason succeeded in his seduction, which continued for some months until he feared they might be discovered. He took her to Madame Costello in the spring of 1845 and had her pregnancy terminated. She remained there in recovery until her parents realized that she was no longer at the Masons' apartment and brought her home with them. Later that summer, warrants were issued for the arrest of Mason, Costello, and Maxwell (for the illegal sale of a body). On August 26, Madame Costello was arrested and committed to the Tombs, her bail having been set at $6,000.[27]

In early September, the grand jury found presentments against both Costello and Mason, which kept them in jail pending someone to bail them out. By mid-September, Costello was out on bail, then re-jailed when her surety surrendered her upon realizing the "enormity of her crimes." Costello's lawyer asked for a reduction in bail, arguing that Costello had been all but convicted by the press already, but this was denied by the court. Finally, on October 2, a little more than a month after she was arrested, Costello was released on bail, which had been guaranteed by Oliver Johnston, who kept a liquor store on Market Street. It is likely that Costello had paid him some fee to act as surety.[28]

The trial began on February 12, and the star witnesses for the prosecution were Emily Dobson and her mother. At the outset of the trial, Dobson herself requested the presence of the mayor, "feeling such confidence in his desire and ability to shield her from self-crimination that she would testify freely and fully with him near to protect her." Taking the stand, "she was dressed in a neat dark silk, with a velvet shawl and hat, and wore a green veil, with which she carefully concealed her features from the gaze of the crowd." The court clarified that Dobson could indeed refuse to answer any question that might prove incriminating, though she could not refrain from answering those that might "disgrace" her. Of course, the two were almost intrinsically linked, the disgrace of the nonmarital sex and the ensuing pregnancy themselves the reasons for the abortion. Over the course of the trial, Dobson would repeatedly refuse to answer certain questions, and the district attorney and the judge then argued about whether she was obligated to do so. After declining to answer a final question at the end of her day of testimony, she was remanded to prison for the duration of the trial. This was at least part of the problem with the new law: one of the only ways to successfully prosecute an abortionist was to use their patients as witnesses, but those patients would be unwilling to testify if they themselves could be prosecuted based on that testimony. This was an early prosecution after the passage of the new statute; over the course of the nineteenth century, it would turn out that New York's prosecutors generally declined to bring charges against the women who had themselves obtained abortions, even though the law said the prosecutors could.[29]

Aside from Dobson's refusal to fully cooperate as a witness, the trial itself was relatively straightforward, lasting only four days. The other highlight—at least to delighted newspapermen—was that Madame Costello's attorney deserted her on the first day of testimony. Costello's second choice also declined the job, and the court had to appoint an attorney for her, Lorenzo B. Shepard. Even he wanted it "distinctly understood by the gentlemen of the press and the public, that he was going into the case as a counsellor at law, and by the order of the court, and not at liberty to refuse doing so." The two principal witnesses— Emily Dobson and Abigail Dobson, Emily's mother—were asked a series of questions designed to confirm the basic outlines of the story. Abigail Dobson simply pled ignorance about her daughter's visits to Costello and the reasons for them but did confirm that Mason had visited the Dobson family in Hoboken and had promised money— she varied the amount between $150 and $400—in return for refusing to testify.[30]

Emily confirmed only that she had visited Costello three times but declined to state the purpose of her visits. The questions and answers at times bordered on the absurd as the prosecution tried to get Dobson to admit to what all in the courtroom understood was an abortion but that Dobson, guided by her appointed attorney, would not say explicitly for fear of implicating herself. At one point Dobson became so exhausted "from the heat of the room which was densely crowded" that she was excused for the moment. The sum total of Dobson's testimony indicated—generally, without saying it explicitly—that Charles Mason had impregnated her and given her abortifacient tablets from Costello, which she then took to no effect. She then visited Costello, who told her to return a week hence, at which point Costello terminated her pregnancy. Dobson then returned to Costello's the next day when she was ill, and stayed there for three days, during which she miscarried the child.[31]

On the fourth and final day of the trial, Monday, February 16, most of the arguments were procedural, the various attorneys making claims about which testimony could be admissible and which charges could be brought before the jury. The defense attorneys, anticipating that the prosecution would have taken longer to finish introducing their evidence, were prepared to present only one witness, a doctor whose testimony seemed to be calling into question whether Dobson could have been pregnant with a quick child. Following the testimony, the judge gave instructions to the jury, explaining that testimony had made it clear that the alleged abortion had taken place *prior* to the passage of the new law. All was not lost, however; according to Judge Ingraham, "the offence charged, was punishable at common law, and if the jury were satisfied of the guilt of the defendants, a verdict of guilty could be rendered under the common law. The jury must be satisfied first that the girl was pregnant, and second that the defendants attempted to, or did produce an abortion. If these facts were clearly proved, it was the duty of the jury to convict." Though newspapers did not carry his precise wording, Judge Ingraham may well have explained that Dobson needed to have been pregnant with a *quick* child for conviction to be possible, because those were the only abortions punishable at common law. The jury deliberated for no more than ten minutes, almost immediately finding both defendants guilty. While Costello's and Mason's counsels requested a stay of judgment to the end of the court's term so that they might prepare a bill of exceptions, Judge Ingraham wasted no time, passing sentences immediately. Mason was to pay a fine of $250 and be imprisoned for four months. Costello was given the same fine and a sentence of six months, also at Blackwell's Island.[32]

A number of newspapers noted that the punishment was not as harsh as they'd hoped it would be. As the *New York Daily Herald* put it, "Thus, one case of abortion is punished, although slightly. It is to be hoped, however, that even this small punishment will have its proper effect." In the months that followed, newspapers noted that Madame Costello seemed to be enjoying much better treatment on Blackwell's Island than was typical for other prisoners. The *Brooklyn Evening Star* alleged that the prison matron, Mrs. Baker, had "taken the bed-clothes from her own bed to accommodate the *guest*, curtaining her chamber, and rendering her situation otherwise comfortable." The *Evening Post* reported that if Madame Costello was even required to wear her uniform prison dress, she "manages to cover it in a most ingenious manner. When we saw her, she was walking around the grounds wearing a handsome shawl and bonnet, and looking as *en bon point* as ever." An anonymous correspondent, identified only as "A Woman," wrote to the editor of the *Tribune* to tell of her visit to Blackwell's Island, which included a tour of the women's workroom, where she observed Costello sitting off to the side reading a newspaper, again not dressed in the prison uniform. As she put it: "Madame Costello has money. Who is guilty of receiving the bribe? Is such corruption in the servants of our public institutions to be allowed?"[33]

Costello was released from Blackwell's Island on August 17, 1846, having served her six-month sentence. As the *New York Evening Express* put it, "She was launched again upon the community yesterday, to renew and to continue her depredations." Catharine Maxwell retired the pseudonym "Madame Costello" soon thereafter, though she continued to advertise under her legal name for decades to come, occasionally running afoul of the law.[34]

Following her own release from prison, Mrs. Bird, Madame Restell's other competitor, maintained a low profile, no longer advertising her services in the newspaper. Vital records and city directories show that she continued to live on the Lower East Side, in various residences on Stanton and Madison Streets. As late as 1862, "Margaret J. Bird, Physician," was listed in the New York directory at 242 Madison Street. If she really was seventy years old at her sentencing in 1844, she would have been almost ninety in the early 1860s. It is also possible that her daughter, Albertina, had taken over the family business, assuming the name Mrs. Bird just as her mother had done.[35]

By the time Mrs. Bird and Madame Costello were released from prison, their fame had already been eclipsed—yet again—by Madame Restell, who in early 1846 had been accused of kidnapping a living, breathing child from its mother.

5

ILLEGITIMACY AND
INFANTICIDE

Around noon on Monday, February 23, 1846, a crowd gathered on Greenwich Street outside Madame Restell's home and office. Some reports estimated the size at more than one thousand people; others thought it was closer to two or three hundred. One noted that it was composed primarily of young men. Those assembled had been summoned by handbills posted around the city the night before, calling on New Yorkers to meet on Cortland Street, where it met the Hudson River, about two blocks from Restell's residence. They were there to hear a speaker on the subject of recent accusations that Madame Restell had kidnapped an infant who had been born to a woman by the name of Mary Applegate, in her lying-in hospital. Too eager to wait on Cortland Street, the crowd bypassed the original location and met on Greenwich, where they began to yell curses and threats at Restell's home. Soon, some forty to fifty police officers arrived and stationed themselves in front of Restell's stoop. The crowd moved to the original location on Cortland, where a speaker, who was later identified as none other than George Washington Dixon, formerly of the *Polyanthos*, stood on a barrel and proceeded to arouse the crowd in their ire against Restell. The demands for Restell were twofold: Give back Mary Applegate's kidnapped child. Leave New York.[1]

Almost no part of Mary Applegate's story is verifiable independent of her own words, so we must rely on them for an account of what happened. On February 5, 1846, she swore out a deposition before New

York's mayor, often the first stop for someone alleging a crime. She explained that she was born in Philadelphia and was living there in 1845, working as a domestic servant in the home of a family named Edwards. At some point Applegate entered into a relationship with Augustus Edwards, one of the sons of that family, who worked in the office of the Reading Railroad. Newspaper advertisements confirm that an Augustus Edwards worked as the general transportation clerk for the Philadelphia and Reading Railroad. In the summer of 1845, Applegate discovered that she had become pregnant as a result of her liaisons with Edwards, which she described as seduction. When Applegate told Edwards about the pregnancy, he at first refused to do anything to help her. Increasingly desperate, Applegate threatened to expose their situation to Edwards's father. Edwards then told Applegate to "pass herself off as a married woman whose husband was absent at sea." She was unable to find a place to live where that would be possible. When she informed Edwards of this, he told her that he had heard of a woman in New York named Madame Restell and that he had made arrangements to send Applegate to Restell during her confinement. There was no mention made in Applegate's deposition about attempting to terminate the pregnancy. This may have been because it was already too advanced, or perhaps Applegate simply did not consider this an option. Applegate resisted the plan of going to stay with Restell because she wanted to remain in Philadelphia, but Edwards was adamant that if she wanted his assistance, this was the form it would take. He claimed that he had already prepaid for her stay. On or about November 20, 1845, Applegate consented to go to New York, and Edwards gave her $14 to pay for her passage. The next morning, she left. Edwards told her that after her boat arrived, she should take a cab to Madame Restell's, on Greenwich Street. Upon arrival, she need only tell Restell that she was from Philadelphia and that she was the person about whom Mr. St. Clair Mason, a pseudonym for Edwards, had written.[2]

When she arrived, Applegate was to find that things were not quite so straightforward. Restell informed Applegate that "Mr. St. Clair

Mason" had not actually paid the bill. Applegate would have to spend the night in a hotel and return the next day once the bill was paid. Mary Applegate was desperate, and she did not know the city. She begged Restell to let her stay with her, and Restell relented. The money arrived the next day by a man who claimed to have been sent by St. Clair Mason. Applegate remained at Restell's residence for about four weeks, the remainder of her confinement, during which time Restell assured her that if she chose to remain in the city, she would find no shortage of men who would be glad to "keep" her, that she might "dress well, and live in great style" if she so chose. While this sort of encouragement might seem crass, Restell was likely being a realist. She knew that many men did not want to marry a woman who had already borne another man's child out of wedlock. A former seamstress herself, Restell was also well aware that wages for women were abysmal. Recognizing that Applegate was not already opposed to sex outside of marriage and that her beauty could serve her well, she was simply alerting her to opportunities in New York that might not have existed in Philadelphia. Applegate recounted that on the 11th of December between 7:00 and 8:00 p.m., she was delivered of a daughter by Restell and Restell's own daughter, who was also in attendance. While what happened next—the eventual disappearance of the child—was certainly what Applegate complained about to New York's mayor in her February 1846 affidavit, it is worth noting that it was not the only part of her story that angered those who assembled on Greenwich Street later that month.[3]

While newspapers reassured readers that the gathering never became violent and that Dixon himself expressed hope that "no one had come there with the desire to create any disturbance, or commit a breach of the peace," this was still the largest gathering in opposition to Restell or any other female physician that had thus far occurred. It also bore some resemblance to the anti-abolitionist riots of the 1830s, where rioters attacked the homes of prominent abolitionists, accusing them of "amalgamation," or interracial sexual mixing, and to the brothel riots that had begun in the 1820s—of which there were at least fifty between 1825 and 1857—where groups of men broke into brothels and ransacked them, sometimes raping and injuring the sex workers who lived within. Historians have seen those riots as a means for mostly working-class men to assert their masculinity and mastery over and above working women, who sometimes refused them service and often earned more than they did working in the sex trade. The brothel riots were, to be sure, more violent and usually more spontaneous than was the demonstration outside Restell's residence, but both were led by men and both drew on masculine anger about changing gender roles and the success of women entrepreneurs. The anti-abolitionist and the brothel riots were also both about sexual politics. That this gathering did not turn violent no doubt owes something to the presence of the police, who were alerted to the demonstration in advance, just as were its attendees.[4]

It is particularly significant that the incident that garnered the crowd was not actually related to an abortion or a death of a woman in Restell's care. Instead, the outrage was about Restell's role in concealing illegitimate pregnancies and in the supposed disposal of the infants that resulted from them. Rather than being ancillary to the concerns of Restell's foes, illegitimacy and the abandonment of infants were central preoccupations, sometimes superseding concerns over Restell's role as a physician who terminated pregnancies. The outburst over Applegate's child was just one moment among many when the three issues were linked. The consequence more broadly was to associate the practice of abortion with that of child abandonment and infanticide, all three depicted as the result of illegitimate pregnancy in a city whose morals and gender order had run amok. The events on Cortland and Greenwich Streets also point toward growing differences in how members of the working and middle classes understood illegitimacy and abortion, and indeed childhood itself. The working-class men who seem to have made up the majority of those gathered that day mostly blamed upper- and middle-class men for seducing working-class women, as well as Madame Restell for helping the men to get away with it. While there is, of course, no way to quantify just how common the practice of seduction was or the numbers of men who got away with it by arranging for abortions or private confinements, the issue rose to prominence during the antebellum era in a way that also influenced the debate on abortion. Middle-class people were more apt to target working-class culture writ large and what they saw as its easy acceptance of illegitimacy and its lax morals. Middle-class reformers, commentators, and lawmakers also targeted Restell for her role in supposedly enabling this kind of licentiousness. Working-class people and middle-class people also differed in their interpretation of Restell's alleged disposal of the child. To working-class people, the issue was that Restell was accused of stealing one woman's child, perhaps at the behest of her lover. Middle-class observers were particularly concerned that Restell seemed to have no regard for infant life of any kind, some believing that she regularly disposed of infants born on her premises. Even as working- and middle-class women quietly and steadily flocked to Restell's door, louder voices indicted her practices, but in ways that were distinctly and differently inflected by social class.[5]

The seduction tale has a long history: innocent girl is tricked into having sex by wicked man under promise of marriage, relents to his advances, and is then abandoned. Her chastity taken, she is now ruined and quickly descends into a life of prostitution, "fallen" from whatever station she may once have occupied. Dissipation and poverty come soon thereafter, followed by misery and death. The tale had been widely read in classics like *Charlotte Temple* (1791) by Susanna Rowson and *The Coquette* (1797) by Hannah Webster Foster. What was new by the 1820s was that larger numbers of poor girls were making their way into cities and often into the homes of wealthy families as domestic servants, the most common form of employment for young women in antebellum America. There were simply more and more young women at risk for seduction. Prostitution, too, was growing exponentially in antebellum cities, and while most in the trade worked because wages were higher than for any other job for which women might be hired, the presence of sex workers in almost every New York neighborhood seemed to serve as proof of the powers of seduction to ruin young women fresh from the country. While estimates of the numbers of sex workers in New York in the antebellum years ranged between two thousand on the low end and the improbable fifty thousand on the high, between 5 and 10 percent of New York's young women aged fifteen to thirty likely sold sex, if only casually, at some point in their lives. Prostitution was highly visible in New York, and many believed that seduction was its cause.[6]

While seduction could occur between two people of the same class, in popular culture it was often portrayed as the crime that a wealthy man perpetrated on a girl with few resources, not just money but also the social capital, in the form of watchful parents, that would allow her to understand that she was being used. When understood this way, it could become a rallying cry for working-class men, like those who assembled on Greenwich Street, to protect "their" women from wealthier rakes and libertines. At times seduction occurred in the public gathering places that proliferated in growing cities, where young single men and women flirted and socialized. In New York, the center of such activities by the 1830s was the Bowery, the wide avenue running up and down Lower Manhattan's east side that housed many shops, bars, and bawdy houses. While young working-class men themselves sought out sexual favors from their peers, they also tried to protect those same women from exploitation by the men, called "aristos" by some, who sometimes came "slumming" in the Bowery, using their cash to impress young women. Other seductions began in private homes. There is no question that young women were at sexual risk living as domestic servants in the homes of middle- and upper-class families, just as Mary Applegate was at risk in the home of the Edwards family. In some cases, this was a risk of outright sexual assault; in others it took the form of single male members of those households courting domestic servants under the guise of possibly marrying them, and then seducing them. The relationships that resulted from such seductions, regardless of how the couple met, were of varying durations and were no doubt brokered under different degrees of forthrightness. While the seduction narrative was framed around the conceit that no woman would willingly have sex without the promise of marriage, women too were interested in sex and some saw distinct advantages in allying themselves sexually with men, especially men of means. Sometimes these encounters ended after only one sexual encounter, but in other circumstances, the relationships were ones of long standing. In some cases, men strung women along for months; in others, men essentially "kept" women as mistresses, paying for their accommodations in exchange for sex. This was what Madame Restell had alluded to when Applegate was staying with her during her confinement. Because she was now "ruined," thanks to the loss of her virginity, Restell presumed that she might be willing to trade sex for security on a more long-term basis.[7]

Concern about seduction and its consequences—single, nonvirginal girls, some of whom were mothers—was widespread enough to prompt reform efforts to update the seduction law that already existed. In early America, most colonies had a civil seduction law that they had inherited under English common law. A seduced girl's father or master (in the case of indentured servants) could sue her seducer for a sum of money meant to represent the labor lost during her pregnancy. In this instance, the wrong was perceived as having been committed by one man against the other; only the father/master could bring an action for seduction. Nor was there a criminal statute on seduction that would result in punishment by the state (fines or imprisonment, for instance). As Americans began to rethink who was really harmed via seduction—the woman and her reputation—and as the practice of seduction itself seemed to be increasing, just as parents' power to pressure seducers to marry their victims was decreasing, reform organizations like the American Female Moral Reform Society (AFMRS) began to ask lawmakers to pass new laws that would criminalize seduction.[8]

In New York State, for instance, the *Advocate for Moral Reform*, the paper of the AFMRS, for years called on legislators to update its seduction law. The AFMRS, which was founded in 1834 both to prevent prostitution and to help the young women who made up the sex trade's ranks, saw a stronger seduction law as an important step for women in

its own right but also as a means to prevent prostitution, the logic being that men would be less likely to seduce women if they knew they
could be punished, which would mean fewer ruined women falling
into sex work. The *Advocate for Moral Reform* published endless stories about seduction—"Have You a Daughter?," "Seduction, Murder,
and Suicide," "Distressing Case of Seduction"—which warned young
women not to trust men and alerted parents about the dangers of allowing one's daughter to move to the city. One story was even titled,
straightforwardly enough, "Do Not Send Your Children to the City."
A typical story, called "Seduction, Maternity, and Suicide," detailed
the story of a young woman who drowned herself in a cistern, "her infant closely pressed to her bosom in death," after she had been seduced
and abandoned and had given birth to an illegitimate child. She was
overcome with guilt and shame. The AFMRS succeeded in having
New York legislators introduce multiple bills making seduction a
crime, though the legislature did not pass a criminal statute until
1848. That statute stipulated that any man who seduced a woman "of
previously chaste character" would be guilty of a misdemeanor and
could be sentenced to up to five years in prison. Others urged that a
woman herself be able to initiate a civil suit against her seducer, instead
of relying on her father to do so. While New York's legislature considered modifying its law to allow for this, ultimately it chose not to do
so. Other states did, however.[9]

Seduction, then, was regarded as a deliberate strategy enacted by
men on women, who were often depicted as too naïve to withstand
clever men's charms. It was also the case that in working-class culture,
it was not uncommon for couples to have sex before marriage. The sex
itself was seen as a man's commitment to that future marriage. This was
also why seduction statutes usually mandated that seduced women be
virgins at the time of the seduction; a woman's ruin could occur only
once. That said, because ruined women were perceived as having so
very few choices, even those who stayed with their seducers (sometimes
for years) were generally regarded with sympathy, even if they would

never fully recover from their falls. The male mob that gathered outside Restell's door was on Mary Applegate's side after all, even though she had had sex out of wedlock. So long as people adhered to the belief that women were tricked by cunning and wealthy men, it was possible to sympathize with the victims.

One particularly celebrated example demonstrates the lengths of that sympathy. On November 1, 1843, a twenty-five-year-old woman named Amelia Norman stabbed a man named Henry Ballard on the steps of New York City's Astor House hotel. She had been his lover for a number of years, had borne him one child (she gave birth at Mrs. Bird's), and had terminated at least one pregnancy with Madame Restell. Ballard survived the attack, which onlookers had witnessed. Norman claimed that Ballard had seduced her in 1841 and then had kept her as a mistress, moving her from boardinghouse to boarding-house, sometimes representing her as his wife. When he finally abandoned her and their child, she went to him to try to get him to support her; he responded that she could "go and get her living as other prosti-tutes do." This, apparently, was what had sent her over the edge and re-sulted in the stabbing. Despite the fact that Norman was quite clearly guilty of the crime, she became a cause célèbre among New Yorkers. Most papers came to her defense. Abolitionists and prison reformers, including Lydia Maria Child, wrote on her behalf and donated funds to pay for her attorneys, who argued that Norman was temporarily insane at the time of the attack. A jury deliberated for under ten min-utes and found her not guilty, and she walked free. As the *Brooklyn Daily Eagle* explained of the verdict,

> It gives us pleasure to record to-day, the *acquittal* of this young woman, on the charge of intent to kill Henry S. Ballard. We say pleasure, because justice would have received a severe wound, had she been convicted. . . . A young woman is villainously betrayed— her ruin accomplished—her unborn offspring nefariously disposed of—and she is cast helpless upon the world—and when she applies

to the heartless and unmeasured scoundrel who does this, is told to get her living as others of the same class do!

While the *Eagle* made clear that it did not condone violence, it also pointed out that there was currently no legal remedy for a woman in Norman's circumstances. No criminal law around seduction existed, and Norman was not recognized as a victim in civil law. Activists intent on reforming seduction law often pointed to Norman's case as a prime example of how young women were betrayed not just by their seducers but also by a legal system that could not protect them.[10]

Even though she had succumbed to Ballard's seduction and had lived with him in sin for more than two years, bearing him one illegitimate child and terminating a pregnancy at a moment when abortion was increasingly vilified, New Yorkers had little problem identifying with her plight. The seduction plot assigned the clear roles of victims and villains to women and men. Just like Amelia Norman, Mary Applegate fit her role very well, as did Augustus Edwards, whom the *Eagle* referred to as a "heartless villain" who went "from city to city and family to family, selecting the choicest flowers of the social garden, and then not only blast[ing] the virtue and name of the victim, and blighting the bloom and beauty of the soul, but hurl[ing] it into a deep abyss of infamy and woe." The difficulty for a practitioner like Restell is that while she served some single women's needs, the best way to sympathize with those women and to condemn their seducers was to depict Restell as an accomplice in crime. For women to be victims, their own sexual choices had to be erased and then female physicians like Restell had to be depicted as aiding the seducers, not the young women themselves, who were painted either as unwilling accomplices in the termination of pregnancies or simply as unable to have made the decision in the first place. Thus, Madame Restell became a target of New Yorkers' rage in February of 1846 partially because she was seen as enabling men like Henry Ballard and Augustus Edwards. Restell could either terminate an illegitimate pregnancy or she could disguise it. Either way, men like Edwards would get off scot-free, enabling them to target more women just like Mary Applegate.[11]

Her story was, of course, not just one of illegitimacy but also one of a disappearing infant. The first inklings of Applegate's ordeal that appeared in print preceded her testimony and largely focused on the missing child. Many of the details of Applegate's story were not known until she swore out her deposition two days later. On February 4, the *Herald*, the *Evening Post*, and other papers reported on what one called "Awful Disclosures" "involving a she-devil, the keeper of a stylish house for the slaughter of *petit innocence*, located in the Third ward." Restell's name was not yet linked with the incidents. The *Herald* noted that a "young man of respectable connexions" from Philadelphia had brought an eighteen-year-old girl whom he had seduced to New York, but that because she was too far along, she gave birth to a child in "this house of horror and death." The *Evening Post* claimed that Applegate was persuaded to part with her child "for a few moments," but the child was never returned. The baby was "cruelly torn from her, and conveyed, she knew not where." Applegate cried, "'My child, my child, bring me my child!" but to no avail. The *Herald* reported that Applegate knew her child had been taken to a wet nurse, but still, "the supposition is that the child has been murdered and thrown off the dock, or burnt, as it is the practice to do in many of these dens." While the language was hyperbolic, infanticide was a growing problem in cities like New York, even if that was not what had occurred in this instance.[12]

In Applegate's deposition, she recounted that during her confinement, Restell had asked her if she would consider giving up her baby for adoption if it should turn out to be a girl. Applegate refused these entreaties. At this moment in U.S. history, adoption was entirely unregulated and far less common than it would become by the twentieth century. While informal adoption—particularly of orphaned minor relatives or of indentured servants—had occurred for centuries, those children grew up without the rights of a biological child in a family. Not until 1851, at first in Massachusetts, did states pass laws to recognize the legal relationship (including inheritance rights) of children adopted into families. New York did not do so until 1873. Prior to adoption law, the only legal way to cement ties between a child and adoptive parents was via an indenture contract or by conferring inheritance rights by naming the child in a will. But that did not mean that some couples, albeit in limited numbers, did not seek out babies to adopt prior to those laws. Babies were adopted away from New York's almshouse, for instance. Restell, who regularly had women give birth to illegitimate children within her walls, was another source for such couples. Eventually, female physicians like Restell who also ran lying-in hospitals would advertise openly that "children can always be adopted" from them.[13]

Applegate recounted that in the days after the delivery, she and the baby remained at Restell's house, but that they did not stay in the same room. Applegate was permitted to see her daughter three times before Restell told her that Edwards had requested that Restell place the baby with a wet nurse. Wet nurses—generally poor women who had themselves given birth quite recently, sometimes to children who later died—were quite common in this era. Wealthier women employed them as live-in servants to nurse and care for their infant children; poor women left their babies with them while they themselves worked at other jobs during the day. And some wet nurses themselves used *other* wet nurses to look after their children full time while they themselves worked in wealthier women's homes. In the mid-1840s in New York, there had not yet been established an institution where poor single mothers could go to give birth and care for their own babies, aside from the almshouse. Those sorts of institutions did not arrive until 1854 in the form of the Nursery for the Children of Poor Women, which itself was designed for wet nurses and their infants.[14]

Mary Applegate met the woman who would serve as her daughter's wet nurse. She was called Catharine Rider, and she said she lived with her husband, a mason, in Harlem, a neighborhood miles north of Restell's home that was still sparsely populated by Euro-Americans. Applegate remained at Restell's for another two weeks and two days and then returned to her home in Philadelphia. Applegate's deposition does not claim that she unwillingly gave up her baby, even though she had earlier said she had refused Restell's suggestion to let her put the child up for adoption. Rather, Applegate claims she told Rider to "take good care of the child," perhaps meaning she hoped to return and claim her at some later date. It is likely she could not take the child with her back to the Edwards household, not only because as a servant she could not bring an infant to live with her but also because it would provoke questions about the infant's origins, questions that the stay at Restell's was meant to prevent.[15]

When she returned to Philadelphia, Applegate asked Augustus Edwards what he meant to do for the child. His response was that he "did not intend to do any thing more than the law allowed," by which he may have meant "required." Applegate attempted to bargain with Edwards, asking that he support the child for one year, during which Applegate would live in Harlem near her daughter. According to Applegate, Edwards agreed to this plan, and they mutually decided that they would both go before a judge in Philadelphia, where Edwards would swear to pay Applegate $100 for support of the child, and she would agree not to make any additional claims on him. At a somewhat later date, Edwards explained to Applegate that he had never instructed Madame Restell to put the child out to nurse nor to prevent Applegate from bringing the child back to Philadelphia. Indeed, according to Applegate, at some point Edwards and her friend, Mrs. Wilson, traveled to New York in pursuit of the infant, though we only have Applegate's testimony that this occurred. Upon calling at Madame Restell's residence, Mrs. Wilson was told that Restell had no knowledge of the child and that no woman had given birth there at any time in the last several months.[16]

Restell's account of how the baby ended up with the wet nurse and what happened after Applegate returned to New York diverges from that of Applegate's and appeared in newspapers the same day as Applegate's affidavit. According to Restell, "When the infant was three days old, [Applegate] requested it to be put to a wet nurse, stating that she intended to return to Philadelphia without it." Restell explained that she then found a wet nurse for Applegate, who herself made all arrangements for payment, before Applegate departed the city three weeks after her confinement. Three weeks later, Applegate returned to Restell's office and asked for the wet nurse, only to be told by Restell that Applegate knew her whereabouts just as much as Restell did. Nevertheless, Restell summoned the wet nurse to her home, and those investigating the incident came to interview her. "They thought proper to take no steps in the matter," and the nurse was released. "Such, simply, are the circumstances of this 'horrid, awful,' &c. affair." Restell made clear that once the authorities talked to the wet nurse, they were no longer interested in pursuing any sort of case against Restell.[17]

What to make of these conflicting claims? A number of scenarios are plausible. Applegate or Edwards could well have instructed Madame Restell to adopt away the baby and then have changed their minds upon Applegate's return to Philadelphia. By the time they had gone back to New York, it was too late and the baby was no longer under the care of Catharine Rider. It is also possible that the child died in Rider's care. Infant survival rates with wet nurses—especially those who were still nursing their own children—were notoriously bad. But Rider surely would have told the police this if it had occurred. Or, conversely, Madame Restell arranged for the adoption of the child against the will of Applegate, who always presumed she would be able to recover the child. But if that was the case, why did she ever consent to have the baby put out to nurse in the first place? While a number of newspapers would later insist that Restell had murdered the child, she had absolutely no incentive to do so; she had nothing to gain by denying a new mother her child. Plenty of living children departed the residence at 148 Greenwich Street, many of them in the arms of their mothers. Restell provided whichever services women asked for. If a single mother wanted to take her baby with her, Restell had no reason to stand in the way. The fact that this case never went to trial also buttresses Restell's account that the authorities did not seem interested in the case following their interview with the wet nurse.[18]

Regardless of what had happened, a number of newspapers pounced on the story as proof that Restell was in the business of infanticide. Under the headline "Another Chapter of Supposed Child Murder," on February 7, the *National Police Gazette*, always interested in scandal and no friend to Restell, printed a specious story about Applegate arriving at Restell's office for an abortion, "but the instruments failed to accomplish the hellish act, and to avoid exposition of such a defeat of her infamous practices, the child was disposed of by Restell's minions, who should be held responsible for its return, dead or alive." With little understanding of how abortion worked, the *Gazette* seemed to imply that a pregnancy capable of being terminated could also result in the birth of a child able to live outside the womb. This was a stretch and actually contradicted the affidavit of Applegate herself, which they printed in full under the story. In essence, the *Gazette* was conflating a fetus and a child as they knowingly misrepresented what had happened in Restell's office.[19]

A number of days after Applegate gave her deposition, a reporter for the *New York Medical and Surgical Reporter* (*NYMSR*), a journal for doctors in New York State, called on the mayor for the purpose of collecting additional facts about the case. According to the *NYMSR*, the mayor summoned Applegate herself to speak to the reporter; Applegate had remained in New York with the hope of recovering her child. According to this report, soon after giving birth, Restell "applied a large plaster of some kind, over each breast, and bade [Applegate] to keep them on," to keep her breasts from leaking and eventually to help her stop lactating. She brought the child back to her for nursing once (at which time a hole was created in the plaster), but otherwise Applegate did not nurse the child, who was kept in a room downstairs. The *NYMSR* speculated that Edwards had explicitly paid Restell to starve the child. This report also directly contradicts Applegate's earlier affidavit that she herself met a wet nurse named Catharine Rider, who took her infant to her own home in Harlem. Applegate was perhaps downplaying her earlier acquiescence to this arrangement.[20]

The rest of the report was dedicated to Applegate's description of the other patients at Restell's, most of whom stayed about four days and seemed to have been there to have their pregnancies terminated, not delivered, though the reporter was not always explicit on this point. The pattern that emerges is that of women attempting to conceal illegitimate pregnancies. A girl of seventeen or eighteen from Boston, who had worked in a factory and been seduced "by a man of wealth," was sent to New York via Restell's Boston office. Another was from Philadelphia, and her stay was being financed by a congressman. Applegate met another young woman, twenty-three years of age, who supported her entire family posing as a milliner, but in point of fact was "kept by a wealthy man of this city." She had supposedly had nine previous abortions, which, if true, inadvertently demonstrated to *NYMSR* readers just how skilled Madame Restell was in her practice. Another very young woman came with her mother, who simply did not believe that her daughter could be pregnant. Upon Restell's confirmation that this was indeed the case, the mother demanded to know the identity of her daughter's seducer, to which the daughter replied that it was a close relative who stayed with them whenever he was in town. On being informed that Restell could "get rid of it" for her daughter if she remained a few days, "the mother said, that she would rather submit to any thing else than the disgrace." "Her *pious mother* had rather submit to any hazardous operation, no matter the criminality of it, rather than be disgraced by her daughter's transgressions. The relative was a married man." While the report—which was also reprinted in the *National Police Gazette*, demonstrating significant overlap between the medical and tabloid press when it suited them—was clearly meant to titillate and shock readers, as well as to condemn those who sought out Restell's services, it also served as a collective portrait in desperation. The majority of the clients in the account were young, had been seduced, or were in dire straits and needed to avoid pregnancy in order to continue to support themselves and their families.[21]

It is unclear why Dixon waited for almost three weeks after Mary Applegate first went to the mayor to give her statement to organize the demonstration near Madame Restell's house. It is possible that he and others were waiting for some action by Restell, the return of

Applegate's child, for instance. Or perhaps he was waiting for the police to pursue charges against Restell. When they seemed unwilling to do so, that may have prompted the demonstration. In addition to objecting to Restell's role in protecting the secrecy of illegitimate pregnancies, some of those gathered with Dixon that day also believed Restell had murdered Applegate's baby, or at the very least had someone else do so. The *National Police Gazette*, for instance, ran an article under the headline "The Child Murderess." It claimed that "the numerous new-born infants that are weekly found sprinkled about our city, as waifs in the highway . . . and but a slight exertion of reflection will assign a due proportion, if not all, to Madame Restell's agency—especially, when it is plain that inevitable destruction would await the mothers who abandon them, from any other source but the mysterious retreats of an abortionist's den." The *Gazette* went on to claim that Restell was also disposing of the bodies of what they suspected were numerous women who had died during childbirth, despite the fact that they had no evidence for this allegation.[22]

While other female physicians, like Mrs. Bird and Madame Costello, had indeed been caught trying to dispose of the bodies of women who had perished in childbirth, Madame Restell had not. And while no evidence exists to connect Restell with infants abandoned throughout the city, the *National Police Gazette* was not fabricating the fact that New York was experiencing something of a crisis in child abandonment and infanticide. Infants were found both alive and dead with surprising regularity in New York. Their bodies were found floating in the Hudson and East Rivers, they were stuffed down privies, left in bins, and buried in backyards. In 1993, archaeologists discovered the remains of two infants, probably twins, and one fetus in a Five Points privy that belonged to a brothel located on that site through the early 1840s. A resident of the brothel had likely given birth to live twins before disposing of them in the privy; the fetus may have been the result of a miscarriage or, more likely, an abortion. Living babies were routinely left on doorsteps or taken to the almshouse. New York coroners' reports for December of 1840 and early 1841 detail far too many infant corpses found on streets, like the "unknown male infant came to his death from some cause unknown" found on Christmas Day on Centre Street. In February of 1845, a woman named Dorothy Moore, alias Margaret Skinner, delivered a child in a lying-in hospital and left it on the doorstep of a Mr. Stuyvesant at 621 Broadway. She was subsequently apprehended and arrested and charged under an 1829 statute that criminalized abandoning any child under the age of six, punishable by up to seven years in state prison. Unlike Moore, most who abandoned their infants were never found.[23]

Sometimes mothers asked a passerby to look after a baby for a moment, never to return. This strategy had the benefit of ensuring the child would not die of exposure before being found. Others left infants with wet nurses and then ceased payment, never to be seen again. While some of these children were no doubt the offspring of impoverished married women, most commentators believed that infanticide and child abandonment were largely the consequence of illegitimacy. It was single women, it was understood, who had the most to lose by bringing a child into the world. Not only could a single woman most likely not afford to care for the child, that child would forever mark her as a fallen woman.[24]

Unlike some European nations, New York did not have a dedicated foundling hospital to accept and care for infant offspring whose mothers could not do so. New York's orphan asylums, of which there were nine by the time of the Civil War, accepted only legitimate children of married couples, one or both of whom had died. No abandoned children, presumed to be illegitimate, were accepted. Not until after the Civil War would a number of institutions be founded to care for abandoned children. In the interim, such infants could be left at New York's Almshouse, though that facility was certainly not dedicated to the care of children and often contracted to have the infants placed with nurses in their own homes. Unless those nurses had themselves recently given birth, they likely bottle-fed the infants, a practice that had staggering mortality rates. There was no safe and nutritious supplement for breast milk until the 1860s, especially when sanitary water was unavailable for New York's poorest residents. As many as 90 percent of such foundlings died.[25]

New Yorkers in the antebellum era debated the feasibility of opening a foundling hospital. In February of 1846, for instance, the *New York Herald* printed an article advocating for a foundling hospital in New York on the grounds that it would lead to a decrease in abortion and infanticide:

> Let this remedy be brought into the United States, and the infamous skill of Madame Costello would produce fewer victims. We should not so often see young and beautiful girls die in horrible tortures, in the effort to destroy the evidence of their weakness and shame; and children that have reached their full terms, will no longer be thrown to fat the fishes of New York, as it is often found to be the case according to the daily statements.

This correspondent argued that the "want of houses devoted to the offspring of seduction and debauchery, does not at all diminish the number of illegitimate births," but others disagreed. Many thought that the very existence of such an institution would only encourage licentiousness and illegitimacy. By the time of Mary Applegate's allegations in 1846, New Yorkers certainly knew that the abandonment of infants occurred with regularity, but they disagreed about who was ultimately responsible. Some, like the *National Police Gazette*, chose to focus on Madame Restell and others like her.[26]

Popular fiction of the period also focused on the role of female physicians like Restell and their supposed role in cases of infanticide. George Thompson, one of the more celebrated authors of sensational fiction of the antebellum era, included an instance of infanticide by accoucheur in his 1849 *City Crimes; Or, Life in New York and Boston.* Miss Julia Fairfield, who lives in one of the "noblest mansions" on Broadway, is one month away from marrying her fiancé, Francis Sydney. The problem is that she has also been carrying on with Nero, a

Black servant in her home, and is enceinte with his child and due to deliver any day now. A few days after the reader meets her, Miss Julia is taken by Nero to a "house of respectable exterior, in Washington street," where she is greeted "by an elderly female." Fairfield remains there through the evening when the carriage returns for her. "The next morning after her visits to the house on Washington street, the newspapers contained a notice of the discovery of the body of a newborn mulatto child, in the water off the Bowery. That child was the offspring of Miss Julia and the black; it had been strangled, and its body thrown in the water." Readers were led to believe that it was the female physician, not Fairfield herself, who had strangled and disposed of the body.[27]

In colonial and early republican America, outright infanticide had been more common than abandonment, because in smaller villages it was simply more challenging for a new mother to abandon an infant without being seen doing so, at least not if she wanted someone to find the child. Abandonment was thus more a product of cities, where mothers could expect that an unwanted child would be found before it died of exposure. That said, infanticide also continued, as did the kind of abandonment that could reasonably be expected to result in death from exposure. It was a challenging crime to prosecute, not just because women could be skilled at hiding the evidence of their crime but also because it was not always simple to tell whether the child had been stillborn or had died sometime after its birth. For this reason, most law on infanticide dating from the colonial period stipulated that simply concealing the body of a stillborn child was itself a crime, precisely because this explanation was so often employed to explain the deceased infant's death. Finally, juries often acquitted women or convicted them of lesser crimes because they sympathized with the women, who were often poor and single and told tales of seduction and their own abandonment. While the discovery and prosecution of infanticide was a preoccupation of the colonial period, especially in New England, by the early decades of the nineteenth century, there was more compassion toward mothers who were accused of infanticide. While poor and single women were always investigated more than married women were, no woman in antebellum New York State was convicted of infanticide after 1825.[28]

By the early nineteenth century, middle- and working-class people were developing distinctly different understandings of the purpose and value of children themselves. Most middle- and upper-class families were limiting the number of children they bore to give those children more financial opportunities, recognizing that each child came at a monetary cost. Providing every opportunity for three children was simply more feasible than doing so for seven. Having fewer children led to a romanticized view of children as priceless innocents, to be celebrated for their intrinsically emotional value. Middle-class reformers could even sometimes extend their understanding of childhood innocence outward to encompass working-class children, as, for instance, when sanitary reformers advocated for children's hospitals to help the children of the laboring poor.[29]

Working-class families, by contrast, understood that while infants were certainly a drain on resources, small children and youth could work to enrich the family's fortunes. Working-class children were loved by their parents, to be sure, but they also came with distinctly utilitarian values. This is why middle-class family birth rates declined much more sharply over the course of the nineteenth century than did those of working-class families. Middle-class women, of course, also had more tools at their disposal to prevent pregnancy. Premarital chastity was also integral to middle-class understandings of respectability, and many middle-class girls married while still virgins, whereas working-class people often took sex as a signal of commitment in the direction of marriage. This led to many more opportunities for exploitation, both by peers in the working class and by middle- or upper-class interlopers. Working-class girls were also placed in positions—especially as domestic servants in middle-class homes—where they were exposed and vulnerable to sexual assault. Finally, those with means had many more opportunities to either prevent or terminate pregnancies than did working-class people. What contraception existed by the 1840s could be unreliable but was also sometimes beyond the means of working-class people. Some women used douches or the "female regulating pills" sold by Restell and others. Condoms, perhaps the most accessible mode of birth control, were made of animal membranes or linen until the 1840s and were often associated with prostitution, meaning that many of the single women who would have benefited most from them were unlikely to have access to them. Finally, middle- and upper-class women were also much more likely to be able to afford to terminate a pregnancy, whether they were married or single. For all these reasons, working-class people may also have been more accepting of child abandonment and infanticide as reasonable solutions to single pregnancy than their middle-class peers would have been.[30]

It was the middle-class viewpoint that came to dominate discussions of infanticide and abandonment and, crucially, to link the practices with abortion. In 1845, at the same time the New York state legislature was updating the abortion statute, which increased the penalties and enlarged the scope of what and who could be prosecuted under its aegis, legislators added two other sections to the statute that are rarely mentioned by historians considering the criminalization of abortion, in part because the sections are not, on their face, explicitly about abortion. Rather, they target mothers who concealed the birth of children. The fourth and fifth sections of chapter 260 of An Act to Punish the Procurement of Abortion, and for Other Purposes, passed May 13, 1845, reads as follows:

Section 4. Any woman who shall endeavor privately, either by herself or the procurement of others, to conceal the death of any issue of her body, which if born alive would by law be a bastard, whether it was born dead or alive, or whether it was murdered or not, shall be deemed guilty of a misdemeanor, and shall, on conviction thereof, be punished by imprisonment in a county jail, not exceeding one year.
Section 5. Any woman who shall be convicted a second time of the offence specified in the fourth section of this act, shall be

imprisoned in a state prison for a term not less than two or more than five years.

This part of the law is worth considering in detail. Bear in mind that murder was already a crime, so what legislators sought to do here was further criminalize a very particular type of murder, and they did so in part by acknowledging how challenging it was to know whether the death of an infant was infanticide in the first place. Regardless, this statute dictates that even if a woman could prove her child had been born dead, if she were herself unmarried and concealed that child, she would be guilty of a misdemeanor. Trying to cover all bases at once, this statute could be used to punish a woman who was acquitted of the murder of her illegitimate child, for instance, if she could be found to have concealed the body of the child, no matter how the infant had died. These legislators believed this practice to be common enough, or perhaps heinous enough, that section five laid out punishments for women who had already been convicted once under section four. Those convicted under section five could expect imprisonment not in county, but rather in state prison, this time for up to five years.[31]

Legislators were technically criminalizing the concealment of a body—no matter how it had come to die—but really they were penalizing illegitimacy because it applied only to children born as bastards. Further, that legislators included these sections in a bill that criminalized abortion, indeed was named for abortion, demonstrates that they saw abortion and infanticide as two sides of the same coin: both as solutions to the problem of illegitimacy, which itself they very much wanted to discourage. Legislators were not actually wrong about this: single pregnant women did both terminate pregnancies and dispose of unwanted children through abandonment and infanticide, the response depending on how early they discovered a pregnancy and whether they had the means to pay for an abortion.

The difficulty, for those like Restell who practiced abortion, was that the procedure came to be seen as if it were similar to the practice of infanticide, which tainted the debate about abortion, and indeed still does. Abortion had plenty of foes on its own grounds—it gave women reproductive autonomy; some women were becoming wealthy as its practitioners; the middle-class birth rate was declining as the immigrant birth rate remained high—but these were all straightforward, if misogynist and nativist, objections. Likening the termination of an early-term pregnancy to the murder of a living child was a symbolic argument but one that animated many antebellum newspapermen and lawmakers who were encouraged to think of abortion as child murder because of both practices' demonstrable links to the rise in illegitimacy during this era. Thinking about abortion as infanticide was a way to take it out of the realm of women's health care, where it had lived for hundreds of years in the United States and its earlier colonies, and place it in the realm of criminal law.

In the wake of the disturbances outside her home, on February 25, 1846, Madame Restell responded with one of her customary letters to the public, this one in the *New-York Tribune*. The letter did little to respond to the concerns voiced by the crowd—that she was helping to conceal illegitimacy and in so doing was likely disposing of bastard infants. Restell began by praising the crowd for maintaining the peace and resisting being "made the tools in the hands of so infamous an instigator," by whom she meant George Washington Dixon. She claimed that she had been "applied to by his emissaries for money," in essence that he had organized the crowd outside her home because she had refused to pay. She claimed further that he had staged the event only to run to newspapers, saying that the crowd was larger than it was and exaggerating its indignance. She claimed that she and her family had remained within the parlor throughout the day because she did not believe that the protesters really meant any harm. This was a clear attempt to downplay the animosity that was on display that day. Restell closed by explaining that she holds herself "amenable to the law, if I have offended, and to its protecting mantle in my person, property, and civil rights, and that every citizen is individually interested in protecting their rights of another from either the designs or machinations of those who, for sinister purposes, would supplant the Majesty of the

Law." Having thus aligned herself with the forces of law and order, which the paper's editors themselves affirmed, she signed off. She made no mention of Mary Applegate or her baby.[32]

Applegate herself disappears from the historical record thereafter. We will likely never know what truly happened to Applegate's child. At least one account at the time—a dispatch from Philadelphia published in the *New-York Tribune*—alleged that the name "Mary Applegate" itself was a pseudonym, which if true makes it that much more difficult to trace her. In this era there were no systematized birth records that can be checked to register the birth of Applegate's child. One Mary Applegate of the same approximate age appears in the 1850 U.S. census; she is twenty-six and living with her one-year-old son, James Carpenter, in Philadelphia. If this is the same Mary Applegate, it appears that she had another child with a different man. Augustus Edwards, whose name is verifiable in Pennsylvania records, appears to have married and remained a resident of Philadelphia for years to come.[33]

Though Restell was never tried for the supposed crime of kidnapping, and Mary Applegate's name soon faded from newspapers, the links between abortion, infanticide, and abandonment had been cemented in the narrative of illegitimacy and connected to the practice of female physicians like Restell. And the increasingly divergent class-based understandings of children and childhood, still only inchoate in the mid-1840s, would only intensify the politics of abortion in the years to come.[34]

6

"A DISGRACE TO HER SEX"

When twenty-six-year-old Maria Bodine's "monthly courses" did not arrive at the normal time in mid-May of 1846, she must have been terrified. She was not married and had been sleeping with her employer, a widower named Joseph Cook, for about a year. She had begun working as his housekeeper in Walden, New York, where he farmed, and then had moved with him to Ramapo, New York, about forty miles northwest of the tip of Manhattan, where he took over the running of a cotton manufactory. While waiting for her courses to arrive, she noticed that she was newly prone to vomiting and that her breasts had become larger and were painful to the touch. Concluding she was likely pregnant, Bodine left Ramapo and went to New York City in June to stay with her sister, Esther Dexter, on Bleecker Street. Bodine had decided that, somehow or other, she needed not to be pregnant any longer. Like many single young women in her situation, she set her sights on finding a solution in the city.[1]

Bodine found Madame Restell's address through one of Restell's many newspaper advertisements. Bodine visited just a few days after arriving in Manhattan, explaining her situation to Restell and asking for her advice. She claimed later that she did not yet know if she was pregnant with any certainty and wanted Restell to tell her. Restell explained that she would have to examine Bodine to determine the best course of action. The examination would cost $5 and an abortion would be $100. At least at first glance, it would seem that Restell's prices had gone up since she had bargained with Ann Maria Purdy over the cost of terminating a pregnancy in 1841. Restell also asked Bodine about what her "beau" did for a living, probably an attempt to ascertain how much Bodine could reasonably afford. When Bodine explained, improbably, that she might be as much as "six months gone," Restell said that she would be happy to have her board there through her confinement at a cost of $5 a week. Bodine responded that Mr. Cook, whom she said was a factory agent, would not approve of that, or perhaps would not be able to pay for it. Bodine left Restell's office without having made a decision. She stopped in at a dry goods store to do a little shopping and was promptly arrested by an officer who had been stationed outside Restell's to observe who came and went. The officer accompanied her back to her sister's house on Bleecker Street, telling her that Bodine had just been "in a bad murderer's house." He asked Bodine if she had bought any medication from Madame Restell, and Bodine said no, explaining that she had visited Restell because she was "very unwell, and I went to consult her as a female physician." There may have been some truth to this claim, as Bodine later also consulted with a Dr. Coles, who resided near her sister, on Carmine Street. She complained of pain in her breasts and sought to find out if she was pregnant.[2]

Without having solved her problem, after another week at her sister's in New York, Bodine returned to her employer and lover, Joseph Cook, in Ramapo. There she resumed her duties as housekeeper, doing "all except the washing," getting up at sunrise and retiring at 9:00 p.m. She remained in Ramapo for a week and a half and then, on July 17, accompanied by an employee of Cook's named John McCann, she returned to New York. This time she went straight to Madame Restell's at 148 Greenwich Street. Restell told her that the charge to terminate her pregnancy would be $75, now $25 less than the original estimate, meaning that Restell was still willing to bargain with those who could not afford full rates. Bodine only had $30, so she alerted McCann that she would need an additional $45 and settled in at Restell's, McCann bringing the balance two days later. That Sunday, Madame Restell ex-

amined Bodine and inserted her hand into Bodine's vagina for the purpose of bringing on a miscarriage. She explained that it was taking
longer than normal because Bodine was "differently situated than anyone else." She gave Bodine pills to take for the subsequent two days, likely
ergot, which would bring on uterine contractions. Later that day Bodine's
courses returned. Restell told Bodine she would likely be fine through
the night, but that she should call on Restell if she needed her. The next
morning the pains were growing, which Restell indicated meant that
"the pills were taking effect." Because she was experiencing pain, however, Restell visited her throughout the day and that night slept with
Bodine so she could be with her in case she was ready to miscarry.
Newspaper reports that describe Restell as only heartless and violent
are certainly belied by this account of her sharing a bed with her client
to comfort her through her pain.[3]

The next morning, Bodine awoke in yet more pain, and Restell had
her sit on "an earthen chamber; narrow at the bottom and broad at
top." Restell inserted her hand into Bodine's vagina, and Bodine heard
something fall from her body into the chamber; this was likely the fetus.
Restell then told her that the pains she was continuing to feel were
"after pains," meaning that she had successfully miscarried. Restell continued to attend to Bodine during the day and night, and Bodine remained with her through Thursday of that week. When Restell found
her crying on the Thursday afternoon because she wanted to go home
but could not afford to get there, Restell gave her money to return to
Ramapo. She told her she must make sure to take a carriage away from
Greenwich Street so that she could avoid the police and also gave her
advice on what to do to stop the pain in her breasts. At the door of her
office, Restell shook Bodine's hand, gave her a kiss, and sent her on her
way.[4]

Bodine returned to Ramapo ready to commence her duties without
a child to support and with very few people knowing she had ever
been pregnant. She had accomplished her goal. Unfortunately, Bodine's
health took a turn for the worse, as it had on prior occasions, and the
involvement of a series of doctors compromised her ability to maintain

her secret. Unable to work because of her illness, she moved to Walden, New York, to live with another sister who could care for her. She stayed in Walden for almost a full year, mostly at her sister's house, and then later in a local almshouse, where a doctor was able to give her more attention. That doctor, Samuel Smith, gave her a gynecological examination in June of 1847 and claimed that he determined that she had either been delivered of a child or had undergone an abortion. It is also possible that Bodine simply admitted this to him. Either way, he believed that her continued suffering was somehow related to the events of a year ago. Smith decided to take action. As a result of the examination and of his questioning of Bodine, on August 2, 1847, he wrote a letter to the mayor of New York City, alerting him to what had happened. More than a full year after Restell had terminated Bodine's pregnancy, police officers ventured to Walden to see Bodine at her sister's house and to hear her story. That account proved to be the evidence necessary to begin criminal proceedings against Madame Restell.[5]

This arrest and trial were more significant than any other had been for Restell thus far. While newspapers in New York and surrounding states had now been covering Restell for nine years, it was during the Bodine trial that she became a household name in many other parts of the country, with newspapers in the South and Midwest regularly re-printing stories from New York newspapers. The Bodine trial made Restell famous. The trial was also significant because it was the first arrest for Restell under the newly passed abortion statute of 1845. Whether or not Bodine's pregnancy had yet quickened would, of course, be key to the trial. Restell's conviction of six years earlier had been over-turned by New York's supreme court on technical grounds, mostly re-lated to how the prosecution had taken testimony from the primary witness who subsequently died of tuberculosis. So long as prosecutors followed proper procedure, Bodine was still very much alive and able to testify on her own behalf. Restell had squeaked out a victory in 1841 via luck and an overzealous police magistrate. Since that time, six years of frustration and anger had been building among some New Yorkers.

THE FEMALE ABORTIONIST.

"The Female Abortionist." This cartoon of Madame Restell ran on the front page of the *National Police Gazette* and is perhaps her most famous likeness. Where Restell's own womb would be sits a bat feasting on a baby. Reprinted from *National Police Gazette*, March 13, 1847, page 1.

The city's newspapers, and especially its tabloids, had of course been steadily building animus toward Restell. Following the demise of the *Polyanthos*, the *National Police Gazette* was perhaps the most active in its opposition to Restell and would rush a trial transcript into production at the end of the case. In March of 1847, it had already debuted what is likely the most famous depiction of Restell under the title "The Female Abortionist."

The depiction of Restell's face is not unsympathetic; she looks sad more than anything else. The disturbing part of the illustration, of course, is the bat-cum-devil feasting on the newborn baby, on which Restell herself rests, as if the creature and Restell are one and the same. Indeed, the devil is situated in the same place on her own body as her womb would be. The illustration essentially made the case that Restell's work of terminating pregnancies had taken her out of the realm of humanity itself. By representing the infant that the devil-bat is eating as fully formed, the illustration served to conflate the practices of abortion and infanticide. The accompanying article claimed,

> In the heart of the metropolis, she holds her bloody empire. In this city, so vain of its good name, she sits in a spacious den, tricked out in gorgeous finery for the superficial eye, but crowded in its extensive labyrinths with groans of misery and death. Her *patients* are of three classes, and her treatment has an equal scope. There is oil of tanzy [*sic*] and steel filings [an abortifacient] for the first; pinioned arms, a probe and a male performer for those who have grown heavier with sin, and a rude delivery and unskilful [*sic*] treatment for others who like the unfortunate Mary Applegate carry the fruit of an illicit love until its perfect time.

Here the *Gazette* presumed that readers were already familiar with the story of Mary Applegate, so well and so recently covered had it been by most newspapers. It then claimed that those children born alive at Restell's office were "sprinkled," alive and dead "about our city on stoops." While the *National Police Gazette* was the most extreme in its coverage and the most overblown in its language, it was hardly alone in its condemnation of Restell's practice, and certainly no newspapers came to her defense, even as many continued to run her advertisements. The stage had been set for Restell's 1847 trial, and all of New York was watching.[6]

* * * *

On September 7, 1847, the grand jury found a true bill of indictment against Madame Restell for manslaughter in the second degree for the abortion of a quick child. The counts of the indictment detail the grand jurors' belief that Restell administered an abortifacient and used an instrument. Remarkably, there were also separate counts for the use of her hands and her fingers in effecting the abortion. If convicted of aborting a quick child, Restell could face up to seven years in state prison. The lesser charge of terminating a pregnancy not yet quick still existed, however, and the jurors could find Restell guilty of a misdemeanor on that charge. The grand jurors also indicted Joseph Cook as a co-conspirator with Restell, and John McCann, Bodine's escort to Restell's, as an accomplice to the abortion. The court of sessions then issued a bench warrant for their apprehension. Restell was arrested the same day, just as she was "stepping into her carriage." She was imprisoned in a cell in the Tombs. A day later, officers returned from Montgomery County, New York, having arrested Cook as well. Both he and McCann were also imprisoned in the Tombs awaiting trial.[7]

Bail for Cook and Restell was set at $10,000 apiece; newspapers do not detail the bail for McCann. On Saturday, September 11, Cook's lawyer was able to have his bail reduced to $5,000, and three men stood as sureties. He was released. The court declined to accept the $10,000 from Restell herself and rejected one potential surety, Joseph A. Jackson, a pawnbroker and recent candidate for alderman in the Fourteenth Ward. Until she could locate someone else to post bail, she remained in jail, though one paper as far away as Maine speculated that "she has too many of our aristocratic merchants in her power to remain long within a prison's walls, when their gold can loose the bars." By September 17, *New York Sun* publisher Benjamin Day had posted bail, which was accepted by the court. The *Evening Post* claimed that Restell's counsel had paid $1,000 for his becoming surety. Restell was "paraded from her cell, in splendid dress" and took her carriage home. The trial was initially scheduled to begin on September 21 and was then postponed until later in October.[8]

Jury selection began on October 20, and it soon became obvious that too many of the men they called—and of course it was only white men who were able to serve on juries at this time—admitted to too much prejudice against Restell, so much so that they could not be impartial. In all, just under one hundred men were set aside for already having formed an opinion about the guilt or innocence of Restell, a testament to how saturated the news media was with coverage of the case and of her prior arrests and trial. Even most of those who were admitted were aware of Restell and the accusations but claimed they were capable of objectivity in judging the evidence. After three days of questioning, the twelve-man jury was made up of a watchmaker, a straw manufacturer, a painter, a tailor, a saddler, a number of merchants (selling, among other things, groceries, hosiery, and thread), and two men whose occupations were not stated in the records that survive. The trial was set to commence following the weekend, on Monday morning.[9]

The trial would be held before recorder John B. Scott, effectively the judge in the proceedings, and two aldermen, Stephen Feeks and Thomas Tappan. In New York City's system of government, the recorder was not only the judge of the court of general sessions but also essentially the deputy mayor and vice president of the board of aldermen, the mayor being president.[10]

The prosecution's opening statement and testimony commenced on October 25, 1847. Newspapers reported that the "court-room was crowded to excess." Prosecuting the case was a team of three lawyers: New York County's district attorney, John McKeon; deputy district attorney, Jonas B. Phillips; and Ogden Hoffman. Phillips gave the opening statement for the prosecution. He characterized Restell as a woman who, "disgracing her sex, forgetting that she is herself a mother, disregarding at once divine and human laws, has amassed a fortune in the daily perpetration of a crime which violates and annuls one of the most sacred ordinances of Almighty God." While Phillips did, of course, detail the facts of the case as he saw them and explain the law under which Restell had been charged, the emotional heart of his appeal was based on two interrelated claims: that Restell had turned her back on womanhood in terminating pregnancies and that she had done so only for money. As Phillips put it, "Nature is appalled, that woman, the last and loveliest of her works, could so unsex herself, as to perpetrate such fiend-like enormities." Because women were uniquely capable of pregnancy, Phillips and others argued that it was, in essence, their duty to carry children to term. Any woman who had gone so far as to aid others in terminating a pregnancy had forfeited the right to womanhood itself. This language was no accident. The jurors lived in a city in which they would have observed women doing many things other than bearing and caring for children. Traditional gender roles had been seriously eroded in the cities of antebellum America, and many men did not like it. Never mind that working-class men depended on the labor of their wives for a family to make ends meet. Wives' labor still inadvertently upset the balance of power within many families in a way that some husbands found profoundly unsettling. While the merchants on the jury might have been able to afford to have wives out of the workforce, and almost certainly employed servants to aid their wives in managing households, other jurors likely relied on the work of their wives. In a city like New York, many women, largely those in the middle class, were having fewer children, slowly but surely lessening the centrality of motherhood in their lives. The argument that Restell was essentially aiding women in rejecting women's supposed destiny as mothers was designed to appeal to men.[11]

Phillips's other point of outrage, and it clearly relates, is that Restell was turning a tidy profit as a female physician. As Phillips explained, "But this defendant destroys the germ of nature—she kills the unborn infant; endangers, if she does not destroy the mother's life, ruins her health; and all for the sake of the base lucre, which she allures the frail, or wicked, who have fallen, to pay her, in the vain hope that she can aid them to conceal their shame." Phillips was criticizing Restell not just for aiding in the cover-up of illegitimacy but for having a job, for charging her clients for the services she performed for them, and for becoming wealthy as a result. It should go without saying that male doctors were generally not criticized for charging their clients or for making a decent living as a result of their profession. While midwives had always charged their clients for their services, they sometimes did so in a barter system, and when delivering babies, they worked with a community of neighbor women and family members, who were not paid for assisting in deliveries. While money might change hands after the birth of a child, it did not outwardly appear to be a monetary transaction in the

way that Restell charged clients whom she did not otherwise know
and for which she advertised her services in the newspaper. Part of the
criticism, though it was certainly never framed this way, was that
Restell was monetizing what had traditionally appeared to be a practice shrouded in a feminine and maternal haze and an act of female
community. The other problem for many observers was that her success
led not just to wealth but also to independence. Brothel madams, some of
whom also became quite wealthy, were similarly criticized and sometimes
harassed and had their brothels ransacked. An independent female entre-
preneur was a threat to the established gender order. Not only was she
working for pay but her earnings were making her richer than the vast
majority of New Yorkers at the time.[12]

By 1847, most newspapers had reported on Restell's husband,
Charles Lohman, so New Yorkers knew that he existed, but their marriage was seen as unconventional, if only because she was such a public
figure. Newspaper reporters often noted their surprise that Restell
could possibly *have* a husband, the implication being that any woman
this independent and successful must not be married because her
husband and family would otherwise be occupying her time. The
Lohman household was anomalous because she was the public face of
their business, and her labor at least gave the appearance of bringing in
the vast majority of their income. This was not how a household was
supposed to operate. In addition to her actual crimes, Restell's guilt
hinged on the ways she upset notions of womanhood itself.

Having given his opening statement, Assistant District Attorney
Phillips called his first witness:

> The complainant Maria Bodine, here came in to Court with a fee-
> ble, tottering walk, and took her seat in the chair usually occupied
> by witnesses. She is a young woman, about 26 years of age, middling
> size, and evidently in a rapid decline of health. She was neatly dressed,
> and her appearance created much excitement and sympathy through-
> out the crowded court-room.

This account comes from a reporter for the *National Police Gazette*, which published a full account at the trial's end. This sympathy for Bodine was not atypical. Restell's attorneys objected to Bodine's testimony on the grounds that she was an accomplice in the alleged crime, but their objections were denied and Bodine was allowed to testify.[13]

Bodine was the star witness for the prosecution, not just because she could describe what had happened at Madame Restell's but because she needed to establish the timeline for when she became pregnant, which then determined just how pregnant she was at the time of the abortion. Much of the testimony on both sides hinged on the timeline of the pregnancy and on Bodine's credibility, with multiple witnesses for both sides praising or maligning her character.

Bodine first recounted how she had come to suspect her pregnancy, her visit to Restell, and her miscarriage. Among the last questions Phillips put to Bodine on that first day of testimony was designed to establish how far along her pregnancy was.

Q. Before going to Madame Restell's had you any sensation in your stomach?
A. Before and about the 17th of July, I had different sensations from what I ever felt before; my breasts were swelled, and my bowels, and I felt something flutter in my womb.

Bodine was testifying that her pregnancy had quickened by the time of the abortion. Bodine's testimony for the day finished by her explaining that she had been ill since she had left Restell's, though no one ever adequately explained what that illness was, the prosecution always intimating that it was related to the abortion, but never explaining how.[14]

The second day's testimony opened with ADA Phillips reviewing elements of the procedure that Bodine alleged occurred at Restell's and trying to establish when, precisely, Bodine had last had her courses. She said the beginning of the month of April 1846. At that point the prosecution rested and attorneys for the defense were permitted to ask Bodine their questions. Restell was represented by James T. Brady and David Graham Jr. Both had already made a name for themselves in legal circles. Restell had obtained among the best counsel money could buy.[15]

Brady first asked that Bodine "put aside her veil and turn to the jury, so that her answers may be heard." He then set about establishing a timeline that would make it much more difficult to believe that Bodine's child could possibly have been quick by mid-July. Bodine admitted that she had last had her courses on April 12 or 13, that she had likely continued to have sex with Cook through the end of that month, possibly as late as May 1, and that it was only in mid-May that she noticed her courses had not arrived. Brady also interrogated her on whether she had ever had intercourse with other men and whether she had told a number of men, including three different doctors, that she had been pregnant prior to 1846. When the prosecution objected to this line of questioning, the court allowed Bodine to decline to answer "provided the answer would tend to degrade or disgrace her." In the end, Bodine chose not to respond to the questions about a prior pregnancy.[16]

Bodine was on the witness stand for three days in total. On the third day, the *National Police Gazette* reported that "the crowd of spectators this morning is immense. The attendance of gentlemen of the Bar from other States, is considerable, including several members of Congress." On this final day of her testimony, Brady asked about the months of medical attention Bodine had received from various doctors in and around Walden. At one point Bodine fainted and was led from the courtroom so that she might rest before proceeding with her testimony. Upon returning to the witness stand, Bodine insisted that all of her ailments—including sores under her arms and pains in her back, which doctors had treated with cupping and leeching—were due to the miscarriage. When asked by Brady and Restell's other attorney, Graham, whether she had ever suffered from venereal disease, she said no. She did admit to having suffered from the whites, a white vaginal discharge that could have been a symptom of gonorrhea and that nineteenth-century Americans often associated with injury to the back, which is why she had been cupped on the back. Finally, Brady walked through Bodine's final months of treatment with Dr. Samuel Smith in Walden, to whom she would ultimately confess the circumstances of the abortion and who would write to the mayor of New York, thus commencing the investigation that had brought everyone to court.[17]

Next the prosecution called a series of doctors, including Smith. Smith testified that he had known Bodine from the time she was a girl and on June 5, 1847, he gave her a gynecological examination, during which he observed that the neck and mouth of the womb indicated that "she must have had a delivery of a child badly managed, or must have had an abortion produced upon her, or by some mechanical injury by an instrument, or by violence of the hand." Bodine told him what had happened at Madame Restell's. One of Restell's attorneys, on cross-examination, had Smith admit that his observations alone were not definitive proof that Bodine had undergone an abortion, though he could not stop Smith from reiterating that the state of her uterus made sense in light of her confession to the abortion. Brady also introduced a line of questioning that would be put to all the medical men, including those who were called as experts and had never actually examined Bodine herself: how to tell if a female body was pregnant and how to discern if a pregnancy had quickened.[18]

The simple answer to both questions was that there was no one definitive way to determine either of these things, at least in the early stages of a pregnancy. Some women didn't have their period for reasons other than pregnancy, just as they might experience nausea and vomiting for other reasons as well. This was precisely why quickening was so important in the legal doctrine of pregnancy and why it eluded regulation: because only women could attest with any certainty to having felt a fetus move within them. And even that, as some of these doctors attested, could be put down to irritable bowels or an upset stomach, some mistaking these other ailments for the "flutters" that a quick fetus produced. On the issue of determining whether a woman was pregnant at an early stage, the main questions asked of the doctors at Restell's trial had to do with a darkening of the areola, though they disagreed about whether that occurred only during a first pregnancy. That the areola did darken during pregnancy they were certain. Doctors also disagreed about whether a woman might be capable of menstruation after she had become pregnant. The prosecution was intent on proving that this was possible because this would backdate the window of conception, given that Bodine had had her courses in mid-April. If she could have been pregnant earlier than that, then there was a much greater likelihood that the pregnancy would have quickened by mid-July, at the time of the alleged termination. On the question of quickening, the district attorney sought to pin down when was the earliest it could occur (twelve weeks emerged as consensus), whereas Restell's lawyers attempted to ascertain the very latest that a pregnancy could quicken (six months was the latest figure cited by one doctor). The two respective sides were arguing either that Bodine's pregnancy *must have* quickened or that it *could not possibly* have done so by July 19. Of course, even Bodine herself did not know precisely when she had conceived, so all of this was a show for the jury to try to sway them either toward or against Bodine's pregnancy having quickened by July 19.

In all, eight doctors testified for the prosecution, taking up about two and a half days of the trial. Of those, three, including Smith, had examined Bodine at some point. The remaining five were called as experts on the practice of midwifery and women's bodies. Significantly, and unlike in earlier eras where midwives would have been called to testify about their examinations of a woman's body, no women were called as experts on medical questions. Perhaps the most significant of the five was Dr. Gunning Bedford, who had begun to make a name for himself as one of the preeminent medical foes of abortion. His anti-abortion writings, which were usually couched in language about women midwives' incompetence, had already appeared in the *New York Journal of Medical and Collateral Sciences* in 1844 and the

New York Medical and Surgical Reporter in 1846. Bedford explained that he occupied "the chair of Obstetrics, including the Diseases of Women and Children," at the College of Physicians and Surgeons in New York (which would later merge with Columbia University's medical school but was still independent at that time). Attorney Ogden Hoffman first asked Bedford whether a woman could menstruate once pregnant, and Bedford responded that indeed she could and that menstruation "does not at all" prove that a woman is not pregnant. This was inaccurate; a woman could certainly experience some bleeding during pregnancy, though menstruation is impossible. Even Bedford's academic medical training clearly had its limits, demonstrating the infancy of the field of gynecology and obstetrics at this time.[19]

Hoffman then asked: "What is the ordinary period when a woman quickens with child?"

"In answering that question," replied Bedford, "I beg to say that physicians consider that life is perfect in the earlier months, the earliest, in fact of pregnancy, and that the child is as much alive then, as at any subsequent period."

One of Restell's attorneys interjected: "Yes, but lawyers do not; there is a distinction between what you regard as life—natural life, and *legal* life."

Dr. B.—I wish distinctly to be understood, and to state only facts, and well received doctrines as I know I am reported.

Q. You are right, sir! I now renew the question.

A. The general rule is that women quicken at four, or four and a half months; women will sometimes quicken at three months, and such is the difference as regards the time, that it is an accepted doctrine with the profession, that from ten to sixteen weeks are the two limits, within which quickening can or will take place.

The second part to Bedford's answer was what Hoffman was after, the idea that Bodine might have quickened at only ten weeks, which made it more possible that Restell had terminated a quick pregnancy. But much more important for the evolving discourse on abortion was Bedford's assertion that life began at conception and his rejection of the law that governed abortion, which relied on quickening. The quickening doctrine existed in part because earlier Americans had believed that this was the moment at which a fetus became "ensouled," that its movement in the womb meant it had become akin to the child it would eventually be if the pregnancy was carried to term. The law relied on quickening, though it was obviously a remarkably imprecise and unreliable measure of development. This was not only because its onset varied among women but also because it depended on those very women's testimony, almost all of whom had a vested interest in denying their pregnancies had quickened if they had already terminated them. Bedford was proposing that in regard to abortion, quickening as a developmental milestone should be thrown out altogether. While New York State's statute did not yet reflect this, as more doctors became organized in their opposition to abortion, legislators would come to embrace this view. Bedford was essentially arguing that a conservative and medical understanding of fetal development should supplant centuries of legal precedent when it came to abortion.[20]

Hoffman also asked Bedford a series of questions about how abortions were performed, about indicators of pregnancy in a woman's body, as well as about possible symptoms a woman might experience if she had had a pregnancy terminated. In turn Brady also cross-examined Bedford, eliciting the admission that almost none of the indicators or symptoms were absolutely infallible, meaning that what doctors had seen on the body of Bodine may or may not have meant she was pregnant, may or may not have meant that she had miscarried. This was, by and large, how the other medical experts were interviewed as well. Unlike the testimony from the doctors who had actually seen Bodine and had had her admit the pregnancy and abortion to them, most of the expert testimony was something of a wash, none of the experts being able to attest to much of anything with definitiveness.[21]

The final witness for the prosecution was John McCann, Joseph Cook's employee who was charged as an accessory in the crime. Despite many objections from Restell's attorneys, all of which were overruled by the court, McCann testified that he had accompanied Bodine from Ramapo to Restell's, that he had gone back to Ramapo for an additional amount of money (the $45 that Bodine needed), which he gained from Cook, and that finally he had returned to Restell's and had given the money to Bodine. The defense asked only one question of McCann, about the time that Bodine had first moved to Ramapo, to which McCann replied that he believed it was in the spring of the prior year. On that anticlimactic note, the court adjourned for the day. The trial, including the initial days of jury selection, had now been in session for eight days.[22]

On the sixth day of testimony, Saturday, October 30, the *National Police Gazette* published a commentary on what it believed had been revealed thus far.

> The dark veil of mystery which has heretofore enveloped the doings of the bloody den in Greenwich street has now been torn aside, and palpable and bold stands out the mistress of its horrors in her true character, as murderess paramount, not only of the unborn, but of the sinning mother who desperately seeks the fearful shelter of her walls to hide her shame.

The *Gazette* claimed that many women must surely die during childbirth in Restell's home and accused her of selling their bodies to medical schools and doctors who might then dissect them, all without any evidence to support the claims. There was, of course, plenty of actual evidence being supplied by witnesses at the trial, but it did not include the disposal of corpses.[23]

That Saturday, the attorneys for the prosecution declared that they were through with their first round of evidence: "May it please the Court, the case is now with the defense." The first order of business was the opening statement by Restell's attorney, Brady, who began by thanking the jurors for their service, telling them how much confidence he had in their ability and "upright minds." He then decried the press, who had reported on Restell as if she was guilty, when in fact the trial had not yet concluded. He argued that Restell was being tried on her reputation, rather than for "a specific offense," and claimed that the evidence purporting to show that Bodine had been pregnant with a quick child was in fact specious. He reassured the courtroom that he did not plan to indict the character of Cook, but when it came to that of Bodine, the eager audience was in for something wholly different. Brady gave a brief preview:

> And this woman, the prosecutrix, it will be our solemn duty to prove, and we have facts to sustain us in this assertion, that that woman is as foul, corrupt, loathsome, guilty thing, as ever polluted God's blessed earth by her pestilential presence.

He went on to assert that they would prove she had earlier in life contracted a venereal disease as a result of "general and promiscuous concubinage." This was not purely a hard-hearted strategy designed to tarnish Bodine's reputation. Rather, in addition to trying to prove that her pregnancy could not have quickened by mid-July, the defense was also attempting to call into doubt whether she had ever been pregnant in the first place, and whether the ill health from which she now suffered might be related to a venereal disease she had contracted years ago and not the alleged termination of her pregnancy. It would, no doubt, be an uphill battle, but given how solid the prosecution's case was, the defense attorneys likely felt they had little choice.[24]

Brady's first witnesses were a series of women and men who had known Bodine in Walden, Montgomery, and Ramapo. All were asked questions about her health prior to July of the previous year, as well as about her character. The difficulty for the defense was that they wanted to cast aspersions on her character, but the ultimate aspersions—sex outside of wedlock and illegitimate pregnancy—were something to which Bodine herself already admitted and of which the defense wanted to disprove, not reinforce. Over the course of a day and a half, the defense called seven witnesses from Walden and the surrounding area, all of whom said that Bodine had a bad reputation and that they would not believe her testimony, even if given under oath. Some said she told lies, and one said that he had been in a public house with her on several occasions, this at a time when such behavior was unseemly for women.[25]

On the eighth day of testimony, the defense called two doctors named Millspaugh, who were father and son. Dr. Peter Millspaugh testified that the signs of pregnancy referred to by earlier doctors—darkening of the areola, hardness of breasts, and so forth—were not absolute indicators of pregnancy. He had had a patient quite recently with these symptoms who turned out not to be pregnant at all. He also called into question the testimony of earlier doctors who claimed that quickening could occur as early as the tenth week and testified that menstruation was not possible following conception. While Dr. Peter Millspaugh had not ever met Bodine, his son, Dr. Thomas Millspaugh, who was called next as a witness, had examined her in Walden. Thomas Millspaugh claimed that Bodine had come to him both because she thought she was "in the family way" and because she suffered from gonorrhea. Millspaugh alleged that this visit occurred prior to Bodine moving from Walden to Ramapo, that is, prior to the pregnancy that Restell was alleged to have terminated. Upon examining her—once by himself and a second time with his brother, yet another Dr. Millspaugh—he concluded that she had syphilis, of which he believed he was able to cure her by removing some ulcers. He did not comment on whether she was pregnant, though when the prosecution cross-examined him, he admitted that at a later time Bodine had told him about an operation she'd had in New York, which he then told the defense she later recanted.[26]

On the ninth day of testimony, the defense read into the record two depositions taken from Delia Morgan and Maria Walden, both sisters-in-law of Joseph Cook, who "hesitated about appearing before the court as witnesses." The two collectively testified that they had seen Bodine in Walden in August of 1845—well before the alleged pregnancy—and on subsequent occasions, where she suffered from a variety of ailments, including a cold and various ulcers that they had witnessed Thomas Millspaugh remove. Morgan claimed that in August of 1845, she had found a certain medicine with a brand name of Velpeau in Bodine's possession, and Bodine had confirmed she was taking it. Both witnesses had nothing but praise for Bodine as a capable servant and excellent dairy woman but said she was almost always ill and usually refused their offers of nursing. With that, the defense rested. The picture they had tried to paint was of a Maria Bodine who not only had a bad reputation and was untrustworthy but who also was almost always ill with one complaint or another. This picture was designed to cast doubt on whether her current condition was really related to the abortion she claimed Restell had administered a year ago.[27]

Beginning with the prosecution, both sides now had the opportunity to recall witnesses and also present testimony designed to rebut that offered by prior witnesses. The prosecution began with Peter T. Clearwater to rebut the testimony of Dr. Thomas Millspaugh. Clearwater recounted that the prior winter, Millspaugh had approached him in Clearwater's capacity as overseer of the poor for Montgomery County to reimburse Millspaugh for the expense of seeing Bodine while she was impoverished and under the care of the county almshouse. Clearwater remembered the conversation this way:

> Says he "you are poor master and I've been attending this girl for a complaint brought on by Mr. Cook, who has knocked her up and sent her to Madame Restell and an abortion has been effected on her person." I think he said "we might probably get the sum, we might extort out of him $500, and we will divide the spoils."

Clearwater reported that he wasn't sure whether Millspaugh was being serious or not, though he did recognize Bodine as having been under his care and he did believe that Millspaugh had treated Bodine during that time. He never accompanied Millspaugh to see Cook at Ramapo and heard no more of the scheme to extort money from him.

If true, however, this was one more piece of evidence that linked Cook and Bodine with Restell.[28]

That evening, the prosecution called two witnesses who had known Bodine and Cook at Ramapo. Both claimed that she was of good character with not a word spoken against her reputation, and one claimed she looked pregnant as early as April of 1846. The prosecution was attempting to salvage Bodine's character as well as backdate the pregnancy as early as possible. The prosecution then called Mrs. Catherine Youngblood, Bodine's sister, with whom she had stayed when she first returned to Walden. She testified to her sister's ill health upon her return from Ramapo. She also relayed the conversation that she had overheard her sister having with Dr. Thomas Millspaugh in which they discussed her pregnancy and abortion. The following day, November 4, the prosecution called a series of witnesses to comment positively on the character of Bodine and negatively on the character of Thomas Millspaugh, the intention being to discredit his testimony that Bodine was ill with syphilis and to bolster the idea that he had always been aware of the true cause of her sickness, but that he had a vested interest in remaining silent because he was hoping to blackmail Cook with the information.[29]

The final witness called by the prosecution was a Dr. Covell, who had recently examined Bodine, looking for signs of past venereal disease. In his words, "There was no appearance of chancre or any venereal sore on her private parts. I have had considerable experience in these cases, and see them every day; if venereal disease had ever existed, there would have been marks." While Bodine might have been relieved to have Covell exonerate her from the stain of having venereal disease, undergoing the examination and knowing that her sexual health was being spoken of in open court and that the particularities of her vagina were being verbally explored by the doctor, the prosecutor, and both defense attorneys must have been excruciating.[30]

The defense recalled five witnesses to testify to the good character of Dr. Thomas Millspaugh. At one point, apparently sick of hearing what amounted to the same statements repeatedly, "several of the Jurors here expressed a decided opinion that they had heard sufficient of this line of testimony." The next day, the defense produced five doctors, all of whom believed that "venereal bubo, chancre, and ulcers, could all be dispersed without leaving a trace," the defense's response to the testimony of Dr. Covell, who claimed he would have been able to tell whether Bodine ever been infected with syphilis or gonorrhea. As the last witness stepped down, the defense rested, and the court adjourned for the weekend. Closing statements would be delivered on Monday morning.[31]

Over the course of two days, attorneys for the defense and for the prosecution would give alternating and lengthy closing arguments focusing on different aspects of their cases. Brady began for the defense, speaking for a total of four hours. He started by laying out just what he believed the prosecution needed to prove for the jurors to convict Restell of manslaughter:

> First, that the principal witness in this case was pregnant; second, that the child was quick; third, that there was an abortion by unlawful means; and, fourth, that the abortion was produced by the defendant; that it was an abortion not produced by the course of nature, not by the act of Maria Bodine herself, but by the defendant . . . and in the last place, the prosecution must prove and establish, that the defendant committed the abortion with the unlawful intent to do so.

Brady was clearly trying to set the bar high. He then explored the laws of evidence, both in New York and in English precedent, essentially arguing that as a matter of law, Bodine's word alone should not be sufficient proof of what she said occurred. Even if her word was acceptable as evidence, Brady was deeply skeptical about whether she was trustworthy: "Is Maria Bodine's testimony so credible? I say it is not, and I shall give you my reasons." Primary among them was that she refused to answer certain questions put to her about her relationship with Cook. For Brady, however, almost all of Bodine's lack of credibility came down to the fact that she was not a chaste woman. As he explained,

> As regards women, when they part with their chastity, disgrace and infamy follow them through life.... In this respect [men and women] differ, because chastity is the basis of character in one instance; and when that departs, no reliance can be placed in her that loses it.

The very fact that she had ever consented to have sex with Cook—and he implied there were others—meant that the jury could not put faith in the veracity of her words. When Brady had finished dissecting Bodine's words, the court took a recess.[32]

When the court reconvened that evening, New York's district attorney, John McKeon, who had been doing some of the interrogation over the course of the trial, rose to speak. Seeking to redirect the jurors' attention away from the remarks made by Brady, McKeon explained,

> The name of Caroline alias Ann Lohman, alias Madame Restell, the person now on trial, in some unaccountable manner, appears to have been abstracted from your sight, and that of another victim, Maria Bodine, substituted.

Restell was on trial here, not Bodine. McKeon also laid out what the jurors must conclude to find her guilty of either manslaughter or a misdemeanor, the difference of course hinging on whether the child was quick. By contrast to Brady, McKeon insisted that Bodine, even though she was technically an accomplice to the crime, was perfectly capable of giving valid evidence at the trial and that he was amply supported both by the trial judge and by legal precedent in this claim. Next, he addressed Brady's allegation that Bodine's lack of chastity undermined credibility:

> The counsel begins by requiring of me a pure and unsullied female, to go on that stand to testify against the prisoner. This, I know, you

know, we all know, cannot be done. He then assails the woman who has lost her virtue, and asks me as public prosecutor, to bring corroborative testimony of a positive character. How am I to do this? Will others, who have been subjected to the same treatment as herself voluntarily come forward and testify against her?

While McKeon effectively acquiesced to the terms of the debate as laid out by Brady, never once contesting that Bodine was a woman fallen from virtue, his greater point to the jury was that there could never be a conviction for abortion unless they were willing to believe the testimony of a woman who had herself obtained one, a woman who by virtue of that decision could never qualify as virtuous:

> Now, if you say by your verdict that you will not believe Maria Bodine, Restell and each one of those wretches engaged in similar infamous pursuits will thank you for your decision, for it makes them safe; because they well know that this girl or any other victim cannot, or rather would not be believed.[33]

The district attorney closed his statement by once again returning to the testimony of Bodine, which he reviewed in full, after which he concluded that it would be "utterly impossible for any human being to invent such a story as has been told by her." After reviewing the medical testimony, McKeon pointed out that the most the defense had been able to muster was "but five persons" from Orange County who said that they would not believe her. With that, he asked for a conviction of the prisoner and took his seat. The court was adjourned for the day.[34]

At the opening of the court's session the next morning, David Graham Jr. spoke on behalf of the defense. He claimed that the prosecution was effectively attempting to prove that Restell was guilty of a misdemeanor, but that she had been indicted for a felony (manslaughter). While Graham was skating dangerously close to admitting that Restell might possibly be guilty of the lesser charge, his point instead was that the jury should not find her guilty on either charge, not just because she was innocent but because, he alleged, the prosecution had committed legal errors in the way they were pursuing the charges. Like his counterpart, he concluded by reviewing the evidence against Restell, which he said was wholly inadequate to justify a conviction and thus asked the members of the jury to acquit.[35]

On the final day of the trial, November 10, the courtroom was packed, filled with "as many persons as the court could well contain, without being on each other's heads." Ogden Hoffman rose to give the final of the closing arguments. Hoffman commenced with a defense of Bodine, who he argued had absolutely nothing to gain by coming forward. Hoffman accused the defense of poor conduct at the trial and then segued into his argument that even if Bodine's testimony should be wholly ignored because the defense had spent so much time painting her as unchaste—not that he believed the jurors should do so—he believed the prosecution still had managed to make its case. He pointed to Dr. Coles's testimony, who asserted that Bodine had indeed been pregnant; to McCann, who had accompanied Bodine to Madame Restell's home and returned with an additional $45. He then focused on the notion that Bodine's testimony was biased because she was an accomplice to the crime:

> To call her—poor victim, who is hardly able to drag her trembling form on the stand—to call her the accomplice of the accused, is idle; why, it is like the lamb being the accomplice of the butcher.

This was a common way to blame female physicians for their trade while maintaining sympathy for their clients, as if the clients had not themselves sought out services in the first place.[36]

Hoffman then focused on how Bodine had come to testify in the first place. She was not actually, as he explained, the complainant and had only told her doctor what had happened, thus only inadvertently setting in motion the chain of events that led to the trial. For that reason the jurors should recognize that she had nothing to gain in testifying: "She is not here willingly. She is brought here by the strong arm of the law, against her will—from reluctant lips her story comes." Hoffman, like McKeon, then focused on some specific details of Bodine's testimony, which he argued a young girl from the country would have been unable to fabricate, thus demonstrating their truthfulness. Further proof of her honesty, Hoffman claimed, was that she did not claim to have missed her courses in February or March or April. Had she been a corrupt witness intent on bringing Restell down, she would have backdated the pregnancy much further, thus making a stronger case that the pregnancy had quickened by the time of the termination. Hoffman took a chance with this strategy because he was essentially admitting whether the pregnancy was quick was still debatable. He clearly wanted a conviction, even if he could not get it for the charge of manslaughter. Because of this, he then returned to the medical indices—the vomiting, the darkening of the areola, the fluttering in her stomach—to argue that it was more than likely a quick pregnancy. But even if it was not, he believed there could be no doubt that Bodine had been impregnated by Cook, a pregnancy that was then terminated by Madame Restell. "It is proved by testimony, independent of Maria Bodine, and proved by Maria, independent of the testimony; I call on you, gentlemen, to discharge your duty."[37]

Hoffman closed with a rousing call to arms for the jurors:

You stand like the Jewish prophet, between the living and the dead. By your verdict, it depends whether this pestilence shall be stayed, or whether it shall continue until the first and noblest in the land be stricken down. Acquit the defendant here, and send her forth again, and what will you do? You will break away the very foundations of female virtue—the dread of discovery of crime—you will render the prayers of the fathers of our land fruitless and the sighs of our mothers unavailing—you will strew weeds in the path of virtue. Think, in God's name, think of the responsibility of what you are about to do. The public look to you; the eyes of your fellow-citizens are riveted on you, your motives and your deeds. The eye of outrage is keenly watching you, and on you are centered the hopes and fears of the best and noblest in the land.

As he finished speaking, almost seeming to threaten the jurors about what might happen to them should they acquit, spectators in the courtroom erupted into applause, which officers in the court were unable to quell for some minutes. Hoffman had clearly made an impression, though it was also the case that almost everyone present was eager to see Restell convicted. He was preaching to the proverbial choir.[38]

It was next the responsibility of the recorder to give the jury instructions about the scope of the charges and their duty in evaluating the evidence. Recorder Scott made seven points to the jury, most of which were a matter of clarifying their duty in relation to the law of evidence and were standard fare. He stipulated that for Madame Restell to be found guilty of manslaughter, the jury must believe that Bodine was pregnant with a quick child on July 19, 1846. At 7:00 p.m. on the evening of November 10, the court convened so that the jury of twelve men, none of whom had ever carried a child, could debate whether Bodine's pregnancy had yet quickened.[39]

It took the jury less than an hour before they returned to the courtroom. The jury's foreman, Richard Venables, a hosiery merchant, announced that the jury had unanimously found Restell guilty of a misdemeanor under the second section of the 1845 statute. They believed she had terminated Bodine's pregnancy, but they did not believe Bodine had quickened at the time of the abortion. Restell's attorneys immediately issued a series of motions, attempting to delay judgment and sentencing and indicating their readiness to file a bill of exceptions, the first step in an appeal of the case. The district attorney also moved to have Restell jailed pending sentencing, and while Restell's attorney objected, the recorder committed Restell to the Tombs overnight. The court then adjourned until the next morning.[40]

Because the verdict had come in relatively late the night before, only a handful of newspapers reported on it that morning. The *Brooklyn Daily Eagle*, under the headline "Conviction of the Child-Murderess

Restell," explained that "this she-wolf was yesterday pronounced *guilty* of a misdemeanor (!) by the jury." In the days to come, sentiments were mixed. While most papers expressed relief that she had been convicted, there were serious misgivings, both with the verdict and with the laws that structured the charges, that she had only been convicted of a misdemeanor and not the higher charge of manslaughter. As the *Herald* explained, "The matter has, however, ended; and the result is, that the law has been vindicated, although not to the extent pressed by the prosecution, and the defendant stands convicted of the crime imputed to her." Getting to the heart of the matter, the paper continued:

> Knowing the prejudice against her in the public mind, and as if brazening it, she has for years past appeared in the streets in her magnificent equipage, and dressed in the most fashionable manner, decorated with costly jewels and ornaments, thereby exciting the jealousy of those who envied her situation; whereas if she had practiced her art—for we are sorry to say it has become an art among us—in secret, and lived in a retired and unostentatious style, she might, like others, have not only escaped public notice and public prejudice, but also her recent conviction.

There was certainly a kernel of truth in this analysis, for, as the *Herald* itself noted, there were likely hundreds of other women performing abortions in much more clandestine ways throughout New York. And "even medical men, who claim a high position in society, constantly practice it to a great extent, and rapidly become rich by it." Restell's great crime then was not just that she was sometimes showy about her success, but that she was also a woman.[41]

The next morning, the courtroom was again packed, many expecting that Restell would be sentenced that day. Restell arrived with her husband. "She was elegantly dressed in a rich black silk gown, handsomely trimmed black velvet mantilla, white satin bonnet, and wore a large, heavy lace veil. She looked excessively pale, however, and was evidently anxious as to the result of the day's proceedings." The recorder declined to sign the bill of exceptions until he had had a chance to re-view it and also declined to delay sentencing any longer. He was intent on proceeding with all deliberate speed. He believed that any delay would be making an exception for Restell, would in effect be giving her special treatment, and "this woman is the same as any other woman con-victed of a similar crime, and we can make no distinction." After giving Restell a chance to speak on the matter of punishment, which she de-clined, the recorder announced,

> Caroline [*sic*] Lohman, alias Madame Restell; you have been con-victed by a jury of a misdemeanor, in procuring a miscarriage, and the Court sentence you to be imprisoned for one year in the peni-tentiary on Blackwell's Island, that being the extent of the punish-ment prescribed by the law for the offence of which you have been found guilty.

The *National Police Gazette* reported that the audience in the court-room immediately began applauding, though officers of the court at-tempted to quiet them. Later that day, Restell's lawyers were successful in gaining a stay from Judge Edmonds of the Supreme Court of the State of New York, meaning that Restell would not be sent immedi-ately to Blackwell's Island. In essence her attorneys were going to make the argument—which they had won the last time she was convicted—that she should remain free on bail while they appealed her case. Newspapers immediately reacted with horror at the idea that she might not see imprisonment. As the *Brooklyn Daily Eagle* ex-claimed, "To have all that has been done [the trial and conviction] thus overturned is pretty nearly intolerable. The moral effect of the whole trial and subsequent proceedings we look upon as disastrous beyond measure." The matter was not yet settled, but many feared that Restell's wealth was effectively buying her out of punishment.[42]

On Monday, November 16, Restell's attorneys, Graham and Brady, argued before Judge Edmonds of New York's supreme court that she should be released on bail. Hoffman and McKeon, appearing for the people, explained that Restell had been found guilty and now must be punished, notwithstanding the appeal that her lawyers had filed. Edmonds surprised many observers in denying her bail and finding that Restell's sentence should begin from the day of her conviction. She was to be remanded to the custody of the sheriff and would remain within the city jail—the Tombs—pending the outcome of her appeal.[43]

The very next day, the *National Police Gazette* began advertising its pamphlet *The Wonderful Trial of Caroline Lohman, Alias Restell*, a complete transcript of the trial. Spurred by interest in this case, another publisher had also come out with *Madame Restell, An Account of Her Life and Horrible Practices, Together with Prostitution in New York, Its Extent—Causes—and Effects*. The first nine chapters of the latter publication documented her life, her entrance into the profession, and her various legal entanglements. It was available for 12½¢, sold by "dealers in cheap books." The latter returned to the connections between abortion and infanticide brought to light in the outrage over Mary Applegate's baby:

> There are infants exposed in our streets, to be frozen, crushed, or at the best, put to the Alms House; there are still more, who float out in the tides of the North and East rivers, or are suffocated in sinks and sewers. The fruit of our rigid virtue is infanticide, murder, and of late, Restellism—a name now fittingly bestowed, in some of our public prints, upon the procurement of abortion, by such medical and mechanical means as are said to be practised by Restell.

These two publications, which were sold beyond the bounds of New York, also serve as evidence of the growing notoriety of Madame Restell. Unlike her other trials, which were primarily covered in New York and its environs, newspapers from across the growing country now regularly reprinted dispatches from New York papers detailing her trial and now her conviction. They did so without much preamble to the articles, suggesting that many newspaper readers were now familiar with the figure of Restell. She had become famous far beyond just New York and even beyond the Northeast.[44]

The writ of error filed by Restell's attorney detailed what were called "exceptions" to the trial. To appeal a case, lawyers had to demonstrate not that they disagreed with the verdict, per se, though that was what motivated them, but that they believed the trial itself was conducted improperly or that the charges were not sustainable as a matter of law. Justices of a higher court could then evaluate the claims about the trial itself, not the evidence of innocence or guilt. In this case, Restell's attorney James Brady alleged many exceptions, the primary being that the indictment itself was flawed. He claimed that the grand jury had indicted Restell for manslaughter, and she had been convicted of a misdemeanor; the misdemeanor conviction could not stand because the grand jurors had not included it in the indictment. He also lodged several exceptions having to do with various witnesses and with one juror who claimed during voir dire that he already had an unfavorable

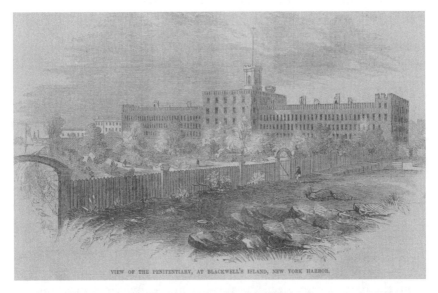

VIEW OF THE PENITENTIARY, AT BLACKWELL'S ISLAND, NEW YORK HARBOR.

William Wade, *View of the Penitentiary at Blackwell's Island*, New York Harbor, 1853. Madame Restell was housed here for one year in 1848. Courtesy of the New York Public Library.

opinion about Restell. On January 20, 1848, Judge Strong, writing for the majority of New York's supreme court, rejected the appeal. He noted that the judges believed the indictment, as it was written, could include both the misdemeanor and the felony versions of the crime of producing a miscarriage. He also rejected the other exceptions, in essence characterizing them as relatively minor errors that, even taken together, did not amount to a serious miscarriage of justice. He noted that "when the act authorizing bills of exceptions in criminal cases was passed, it could not have been intended that convictions should be reversed for any and every error which may have been committed on the trial." The judges did not feel that the rights of the accused had been affected via these minor errors, and they affirmed the lower court's decision, ordering that Restell be taken from the city jail, where she continued to be held, to Blackwell's Island. Brady immediately applied for a stay of proceedings to allow him to file an appeal to the New York State Court of Appeals, which the judges granted.[45]

In the meantime, Brady was hard at work trying to secure Restell's release on bail while she awaited a hearing with the court of appeals. In February, the Supreme Court of the State of New York denied Brady's application for a writ of habeas corpus and ordered that Restell remain under the custody of the New York sheriff until the time of her hearing with the appeals court. As Justice Hurlburt wrote in his opinion, "She presents nothing upon which to argue that a doubt exists as to her guilt—and even if her guilt were doubtful, I am by no means satisfied that bail would secure her appearance to answer the demands of the law." Restell remained in the Tombs.[46]

Finally, in June of 1848, the New York State Court of Appeals heard Restell's case, and they were no more sympathetic to her exceptions than had been the supreme court. Restell had lost, this time decisively. She would now be moved to the penitentiary on Blackwell's Island. In the court's decision, Restell's year-long sentence would begin from the date of their decision, not her first conviction, meaning she would be imprisoned for longer than a year total.[47]

Blackwell's Island is the two-mile-long narrow strip of land in the East River between Manhattan and Queens that is now called Roosevelt Island. New York City took possession of the island in 1828 and erected a county prison there in 1832, the same prison where Mrs. Bird and Madame Costello also served their sentences. The penitentiary was six hundred feet long and four stories high and constructed of gray stone taken from quarries on the island itself. The prison contained at least seven hundred cells and women were housed separately from men. In the next two decades, a lunatic asylum (1839), an almshouse (1848), and a workhouse (1852) were constructed on the island. The penitentiary at Blackwell's Island was designed for mid-range sentences, anywhere from one to ten years. Those serving more went to Sing Sing or Auburn. In practice, however, many served sentences of under six months on the island, and some were transferred between the prison, the almshouse, the workhouse, and the asylum.[48]

The prison at Blackwell's Island enjoyed a truly horrible reputation, not least because it was so close to Manhattan that prisoners could see, from almost any vantage point, exactly where most had come from but to which they could not yet return. When Charles Dickens toured Blackwell's Island in 1842, he saw the almshouse, the asylum, and the prison. Of the last, he wrote,

> The women work in covered sheds, erected for that purpose. If I remember right, there are no shops for the men, but be that as it may, the greater part of them labour in certain stone-quarries near at hand. The day being very wet indeed, this labour was suspended, and the prisoners were in their cells. Imagine these cells, some two or three hundred in number, and in every one a man, locked up: this one at his door for air, with his hand thrust through the grate; this one in bed (in the middle of the day, remember); and this one flung down in a heap on the ground, with his head against the bars, like a wild beast. . . . Put the everlasting stove in the midst: hot, and suffocating, and vaporous, as a witch's cauldron. Add a collection of

gentle odours, such as would arise from a thousand mildewed umbrellas, wet through, and a thousand buck-baskets, full of half-washed linen—and there is the prison, as it was that day.

Dickens had much better things to say about the state prison at Sing Sing, which he found to be a model jail.[49]

Prisoners of renown, however, and those with money were generally able to buy themselves better treatment, just as Madame Costello had done during her imprisonment two years earlier. Less than a month into Restell's stay on Blackwell's Island, the mayor, grand jurors, and others visited the facility, and their impressions were detailed in newspapers. The *Trenton State Gazette* explained that there was "a marked difference in the treatment of this infamous convict [Restell] from that of the other prisoners."

> Her delicate hands, although stained with the blood of numberless innocents, were covered with silk mits; her diamonds and other jewels still glistened on her fingers; although she wore the convict's frock, yet a silk apron partially concealed it; while, lest the sun's rays might peradventure be too severe for her neck, a handsome barege cape was thrown over her shoulders.

The description of Restell dripping in jewels is hard to believe, though it is quite likely she did enjoy better treatment, probably by paying extra to guards and the warden. The same article also reported that she ate better food than did her fellow inmates, brought by private servants from the warden's kitchen. It also claimed that she might not even sleep in a cell but instead lodge in the attic of the warden's private residence. By the end of 1848, the district attorney and the recorder (McKeon and Scott, who had tried Restell) had commenced an investigation into differential treatment on Blackwell's Island, not just for Restell but in light of confirmations that one John Harrison, convicted of keeping a gambling house, was also receiving preferential treatment.[50]

The outcome of the investigation would have no effect for Madame Restell, who was released from Blackwell's Island in mid-November 1848. While this date was exactly a year after her conviction, earlier accounts of the denial of her appeal made clear that the seven months she spent in the Tombs would not count against the year's sentence on Blackwell's Island, meaning that she had been set free early. Restell had been released and was able to return home to a new house her husband had purchased on Chambers Street during her time in jail.[51]

And what of the others indicted in the scandal, or indeed what of Maria Bodine herself? It appears that neither John McCann nor Joseph Cook were ever tried. They almost entirely disappeared from newspapers after the trial ended, reporters seeming to have lost interest in them. The indictment against McCann was likely dropped in exchange for his testimony against Restell. Why Cook was not tried is more curious. The conviction of accomplices in Madame Costello's case certainly demonstrated that it was possible. One historian has speculated that prosecutors may not have wanted the expense of bringing back the witnesses from Orange and Montgomery Counties that would be necessary to try Cook, especially in the winter months, when parts of the Hudson River were frozen. It could also be that prosecutors were unwilling to make Bodine, by most accounts virtually an invalid, testify again. In July of 1848, the *Brooklyn Evening Star* reported that "this poor girl, whose health has been forever destroyed by Restell's practice, still lingers out a wretched existence . . . prostrated by bodily infirmity, ruined in reputation, and neglected by every one save those in whose immediate charge she has been placed." It is likely that she returned home to Walden or Montgomery to live with her sister, Mrs. Youngblood. Census records show a number of Maria or Mary Bodines in the general area of Montgomery, but none can positively be confirmed to be this particular Maria Bodine. In all likelihood, Bodine wanted nothing more than to fade forever into obscurity.[52]

7

A.M. MAURICEAU, PROFESSOR OF DISEASES OF WOMEN

While Madame Restell spent a year behind bars, first in the Tombs and later on Blackwell's Island, one might think that business as usual would cease. In one way, that was true: advertisements for Madame Restell herself and her services did not appear in New York newspapers during the time of her imprisonment. New Yorkers would have been surprised if they had, so widespread had news of her conviction been. But within the Restell household, business continued apace. This was due to the labor of Restell's husband, Charles Lohman, and her brother, Joseph Trow. Together, the three constituted a veritable reproductive services empire. While Madame Restell was generally the public face of the operation, Lohman and Trow—using a slew of pseudonyms—also sold a variety of medicines, provided medical services for women, and, in 1847, published a book of medical advice. Beginning business in 1840, Lohman operated out of an office at the corner of Grand and Allen Streets for about three years, moving in 1843 to an office at 129 Liberty Street, just around the corner from their home. The primary pseudonym that Lohman used was A.M. Mauriceau, an identity that both Lohman and Trow assumed as they navigated the world of women's medicine and drugs designed to prevent and end pregnancy, as well as cure infertility. The Lohman fortune was partially of Madame Restell's making, but the sheer volume of advertising placed under the name of Mauriceau and other pseudonyms indicates that Lohman also must have contributed substantially to their financial success. The fact that both ran independent but loosely related businesses also helped one or the other to take time off, as when Restell and her daughter, Caroline, returned to England for the summer in 1845. She could do so knowing that business continued in her absence. The Lohmans were true partners in their work.[1]

* * * *

Between 1833 and 1840, when Lohman first went into business selling medicine under a pseudonym, he both married Ann Summers and helped her to establish herself as Madame Restell. By 1840, the couple had clearly decided to expand their operation. On February 10, the *New York Daily Herald* ran an advertisement—the first of many hundreds—for Portuguese Female Pills, which it claimed had been "invented and prepared by M. De Boudeloque, M.D." of Lisbon, Portugal:

> The scientific combination of ingredients of which these pills are composed have made them the wonder and admiration of the world. They are known all over Europe to be the only preparation ever discovered that has proved invariably certain in producing the monthly turns. Their certainty, in all cases, being such that they must not be used during pregnancy, for, though mild, safe, and healthy, they are certain to produce miscarriage if used during that period.

The ad further explained that directions accompanied the pills from Dr. De Boudeloque, which had been translated into English by Dr. F. Melveau, who was also the authorized agent for their distribution in the United States. The advertisement assured readers that the pills could be sent anywhere in the country and gave a post office box for inquiries and orders and an address at 264 Grand Street, where New Yorkers could visit Dr. Melveau to purchase a box for $5 or a half-box for $3.[2]

This was the introduction to two of Lohman's fictitious medical men. Dr. De Boudeloque made appearances, always associated with

Portuguese Monthly Pills, in newspapers between 1840 and May of 1845, after which he was retired. Lohman chose the name "De Boudeloque" for its similarity to that of Jean-Louis Baudelocque, the first chair of obstetrics in France, appointed by Napoleon in 1806, and physician in chief at what was eventually named the Maternité Baudelocque. Unlike with some of the other identities, Lohman never claimed to actually *be* De Boudeloque, who always remained in Lisbon, the source of the famed Portuguese Female Pills. There is no reason to believe the pills were not the very same medication, just with different packaging, that Madame Restell was selling. Indeed, for a time in the early 1840s, those wanting to purchase Restell's own Female Monthly Pills were also encouraged to visit the same address on Grand Street, even as Restell offered services out of the office on Greenwich. Both Restell's pills and De Boudeloque's were abortifacients, the advertisement making clear that pregnant women should not take them if they wished to remain pregnant. It is likely they were made of ergot, and perhaps cantharides, just as were the pills sold to Anna Dall in 1839. Of course pregnancy was not the only reason a woman might not have her monthly turns, and just as in Restell's advertisements, Lohman used innuendo to subtly appeal to those who might want to terminate a pregnancy as well as to those who might genuinely believe they were not menstruating for other reasons.[3]

For the four years Dr. F. Melveau acted as agent for Portuguese Monthly Pills, and immediately after his move to 129 Liberty Street, Lohman expanded his medical services. By 1843, his advertisements for the pills also noted that "Dr. Melveau can be consulted on all complaints incident to females with the strictest confidence." Beginning in 1844, Lohman began addressing women who were in a very different position from those wanting to end their pregnancies. The headline for a new series of ads read: "To Those Without Children. A Procreative Elixir Cordial." This advertisement also introduced a new doctor to Lohman's lineup. "The greatest discovery in medical science is that of M. M. Desomeaux, of Paris. He has entirely exploded the generally received opinion of the existence of incurable sterility or barrenness, except indeed in cases of malformation, which are extremely rare." The use of the name "Desomeaux" was a nod to the French physician Antonin Jean Desormeaux, who had revolutionized gynecological surgery in France and whose name appeared frequently in midwifery textbooks in the United States. The elixir was designed to help women "who for years pined in childless loneliness." The ad explained that more than fifty thousand bottles and packages of it had already been sold, surely a testament to its efficacy, and that it was "pleasant and agreeable to the taste." Just as with the Portuguese pills, Dr. F. Melveau was the "only authorized agent in the country." And just as with those pills, one might have the elixir mailed to them, while New Yorkers could visit Melveau at his office at 129 Liberty, where "ladies calling for the 'Elixir' will be waited on by a lady in attendance."[4]

Unlike with the Portuguese Monthly Pills or with Restell's own pills, Dr. Desomeaux's cordial elixir was likely junk. Scientists still have not managed a quick and easy over-the-counter medicine to treat infertility. Lohman was selling false hope in this advertisement. Ads like this one were generally assembled on one page of a newspaper that contained nothing but scores of advertisements, some of them for perfectly legitimate products and services, others for quack medicine or other junk. One version of this ad appears in between ads for "The Invisible Wig" (guaranteed to "defy detection") and "Jones's Soap," which promised to cure "Pimples, Blotches, Freckles, Tan, Morphew, Salt Rheum, Scurvy, Erysipelas, Barber's Itch, Ringworm, Old Sores, and Sore Heads." Lohman was hardly alone in this kind of fraudulent advertising. Recall that one of the reasons for the passage of a revised 1829 statute on abortion was to target the manufacturing, marketing, and selling of quack medicines that were sometimes dangerous but more often a harmless waste of money. While all members of the Lohman household, including Restell herself, certainly benefited from Lohman's crooked marketing, Restell never advertised these other sorts of products, confining her work to midwifery, abortion, and abortifacients.[5]

The advertisement for Desomeaux's cordial elixir noted that women visiting the office could be seen by a woman, Lohman indicating that

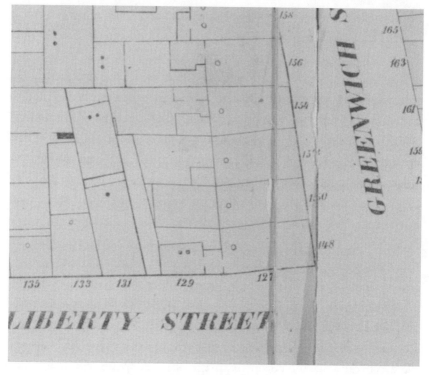

The map detail shows that 129 Liberty Street was directly behind 148 Greenwich Street, allowing for easy access between the offices of Restell and Mauriceau. Detail of plate 7, map bounded by Vesey Street, Broadway, Liberty Street, West Street. Map by William Perris, 1852, Lionel Pincus and Princess Firyal Map Division. Courtesy of the New York Public Library.

married women might want to discuss the delicate issue of infertility with one of their own. Restell and Lohman employed servants in their home. It is possible that one of them also worked double-duty as a salesclerk for Lohman when women called for certain medicines. It was also the case, however, that while the Lohmans lived at 148 Greenwich Street, Lohman's office was directly behind their home. An 1847 newspaper account of Lohman's business dealings claimed that there were passageways between the office and the home that would have allowed Lohman to quickly summon his wife or a servant if he needed the assistance of a woman to see to a female customer.[6]

That might well have worked as a last-minute solution or as a way to conduct a customer in need of medical care from Lohman's office to Madame Restell's, where she might make an appointment to terminate a pregnancy. But it worked only as long as the Lohmans remained occupants of both spaces, which ceased to be the case in 1848. In that year, Charles Lohman bought a large home at 162 Chambers Street, about half a mile farther uptown from the former residence and his office. Restell would use the Chambers Street house as her own place of work following her release from Blackwell's Island. It was also to be their home for the next seventeen years. And its occupants included not just Restell, Lohman, and Restell's daughter, Caroline Summers. Also living there were four servants, a clerk named George Howe, and Restell's brother, Joseph Trow, who helped Restell and Lohman with almost all aspects of their joint businesses. Lohman and Trow both listed "Publisher" as their occupation in the 1850 federal census. Ann Lohman was without an occupation of any kind, which was not atypical for women in the census, even if untrue in this instance.[7]

Restell's brother Joseph was christened in Stroud, Gloucestershire, on October 7, 1821, making him eleven years younger than his sister Ann. He came to the United States in 1841 or 1842, likely at the expense of his sister, who saw the potential in having a relative work for her. He was apt to remain loyal to his sister, even as she and her husband regularly broke the law. Trow and his niece, Caroline Summers, both declared their intentions to become citizens of the United States on the same day, March 21, 1848. Until the time of his marriage some thirty years later, and with the exception of one trip to Europe in the 1850s, Trow lived with the Lohmans. Trow may have had reasons of his own for seeking out employment with his sister. At some point during his childhood or youth he had injured himself, and he walked with the help of a prosthetic wooden leg. This disability left him unsuited to some forms of manual labor. Restell would later buy farms in Upstate New York for two other brothers, but Trow was unable to take up farming because of his leg. The evidence is inconclusive about whether the Lohmans paid Trow a regular paycheck or if they gave him money irregularly, though they certainly did pay him at times. Trow lived with his sister rent-free, as a part of her family, taking all his meals with the Lohmans. Presumably what was theirs was also his to enjoy. As the Lohman fortune grew, this arrangement clearly had certain advantages, but it also left him almost entirely reliant on his sister and brother-in-law for any funds to pursue an independent life. This may be one reason why he did not marry until he was in his early fifties, certainly much later than the average age of marriage for men during this era.[8]

Trow was an integral part of the Restell business almost from its inception, something of a jack-of-all-trades who was part household manager and part salesman and, as one census enumerated for an occupation, a "Retail Medicine Manufacturer." As Trow himself put it, "I did all her marketing, took care of the house, superintended her carriages and horses, bought the feed, put up the medicine for sale, attended to her financial business, cashed coupons, and everything of that kind; in fact everything that was to be done." He was also in the habit of "attending to Mr. Lohman; and doing all his errands." By Trow's own telling, he and the Lohmans did not actually manufacture the medicines themselves. Instead, they contracted with an outfit called Hegeman and Company, which compounded them out of offices that had been established in 1837 on Broadway. In an era long before drugs were regulated by the FDA, all drugs were available on an open market. Trow's great-niece remembered that on Saturday mornings "he used to get up early and wash the sidewalk, pump the water over it, and in the winter he would attend to the furnace." Given that he was responsible for sales, marketing, and the organization of the medicines themselves, in some respects Trow was as much any of the pseudonymous French physicians as Lohman was. In part that was the beauty of using so many different names—anyone could play the part when necessary.[9]

By far the longest-running and most famous of those names was A.M. Mauriceau, who represented himself as a French-born and trained "professor of diseases of women," or occasionally, of midwifery. He was named for the seventeenth-century French physician François

Mauriceau, who wrote on obstetrics and gynecology. In 1847, A.M. Mauriceau would announce the publication of *The Married Woman's Private Medical Companion*, which he advertised well into the 1860s. The book was supposedly authored by Mauriceau, though the inside cover displayed the statement: "Entered according to Act of Congress, in the year 1847, by JOSEPH TROW, In the Clerk's Office of the District Court of the Southern District, New York." While Lohman's own claim about the number of copies sold was surely exaggerated—by 1856, he boasted two hundred thousand—the multiple editions do make clear that it was reprinted several times, so there must have been some demand. In one of the initial advertisements announcing the availability of the book, Lohman—or perhaps Trow—wrote of the book that "the important secrets here contained, though of a nature strictly intended for the married yet to those contemplating marriage, it is equally important." The advertisement boasted of secret French knowledge that allowed women, if one read between the lines, to avoid pregnancy. The book would also aid women "afflicted with the various complaints arising from a stoppage, irregularity, decline or retention of the menses." Never one to exclude possible customers, Lohman also advised that "every husband and every father, as also every young man contemplating to become one, will here find suggestions, which once possessed, no pecuniary consideration will induce them to part with. Their own happiness, the future happiness of their children, depend upon being possessed of the important secrets contained in this work." The volume was on sale for $1 per copy and Lohman was willing to mail it—no charge for shipping—anywhere in the United States. Those who ordered in bulk for resale would be offered generous discounts. By the next year, the advertisements also included agents in Albany, Boston, and Philadelphia where the book could be purchased and he was advertising in papers up and down the East Coast, including in the French language newspaper *Courrier des États-Unis*, for French-speaking residents of the United States.[10]

The Married Woman's Private Medical Companion, as was typical for volumes like it published in the nineteenth century, had an exceedingly

> THE MARRIED WOMAN'S
> PRIVATE MEDICAL COMPANION,
> EMBRACING THE TREATMENT OF
> MENSTRUATION, OR MONTHLY TURNS,
> DURING THEIR
> STOPPAGE, IRREGULARITY, OR ENTIRE SUPPRESSIO;
> PREGNANCY,
> AND
> HOW IT MAY BE DETERMINED;
> WITH THE TREATMENT OF ITS VARIOUS DISEASES.
> DISCOVERY TO
> PREVENT PREGNANCY;
> THE GREAT AND IMPORTANT NECESSITY WHERE
> MALFORMATION OR INABILITY EXISTS
> TO GIVE BIRTH.
> TO PREVENT MISCARRIAGE OR ABORTION.
> WHEN PROPER AND NECESSARY
> TO EFFECT MISCARRIAGE.
> WHEN ATTENDED WITH ENTIRE SAFETY.
> CAUSES AND MODE OF CURE OF BARRENNESS,
> OR STERILITY.
> BY DR. A. M. MAURICEAU,
> Professor of Diseases of Women
>
> Office, 129 Liberty street.
>
> NEW YORK
> 1849.

Cover page of the 1849 edition of *The Married Woman's Private Medical Companion*, which was originally published in 1847. It went through numerous printings, a testament to its popularity and to how frequently Charles Lohman advertised it.

lengthy full title. Following the initial main title, the subtitle explained that the book was *Embracing the Treatment of Menstruation, or Monthly Turns, During Their Stoppage, Irregularity, or Entire Suppression, Pregnancy, And How It May Be Determined; With the Treatment of Its Various Diseases. Discovery to Prevent Pregnancy; The Great and Important Necessity Where Malformation or Inability Exists to Give Birth. To Prevent Miscarriage or Abortion. When Proper and Necessary to Effect Mis-*

carriage When Attended with Entire Safety. Causes and Mode of Cure of Barrenness, or Sterility. If the title was not enough to describe the contents, Lohman used an index, instead of a table of contents, in the first few pages to give prospective readers a handy way of finding what interested them most. Alphabetically, the index ranged from "Abortion, Symptoms of," to "Womb, Falling down of the," and included extensive entries on menstruation, labor, and pregnancy, as well as brief entries on the raising of children, flooding (excessive menstrual bleeding), and stillborn infants.[11]

With a few important caveats, the book was entirely typical of its time. Lohman was writing in the tradition of reform physiologists, a group of doctors and health reformers who spoke to audiences and published about the human body so as to empower and inform listeners and readers. They believed that people would be better off if they could understand how their bodies worked. Most controversial about this was their frank discussions of sex, conception, pregnancy, menstruation, and masturbation, the last of which they urged against. By the time Lohman published *The Married Woman's Private Medical Companion*, Robert Dale Owen's *Moral Physiology* was already sixteen years old, "the first book written and printed in the United States that discussed contraception and gave practical advice." Charles Knowlton's *Fruits of Philosophy: Or, The Private Companion of Young Married People* followed in 1832. While these publications were not without some attendant controversy—Knowlton was tried three times for obscenity, though never convicted—by 1847, what Lohman was doing was hardly groundbreaking.[12]

The preface explained that "whether married or unmarried, [the reader] can, from these pages, compare her own symptoms with those described, and act in accordance with the mode of treatment prescribed." Despite the fact that the book was billed as the *married* woman's medical companion, it was clear that Lohman was well aware that some single women were also sexually active, and he was speaking to them as well, which made it more controversial. Anticipating some objections, he noted in the "Introductory Remarks" that "it is because prejudice or ignorance thinks that if men and women acquired the knowledge whereby to improve their condition as social moral beings, guard against disease, and preserve their health, that *perhaps*, it might lead to immorality and vice. This is ever the pretext to arrest the progress of physiological discovery." Just as the reform physiologists did, Mauriceau placed himself on the side of enlightenment, science, and knowledge.[13]

Many of the sections of the book were largely descriptive and anodyne, even if by today's standards, the science was inaccurate. Lohman's accounting of the varied temporal onset of menstruation, for instance, was unlikely to cause offense, even though his account of a woman menstruating till the age of ninety-four or pregnant at ten might give the contemporary, or indeed the nineteenth-century, reader pause. The first important difference between this book and those by other physiologists was that Mauriceau advertised his own products, usually in footnotes that accompanied the sections of various entries related to medical ailments. A footnote in the section on "Suppression of the Menses," for instance, notes that "the most successful specific, and one almost invariably certain in removing a stoppage, irregularity, or suppression of the menses (monthly turn), is a compound invented by M. M. Desomeaux, of Lisbon, Portugal, called the Portuguese Female Pills. It would appear that they are infallible, and would, undoubtedly, even produce miscarriage, if exhibited during pregnancy." The footnote closed by noting that M.M. Desomeaux's remedies were available through Dr. A.M. Mauriceau himself, at a P.O. box or by visiting his office at 129 Liberty Street, where he "attends to all the diseases of women, especially those arising from suppression of the menses." While Lohman was now claiming that Desomeaux, and not Boudeloque, was the originator of the Portuguese Female Pills, Mauriceau had replaced Dr. F. Melveau as the sole agent for their sale in the United States. He was effectively commercializing what was otherwise a relatively straightforward book of advice, first in its sale and again by advertising products within its pages. Lohman plugged Desomeaux's pills three additional times in the book and also advocated for a product called Morand's Elixir in the section on barrenness. It, too, was available at Mauriceau's office at 129 Liberty. Because Lohman had switched the name of the doctor who had discovered the pills to "Desomeaux," for reasons that remain unclear, he now needed to invent a new name for drugs that would assist with the opposite problem, infertility. While Mauriceau was no great fan of condoms, which he mostly linked to prostitution and the prevention of venereal disease, he was not above advertising them for sale in a footnote: $5 for a dozen.[14]

Lohman's advice on pregnancy, contraception, birth, and abortion is worth exploring, precisely because he and his wife were in the business of attending to women who were pregnant or were hoping not to be so. Lohman included an entire section titled "Of the Mode by Which Pregnancy May Be Determined," in which he outlined many of the symptoms that might attend a woman during the early stages of pregnancy. Like a number of the doctors during his wife's trial, however, he was adamant that none of them were definitive proof and that suppression of menstruation alone was certainly not enough evidence of pregnancy. This was always the fine line walked by the Lohmans when selling abortifacients, which could be marketed simply as emmenagogues, medicines designed to restore the monthly turns. As did the doctors called as expert witnesses at his wife's trial, Lohman also noted that the onset of quickening varied in women, and sometimes varied among pregnancies in the same woman. Again, noting the variability in quickening served to expand the window of time during which his wife, and perhaps Lohman himself, might terminate pregnancies without the abortions being considered felonies.[15]

In the section on "Prevention to Conception," Lohman rehearsed many of the same arguments that Madame Restell made in her advertisements. Pregnancy was a "peril to life" for some women. "And even when life is spared, the birth of every child snatches many years from the life of the mother, hurrying her, with a constitution shattered, and health destroyed, to a premature grave." Some women did not want to procreate for fear of passing on inheritable diseases or insanity.

Lohman also advocated for contraception as a way to encourage youthful marriage—young people could marry without worrying about supporting a family while youthful—which itself would cut down on licentiousness. Finally, contraception would itself reduce illegitimacy, which, while a problem in and of itself, was made visible via pregnancy and which led to the downfall of young women into prostitution. In short, while some argued that contraception would lead to *more* vice, Dr. A.M. Mauriceau believed it would prevent vice. Lohman believed that there were ways to prevent pregnancy "without the least sacrifice of those pleasurable sensations experienced in the connubial embrace." The answer was Desomeaux's pills:

> The principle upon which it prevents conception, is to neutralize the fecundating properties in semen, and it preserves and conduces to the health of the female, by eradicating all predisposition to sexual weakness, fluor albus, or whites, the falling of the womb, &c., and restores and maintains that elasticity and firmness of the generative functions (appertaining only to a young female) for many years.

We know that some of the ingredients in the abortifacients sold by Restell really could bring on a miscarriage, but the medicine Lohman is describing here seems far too good to be true. It both neutralized the fertility of sperm *and* aided in the health of the woman who took it, preventing a number of the illnesses that sometimes beset women's reproductive organs, like leukorrhea (fluor albus, or "the whites").[16]

Beginning in this section, which is about halfway through the book, and continuing for the duration, Lohman places certain passages in quotation marks, occasionally makes note of "the author" of these passages, and quotes other people for pages on end. At other times he does not attribute authorship to those who wrote the words. In total, at least half of *The Married Woman's Private Medical Companion* is cribbed from other sources, sometimes in ways that are acknowledged, other times not at all. Perhaps the greatest "contributor" to the book is Owen's *Moral Physiology* itself. Lohman shamelessly copied many pages outright, even changing some of the wording to suit his purposes. For instance, in quoting a letter Owen received from a satisfied reader, Lohman removed the title of Owen's book and instead uses the phrase "your valuable work," to make it seem as if Mauriceau himself had received the letter of thanks. In another instance, where Owen had received a letter from a man extolling the virtues of withdrawal as a means of contraception, Lohman had substituted "preventive" for the word "withdrawal," which had the effect of making it seem as if the preventive that Mauriceau himself was selling (Desomeaux's pills) was responsible for this man's satisfaction with his wife's reduced birth rate. When Lohman first starts quoting from Owen, about halfway through the volume, he uses quotation marks around the lifted material and refers to another author, by which he seems to mean Owen. But the quotation marks are not present for all the parts plagiarized from Owen.[17]

Owen was not the only source of Mauriceau's plagiarism. He also lifted from Andrew Combe's 1836 *The Physiology of Digestion: Considered with Relation to the Principles of Dietetics*, Wooster Beach's 1846 *The American Practice Abridged, Or the Family Physician*, and James Ewell's 1827 *The Medical Companion; Or Family Physician*. In his plagiarism, Lohman was practicing copyright infringement if the various authors he quotes had registered their works, but the overall effect of his constant mentioning of other doctors and their expertise was to place the fictitious Dr. Mauriceau in their company, to allow their accomplishments and expertise to enhance his own, thus lending credibility to *The Married Woman's Private Medical Companion*.[18]

A.M. Mauriceau was especially noteworthy on two issues. In one issue, he was in keeping with his wife's practice, though he was decidedly inconsistent with most formally trained medical doctors of the era. In another, he was surprisingly inconsistent with his wife and congruent with formally trained doctors. First, he expressed great skepticism about doctors' interference with labor, this at a moment when formally trained doctors with MDs were increasingly using forceps and painkillers to deliver babies. Historians of medicine have demonstrated that the increased use of forceps led to higher rates of infant mortality and injury. Here, Mauriceau stood on the side of midwives like his wife, who delivered babies in ways that women had been doing for thousands of years. As he put it, "When it has been ascertained that the labor is natural, or that there are no impediments or obstacles, there will be very little more to do than superintend the process." He also noted that physicians and midwives "who watch only the process of labor, or do little or nothing, are pronounced inhuman and cruel, or perhaps ignorant, because they are honest in not interfering with the simple and beautiful process of labor." He went on to indict, albeit subtly, the women who believed it necessary to call in a doctor to attend her hours before it was necessary or who demanded medical interference in what should otherwise be a natural process. Lohman was directly plagiarizing from Beach's *The American Practice Abridged*, but even that is telling. Beach was one of the founders of a movement called eclectic medicine, which relied on traditional cures found in nature and eschewed heroic measures and interventions into what were otherwise natural practices. Eclectic or "reformed" medical men were essentially reacting to the rise of formally trained "regular physicians," who advocated more intervention during labor and other procedures. It is not surprising that Madame Restell's husband, who was not really a medically trained doctor, should advocate for these positions, except that he was pretending to be a "Professor of Diseases of Women," or a man trained in the emerging field of gynecology, the very kind of man who usually *did* advocate for a greater role in regulating birth, precisely so that his expertise could be recognized. Beach, and by extension Lohman, espoused a traditional or conservative approach to childbirth but one that most experts in home birth and midwifery would today support as being in the best interests of both mothers and babies.[19]

The second matter in which Mauriceau's official stance largely accorded with that of his wife's was in his attitude toward abortion. If anything, he was slightly more conservative than she, at least in regard to when terminating a pregnancy might be justified. He began by dismissing fears of miscarriage and abortion as overblown, saying that when produced externally (by a fall or kick of a horse) or internally (by ruptured blood vessels or disease of the uterus), the causes of a spontaneous miscarriage were much more dangerous to a woman's health than the miscarriage itself was. That is, whatever had caused the end of the pregnancy could well injure a woman in ways that lasted longer than the miscarriage itself. He then stated absolutely that

> it is well known by those versed in obstetrics that, where it is deemed indispensable to effect a miscarriage, either because of the existence of a deformed pelvis, diseased uterus, or other causes, if skillfully effected, it is attended with no danger, especially in the earlier stages of pregnancy.

This was as true then as it is now and was generally acknowledged to be so by most practicing physicians, as well as in textbooks of medicine and midwifery published in that era. The point of contention was not about whether abortion was possible or safe, it was about when it should be permissible for a woman to choose it.[20]

On that point, Mauriceau was not as radical as one might imagine. Following remarks on the symptoms of spontaneous abortion and its prevention, the next section was titled "When Necessary to Effect Miscarriage or Artificial Delivery." Here, Mauriceau reviewed the reasons that it might be dangerous for a woman to deliver an infant, among which he claimed were pelvic deformities, rickets, and curvature of the spine. Before exploring abortion itself, he once again recommended Desomeaux's pills for the prevention of pregnancy in those for whom it would be dangerous. He then moved on to what he called "Premature Artificial Delivery." He first dealt with cesarean section, which he claimed was not possible to perform whilst ensuring the mother and child would survive. While historians debate when the first cesarean section was successfully performed, it is certainly the case that the procedure was not done frequently in the United States until later in the nineteenth century, so Lohman was on solid ground in this assertion. He then essentially posed the problem as being relevant only to women for whom delivery of a child would be life threatening.

> During pregnancy, abortion will present an extreme and last resource. And it would seem more humane to sacrifice, before the period of viability, an embryo whose existence is so uncertain, in order to protect the mother from the perilous chances of symphyscotomy and the Caesarean section.
>
> The abuse and criminal extension of such a resource is reprehensible, but not its proper and authorized employment. This operation should always be undertaken with great care and all necessary precaution used to satisfy the public mind of its necessity.

This is hardly a ringing endorsement of women's right to choose and it runs entirely counter to his wife's practice, where women were regularly terminating pregnancies based on many reasons, only a small percentage of which were likely related to direct and provable fears about the ability of a woman to safely deliver a child. It is also plagiarized directly from the celebrated French obstetrician M. Chailly's *Practical Treatise on Midwifery*, first translated and published in the United States in 1844. The real irony is that the translator and editor of Chailly's work was none other than Gunning S. Bedford, who himself had already been quite critical of Madame Restell in medical journals and had testified against her at the trial for Maria Bodine's abortion. The trial took place a few months after the publication of the book, but Lohman must have been well aware of Bedford's views about his wife as he assembled *The Married Woman's Private Medical Companion*. Indeed, he may have taken a certain measure of amusement in plagiarizing from Bedford, knowing how divergent their views were on contraception and abortion. Nevertheless, and because of his use of Chailly/Bedford's words, *The Married Woman's Private Medical Companion* was not an advocate of abortion on demand and makes no mention of abortion post-quickening at all, meaning that it largely stands to the side of the abortion debates that were consuming New Yorkers and their legislators.[21]

Lohman had begun to advertise *The Married Woman's Private Medical Companion* in the *New York Herald* in early March of 1847. He slowly expanded across the country until September of 1847. For most of that year it was just one more book advertised among many other products and services in most of these newspapers' third or fourth page, filled with scores of similar ads. That changed at almost exactly the time his wife was indicted and arrested for performing an abortion on Maria Bodine. It seems likely that this was why the police and the public more broadly realized who A.M. Mauriceau really was. On September 15, the *Brooklyn Evening Star* explained that someone had written to the Sunday *Times* to report that "*Dr. Mauriceau* of Liberty-street, New-York, whose infamous advertisements have been so long presented to the public, by the New-York papers, is no less a person than Charles Lohman, the husband, or whatever he calls himself, of the woman Restell." The article appeared under the title "Restell Case," indicating that the discovery was noteworthy as it related to Restell's arrest the week before. Also of note in this account is the way Lohman's status as Restell's husband is both revealed and simultaneously derided, as if a woman like Restell was actually incapable of having a husband, so much had she unsexed herself through her trade. Perhaps as a result of the attention garnered through his now-revealed relationship, the *Herald*, the same newspaper that had been advertising Lohman's book at least five times per month for the better part of a year, announced that Lohman had been arrested "on a warrant issued by the Court of Sessions, as having been indicted by the grand jury on a charge of publishing an obscene book, under the fictitious name of Dr. Moriceau [*sic*]." Lohman was being represented by two attorneys who had represented Restell in the Ann Maria Purdy trial in 1841. He was released on bail the next week.[22]

At that point, newspapers in other locations picked up on the story. The *Louisville Courier* announced on September 27 that it would discontinue running advertisements for *The Married Woman's Private*

Medical Companion. It explained in some detail just who Mauriceau's wife was, in a story taken from the *National Police Gazette*, noting also that she had recently been arrested. The *Courier* reported that "as soon as [they] received a hint of the character of the book," they sent away for a copy of it. There was a "good deal of minor villainy" in it, and

> in the middle of the book, there are fifty-two pages devoted to the schemes of Madame RESTELL, and designed for her express benefit.—Not content with debauching society in the city of New York, not content with proclaiming immunity to libertinism, and with daily communion with the murderous orgies of her avocation, she has sent her emissaries over the land, to obtain the aid of unsuspecting publishers in furtherance of her hellish schemes. Of course we cannot become accessories to her crimes, and we are sure that no virtuous publisher, will lend his aid after he finds out the character of her book.

Completely out of step with how most nineteenth-century Americans understood patriarchal marriage to function, the editors of the *Courier* assumed that Madame Restell, who was certainly the more famous of the pair, must be responsible not just for the publication of the book itself but for its content, even though she is never named in it and her husband was running a sizable side business under his own pseudonym.[23]

The *Courier* did note that these fifty-two pages were taken directly from Owen, whom the editors believed was honest and innocent in his intentions, but not so Restell: "Throughout the matter that RESTELL has plundered from him are advertisements of her infamous means, and knowing the desperate character she has obtained under her common sobriquet, she has adopted in this book, the name *A. M. Mauriceau.*" Despite the fact that Charles, not Restell, had been indicted for publishing an obscene book, the *Courier* had entirely erased his existence, so consumed were they by the evils of Restell.[24]

Lohman was never prosecuted for obscenity. In December of 1847, after Restell herself had already been convicted of a misdemeanor and was jailed in the Tombs, Lohman's lawyer asked for a postponement in the obscenity case. He claimed that Owen was a material witness for the defendant, and because Owen was an Indiana resident, the defense would require more time to examine Owen, presumably in Indiana. The postponement was granted and the trial never took place. Presumably Lohman's lawyer was going to argue that because Owen had never been charged with obscenity, and the most controversial parts of Lohman's book were plagiarized from Owen, Lohman could not be guilty. It is unclear whether that strategy worked or whether prosecutors simply lost interest in pursuing the case. Either way, Lohman never stood trial. While New Yorkers were now aware that the infamous Restell did indeed have a husband, Lohman's and Trow's roles in the family business never again saw so much attention, even though they continued to advertise until the 1880s, indeed after the time of both Lohman's and Restell's deaths. In 1860, when the census taker came to the door at 162 Chambers Street, the residents were reported as being three servants; Charles R. Lohman, physician, 48; Annie, 46; and Joseph Mauriceau, 28 [sic], physician. In this official accounting of the residents, Charles was head of household, Madame Restell was reduced to a first name, and her brother had assumed the pseudonym of Mauriceau, just as he was when he clerked daily at 129 Liberty Street.[25]

8

SEDUCED AND ABANDONED

As the 1840s gave way to the 1850s, Madame Restell mostly had managed to remain out of the news after her release from Blackwell's Island in 1848. She continued to sell ladies' monthly pills from her office at 162 Chambers Street, where she also saw pregnant women for their confinements and to terminate their pregnancies, depending on their desires and on how far along they were. Her advertisements—as well as those placed using her husband's pseudonym, Dr. A.M. Mauriceau—appeared in newspapers regularly in cities along the Eastern Seaboard. Their fortunes grew. The year 1853 also brought good news. In June of that year, Restell's only daughter, Caroline Summers, married Isaac Lent Purdy of Greenburgh, New York, just outside the city, near Tarrytown. Purdy was the only son of Gabriel and Eleanor Purdy. The Purdys were an old and established family in Westchester County, and Gabriel served in a number of elected positions. It is likely that Restell was pleased with the match, though what Gabriel and Eleanor thought of their son marrying the daughter of the notorious Madame Restell we will never know. Following the marriage, Caroline moved out of her mother's home and in with her new husband, in Greenburgh, where Isaac worked as a carpenter. They lived comfortably, with two Irish servants tending to their needs. A first child, Caroline Summers Purdy, named for her mother, followed in May of 1854. The summer of 1853 brought more family to New York as well. Madame Restell's younger brother, Stephen, arrived from England in mid-August with his two sons. Stephen had been widowed in Gloucestershire, and his sister had assured him she could provide him with a farm if he moved to the United States. He settled upstate, with his two sons, in Barre, about thirty-five miles west of Rochester, and soon remarried and had two daughters.[1]

Restell's luck, however, did not hold. On February 13, 1854, headlines across the city announced her arrest by Captain Walling of the Eighteenth Ward Police. A beautiful young woman named Cordelia Grant had sworn out a statement against Madame Restell in police court, alleging that Restell had performed no fewer than three abortions on her person, which she claimed had been paid for by the man who had seduced and subsequently abandoned her, "Mr. George Shackford, a wealthy gentleman occupying a splendid mansion at Fordham, Westchester county." They had been living in sin for more than six years, claiming variously to be husband and wife, uncle and niece, or guardian and ward. Police court justice Stuart also issued a warrant for the arrest of Shackford as an accessory to the most recent abortion, the only one to fall within the statute of limitations. Miss Grant's attorney also made clear that she would be bringing a civil suit against Shackford for breach of promise, alleging that she had only consented to sexual relations with him because she believed they would marry. Instead, Shackford had continually strung her along and ultimately abandoned her. For the next month, readers of New York City newspapers were rapt, as the case took some unpredictable twists and turns. Would there be a trial that would put Restell away for more than a year? The presence of a complaining witness, always difficult to obtain in cases like these where former clients usually wanted to preserve their privacy, did not bode well for Restell. Grant's testimony before a New York jury might be enough to gain a conviction on the charge of second-degree manslaughter, which would result in up to seven years' imprisonment, rather than the one year she had served in the case of Maria Bodine.[2]

Grant chose to go public with her story and to initiate legal proceedings by making a criminal complaint in police court. This was not unusual. Police courts in New York City provided a forum for every-day residents to make claims against one another for violations of the law, usually without lawyers there to represent them. In essence, this was individualized prosecution of crime. Police court justices, who often had little training in the law, were authorized to send police officers to execute arrest warrants, hold investigative hearings, imprison suspects and witnesses, and pass judgment on cases, usually those cases that did not rise to the level of a felony. In cases deemed more serious, police court justices might hand off cases to the district attorney and grand jury, who would initiate proceedings in the more elevated court of general sessions. The police court, which was founded in 1798 and continued till 1895, was in some ways a holdover from an era in which there was no police force to investigate crime. Instead, police courts relied on everyday citizens to do that work, aided by police justices who could be paid fees to issue arrest warrants, fees paid by the complaining witnesses. Once a police force was established in 1845, some of these prosecutions became public, brought before the police court by a police officer who had arrested someone he believed had committed a crime, but individual prosecutions, like the one initiated by Grant, also continued. The evidence from a number of antebellum cities shows that police courts were also often used to effect blackmail; a complaining witness could call off a trial once the accused paid him or her off.[3]

Grant's affidavit laid out the story of her ruin. New York newspapers printed it verbatim. Grant was from Portland, Maine, and said that she was about to turn twenty-one. Six years earlier, when she was but fifteen years old, she had met Shackford when she and some friends were out "on a pleasure party" in Portland. Shackford "singled out Miss Grant, and insisted upon paying her attentions, despite the disinclination of her brother-in-law to permit them from a stranger, and also of the young lady's efforts to be free of him." Eventually, Shackford managed to obtain admission to Miss Grant's sister's home, where she was then living, and began to make regular calls on her there. Shackford persuaded her that his intentions were true, promising her that he wanted to marry her but explaining that family circumstances did not permit it at the time. He asked her to elope with him, and according to the *National Police Gazette*, "Miss Grant, being young and giddy, listened to his honied softness" with "credulity and curiosity," and while she resisted for some time, at last relented, but only on the condition that Shackford take her to his mother's home in St. Louis and marry her there.[4]

Shackford, a widower, had a young son from his prior marriage with him in Portland. The three planned on taking a steamer to New Orleans and then making their way to St. Louis. As the *Gazette* explained, Grant, Shackford, and the boy fled from her sister's house in Portland, without permission from the sister and brother-in-law, taking a small boat across the bay to a steamer and at that point, as the newspaper explained in high melodrama, "Miss Grant was in the power of a man without a heart, without one sympathetic feeling of kindness, and the home of her childhood and her innocence was left forever, and she, trusting in his plighted word, saw not the horrors of her future. Her guardian angel was sleeping on its post, or she was unmindful of the promptings she received." Drawing on literary representations like the American bestseller *Charlotte Temple* (1792), by English author Susanna Rowson, newspaper editors and the American public often depicted the decision to accompany a man away from a girl's parents' home as just as decisive a break from purity as the sex that was presumed to follow afterward. Grant was following in a well-established tradition, though the presence of Shackford's son was certainly an unusual twist. Running away with Shackford, whatever happened immediately thereafter, was enough to ruin her reputation for good. On the course of the journey, tragedy struck: Shackford's son fell overboard and drowned. "[Shackford] received the intelligence unmoved, whilst she, to whom the child had become endeared, grieved for him, and yet, in the father's indifference she did not perceive a foreshadowing of the treatment destined for her."[5]

The representation of Grant's downfall as a seduction narrative was a combination of what Grant herself told to newspapermen and those reporters' propensity to tell the story in that way. It was a familiar

cultural script that framed the tale in the blunt terms of Grant's innocence corrupted by evil in the form of Shackford and Restell. Key
details of the story, however, can be confirmed from sources prior to
Grant's 1854 revelations. Vital records show that George R. Shackford was born in Rockingham County, New Hampshire, in 1818, the
child of Samuel and Hannah (Currier) Shackford, grew up in St. Louis,
later moved to Philadelphia, and returned to New Hampshire in 1841
on a trip, where he met and married Margaret E. Robinson in Brentwood that year. At some point following their marriage, they relocated
to New York City, where they lived on Greenwich Street, just a block
from Madame Restell's office. Margaret Shackford died in 1845 in
New York, and in subsequent years Shackford lived variously in Philadelphia and Portsmouth, New Hampshire, only about fifty miles
down the coast from Portland, Maine, where he met Grant. Newspapers claimed he worked, at various times, in the wool business and
in construction and was worth at least $100,000. A Portsmouth, New
Hampshire, newspaper in April 1848 also confirmed that Shackford's
son, Daniel, almost six years old, did fall from a steamer cabin window
on a voyage from Portland, Maine, to New Orleans, at exactly the time
that Grant alleged she was seduced by Shackford.[6]

In the affidavit she swore out in New York in 1854, Grant detailed
the abortions she had had at Restell's hands and, one can't help but
imagine, told a tale that was designed to evoke the sympathy of the
audience she knew she would soon have. Grant's affidavit was a legal
document, which, if found credible by the police court magistrate,
might lead the district attorney to press charges against Restell and
Shackford and eventually bring them to trial. But it was also printed
verbatim in newspapers, just as Grant probably knew it would be. She
needed to make sure she had readers on her side, and the best way to do
that was to portray herself as a victim. Grant's story was somewhat
more complicated, in that she remained with Shackford for a period of
more than six years. But the most important part of the tale was that
he had promised her marriage as a means to have sex with her and then
refused to actually follow through. After that, many would have be-

lieved she had little choice but to remain with him. A fallen woman would have been disgraced in her home and likely destined for a life of prostitution. By contrast, many readers might be able to understand how living as a kept woman was preferable to working in a brothel, even if different only by degrees.

By 1854, seduction was criminalized by statute. While New York never passed a civil statute that allowed a woman to sue for damages on her own behalf, a man could be prosecuted under a criminal seduction statute passed in 1848. If Grant went to the police accusing Shackford of seduction, she could also use the charges as leverage to extract compensation, albeit extralegally. She could also sue him for breach of promise, an allegation that he had promised marriage and then reneged. The harm done to Grant—to her reputation and to her marriage prospects—was understood by most Americans to be real and to have demonstrable economic consequences. Because Grant had remained with Shackford for more than five years after the alleged crime, however, it is unlikely that a New York prosecutor (or a prosecutor in Maine, where the seduction had likely taken place) would have taken on the case. When crafting her affidavit, Grant made sure to fit herself and Shackford into roles with which most papers' readers would already be familiar. At the same time, the affidavit was confined to details of the abortions themselves, though Grant and her lawyer also made sure that reporters were aware of the broad outlines of her story.[7]

Grant explained that she had been made enceinte (the French word for pregnant and a common way to describe the condition in print at the time) by Shackford five times; in each case he had insisted that she procure an abortion. Twice, the abortion took place in Massachusetts, and the other three pregnancies were terminated in New York, by Madame Restell. On the first occasion, on the 21st of January 1850, Grant explained that she was boarding with Shackford "as man and wife" at the home of Michael Henry, and she was between three and four months pregnant. Shackford arranged the abortion with Charles Lohman. When Shackford and Grant arrived at 162 Chambers Street,

Shackford paid Lohman $50, and Lohman explained that Grant could be attended by a woman. Restell appeared at this point and led Grant upstairs, where "Madame Restell then conversed about other matters for the purpose of keeping up my spirits." She then performed the operation, which Grant found to be quite painful, and she was delivered of the fetus the next day at Henry's residence. Shackford burned her soiled clothing and presumably disposed of the fetus.[8]

The occasion of the second abortion was almost exactly a year later. Shackford and Grant were boarding about a half mile downtown from Restell's office. Shackford was by this point claiming that Grant was his niece and she "was at that time going to school at Mrs. Hannah Parker's in Spring street, Mr. Shackford telling the school teacher and the persons where [they] boarded that [she] was his ward." Again between three and four months pregnant, Shackford insisted that Grant terminate her pregnancy, which Grant resisted. On this occasion, Shackford made arrangements with Lohman and Restell for Grant to stay with Restell after the procedure. This was not uncommon for Restell's patients; as a midwife and the operator of a lying-in hospital, Restell regularly had clients who had terminated pregnancies or were confined and awaiting delivery stay with her. Grant packed a trunk and they took a carriage to Lohman's office, where Joseph Trow, Restell's brother, subsequently picked up the trunk and transported it to Restell's office and home. This may have been because Shackford and Grant believed that Restell's residence was under surveillance and they wanted to avoid the scrutiny they might garner by arriving with luggage. Grant and Shackford then proceeded to Restell's, where Shackford paid Restell both for the operation and for two weeks' stay for Grant. That night Restell terminated the pregnancy and, in Grant's telling, informed her when Grant asked about the fate of the fetus that she had burned it. Grant remained at Restell's home for another two weeks. She explained that Restell's husband, Lohman, was also present during those two weeks "and knew perfectly well the object of my visit." Other reports indicate that women who stayed at 162 Chambers Street either for the purposes of abortion or for the delivery of a child stayed in an upstairs bedroom and thus saw Restell, Lohman, and the servants regularly. By including this information in her affidavit, Grant seems to have been trying to make sure the magistrate understood the degree to which Restell, Lohman, and Trow were all implicated in the workings of the family business.[9]

After two weeks, Shackford returned from Boston, where he had been conducting business, and he and Grant again resumed boarding together. At the spring, they left New York to spend the summer traveling. While in Cape May, New Jersey, at the beginning of the autumn, Grant again became pregnant, and they returned to New York on a Sunday in October 1852. The next morning, Shackford sent her to 162 Chambers Street, again with $50. When she arrived, Restell was not in and a servant informed her that Restell was at Lohman's office. Upon arrival at the office, Grant found Restell with her brother, Joseph. Lohman, Grant was told, was away in Europe. Restell and Grant returned to Chambers Street, where Grant paid Restell, who once again terminated her pregnancy "in the same manner as on the previous occasions." Upon returning to their boardinghouse, Grant found Shackford with packed bags; they stayed that night at a hotel called the Westchester House, at the corner of Broome and the Bowery— coincidentally the same location where Ann Maria Purdy had given her testimony about ten years earlier. Grant was delivered of a premature fetus that evening as Shackford attended her. They remained there for an additional two weeks as Grant became well.[10]

In Grant's telling, this was the end of her sexual relationship with Shackford. She explained that after leaving the Westchester House, she went east to see friends for a period of three weeks. Shackford retrieved her at that time and as Grant explained, "Since that time I have not been *enceinte*, nor had any intercourse with him, and since we left the Westchester House I have continued to live with him as his ward." They boarded in New York for a time, and eventually Shackford acquired a home in Fordham, in Westchester County, where he took Grant in October 1853, and she assumed the duties of the mistress of the house.[11]

As a result of the affidavit, the magistrate issued a warrant for the apprehension of Shackford. Upon hearing this, Shackford voluntarily appeared before the court with counsel and demanded a hearing to answer the allegations. What Cordelia Grant does not make clear in this account is why she chose this moment to come forward and make her claims. That is, if her circumstances would seem to have improved—no more intercourse, no more pregnancies, residence in a fine Westchester mansion—why now? Reporters claimed that Grant had begun to worry that Shackford was planning to abandon her and proposed to him a one-time settlement of $5,000 and a clean separation. He refused and she filed this complaint with the police justice as a means of exposing him and perhaps pressuring him into settling with her. What Grant did not say, and possibly did not actually know, is that George Shackford had married, in April of 1853, to Rutha E. Crosby, in Boston. By 1854 and the time of this indictment, Shackford was already father to a son, also named George. Rutha Shackford's existence, whether or not Grant knew about her, is no doubt the cause for the rupture between the two.[12]

Why did Shackford marry Crosby and not Grant? While we cannot know with any certainty, by 1853 George had already demonstrated that he did not consider Grant suitable for marriage. He had avoided marriage to her for five years, during five alleged pregnancies, any of which might have prompted another couple to take a trip to the altar. Perhaps Grant was not of a suitable social class for a wealthy man like Shackford. Perhaps he realized early on that while he was very much attracted to her, he could never love her. It is quite likely that Grant's willingness to have sex with him prior to marriage was precisely what had made her ineligible to become his wife. A powerful double standard governed sexual conduct in the nineteenth-century United States. It is probable that Shackford had never intended to marry Grant, and his ongoing dalliance with her was never meant to stand in the way of his marrying for a second time and beginning a new, respectable family. By 1854, the demands of that family may finally have increased to the point that maintaining Grant as well was simply no longer tenable.

The initial examination of Grant was set for Wednesday, February 15, before the police court magistrate, Justice Stuart. This was not yet a trial, no indictment having been filed by the grand jury. Instead, this was an investigative hearing that would allow Stuart to determine whether Grant herself was credible, during which the defendants' lawyers could pose questions. In a high-profile case like this, it was likely that if Stuart found Grant's allegations credible, he would pass the case on to the district attorney, though with lesser charges, he did have the right to pass sentence himself. On February 15, Shackford, Restell, and their lawyers appeared, but Grant, "being very severely indisposed with a cold," was unable to be present. The magistrate postponed until the next Wednesday. That day, as the *Herald* explained, "at an early hour in the afternoon, the court room began to fill with mysterious personages, who stepped lightly into the court, their eyes wandering all around the room and ultimately fixing on the magistrate, as if that functionary had really got concealed in his pocket Miss Grant, Madame Restell, or Mr. Shackford, or, perchance, all three, for what they knew." The courtroom became steadily more crowded with women and men as the time to commence approached, "and when Miss Grant arrived, under the escort of Counsellor Busteed, a tremendous rush was made toward her, each one wishing to see as much as he could." Grant was wearing "a black watered silk, fur tippet and cuffs, a dark blue satin hat trimmed with black velvet, a brown veil drawn over her face, and dove colored gloves." Presently, Shackford also arrived, "dressed in a suit of black, with gloves corresponding in color exactly to those of Miss Grant." Restell and Lohman were seated nearby with counsel. Justice Stuart announced that he was now prepared to examine Miss Grant.[13]

After a brief back-and-forth between counselors about the calling of various other witnesses, the examination of Grant began. The initial questions, posed by Justice Stuart, focused on ascertaining the basic facts of Grant's identity and her allegations about the 1852 abortion, the only one that fell within the statute of limitations. At one point the counsel for the defense applied to compel Grant to remove her veil so that they might see her face and be able to identify her. Her counsel objected and was overruled, and Grant removed her veil, revealing her beautiful countenance to all those assembled. The questions then continued, with Grant giving answers that confirmed the facts she had given in her affidavit: she and Shackford had come from Cape May, New Jersey, in October of 1852 for the purpose of procuring an abortion by Madame Restell at 162 Chambers Street. When asked why Shackford had chosen Restell for the procedure, Grant replied that Restell had terminated earlier pregnancies of hers. Counsel for the defense objected, noting that prior acts were inadmissible, and the magistrate sustained the objection. The questioning resumed and Grant recounted the details of the day on which she had obtained the abortion. Grant extended somewhat the testimony from her affidavit, explaining that afterward she and Shackford walked from Restell's office to the Westchester House. There she was delivered of the fetus at eleven that evening, Shackford being in bed with her at the time. Following the delivery, Grant recounted that Shackford said he had burned the remains and that he had taken the soiled blanket to a "colored woman" to be washed. She said that during her two-week stay at the Westchester, "Mr. Shackford attended to all my wants and nursed me; the head waiter brought the meals to the room; there was no medical assistance procured or spoken of for me by Mr. Shackford."[14]

When asked if she had felt motion of "the child" prior to the abortion, Grant confirmed, "I felt a motion of the child about ten days prior to the abortion," later explaining that she was "certain" about this. This detail would be key to any case brought by the district attorney, for Grant alleged that Restell had performed an abortion on a "quick" child, which upgraded the crime to that of second-degree manslaughter. The examination continued with questions relating to whether Shackford and Grant had known Restell before and whether the Lohman family was also acquainted with Shackford. Grant replied in the affirmative to these questions. The magistrate then asked Grant if she was familiar with Restell's handwriting; indeed, she was. The magistrate explained that he had in his possession a letter that he wished Grant to testify was written by Restell, to which the defense objected strenuously. Grant's counsel explained that he would not reveal the contents of the letter at present as he was also in the process of bringing a civil suit against Shackford for breach of promise for $30,000, on which the letter had bearing, but that he had already revealed its contents to the magistrate. Much objecting ensued, and little resolution. The court adjourned for the day at 6:00 p.m., with plans to continue the following week as the magistrate himself had business to attend to in Albany that prevented a resumption of the case on the following day.[15]

The next Thursday, Madame Restell appeared in court at the appointed hour with her counsel, Ambrose L. Jordan. There was no sign of Miss Grant and Mr. Shackford. All assembled waited for upward of two hours before Justice Stuart was forced to postpone the examination indefinitely. Cordelia Grant had disappeared. The magistrate explained that after Grant had made her complaint, he had placed her in the home of a police officer in the Eighteenth Ward, where she had resided since. New York State's revised statutes of 1829 gave Stuart the power to detain Grant as a material witness. The day before she had been at the policeman's house and had received a note in the morning. She answered that note with one of her own and soon thereafter dressed and went out, leaving her trunks behind. One newspaper claimed she "had an interview" with Shackford, but most New York papers did not print that particular rumor. She had not been seen since. The magistrate explained that, as a matter of law, no case could proceed based on the affidavit alone without a completed cross-examination.[16]

Where was Cordelia Grant? Some believed she had been abducted and perhaps murdered, others that she had been paid off by Restell, Shackford, or the two together. The *Daily National Era*, a Washington, DC newspaper, pointed out that both certainly had plenty of money to buy her silence. One paper intimated the payoff was $10,000. Writing before Grant had disappeared, the *Sunday Dispatch* of

Philadelphia, where Shackford had been an on-again, off-again resident, anticipated the disappearance by some weeks and predicted its cause:

> We may say, however, that the complainant, Miss Grant, is really a very handsome arrangement of feminine flesh and blood, and we may whisper (mind! it is only a whisper) that measures are in active progress to occasion her sudden absence when the accused shall have boldly summoned her to come forth and substantiate her fearful charge. If we may believe the public press, she only wanted $6000 to quiet her conscience and bind her to eternal silence as to the past. How much more ointment will be needed, under the present exasperating circumstances, "to bind up her wounds" and give her "another horse," we can only conjecture. Spermaceti, Hotspur tells us, is good for "an inward bruise," but modern science has furnished a remedy far more efficacious, or else the annals of Wall street are pure romance, and have none of the elements of veritable history.

Referencing a character, Hotspur, in Shakespeare's *Henry IV,* who reported on the use of spermaceti—a waxy substance produced by sperm whales often used in medicinal ointments—the editorial intimates that the "inward bruise" of Grant's heartache will be far better healed by money than by medicine. Because spermaceti continued to be used well into the nineteenth century, this was also a double reference to Grant's supposedly damaged womb, figured as the "inward wound." Indeed, the paper asked, if she originally asked for $6,000, how much more will she want now to "bind up her wounds" and keep her silent?[17]

The magistrate overseeing the case went to some trouble to find Grant, taking additional affidavits, according to the *New York Herald*, and sending police to search several houses, among them the home of Madame Restell. When the police arrived with a search warrant at 162 Chambers Street, Restell was surprised but granted them full access to the home, which they searched "from cellar to garret, but no Miss Grant was found." In the meantime, Grant's lawyer, Richard Busteed, issued a long and rambling statement, explaining why he had been absent from court that day. According to Busteed, he last saw Grant on Monday, February 27, the week the examination was to resume. At that time he arranged to meet with her at his office at noon on Thursday in order to travel to the police court together. In the interim, Busteed was called to Staten Island to work on a different case and was unable to make it back to Manhattan on time. He left word with a partner to attend to Grant, but she had vanished. "In conclusion, I have not seen Miss Grant since Monday evening. I do not know, and have not even the faintest idea, where she is, when she left, or how, or with whom, or by whose procurement, or who was privy to it. I do not know whether she has been abducted forcibly or has voluntarily absented herself." As a number of newspapers reported, "The theory that the young woman has gone off on her own accord, does not have many disciples." In the absence of Grant and thus the inability to cross-examine her, Justice Stuart released Shackford and Restell from their arrests (they had never been held in custody), vowing to revisit the case in two weeks' time.[18]

On Thursday, March 16, exactly two weeks after Grant went missing, the body of a drowned woman was discovered in the East River, close to the Brooklyn side. There were enough similarities between the young woman and Cordelia Grant that many speculated they were one and the same. For a day, New Yorkers were abuzz with the possibility that Grant had been murdered and dumped in the East River in circumstances eerily reminiscent of the death of Mary Rogers, who was found washed up in the Hudson River near Hoboken in the summer of 1841. Within a day, however, the body in the East River was identified as Sarah Ann Jacobs, who had been missing for about two months, dead from an apparent suicide "while laboring under mental derangement," as the *Brooklyn Eagle* explained. Grant was still missing. That many found it possible that she could be found drowned, presumed murdered, attested both to the powerful evidence she had brought against Shackford and Restell and to Restell's reputation by the early 1850s. Murder to preserve her fortune and profession was not thought to be beyond the pale for someone so universally portrayed as evil in the press.[19]

A week later, Justice Stuart of the police court, on appeal of Restell's and Shackford's counselors, dropped the case entirely. He was unable to proceed without a complaining witness. As he explained, "I have used every effort within my means to find Miss Grant, and have failed in so doing." He had not dismissed the case earlier because he believed that Restell or Shackford, or both, had been instrumental in removing Grant from the city and he had hoped to prove this and bring Grant back to testify. He had also explored the possibility of introducing her affidavit and the prior examination into evidence against the defendants, believing that if they had removed her from the city, they should not also benefit from her absence, but instead should have the testimony used against them. The district attorney had advised him that this would abrogate the legal rights of Restell and Shackford.[20]

In the meantime—one can imagine the gasps in the courtroom—Stuart had also received a letter purporting to be from Cordelia Grant herself. It was posted on March 10 from New Brunswick, New Jersey, about forty miles southwest of the city. The letter read:

Justice Stewart [sic]—As I have voluntarily withdrawn from the State, and do not intend ever to renew my criminal prosecution against Mr. Shackford, I trust you will be so good as to allow me to have possession of my baggage, of which I am in great need. For your uniform courtesy to me, I am very grateful and were it practical I would gladly express the same to you in person. But the fear of falling under the influence of others, who have deceived and misled me in this most unfortunate affair, as well as other important considerations, deters, and must deter me, for a long time, from returning to New York. I am very truly yours.

Cordelia A. Grant.[21]

It is possible that the letter did not come from Grant and was simply designed to get the police court to drop the charges and throw them off the scent, though that was not how Stuart or the press interpreted it. Indeed, the fact that Grant mentioned her baggage, which reporters had earlier noted she left behind, led them to believe this letter was genuine. Though the letter printed in the papers did not include Grant's return address in New Brunswick, it is certainly possible that the original did, leading Stuart to believe the letter genuine. He may well have returned the baggage. Finally, the fact that Stuart did not attempt to find Grant in New Jersey, at least so far as we know, indicates that he believed her withdrawal from the case to be genuine. While he had earlier wanted to ascertain that she had not met with foul play, once she voluntarily chose to withdraw her complaint, there was little he could do to compel the testimony of a witness in a proceeding that had not even advanced to the trial stage. A few weeks later, the letter made one final appearance in the press, when an anonymous source alleged the letter had been forged. New York's recorder—essentially the city's chief judge—instructed the grand jury to "give the matter their earliest and most earnest attention." Even as the original charges were dismissed in late March, Stuart had made it clear that he would have no hesitation in bringing them again should new evidence be brought to light. As it turned out, no additional charges were ever brought related to the Grant case. Madame Restell had escaped again.[22]

So what became of Cordelia Grant and why did she disappear? The latter question will likely never be answered satisfactorily, but it is highly likely that Madame Restell and George Shackford paid her off. Grant's initial appeal to Shackford had been for money. She had been a kept woman for more than six years, and she believed that her chances at marriage, which she had once thought would occur with Shackford himself, were over. Indeed, her discovery that Shackford himself was remarried may have prompted her demands in the first place. If it was money she wanted to secure some sort of future for herself—an entirely reasonable demand given her chances otherwise and given her new notoriety—money was something Shackford and Restell both could provide. Both Restell and Shackford had plenty to lose if Grant gave testimony. While Restell's punishment for administering the abortion would be stiffer than Shackford's as an accessory would be, Grant was also suing Shackford for breach of promise, further indicating that she believed she was entitled to compensation as a result of his treatment of her. Shackford may also have feared that the longer the suit dragged out in court, the more likely it was to affect his marriage with Rutha and his relationship with the son they shared. Both, in sum, had much to gain if Grant went away, and the cost, whatever it might have been, was likely within their means, especially if they pooled resources. That Grant is reported to have left the home where she boarded upon receiving a note makes Shackford a more compelling suspect as the briber. Would Grant have felt comfortable leaving the safety of the policeman's home to go meet Madame Restell on her own, for instance? Unlikely, though perhaps yes, if the note made quite clear what Restell was offering.

On the question of Grant's whereabouts, however, the evidence is much more conclusive: Cordelia Grant returned home to Maine. On February 25, 1855, less than a year after she brought the charges and then disappeared, she was married to Samuel J. Noble, originally from New York but then a resident of Portland. Soon thereafter, Cordelia gave birth to a daughter. In 1857, the *National Police Gazette* reported that Grant, still a resident of Portland, had written to her former counsel, Richard Busteed, enclosing a bond, payment on which she asked him to collect from Shackford. If this report is to be believed, it indicates that Shackford had indeed bribed her to leave New York and drop the charges. This was certainly the conclusion drawn by the editors of the *Police Gazette*, though their reporting could sometimes be specious. Ever resentful of the role he had been made to play in the affair, "Mr. Busteed, we learn, has indignantly returned the document, having no desire for a client who played him such a trick."[23]

By 1870, Cordelia and Samuel Noble had relocated to Boston, where they lived with their two daughters. Noble worked as an apothecary, or druggist. In 1870, George and Rutha Shackford also lived in Boston—had resided there since their marriage—with their son and daughter, Hannah, who was the same age as Cordelia's eldest. The

Nobles and Shackfords did not live particularly close to one another. George was in East Boston and Cordelia lived in the Eighth Ward, which was southwest of George's house, encompassing parts of North Dorchester and Roxbury. That said, the city of Boston in 1870 had a population of only just over 250,000; it is not hard to imagine them happening on one another while shopping or strolling with their children in a park. If Shackford had finally paid off Grant, it is even possible that they could meet each other amicably.[24]

Restell had succeeded once again in eluding imprisonment, but she was soon to find that her growing notoriety had made her a target for more than just the police and their courts.

9

IN THE PUBLIC EYE

In July of 1855, a poor German woman named Frederica Wilhelmina Neidlinger knocked on Madame Restell's door at 162 Chambers Street. Mina, as she was called, explained that she was pregnant and expected to give birth within weeks and she had nowhere to go and no money. She told Restell that she was not married and currently worked as a domestic servant, and she asked Restell if it would be possible to stay at the lying-in hospital in exchange for her labor. She had nothing else to give and nowhere else to go. Within days, she arrived with her trunks and began working in Restell's home. On August 30, Neidlinger went into labor in a third-floor bedroom of the home and was delivered of a son by Madame Restell. Neidlinger named him George Meyers, using what she claimed was her cousin's surname. She continued to work in Restell's home for several more months, laboring to pay off the expense of the delivery, room, and board.[1]

On these fundamental elements of the story, Restell and Neidlinger agreed, but about almost everything else related to the case, they were at odds. Almost one full year after Neidlinger had given birth, and well after she had left Restell's employ, Neidlinger swore out an affidavit claiming that Restell had stolen her baby and given it away to persons unknown. She demanded that Restell reveal the name of the person who had adopted the baby and that the baby be returned to her. Restell claimed that she had indeed found a new home for the infant, but only at the behest of Neidlinger, who had supposedly said she wanted a better life for her son than any she could provide for him. The fight between Neidlinger and Restell played out in the courts for almost six years, each claiming the other was lying. This case was more complicated and more contentious than the case of Mary Applegate and her own missing child a decade earlier. For one, by the mid-1850s, Madame Restell was even more wealthy and famous. Following her imprisonment on Blackwell's Island, which some thought had been far too short, many New Yorkers wanted to see her prosecuted again. Also, unlike with the case of Applegate, whose child everyone agreed had been placed with a wet nurse with Applegate's own permission, Restell claimed that Neidlinger's son had been adopted. Testimony in the case reveals the shadowy, and growing, world of unregulated adoption at midcentury. The testimony also suggests what might really be behind Neidlinger's accusation. If, as Restell contended, she put the child up for adoption only because Neidlinger asked her to, what was behind the claim that Restell had abducted the child? And why would New York's judiciary take these claims so seriously, continuing to revisit and investigate the case until 1862?

* * * *

On August 20, 1856, almost all of New York's newspapers reported the "Re-Arrest of Madame Restell—Attempted Abortion and Abduction." Newspapers up and down the East Coast, and as far away as Sacramento, also covered the case in the days to come. The headline read "re-arrest" because Restell had only recently been released on bail after a different German woman, Elizabeth Kaiser, had accused her of performing an abortion on her person and against her will, while simultaneously accusing her fiancé of breach of promise. Kaiser claimed she had been a housekeeper to a Mr. Schultz, a widower, and he had promised he would marry her when a year had lapsed after the death of his wife. When Kaiser became pregnant, he had taken her to Madame Restell's, where, in Kaiser's telling, Restell had terminated the pregnancy without telling her she was doing so, a version of the story likely told so that Kaiser could avoid being charged herself. She had been in poor health ever since, and Schultz had still not married her. The accusations in police court were designed to effect precisely that goal.[2]

The case of Mina Neidlinger, however, was altogether different from that of Elizabeth Kaiser, precisely because Neidlinger had given birth to her child in Restell's care. The *Herald* reported that the affidavit sworn out by Neidlinger (whose name they occasionally misspelled as Medinger) claimed that "on the 27th of July, 1855, she was induced to become a boarder in the house of the accused, 162 Chambers street, under the belief that it was a respectable private boardinghouse, her object being merely to stay until a child, with which she was then pregnant, should be born." Already the allegation strains belief. Even if Neidlinger was not fluent or literate in English, she had found out about Restell from someone. The idea that she would *only* have known about Restell's services as a midwife, and not as an abortionist, is implausible given that most people were surprised to learn that Restell did anything other than terminate pregnancies. The *Herald* continued, explaining that Neidlinger only realized that Restell was an abortionist after two weeks in the home, by which point her time of confinement was too soon to think of leaving. Soon thereafter, Restell "persuaded her to take six pills, which she said would be of great benefit to her; that soon after taking the pills, she was confined and delivered of a living child." These pills were the "attempted abortion" of the August 20 headline. According to Neidlinger, the child remained with her for a few hours, at which point Restell took him and Neidlinger never saw him again. She claimed that Restell subsequently told her she had sent the child to Philadelphia, "by the direction of the gentleman who had placed her there," that is, at Madame Restell's. Neidlinger, by her telling, went to Philadelphia in search of the child, and when she could not find him, Restell informed her that the child had since died. On the strength of this testimony, the police court issued a warrant for Restell's arrest, and she was taken into custody and charged with abducting the child of Frederica Wilhelmina Neidlinger. A Mr. Levy stood as Restell's bondsman and she was subsequently released on $1,000 bail.[3]

Many elements of this story rang false for anyone who knew how Restell did business or how she and Neidlinger came to know each other. Restell herself responded the very next day in a long letter in the *Herald* in which she called the accusations "baseless and improbable" and her accuser "wicked, unprincipled and mendacious." She first bemoaned the fact that the *Herald* (and other papers, many of which had simply reprinted the *Herald* story) had printed all of the accusations in Neidlinger's affidavit, but no one had seen fit to include any of the rebuttal that Restell herself had issued; readers thus had only one side of the story. As for the accusations themselves, Restell inquired why no one had asked Neidlinger why she had remained at Restell's home for four months after the delivery and supposed abduction of the child, "a fact which cannot be denied, or if denied, can be proved." With words practically dripping in sarcasm, Restell pointed out that "though a woman is confined at full time, in some way or other 'abortion' must be dragged in; also by insinuation, by the administration of some wonderful 'six pills,' from the effects of which, of course, there was a bare escape of life." This "simple administration of medicine" to a woman who was but two weeks away from delivery had now been "tortured" into an attempt to commit abortion. Restell was perfectly correct. She did not possess a medicine that could possibly have caused an abortion of a pregnancy nearing the end of its ninth month, at least not if the goal was the death of the fetus, as the newspapers implied.[4]

Restell then pointed to what was perhaps the issue deserving of the most skepticism. Why, if the abduction had taken place in August of 1855, was Neidlinger only coming forward with this accusation a year later, in August of 1856? "If a person has a pocketbook 'abducted' from his pocket, he is not apt to take a year to discover its abduction, or to omit mentioning the circumstance until the expiration of that time. On the contrary, he would mention it to everyone with whom he had communication." Restell claimed that Neidlinger had been in regular communication with Restell's other servants, none of whom said Neidlinger had ever mentioned anything about an abduction. Restell believed that "the affidavit is 'made to order' by some 'briefless member of the bar' whose practice is confined within the narrowest bounds, and whose reputation and standing is co-extensive with his practice." Restell was essentially accusing Neidlinger's attorney, Mr. R. Johnson, of attempting to extort money from her. Proof of this, she believed, was the affidavit's failure to mention Neidlinger's seducer, which served to "scapegoat" Madame Restell alone. She intimated that Neidlinger was making a show of accusing Restell also as a way to pressure her seducer into doing what she wanted. She further claimed that Neidlinger had falsely represented to her seducer that she had kept the child at a friend's house in an attempt to extort payment from its father. All, Restell claimed, would be revealed in due time. Other newspapers up and down the East Coast reported on the letter's publication, noting that Restell "says the missing child was voluntarily given by the mother to a lady for adopting."[5]

Over the next few months, a series of witnesses were called on to give testimony in the case, and some of the testimonies were printed in newspapers. One of these was from a married woman from Port Richmond, New York, named Helen Baker. She deposed that she had herself been a boarder at Madame Restell's in August of 1855 and given birth to a child there on August 22. She met Neidlinger there on August 27 when the latter arrived for her own confinement. Baker confirmed that Neidlinger had given birth to a son on August 30. Baker then recounted that Neidlinger had informed her the next day that "*she had given the child away.*" Soon thereafter, Baker left Restell's with her newborn daughter and returned home. In November of that year, Baker called at Restell's home and saw Neidlinger again, who informed Baker that she had heard from the woman who had adopted her son and that he, having been sickly from birth, had died about a month later. Neidlinger told Baker this news with great sorrow "and shed tears when talking of the death of her child." In addition to rebutting most of the other elements of Neidlinger's story, Baker attested that she had never known any child to be neglected at Restell's lying-in hospital and claimed both that she knew of other babies who had been adopted via Restell and that until the prior week, Neidlinger had represented the choice to give away her baby as her own. Baker finally testified that while she had never heard Neidlinger express a desire to find her child, she had often heard her "talk about suing her seducer to get money."[6]

Testimony continued through the autumn of 1856, and Restell and Neidlinger appeared before a special term of New York's supreme court on December 16, 1856, on a writ of habeas corpus. Restell was commanded to produce Neidlinger's child. During this hearing, Restell denied outright that she had ever had the child in her custody and explained that she was unable to produce the child now. Restell also explained in greater depth the circumstances that led to the adoption of Neidlinger's child. Several days prior to Neidlinger's delivery, Restell "had an application from a lady who desired to adopt a child, at which petitioner [Neidlinger] manifested such joy, and desired respondent [Restell] to secure the opportunity for her." Restell explained that following delivery of the child, Neidlinger freely gave it up "to one Mrs. Wright, with a request that the [boy] might be given to the lady who desired to adopt it." According to Restell, Neidlinger never again asked after her son and remained in service to Restell for another four months, until such point as she was dismissed for "unbecoming conduct."[7]

Restell also elaborated on the rumors that Neidlinger was using the missing child to extort money from his father. Neidlinger had represented another baby as being her own, claiming that she needed money to keep it boarding in Brooklyn. But when a friend of the purported father interviewed the woman who was keeping the baby, the woman admitted that it was her own, not Neidlinger's. Earlier in the fall, Judge Connolly had dismissed the charges against Restell as "groundless and unproven." Nevertheless, Neidlinger went on to file two more habeas corpus suits, both of which were also dismissed for insufficient proof. During this hearing, Restell testified that she believed Neidlinger was motivated by a desire to extort money from her "and she prays that said suit may be dismissed and the petitioner dealt with according to law."[8]

Restell was not going to see her wish honored just yet. Instead of dismissing the case, like prior judges had done, Judge Clarke ordered that the case be turned over to a Mr. Charles Edwards, who would act as referee, investigating the claim on its merits and making a recommendation based on the evidence. The policy of using a referee has its history in English chancery courts. In most cases, judges can hear evidence themselves and they or juries can rule on it; referees were usually used when the evidence was particularly complex. While that was not the case in this suit, it may be that Judge Clarke sought out further investigation only because Neidlinger kept returning with the same complaints and the same suit. Her persistence itself might have been convincing, even though there were large discrepancies in the evidence she presented to the court and that it diverged so dramatically from the evidence presented by Restell and some other witnesses. It is also possible that Clarke was curious about the precise circumstances of the adoption and how it was that Restell could claim she had no knowledge whatsoever of the home of the baby, which was unlikely. Who, for instance, was the mysterious "Mrs. Wright" who acted as intermediary between Restell and the baby's adoptive parents? Adoption was entirely unregulated at this time, but a judge might well have wanted to know how an infant changed hands with no involvement of the law whatsoever. Edwards's explicit charge as referee was that "he report thereon with all convenient speed to whether the said infant was at any time in the possession or under the control of the said defendant [Restell], and whether the said defendant has parted with the custody of the said infant, and if so to whom and under what authority she disposed of the said infant, and if the defendant knows or has any means of knowing in whose custody the said infant is."[9]

It is unclear why it took him so long to conduct his investigation, but in October 1857, Edwards filed a report with the court. He believed that Restell did have the child in August of 1855, at least briefly:

I report in all the purposes of this proceeding that she the said Mary [*sic*] Lohman alias Madame Restell has not parted with said child and that she is answerable and responsible to this court for the same.

Also I certify that she has or has the means of knowing in whose custody the said infant is.

There is no evidence to suggest that Restell kept Neidlinger's child herself, but she probably did know where the child was placed, and she refused to tell Edwards. It was possible that whoever had adopted the baby had represented it as being her own biological child and, in an era before adoption was widespread and socially acceptable, Restell did not want to reveal the woman's identity. Restell's business was built on her discretion. Newspapers regularly intimated that society matrons visited Restell for contraception and abortion, but she would never reveal the identities of her clientele. Even if the adoptive mother of Neidlinger's son was not a known figure—and there is no evidence to indicate she was—if Restell revealed her name, she could become known as someone who revealed *any* client's name, and that was not something she could afford to do.[10]

For all that New Yorkers, including some in the judiciary, were prejudiced against Restell, and even though this was a case that did not actually involve abortion at all, the transfer of an infant child's custody from its biological mother to another unknown person was worthy of investigation, especially if that mother now claimed it had occurred against her will. If Restell had simply been willing to name the new parents, they might have been able to confirm whether they had interacted with Neidlinger at all and whether the child was still alive. These details could have cleared up Restell's legal troubles quite quickly. Her unwillingness to budge meant that the case continued. And the longer it did so, the more the court learned about the circumstances of the adoption, at least as Restell represented them.

The October 1857 report from the referee prompted the court to revisit the case during the winter and spring of 1858. In essence, the court was convinced that either Restell had the child or knew where he was or she had somehow disposed of the child in an illicit manner. Even the possibility that Restell had simply aided Neidlinger in placing the child for adoption did not sit well with the judges:

For it may with some plausibility be affirmed that a Mother, who was willing and even anxious to part with her infant immediately after his birth, must be destitute of that affection, without which, no person is capable of suitably rearing and bringing up a child. As far as the defendant [Restell] is concerned, she cannot avail herself of such an allegation. A child cannot be disposed of or alienated like a chattel. A father, even, cannot contract away the custody of his legitimate children.

In their very most charitable reading of the case, where Restell was just abiding by the wishes of Neidlinger, the court still saw her as taking advantage of Neidlinger's supposed lack of affection for her infant postpartum. The court could not seem to conceive of the real financial and logistical reasons that might bring a new mother to feel forced to part with her infant, nor did the court offer up any reason that Restell benefited from taking advantage of her client. If nothing else, arranging for an adoption would take time; simply allowing Neidlinger to leave her home with her own infant was by far the easier and less complicated route. That said, the court was quite right that there was not yet any legal mechanism in place that would allow even a legal parent or guardian to simply give away a child. A parent might indenture one's child, which was sometimes used as an informal substitute for adoption. The judge's ruling in this case makes mention of New York's habeas corpus statute, by which someone holding another against the latter's will would be commanded to produce that person. The judge wanted to call on Restell to ascertain, in the words of the statute, "whether he [or she] have or have not the party in his custody or power, or under his power or restraint." The court also issued what was called an attachment against Restell, unless, within ten days, she could either produce the child or be able to reveal its whereabouts. In the realm of the law, an attachment was the seizure of property or funds that could be used to ensure payment of a future judgment. While the documents do not say how much would be seized if Restell did not comply, the court was either readying itself to be able to make an award to Neidlinger to compensate her for the loss of her child or attempting to secure Restell's compliance with the judicial proceedings by gaining an attachment of some property.[11]

As a result of this additional order, Restell appeared on May 3, 1858, just barely complying with the court's order that she do so within ten days. In a deposition she signed that day, Restell first "denies that the son of Frederica Neidlinger, the relator in the said writ of habeas corpus named, or any son or any child of the said relator born at respondent's home on the 30th day of August 1855, or born at any other place or time viz or at any time has been, imprisoned or detained in any way restrained of liberty by respondent or by her direction, procurement or consent." She did not have the child nor, she claimed, had she ever had the child, with one exception that she then explained. She admitted that on August 30, 1855, Frederica Neidlinger had given birth to an illegitimate son at Restell's home, attended by Restell in her capacity as a midwife. None of this was news, however. In what came next, however, Restell shed light on the shadowy world of unregulated adoption in antebellum America.[12]

Around the time that Neidlinger came to her home for her confinement, Madame Restell met the woman who wanted a child, "should it appear to be a sound, healthy, well-formed child and the relator [Neidlinger] should still feel inclined to give it away for adoption." According to Restell, "The lady referred to was an entire stranger to respondent [Restell], apparently between 20 and 30 years of age of genteel and pleasing deportment and by her dress + paraphernalia apparently a woman of wealth and she gave as her name + place of residence respondent a name + place, which deponent at the time saw no reason to doubt and did not doubt were the true name and place of residence."[13]

If all of this made some degree of sense, what happened next was somewhat more convoluted. Restell called on the services of two other women following the birth of Neidlinger's son. One was a wet nurse named Rachel Ann Smith. The other was a Mrs. Adeline M. Wright, who acted as a sort of middlewoman between Restell and the adoptive mother. Restell claimed that on the day Neidlinger gave birth, she called on Mrs. Wright to visit Neidlinger in her bedroom and ask her if she "was still desirous to give away said child for adoption." She also conveyed the name and address of the woman who was interested in adopting the child, all using Wright as an intermediary. According to Restell, Neidlinger then wrote down, in a small book in her room, the name and address of the mysterious "lady" who would adopt her child and gave her son to Adeline Wright, fully consenting to the adoption.[14]

At that point, Restell explained that she had arranged for the child to be taken to the wet nurse, who herself had recently lost an infant child, which was what made her capable of commercial wet-nursing. Neidlinger's son would stay there "to be nursed until the aforesaid Lady should take it away as her own by adoption." The next day, Restell met the "lady" at Mrs. Smith's home "at about 11 or 12 o'clock" where the lady "received him kindly + tenderly into her arms from the said Mrs. Smith." Once again, there was nothing particularly unusual about a baby going to a wet nurse if his or her own mother was unable or unwilling to nurse the child. Restell likely had multiple wet nurses on call for precisely this purpose, though nurses were available or un- available depending on whether they were lactating at any given time. The adoptive mother then examined him and "pronounced him well- formed, sound, healthy male child which she was well satisfied to *take* and adopt as her own and promised to call the next morning and re- ceive him." The next morning between 8:00 and 9:00 a.m., everyone returned to Mrs. Smith's, where she was given the child. According to Restell, she and the new mother left Mrs. Smith's together and parted ways on the street, Restell never seeing or hearing from her again. She claimed also to have no knowledge of the baby's whereabouts. Restell then explained that within a month or two she had received a letter telling her the baby had died, but she was skeptical. She believed that the letter was "designed merely to prevent any inquiry" that might lead someone to discover "who was in fact the real mother of said child."[15]

Restell then doubled back on her story to explain that she had gone into the room occupied by Neidlinger shortly after Mrs. Wright had been in the room, and Neidlinger showed Restell the book into which she had recorded the adoptive mother's name and address. Restell claimed that she saw the words in the book but did not understand them because they were written in German, which is unlikely given that German employs the same alphabet as English. Because Neidlinger was now in possession of the name and address of her son's new mother, Restell allowed the information to "pass out of her mind without any effort to retain a recollection of any of the particulars." While she claimed not to remember the name or address, she vaguely recalled that it was not a common name, perhaps of French origin, and that the address was not in New York but in one of the neighboring states. She then explained, as she had done before, that Neidlinger never mentioned the child or his adoptive mother again during the time she continued to work for Restell, or indeed for almost a full year after the birth of the child, except to express "satisfaction that said child had been given away as it was." Restell was here not only reiterating one of her main arguments—that it was suspicious that Neidlinger had waited so long to complain—but also emphasizing as much as possible that Restell herself did not remember the name of the adoptive mother but that Neidlinger herself had *always* known her name and address, and had indeed recorded them in her notebook, making a suit of habeas corpus against Restell particularly absurd. The use of the intermediary, Mrs. Wright, is the one real curiosity in the entire affair, especially because Restell herself had found the adoptive mother and had not needed to rely on Wright as a go-between. Perhaps Restell was using Wright in order to have a witness to Neidlinger's willingness to part with her child, but if that was the case, it remains unclear why Wright was not called during these proceedings.[16]

Restell's statement closed by again stressing that all she had done had been at the behest of Neidlinger and emphasizing that she had already been arrested and appeared before the court and that the charges had been dismissed by Justice Connolly as "groundless and unproven." After that, she reminded the judge that two prior writs of habeas corpus, similar to this one, were dismissed for insufficient proof.

Because the current writ was effectively the same as the prior writs, she asked to have it discharged. With that, Restell signed her name as Ann Lohman. Like prior judges, this one seems to have been convinced, because for the next two and a half years, Restell and Neidlinger stayed out of court. For a time, it seemed as if Mina Neidlinger had given up.[17]

In the interim, however, Restell's fame only increased, as did her wealth. By early 1860, newspapers across the country were running stories whose only purpose seemed to be to note how much money she had. In late February of that year, multiple newspapers printed a story claiming that Restell had recently arrived on a ship in Philadelphia from Havana, Cuba. The story, which called Restell "the Mrs. Herod of America," a reference to the King of Judea's killing of infants, known as the Massacre of the Innocents, mostly focused on her wealth: "By the way, she is rich. She owns blocks and acres of lots and stocks of all kinds. Her income from books and other sources is $21,000 per annum." The story then explained, erroneously, that she had three children (some said grandchildren, also incorrect), who would inherit about $400,000 "when Madame Restell turns up her toes." The story closed by wishing that Restell could simply "retire from active business and live upon her splendid property." In the *Boston Investigator*, the same reprinted story was simply titled "Rich."[18]

While the various newspaper accounts may well have been exaggerating the extent of Restell's wealth, they would have been shocked to learn that Restell and Lohman did have plans for a brand-new residence that would be far more luxurious than the house at 162 Chambers Street. In 1857, Charles Lohman had purchased ten lots on the corner of Fifth Avenue and Fifty-Second Street, lots on which he was planning to build an impressive mansion. Fifth Avenue was still undeveloped at that point, but plans had already been made for Central Park, whose southern border is Fifty-Ninth Street. Other wealthy Manhattanites were also moving uptown, escaping the more commercial areas below Houston Street. The New York diocese of the Catholic Church had also secured the block of Fifth Avenue between Fiftieth and Fifty-

First Streets prior to Lohman's purchase. Work on St. Patrick's Cathedral began in 1858, and rumor had it that the other bidder on the Lohman land was an agent on behalf of Archbishop John Hughes, who was said to want that corner for his official residence. The Lohmans outbid him. When nearby owners found out who had made the purchase, they tried to buy the land from Lohman, not wanting the infamous Madame Restell as their neighbor. Lohman refused the offers. While the general public did not yet know about the future Lohman residence, coverage of Restell's fortune only made her more vulnerable to schemers like Neidlinger, who hoped to extort money from her.

In the midst of all of this, in what seemed a world away, the southern states formed themselves into the Confederate States of America and seceded. The Civil War began on April 12, 1861, with the Confederate attack on Fort Sumter in South Carolina. About a week later, crowds gathered in New York City in support of the Union, and newly elected president Abraham Lincoln called for volunteers from the North to take back captured Fort Sumter. As the war effort geared up, most things in a city like New York, well removed from battle sites, continued normally. Because of this, there is little reason to imagine that much of anything changed for Madame Restell, at least initially. After all, women continued to become pregnant. Indeed, just the day after the Civil War began, and presumably because she felt that the business with Neidlinger was behind her, Restell placed an ad in the *New York Herald*: "Any lady wishing to adopt an infant from its birth; about the first of the month, will hear of an opportunity by applying to Madame Restell, 162 Chambers street." Clearly, Restell was expecting one of her patients to give birth around the first of May.[19]

If Restell believed that Neidlinger's silence in 1859 and 1860 meant she was gone for good, she must have been disappointed when, on October 21, 1861, Neidlinger once again went to court, this time applying for an attachment, claiming that the mode by which Restell had previously responded to requests for her cooperation was not in compliance with the judges' orders and that Restell should also be held in contempt. In essence, Neidlinger's attorney was arguing that Restell *still* had not complied with the court's orders. Judge Leonard, of the Supreme Court of the State of New York, which was sitting in Manhattan, "decided that Madame Restell must present herself to the Court, and must be sworn and examined as to her knowledge of the disposition and whereabouts of the child." He ordered on December 9, 1861, that she appear before him on December 21, about two weeks later. In the previous legal wrangling about Neidlinger's baby, it had almost always been referred to as an infant; if the child had survived, he would now be six years old, a living testament to just how long this case had been dragging on.[20]

On this appearance in court, instead of Restell offering up her own version of the events of the summer of 1855 and then attesting to their veracity, she would be questioned, first by Neidlinger's attorney and later by her own. This testimony would determine whether the motion for an attachment would be granted. For whatever set of reasons, Restell did not appear before the judge until December 31, but the examination did indeed take place. Asked to identify herself, Restell responded: "I am a midwife and ladies physician." Much of the information heard that day in court was not particularly new, but there were some revelations. She explained how she had come to know the woman who was called Mina Neidlinger: "The first time I saw her she told me she expected to be confined in a few weeks and she said I am poor + unprotected, living out to service. The man that is the cause of my difficulty is my cousin working in a coach factory in Harlem but now gone to California." This was the first time anyone had publicly revealed who Mina had claimed was the father.[21]

Restell also recounted how she had come to know the adoptive mother, referred to consistently in her testimony as "the lady." "The first time I saw the lady was I thought about a week or 10 days after Mina came to the home. She called at my house. She asked me if I had one she could adopt and I said I expected one before long, and the mother was so circumstanced that she would like to have it adopted by someone." According to Restell, "she had been married 7 or 8 years +

had no children of her own. She said she would prefer a boy but she would take either." Restell explained that she did not ask "about the business of the husband. I did not make inquiry of any other person respecting the lady. I did not know anyone that was acquainted with her. All the information I had I obtained from the lady herself. She did not give me any references."[22]

Restell also shed light on Neidlinger's state of mind in the days after the birth. She explained, "I also observed 'Mina you have a choice of this.' You can put it to the breast + nurse it; you can put it out to nurse; or adopt it as you proposed. Her answer was 'for the sake of the child, I wish to adopt it.'" By this she meant she wanted to have it adopted. Next, Mrs. Adeline Wright arrived and went to Neidlinger's bedroom. Restell overheard Neidlinger tell Wright that she "would like to have the child called 'George' for one of his names if the lady had no objection." Mrs. Wright observed that she did not think that the lady would object.[23]

The next morning, Restell met the prospective adoptive mother at the wet nurse Mrs. Smith's home, which she explained was also a store. Keeping a store and also working as a wet nurse would not have been uncommon at the time; many in New York's working class worked a variety of jobs to make ends meet. Smith explained that "the babe was sleeping in the cradle in the front room + she would go + bring it. She observed that Mr. Smith, who was a policeman, was sleeping in the room where the baby was, which was the reason she did not take us in the front room." Mr. Smith was likely well aware for whom his wife was nursing babies and that she was doing so for illegitimate children, and yet he did not see enough wrong with either circumstance to arrest Restell or to stop his wife from making money by nursing such babies. All parties agreed that the adoptive mother would return the next day, once she had procured a nurse of her own and bought a wardrobe for the infant.[24]

On the following day, Mrs. Smith gave "the lady" the baby. Restell "left the lady with the child in her arms in Canal St." Among Restell's final answers to the lawyers' questions was the following: "I have stated everything within my knowledge. It is utterly impossible for me to give any further information respecting that child than what I have already stated."[25]

No final judgment was issued until July 21 of the next year; the delay is not explained in the court documents. On that day, however, the Honorable J.W. Clarke, Justice of the Supreme Court of the State of New York, issued his ruling in the case of *Frederica Neidlinger v. Ann Lohman*: "Ordered that the attachment against the Respondent is denied and the suit of Habeas Corpus heretofore issued, is and the same is hereby discharged." After six years, the case was finally over. No doubt Madame Restell and her husband were relieved. If she is to be believed—and evidence and logic both guide us in that direction—this case stands as a testament to how vulnerable Restell had become. Her notoriety and unpopularity meant that a disgruntled former client could bring a specious lawsuit and tie her up in court on and off for a period of six years. It is possible that Neidlinger hoped that Restell would attempt to avoid going to trial repeatedly by simply paying her off, as Restell may have done with Cordelia Grant. If that had been her hope, it was not to be realized. Restell had finally prevailed, and thereafter Frederica "Mina" Neidlinger disappears from the historical record.[26]

During the years after the suit began, Restell was also preoccupied with major upheavals in her family. Restell's daughter, Caroline, already mother to daughter Carrie, had had three additional children. Frances Ann Purdy was born on May 7, 1856 and died three years later on February 1, 1859. Son Charles Robert Purdy was born on August 15, 1859. On December 1, 1860, Caroline gave birth to a fourth child, Florence Annie Purdy. Perhaps even more momentously, Caroline's husband, Isaac Lent Purdy, enlisted in the Union army on August 13, 1862. This was prior to the passage of the Civil War Military Draft Act, meaning that Purdy volunteered to serve his country, leaving his wife and three children behind in Tarrytown, New York. Purdy was not a model soldier. He was court-martialed and fined and spent time in a military prison for drunkenness on duty and carousing with prisoners he was meant to be guarding. The Lohmans had clearly become disillusioned with Purdy even before this incident. In an 1862 version of his will that left an annuity to Caroline Purdy, Charles Lohman specified that no part of the annuity could be used "for the support of her husband in idleness and intemperance." As a result of Isaac's extended absence at war, Caroline sold the house in Tarrytown in 1863 and with her three children moved in with her mother and stepfather in New York. Then in May of that year, little Florence Purdy also passed away. The Lohmans erected a large marble obelisk containing a carving of a sleeping baby to commemorate both Frances and Florence at the Sleepy Hollow Cemetery near Tarrytown, where the Purdys had lived and where Isaac's family still resided.[27]

In May of 1864, Isaac Purdy's regiment was ordered to the front to serve as infantry and met up with General Ulysses S. Grant's army near Spotsylvania, Virginia. The next month the Seventh Regiment was one of many engaged in the four-day Battle of Petersburg, Grant's failed attempt to capture one of the key sites of Confederate communications and supplies. Purdy went missing on June 16, 1864. Approximately 104,000 troops fought during the battle that lasted from June 15 to June 18, and of those, 11,386 lost their lives. Purdy survived the battle, but his wife and children knew nothing of his fate for months. He was being held at the prison camp in Andersonville, Georgia. Isaac Lent Purdy died on November 15, 1864, in Andersonville. His enlistment card enumerates the cause of death simply as "disease." Andersonville was massively overcrowded, housing about four times its actual capacity. Nearly 13,000 died there of diarrhea, dysentery, and scurvy. In part because of the appalling mortality rate, but also because of his own personal cruelty toward prisoners, the man in charge of Andersonville, Henry Wirz, was tried, convicted, and executed for war crimes in November of 1865. It was a truly terrible place to be imprisoned and had Purdy been housed elsewhere, it is quite likely he would have survived and returned to his family in New York. Instead, Caroline Summers Purdy was now a widow with two young children.[28]

Meanwhile, in 1861, the house located beside the Lohmans' home and Restell's business on Chambers Street went up for sale. The city of New York bought it for $20,000 with the object of turning it into the police station for the Third Precinct, which was to be located directly beside Madame Restell's place of business. The Lohmans broke ground for their new home on Fifth Avenue the very next year. Though it is impossible to know whether the arrival of the police hastened their construction project, clearly there was now some pressure to exit the residence at 162 Chambers Street as soon as possible. While Restell's business as a midwife was perfectly legal, much of the rest of her operation was in direct defiance of the law that her new neighbors were charged with enforcing. Add to this that her clients might be increasingly leery of visiting Restell's offices if they knew they might be spotted by the police.[29]

For two more years, however, the Lohmans lived beside the police station, which gave them plenty of time to interact with their new neighbors. Some of that interaction apparently turned romantic, because on September 11, 1865, less than a year after the death of her husband, Caroline Summers Purdy married William Farrell, an Irish police officer in the Third Precinct. By most accounts, this did not please Madame Restell, who had worked hard to raise her family from the poverty she had first experienced as a single mother on the Lower East Side. Now the Lohmans were planning a move uptown to a colossal Fifth Avenue mansion, and Caroline had married an Irish immigrant who was five years her junior. He was also a policeman, and Restell obviously had a vexed relationship with the police. That Caroline had married one of them was no doubt seen as a betrayal of her mother. The Irish in 1860s New York City were likely to be poor. Many had arrived during the potato famine of the 1840s, and Farrell's profession did not pay well. Caroline had chosen a working-class life at a moment when her mother was prepared to offer her so much more than that. The 1870 census lists the sum total of the Farrells' personal effects at $1,500 and shows that they rented, and did not own, their apartment. Furthermore, Farrell, by virtue of being Irish, was likely to be Catholic, though Purdy and Farrell were married in St. John's Episcopal Church, and it would not be surprising if Restell disapproved of his religion.[30]

The marriage caused a rift in the relationship between Caroline and her mother that was never fully repaired. For the first few years follow-

Charles R. Lohman residence, 657 Fifth Avenue, New York City, undated. The home and staircase fronted Fifth Avenue, while Restell's office was in the basement of the building on Fifty-Second Street. The Lohmans also owned the adjoining lots on Fifth Avenue and stables on Fifty-Second Street. Color lithograph by Hatch and Company, geographic images file, PR 020, New-York Historical Society, 100059d.

ing their marriage, the Farrells lived in a variety of apartments within about half a mile of the police station. While Caroline's son, Charles, lived with his mother and stepfather, her daughter, Carrie, moved with her grandparents uptown to the house on Fifth Avenue. She was then ten years old and would never live with her mother again.[31]

Before the Lohmans moved into their new residence, it was already garnering attention for just how large and luxurious it was. Some newspapers estimated the cost of construction at $165,000, about $2.5 million in today's dollars. As the *New York News* wrote, rumors abounded about who might occupy the "rather unique edifice" on the corner of Fifth Avenue and Fifty-Second Street. "By some it has been represented as the future residence of a foreign count, or possibly of a prince of the blood royal." The real owner, however, was "Dr. Lohman, husband of Madame Restell, the well-known female physician of this city." The *News* believed that the house, once completed, which the paper estimated would be on the first of June, "promises to be unsurpassed in elegance by any private residence in this city." While some headlines covering the story were relatively innocuous, others tied Restell's fortune directly to her work, which they indicted: "The Wages and Work of Sin—Palatial Residence of Madame Restell, the Abortionist" and "A Palace of Blood." The house was destined to become a symbol of what many saw as Restell's flagrant violation of societal norms.[32]

While the house was being constructed and in the early days of the Lohmans' occupancy of the residence, reporters mostly just observed the outside of the dwelling. It was five stories of brown stone, occupying about fifty feet of Fifth Avenue. "The portico is formed of graceful Corinthian columns upon which rests a heavy and uniquely ornamented spandrill, and the windows have that peculiar form, appearance, or (shall we say?) expression which makes them seem like deep-set gracefully shaded eyes." The *New York Evening Express* went on to compliment the "general good taste of the edifice," noting that "the general merit of the building is its almost absolute combination of beauty, simplicity, and boldness."[33]

Not all depictions were so complimentary. Especially after the Lohmans moved in and people started visiting the residence, criticism generally coalesced around the Lohmans' taste in furniture and decoration, which some considered to be extravagant, a reflection of their status as nouveaux riches. The Lohmans were tacky, in other words. They might live *on* Fifth Avenue, but they were not *of* Fifth Avenue the way their neighbors were. Given that Fifth Avenue was itself only recently settled by New Yorkers, meaning that all the houses were newly constructed and most were extravagant, this was a challenging criticism to pull off successfully. But really, observers who mocked the Lohmans simply did not approve of how they became wealthy, contrasted with the generational wealth of some of their neighbors and the other forms of business in which they were engaged. In his 1870 *Women of New York*, in a chapter called the "Wickedest Woman in New York," author George Ellington allowed that the house was "one of the finest on the avenue" but also explained that "shades of a most gaudy, though very vulgar, pattern, are at the windows. No other house in Fifth avenue or in New York possesses such shades, or, indeed, would any one else in the city want to."[34]

According to Ellington, on the first floor were a "grand hall of tessellated marble, lined with mirrors," three "immense dining rooms, furnished in bronze and gold, with yellow satin hangings," more parlors and reception rooms, and a butler's pantry. On the floor above were more parlors, a guest chamber, the bedrooms of Restell, Lohman, and Carrie Purdy, a "news room," and a study. Each bedroom had its own "boudoir for dressing." The third floor was occupied by servants and the fourth floor had "a magnificent billiard-room, dancing-hall, with pictures, piano, etc., and . . . a fine view of Fifth avenue." In the basement, with an entrance on Fifty-Second Street, was Madame Restell's office. The whole house was "filled with statuettes, paintings, rare bronzes, ornamental and valuable clocks, candelabras, silver globes and articles of *vertu*, chosen with unexceptionable taste." Reasonable people might disagree about whether the home was tasteful, but everyone could see that it was enormous and expensive. The 1870 census estimated the value of this real estate (they owned the lots next door as well) at $200,000. Restell could be seen regularly in her carriage in both summer and winter: "In winter she drives in tandem, with large ermine sleigh-robes. On every afternoon in summer she may be seen out alone driving in the Central Park. Her carriage is noted for its extraordinary showiness."[35]

All the attention Restell garnered, because of her profession and her lavish spending on the Fifth Avenue mansion, would ultimately prove her downfall when a mysterious figure visited her in that mansion's basement office. But not before New York City was roiled with a series of shocking deaths by Restell's less skilled competitors, and the city's doctors joined together to try to put them out of business once and for all.

10

DOCTORS AGAINST
DOCTORS

In 1860, Madame Costello published a book. She called it *A Female Physician to the Ladies of the United States: Being a Familiar and Practical Treatise on Matters of Utmost Importance Peculiar to Women*. She published it under her married name, Mrs. W.H. Maxwell, to which she appended "M.D.," though no evidence exists to indicate that Catharine Maxwell had ever earned such a degree. In 1860, only a handful of women had done so. The title page of the book noted that she was a "Physician of 30 Years' Practice" and included the helpful aphorism "Experience is the best Teacher." The introduction situates her expertise firmly in that experience: "After a woman's experience of three score years, and a medical practice of thirty, she can surely claim something more of knowledge than ordinarily falls to the lot of female or other physicians.... Only a woman can know what woman has suffered, or is suffering." She continued,

> The female physician must necessarily possess sources of knowledge denied and inaccessible to the most studious and skillful man.... The amount of relief, and above all, the mental ease a woman can give another in sickness, where implicit confidence exists, are so great as to merit a thorough discussion, and the importance of the obvious aid so bestowed, will in all cases serve to establish the (to the writer, at least,) self-evident truth, that in the majority of diseases peculiar to women, no one but a woman educated in medicine, is the proper physician.[1]

Maxwell self-published this otherwise unremarkable volume, which was similar in content to many others available at the time. It was unlikely that it ever reached a particularly large audience. Most noteworthy about the book is that it is an almost perfect encapsulation of everything that formally trained medical doctors objected to about female physicians. Not only was Maxwell lying about her qualifications (claiming an MD she did not have), at every turn she claimed that her experience and her femaleness trumped any formal training that any male doctor might have, no matter how exclusive and extensive his education. By 1860, when Maxwell published this book, the war between the "regular" physicians—men with MDs—and the likes of Maxwell, Madame Restell, and countless others who had joined the ranks of what were called "irregulars" was approaching its apex. The fight over abortion was one of the ways regular physicians sought to drive the irregulars out of business. In some ways, legal abortion was the casualty of a fight that was really about money, prestige, and professional recognition. By further criminalizing abortion, doctors could drive their competition out of business and lay claim to both the medical market and the professional status they believed their education had earned them. But one could imagine a campaign in which male doctors simply tried to push their competition out of business, leaving male doctors free to perform abortions and provide all other medical care as well. There was certainly money to be had in such a practice, as the fortunes of female physicians like Madame Restell made amply clear.

The regulars did not choose this route. There was something particular about abortion that enraged them enough to insist on the further criminalization of a procedure that was already illegal and until the 1820s had been largely unremarkable for centuries. One of the objections was that women were suffering at the hands of unskilled practitioners as more irregular doctors entered the business. But this was not the whole story. Today, most arguments against abortion center on the fetus and debates about the beginning of life—and some doctors did advance such arguments in the antebellum period as well—but this was not the primary focus at the time. Instead, they were clearly resentful of those like Restell and Maxwell, whom they perceived to be interlopers in a field they had been promised would be theirs alone. Successful professional women were threatening, both symbolically and also monetarily, especially to those men who had trained in the relatively new field of obstetrics and gynecology.

Even more significant, however, was the perception of the women who were choosing to terminate their pregnancies, women who were purposefully limiting their families and who had the means to seek out the medical services they desired, even when their male doctors recommended against those services. Reacting to the perceived threat from irregulars and to the middle- and upper-class women who sought their services, between the 1850s and the 1870s, formally trained doctors banded together to criminalize abortion across the nation, no matter the stage of the pregnancy or the needs of pregnant women. No one was more responsible for this legislative coup than Horatio Robinson Storer, MD, and the American Medical Association.[2]

* * * *

When the American Medical Association (AMA) was founded in 1847, its members came together to represent the interests of doctors with formal training, to insist that scientific medicine was superior to a wide variety of other traditions, including eclecticism, Thomsonianism, hydropathy, homeopathy, and female midwifery. An MD was a requirement for membership, the AMA in essence closing ranks around who laid claim to the title of "doctor" or "physician." The regulation of abortion was by no means the only issue about which the AMA cared, but abortion had for at least a decade already been associated in the public consciousness with those who practiced medicine without formal education, in large part because of the commercialization of midwifery, lying-in hospitals, and the other services offered by female physicians who had no access to medical schools.[3]

Some doctors from the 1830s through the early 1850s had already opposed abortion, even going so far as to influence their legislators, who passed increasingly restrictive legislation in some states, including New York. But there was no unified medical opinion on the practice until the AMA was formed, no other organization that purported to speak on behalf of learned medical men. Horatio Robinson Storer led the efforts of the AMA regarding abortion. Storer was born in Boston on February 27, 1830, and was the son of Dr. D. Humphreys Storer, who lectured on obstetrics and medical jurisprudence at Harvard University. Storer obtained his medical degree in 1853, also at Harvard, and soon set his sights on the question of abortion. Among his first steps was an 1857 letter to influential doctors across the United States, asking them about the legal status of abortion where they lived, in essence taking the temperature of his fellow doctors at the same time that he was priming them for a fight. Dr. Thomas Blatchford of Troy, New York, responded to Storer:

> I am glad, right glad, you have got hold of the subject of criminal abortion—a crime which 40 years ago, when I was a young practitioner, was of *rare* and *secret* occurrence has become *frequent* and *bold*. It is high time it was taken hold of in good earnest, but you will find its roots deep and its branches very spreading. It is so here[,] our enactments to the contrary notwithstanding. . . . Don[']t let it go until you have made your exertions tell on [the] community.

Blatchford was among many physicians to respond to Storer expressing their opposition to the practice of abortion. Storer's goal in soliciting these responses was to assemble enough evidence from varied states to press the AMA into taking a formal position on the practice, which could then be utilized to pressure state governments into legal reform, further criminalizing abortion.[4]

In May of 1857 Storer also brought a resolution to Boston's Suffolk District Medical Society, asking his colleagues "that a Committee be appointed to consider whether any further legislation is necessary in this Commonwealth [Massachusetts], on the subject of *criminal abortion*, and to report to the Society such other means as may be necessary

Horatio Robinson Storer led the campaign to outlaw abortion on behalf of the American Medical Association. This image, dating from later in his life, was featured in a *Biographical Sketch of Dr. Horatio R. Storer*. Courtesy of the National Library of Medicine.

for the suppression of this abominable, unnatural, and yet common crime." At the suggestion of another attendee, Storer amended his resolution to stipulate that any report produced by the committee would then be forwarded to the Massachusetts Medical Society "as a basis for its further action." The report, which Storer's committee produced with some alacrity by late May, met with resistance, some physicians arguing that it did not take into consideration the necessity of abortion for saving some potential mothers' lives, among other things. As the *Boston Medical and Surgical Journal* explained: "The writer of it seems to have thrown out of consideration the life of the mother, making that of the unborn child appear of far more consequence, even should the mother have a dozen dependent on her for their daily bread." Early on in this debate among MDs there was disagreement about abortion and its necessity, not just for saving the life of the mother but for acknowledging circumstances like family limitation. And of course, some MDs themselves performed abortions with regularity. These men also clearly disagreed with the likes of Storer, even if they were in the minority.[5]

The Boston-based criticism of the initial report actually worked in Storer's favor, igniting a firestorm of defense of the report up and down the Eastern Seaboard in various medical journals. Storer had been correct in assessing his fellow doctors in advance, having accurately gauged their opposition to abortion. While a committee of men was appointed to make the case at the Massachusetts Medical Society, Storer took his crusade to the organization he had always planned on: the AMA. At the May 1857 meeting of the special committee "on criminal abortion, with a view to its general suppression," which was led by Storer, the committee voted to constitute yet another committee to issue a report on the subject. Storer would lead that group. He also began drumming up support from prominent doctors and medical societies across the country.[6]

In May of 1859, when the AMA met in Louisville for their twelfth annual meeting, they endorsed Storer's report, which outlined his and his fellow committee members' beliefs about abortion. They claimed that abortion had become widespread because of a general demoralization in society and blamed three factors in particular. First, they cited the "belief, even among mothers themselves, that the foetus is not alive till after the period of quickening." Second, they believed that some of their medical colleagues themselves might be ignorant of fetal life, that they might "omit precautions or measures that might prevent the occurrence of so unfortunate an event." Third, they blamed laws that they claimed were based "upon mistaken and exploded medical dogmas." Here they referred implicitly to the quickening doctrine, under which most state statutes (and the common law as well) had always differentiated between a pregnancy terminated before or after the moment when a woman first felt fetal movement. They vowed to do all in their power to outlaw abortion. As they put it, "We are the physical guardians of women; we, alone, thus far, of their offspring in utero. The case is here of life or death—the life or death of thousands—and it depends, almost wholly, upon ourselves. As a profession we are unanimous in our condemnation of the crime. Mere resolutions to this effect, and nothing more, are therefore useless, evasive, and cruel." The language here is noteworthy: only formally trained doctors, they claimed, which at that time was almost exclusively men, knew what was best for women.[7]

Because "mere resolutions" were not enough, the AMA vowed to work with state legislatures to pass more restrictive legislation banning the procedure. They noted particularly that the evidence for why abortion should be made criminal was "especially of a medical nature," and because it was their duty as doctors to correct any past medical doctrine that countenanced abortion, they resolved to "present this subject to the attention of the several legislative assemblies of the Union, with the prayer that the laws by which the crime of procuring abortion is attempted to be controlled may be revised." They also requested the "zealous co-operation of the various State Medical Societies" in lobbying their respective state legislatures.[8]

This was the beginning of the coordinated effort by doctors to outlaw abortion across the nation, including in New York State, where Madame Restell and many other female physicians continued to practice. The AMA was relatively clear in its evaluation of why abortion was wrong—life begins at conception, not quickening—and in its belief that widespread abortion was, in its words, "the slaughter of countless children," the AMA eliding the difference between a child and a fetus. It is possible, of course, that after centuries of Americans ignoring abortion, doctors had suddenly come to their senses, imbued with new medical knowledge that made it possible to understand abortion differently from the way past generations had. Except there was no new knowledge. It was not like doctors now understood pregnancies to be nine months in duration, when previously they had believed them to last only six. There was little new knowledge about pregnancy, but there were new practitioners.

Within the AMA, the doctors most responsible for the campaign against abortion were specialists in the relatively new field of obstetrics and gynecology. These were men who had every incentive to insist that they, and they alone, were experts on pregnancy and women's bodies. Gynecology was still very much associated with women, not just for the obvious reason that it was a specialty *in* women and their bodies, but also because it was work that had been done for centuries *by* women, in the form of midwives. One way of asserting medical expertise in gynecology was an explicit rejection of prior medical knowledge like the quickening doctrine, which doctors cast as ill-informed and now replaced with their more specialized approach. Neither medical interpretation was necessarily correct or incorrect, but the rejection of thousands of years of medical belief at this precise moment makes sense in the context of the growth of the field of gynecology as a specialty within formal medical education.[9]

A change in attitudes toward abortion also owes something to the changing landscape of gender, marriage, and reproduction in antebellum cities, to which the report also alludes, and which attitudes toward Madame Restell and her colleagues have already attested. Storer's AMA report first noted that abortion was practiced with great frequency, "among all classes of society, rich and poor, single and married." This claim was demonstrable because the "rates of increase," or birth rate, were declining. Storer was correct about this; among the white middle classes of the Northeast, the birth rate essentially halved over the course of the nineteenth century. Abortion, contraception, delayed first marriage, and abstinence were the means by which American women had achieved family limitation. They did so sometimes with the deliberate assistance of their husbands, who were primarily charged with supporting however many children a family produced. As more and more Americans moved to cities and towns over the course of the nineteenth century, leaving behind rural farming lives, they opted to have fewer children because offspring were more of a financial liability in the city. As the middle class developed over the same period, families were better able to afford the perquisites of a middle-class existence if they had fewer children to feed, clothe, and, sometimes, educate. Poor and immigrant families did not practice family limitation in the same ways the middle class did, not only because many were unable to afford abortion or contraception but also because they continued to rely on their children's labor both within and outside their homes. While almost all American families decreased in size, on average, by the twentieth century, initially during the nineteenth century this shrinkage was a middle- and upper-class phenomenon.[10]

And this had many native-born white Americans worried, some of them the very doctors who advocated for an end to abortion. They bemoaned the fact that respectable white married ladies, the very people who should be producing the next generation of upstanding American citizens, were reneging on their duties in favor of family limitation. If they had fewer children, while the poor and immigrants continued to have such large families, would old-stock Americans eventually be outnumbered, even replaced altogether? And what of the fate of the republic if such a thing should happen? Thus, for some the debate about abortion was essentially one of Anglo nationalism. This nativist argument was most fully developed in the 1860s and 1870s, just as immigration to the United States from southern Europe itself also increased. In a lecture to the American Academy of Arts and Sciences in 1858, Storer himself made the connection that the "increase of the population, or the excess of the births over the deaths, has been *wholly* of those of *recent foreign origin*." He also noted of his home state of Massachusetts that "the immense proportion of living births in the foreign as compared with the native and protestant population . . . is to be explained by the watchful protection exercised by the Catholic church over foetal life." In *Woman's Great Crime!*, J.T. Cook beseeched women to "stop murdering their children, and stop trying to defeat nature in *any* way, so that our American homes may again become populous with incipient citizens and voters, and incipient mothers of citizens and voters, and so that the American family shall not become an extinct institution in this country." Similarly, in his

1867 AMA prize–winning *Why Not? A Book for Every Woman*, which was designed to convince women not to terminate their pregnancies, Storer contemplated the fate of the nation, particularly the land opened in the South and the West in the wake of the Civil War:

> All the fruitfulness of the present generation, tasked to its utmost, can hardly fill the gaps that have of late been made by disease and the sword, while the great territories of the far West, just opening to civilization, and the fertile savannas of the South, now disinthralled [*sic*] and first made habitable by freemen, offer homes for countless millions yet unborn. Shall they be filled by our children or by those of aliens? This is a question that our women must answer; upon their loins depends the future of destiny of the nation.

Nothing less than the civilization and future whiteness of the United States of America rested on Anglo-Saxon women being barred from terminating their pregnancies and fulfilling their duty to their nation.[11]

If racial degeneration and a nation overrun with immigrant children were supposedly the consequences of too much abortion, why, in the eyes of its critics, was it so popular? According to doctors, as well as many other commentators, married women's laziness was to blame. Earlier Americans had generally tolerated abortion in part because they believed that single women were resorting to it, and they were doing so to cover an actual sin: sex outside of wedlock. As one doctor explained of an earlier era, "Formerly it was almost exclusively adopted to rid of the encumbrance and shame of illicit intercourse; it was considered as the natural result of such carnal indulgence." This doctor was not countenancing the decision to abort, but he was explaining why there may have been tolerance for it. By the 1850s, by contrast, both the declining birth rate and the inquiries of married ladies to their doctors made it abundantly clear that it was not just single women who were terminating their pregnancies. For wives, abortion was clearly a proven strategy for family limitation; critics railed against their supposed motivations for choosing to have smaller families.[12]

Dr. Hugh Hodge, for instance, explained to his medical students that "married women also, from the fear of labor, from indisposition to have the care, the expense, or the trouble of children, or some motive equally trifling and degrading, have solicited that the embryo be destroyed by their medical attendant." Dismissing out of hand the exceedingly real dangers of carrying a pregnancy to term, Hodge cast women's other reasons for choosing to terminate a pregnancy as frivolous or "trifling." An 1866 editorial from Philadelphia in the *Medical and Surgical Reporter* explained that "the *inconvenience* of having children" was the cause: "There is no plea of inability to raise children on account of poverty, but in the great majority of cases, the simple desire not to be bothered by babies, and not to be prevented by fulfilling maternal destiny, from running about town, visiting friends, dressing finely, and attending parties, theatres, balls and the like, is the only reason given for these abominable deeds. This is certainly carrying the law of convenience as far as the devil would wish." Though not a doctor, the Reverend John Todd's 1867 "Fashionable Murder" made it clear that he was writing at the urging of doctors like Horatio Storer. He decried the tendency among Protestants to terminate pregnancies and then also noted that "it is the testimony, too, of those who know, that in proportion as people become indolent, or fashionable, the temptation to produce abortion is increased; that in many circles it is absolutely a matter of boasting and vanity to tell the number of times they and their friends have been guilty of the deed." Perhaps no explanation for the rise of abortion is more misogynist than this one. Doctors who dismissed the dangers of pregnancy and childbirth as trifling also paid little attention to the duties of mothering itself, which obviously increased with the number of children one had.[13]

Another issue doctors found vexing was that some of the married, middle-class female patients who came to them and asked them to terminate their pregnancies as if it were only a minor matter, when refused abortions, ignored the doctors' advice and sought treatment elsewhere. Women, who themselves had no medical training of their own, simply turned their backs on trained professionals with medical degrees and took their business away, either to another MD with a different position on abortion or, more likely, to a female physician or other irregular who was more than happy to provide an abortion. Dr. Andrew Nebinger spoke to his colleagues at length in 1860 about what to do when they are waited on "by married ladies, and invited to bring them treatment to bring them regular, because they have missed their flow." He believed it was incumbent on doctors to instruct women on the true nature of the embryo. "If, after being properly instructed, they still persevere in importuning us, do we inform them that they are not only inviting us to step far, far down from our high positions as physicians, but that they are offering an indignity to our manhood?" Nebinger believed his own manhood was threatened by abortion. As Dr. Montrose Pallen explained to his colleagues at the Missouri State Medical Association (and later reprinted in *Medical Archives*):

> Married women . . . have solicited that the embryo should be destroyed by their medical attendant, and when such individuals are informed of the nature of the transaction, there is an expression of real or pretended surprise, that any one of them should deem the act improper, much more guilty; yea, in spite of the solemn warning of the physician, they will resort to the debased and murderous charlatan, who for a piece of silver, will annihilate the life of the foetus and endanger even that of its ignorant and guilty mother.

Pallen here certainly indicted the abortion provider, but he seemed particularly offended that the pregnant woman would ignore the warning of her learned physician and that she had options once she had done so, that she would turn to someone willing to perform the procedure even when her doctor was not.[14]

Doctors also advanced many arguments about the supposed harms of abortion, ranging from the patently false to the deeply paternalistic. It was true, of course, that an abortion performed by an unskilled practitioner could be deadly, but doctors went much further, greatly exaggerating the dangers of abortion, especially when compared with childbirth. Horatio Storer explained that abortion was "often a thousand fold more dangerous" than carrying a pregnancy to term. This was not just false, it was absurd. Some went so far as to say that abortion was almost always fatal. They claimed that after terminating a pregnancy, women were invariably scarred mentally or would meet with future medical dangers like cancer: "A very large proportion of women become invalids, perhaps for life." Storer said that some of these diseases remained "latent for many years, at times not showing themselves until the so-called turn of life [menopause], and then giving rise to uncontrollable and fatal hemorrhage, or to the development of cancer, or other incurable disease." Insanity was also a likely outcome, according to doctors. One state lunatic asylum superintendent claimed that he had "treated patients whose insanity was directly traceable to this crime, through its moral and physical effects." Doctors were perfectly forthcoming about *why* all these things happened to women, in their estimation: they had refused their duty in life, which was motherhood. In terminating a pregnancy, women had run counter to what God and nature had intended for them. The consequences were only to be expected. In *Why Not?*, Storer summarized this view: it was "the holiest duty of her sex to bring forth living children." Any woman who turned her back on that duty risked no longer being a woman at all.[15]

If all these arguments were compelling to Americans at midcentury, it was largely thanks to the increased emphasis on middle-class women's role as mothers and the new valuation on the individuality of middle-class white children. It is no small irony, of course, that abortion was one of the ways American families managed to have fewer children, which led them to value those children differently, which in turn made the specter of "child murder" such a persuasive argument against abortion itself. That is, abortion itself was partially responsible for being able to leverage these arguments against abortion.[16]

All this operated at a level beneath the surface, however, and is visible to us in hindsight in a way that might not have been apparent to nineteenth-century Americans. More obvious was the language that doctors, and the AMA particularly, used to describe female physicians themselves, much of which was not terribly dissimilar from that which newspapermen like George Washington Dixon had used in the 1830s and 1840s. Collectively, they all emphasized how evil female physicians were, how much they took advantage of their patients, and how in helping to terminate pregnancies they had also unsexed themselves. One medical journal referred to female physicians as "those fiends in human shape who practice their iniquitous trade to so large an extent in our city."[17]

In his 1860 *On Criminal Abortion in America*, Storer found that nurses, midwives, and female physicians were likely responsible for most cases of criminal abortion, though he also blamed the mothers themselves and their female friends for influencing them into termination. Of midwives and female physicians, he complained, "These make it their claim, in rivalry of the male physician, that their schools and their practices are, like his, founded on those abroad, especially of Paris." He could well have been writing of Madame Restell in this instance, and of her fictionalized midwife grandmother. Another contributor to the *Medical and Surgical Reporter* referred to female physicians as "loafing pretenders" and "vile imposters." Montrose Pallen specifically objected to the way "abortionists" advertised as having trained in medicine. He exhorted his fellow physicians to unite, to "strenuously act to manufacture a public opinion," to arrest those who performed abortion, and to "shame any decent editor into an absolute refusal to publish the vulgar, obscene, and criminal advertisements, which are constantly printed under the head of 'MEDICAL' in flaming capitals in most of our secular and some of our religious papers." It should come as no surprise that it irked MDs that some female physicians claimed expertise when medical men insisted that their formal training is what set them apart.[18]

The AMA's lobbying paid off across the country, and in New York State in particular. In 1869, New York's legislature passed a new abortion statute that repealed and replaced the 1845 statute. The prior year they had also passed a separate new statute that criminalized the selling or giving away of any "obscene and indecent" articles, which included any "article or medicine for the prevention of conception or procuring of abortion." The punishment was up to a year in county jail and a fine of up to $1,000, one-third of which was to be awarded to whoever had informed on the alleged offender. This statute presaged the federal statute that would come five years later under Anthony Comstock.[19]

The 1869 statute, by contrast, focused squarely on the practice of abortion. Passed on May 6, this statute applied to anyone who prescribed or procured or administered anything to terminate a pregnancy. If the abortion was successful—notably described as "the death of such child"—or if the woman receiving the abortion should die, the person was guilty of manslaughter in the second degree; that part was unchanged from 1845. It further stipulated that anyone who procured "any medicine, drug, substance or any thing whatever" that was intended to bring on a miscarriage "of any woman, whether she be or be not pregnant" was guilty of a misdemeanor, punishable by between three months and a year in jail and a fine of up to $1,000. In other words, while the 1868 statute had criminalized *selling* an abortifacient, this statute declared that simply *purchasing* an abortifacient was now a crime, regardless of whether it was used and irrespective of whether a woman who used it was even pregnant in the first place. It further stipulated that any person violating either part of this statute could be compelled to testify against a co-conspirator in breaking the law and their testimony would not be used against them at trial. The legislature was both widening the net in terms of who they believed was complicit in the crime of abortion while also recognizing how difficult it was to successfully prosecute these cases because all parties involved in the selling, buying, procuring, administering, and receiving of an abortifacient or abortion had no interest whatsoever in revealing themselves.[20]

From the 1850s onward, Madame Restell and her colleagues operated in an environment of increasing hostility, their livelihoods and liberty at stake as formally trained doctors set their sights on running them out of business and putting them behind bars. And yet, even though Restell and her colleagues did not usually hesitate to respond when they felt they were being persecuted, on this issue female physicians remained largely silent. As women, they had no formal representation in the legislative process; they could not vote. More importantly, it was just too dangerous for them to come forward and publicly defend a practice that was already illegal no matter when it occurred in a pregnancy, because it would be perceived, accurately, as an admission that they were regularly breaking the law. The women who sought out female physicians' reproductive services were similarly silent on the issue, at least in the public sphere, not wishing to admit to the importance of abortion to their own bodily autonomy.

If practitioners like Madame Restell and Madame Costello thought that the 1869 statute might be the last word on their practice, they would have been disappointed. In the late 1860s and early 1870s, a series of scandals brought renewed attention to the illegal abortion trade. These stories also played neatly into the AMA's agenda to criminalize abortion, equating abortion with danger and death, even though the vast majority of abortions never came to light precisely because they were completed successfully.[21]

In November of 1870, Dr. Thomas Lookup Evans, sometimes known as Dr. Walter Power, was arrested after the death of one Mary Geary. Evans, who operated a lying-in hospital at 94 Chatham Street and claimed to have been educated at the University of Edinburgh, sounds suspiciously like William Evans, to whom Madame Restell was apprenticed in the 1830s. Either way, in this instance, Geary died of puerperal fever following childbirth at Evans's lying-in hospital and residence. The jury only censured Evans, finding him guilty of malpractice, but certainly no greater crime. In the wake of that trial, however, one Ann O'Neill came forward and testified that he had both sold her an abortifacient and attempted to perform an abortion on her person. Neither had been successful and she gave birth to twins at Bellevue Hospital, both of whom died. Evans was once again put on trial in the spring of 1871, and this time, given that a complaining witness was able to testify, he was found guilty of assault on the person of O'Neill with the intent to commit manslaughter in the second degree. In imposing his sentence, the judge told Evans,

> I believe you to be the most consummate villain ever convicted in any court of justice. You are a professional abortionist. You have lived, thrived and prospered in your wicked career and have accumulated by reason of your dark undertakings an immense fortune. Let your conviction be a stern lesson to the many professional abortionists of this city, for on conviction they will learn that neither their ill-gotten wealth nor their alleged great influence will be of any avail when tried in this court room.

Evans was sentenced to three years and six months in the state prison, the maximum allowable by law, because in this instance Evans had actually been unsuccessful in his attempt to produce an abortion. What is strange about the two Evans cases is that neither of them stemmed from a successful abortion. One patient died of a very common infection following childbirth. Evans was clearly targeted because he was also known to perform abortions in his lying-in hospital. In the second case, Dr. Evans did not actually succeed in terminating her pregnancy, perhaps demonstrating his lack of skill. But so heated had the abortion debate become in New York City and given the new 1869 law that targeted even attempted abortion, he was easily found guilty.[22]

In August of 1871, the *New York Times* published a multipart exposé about the abortion trade in New York City called "The Evil of the Age"; the subtitle was "Slaughter of the Innocents." It created a minor sensation at the time and parts of it were reprinted in other newspapers. The author, Augustus St. Clair, had visited the offices of multiple female and male physicians who provided abortions and sold various forms of contraception and abortifacients. Picking up on arguments promulgated by the AMA, he noted that "the men and women who are engaged in this outrageous business are, with few exceptions, the worst class of impostors. Very few have genuine medical diplomas."

He noted the recently settled Evans case and then told of visits to a variety of establishments, including that of Dr. A.M. Mauriceau, described as "of comely exterior, about fifty years of age, and of bland and courteous manner.... More like a benevolent Samaritan than a designing adventurer." Mauriceau told him that he could certainly "relieve a lady of a physical difficulty" but would need to see the lady in question first. Next St. Clair reported that a man and woman had called on Madame Restell at her office at Fifty-Second Street and Fifth Avenue with the same query: Could she relieve a lady of a physical difficulty? Restell at first told them that it would be no problem, but upon quick consultation with someone else in the office, returned to the pair, explaining, "I can sell you some pills, but really we do no other business. We have had so much trouble about these matters we don't take any more risks." The article also detailed visits to Dr. and Madame Grindle, a Dr. Selden, and a Dr. Ascher, "alias Rosenzweig," of South Fifth Avenue, "who claims to be a Russian, but his voice has the twang of a German Jew."[23]

Not three days later, a baggage master discovered the body of Alice Bowlsby, a beautiful, middle-class young white woman, stuffed in a trunk in the Hudson River Railroad Depot. She had died of peritonitis following an abortion. The trunk was eventually identified as belonging to Jacob Rosenzweig. A handkerchief belonging to Bowlsby was found at Rosenzweig's home, and he was arrested, tried, and found guilty of manslaughter and sentenced to seven years' hard labor. Then, in September and October of 1871, a court in Brooklyn heard a case against one Madame Mary Van Buskirk, female physician, and a Dr. Benjamin Perry, both of whom were charged with manslaughter in the death of Emily Post and her unborn child. Newspapers in New York gave extensive coverage to the trial. As the demand for abortion grew, so did the ranks of those willing to provide the service, including some who had none of the skill or training of Madame Restell.[24]

In the wake of these scandals, in January of 1872, the New York Medico-Legal Society published a "Report on Criminal Abortion" in the *New York Medical Journal*, a monthly journal focusing on issues of interest to New York's doctors. The report documented a subcommittee's findings on "the practical value of the existing statutes in this state relating to the prevention of criminal abortion." The report found the practical value lacking, to say the least. The authors, who included among their number Gunning S. Bedford, who had earlier testified against Madame Restell, began with a lengthy investigation of the regulation (or lack thereof) of abortion. Joining with many other doctors, their chief criticism was with the medical understanding of the beginnings of life, which they concluded began at conception. They rejected the doctrine of quickening completely: "*The foetus is alive from conception, and all intentional killing of it is murder.*"[25]

Given that from 1869 onward, the quickening distinction was already moot in New York law, they focused on other parts of the law they found lacking. While the current statute allowed for abortion if a physician approved it to save the life of the mother, they believed that it should also recognize circumstances where, "in the judgement of an experienced medical man, premature labor should be induced, and be absolutely necessary to save the life of *the child*." Because abortion was murder in their eyes, they believed that the punishment should also be changed. Under the 1869 statute, abortion was manslaughter in the second degree. If considered murder—in their words, "an act of cool, deliberate, unrelenting murder"—the report's authors believed that the crime should be a capital felony. They recognized, however, that it was difficult to get jurors to convict abortion providers even under this more lenient statute, so instead they recommended that the sentence, not the denomination, of the crime be changed. While they believed that "punishing the crime with death would be the most effectual preventive," they did not think this feasible. Instead they recommended that the mandatory minimum sentence be changed to four years in a state prison, with the maximum sentence at the discretion of the sentencing judge, who could take into consideration the circumstances of the abortion and whether the offender was a "professional abortionist" "who recognizes no higher power than his own base interests, whose heart has long ceased to know a humane feeling, whose hands are stained with the blood of innocent children, victims of his foul lust for gain." Finally, they advocated for a change in the portion of the 1869 statute that punished anyone who procured an abortifacient for another person to also criminalize anyone who procured *instruments* to terminate a pregnancy.[26]

The New York state legislature passed a law very similar to that recommended by the Medico-Legal Committee, going perhaps even further than the committee had envisioned. On April 6, 1872, they expanded one section of the law to criminalize anyone who procured instruments as well as medicines for the purpose of effecting an abortion. They did name the crime a felony, which "upon conviction shall be punished by imprisonment in a State prison for a term not less than four years or more than twenty years." This statute went much further, however. The second section declared it a felony for any woman found guilty of procuring an abortion on her own person and specified the punishment as between four and ten years in a state prison. This punishment was far more severe than earlier versions of the law. It also expanded the punishment for those who might sell or procure for such a woman an instrument or abortifacient; the punishment was now between one and three years in a state prison. This statute repealed the 1869 exception for those who might be excused from punishment if they testified against their co-conspirators in an abortion. The legislature was doubling down. All parties involved in an abortion, including the woman herself, were now subject to arrest and imprisonment. It was, far and away, the harshest law that New York State had ever seen regarding abortion, though state legislatures across the country were also moving in this direction.[27]

Aside from her appearance in Augustus St. Clair's exposé, where was Madame Restell as these laws that further criminalized her profession were being debated and enacted? Surely she had opinions about them. They threatened her livelihood as well as her own personal freedom. She did not speak out as she did when she was personally attacked in the press or charged with a crime. In fact, very few women spoke publicly about abortion in this era. Even women's rights advocates, so vocal about so many aspects of women's second-class citizenship, often shied away from discussion of abortion. Those who did address abortion head on, like Matilda Joslyn Gage or Elizabeth Cady Stanton, generally offered sympathy for women who found abortion necessary because they saw it—along with prostitution and infanticide—as a by-product of men's inability to control their lust, which led to "forced motherhood." While women's rights advocates did not support an inherent right to abortion, they did believe in women's bodily autonomy and opposed anti-abortion laws, mostly because they did not believe that criminalization would solve the problem. For them, only a national campaign for women's rights could address the root cause of the need for abortion in the first place. No doubt Restell would have disagreed with them. She was well aware that plenty of women found themselves pregnant as a result of women's own sexual desire. In this, Restell was more nuanced in her thinking than were her sisters in the women's rights movement, however much they might have agreed about other matters.[28]

11

NEMESIS

Even though the New York state legislature and lawmakers across the country were increasing the punishments for abortion, Madame Restell's practice continued on, precisely because there was so much demand. Things were not well at home, however. Restell remained partially estranged from her daughter, Caroline, following Caroline's marriage to New York City policeman William Farrell. They were not on speaking terms for most of the 1870s. That said, Restell's grandchildren were living with their grandmother in the mansion on Fifth Avenue. She had essentially become their primary caretaker. Also resident was Restell's brother, Joseph Trow. Restell had been depending on her brother since his arrival in New York three decades earlier. He managed much of the day-to-day business of both her office and her husband's. And she, in turn, had done her best to help him, always providing for his room and board, along with her husband giving him cash payments from time to time. At one point she also paid for his stay at a New York hospital, for what Trow described as "the purpose of stopping drink." In the late 1850s, he spent some time in Europe, also at her expense. In recognition of all he had done for her, often without direct pay aside from room and board, in 1870 she gave him $10,000 in savings bonds, which they kept in the office in the house on Fifth Avenue. As one witness recounted, Restell explained that "he cannot work and pa [Charles Lohman] gives him very little in the office, but I have given him $10,000 in bonds, as I thought it was my duty to provide for him whilst I lived." Restell's description of Trow's inability to work may refer to his wooden leg and her belief that he would not be able to find work beyond her employ, or it may have been a disparaging comment that reflected the increasing strain developing between herself and Trow.[1]

The relationship between the Trow siblings held steady until the fifty-one-year-old Joseph announced in 1872 that he would soon marry one Marie Sherwood Clark, a twenty-five-year-old widow who was native to New York and daughter to a barber. The couple were wed on September 24, 1872. There is no doubt that Restell objected to her brother's marriage. The reasons seemed to be twofold. Restell had by this point counted on his service for three decades, since his arrival in New York in 1841. She was now in danger of losing what she called "my right hand," even while at other times she downplayed his capabilities. While Trow could, of course, continue to work for his sister following his marriage, it is likely that he would have wanted to renegotiate the terms of his employment if he were to live with his wife outside of the mansion on Fifth Avenue. Marriage would mean that Trow would no longer be available at all times to see to his sister's needs. Restell also objected to the bride's family, one friend explaining that Restell didn't "intend [that] any of that family shall have any of that money that I have made." At some point, either at the time of the wedding or later on, Joseph Trow and his wife moved out of his sister's home. They would eventually relocate to Greenport, on Long Island. Most of the evidence indicates that he continued to be involved in the family business.[2]

Charles and Ann Lohman were undergoing other changes in their living arrangements. Early in the 1870s, they moved into separate bedrooms. While accounts differ about why they chose to do so—and while sleeping in separate bedrooms, especially for those wealthy enough to afford them, was hardly unusual—this was a change from how they had lived until the 1870s. It could be that they were not getting along or, as their granddaughter would later insist, "there was no trouble between them." Either way, the residents of the mansion at the corner of Fifty-Second Street and Fifth Avenue were experiencing changes.

It turned out these changes would be the very least of Madame Restell's woes. Trouble was brewing from a new set of foes. Because Restell had managed to remain relatively unscathed by the doctors' crusade to put her out of business and to outlaw large portions of her trade, she may have thought that the worst was behind her. It was not to be. In 1870, the man who would bring about her downfall, Anthony Comstock, was just getting started.[3]

* * * *

The man who would leave an indelible mark on American regulation of vice, obscenity, and so-called morals came from humble origins. Comstock was born March 7, 1844, in New Canaan, Connecticut, one of ten children (seven surviving). Thomas, his father, owned a farm and sawmills, and the Comstock children grew up working on the farm. Anthony's mother died when he was only ten years old, but she left an impression on him, particularly in the realm of her faith. The Comstocks were descendants of New England's Puritan settlers and attended New Canaan's Congregational Church. Comstock grew up with a strong belief in good and evil, with an awareness that he might be tempted toward sin at any moment. His youthful journals recount episodes of masturbation, for which he was endlessly apologetic and regretful. His faith in God was coupled with a belief in the Devil's powers to lead one into temptation, which he sought to resist. Journal entries that date from his twenties continue the theme: "Today Satan has sorely tried me; yet by God's grace did not yeild [sic]." "This morning was severely tempted by Satan and after some time in my own weakness I failed." His religious upbringing, combined with a regard for his deceased mother, also left an imprint on his ideas about womanhood. Like many Christians of the mid-nineteenth century, Comstock believed that a single woman's value resided in her chastity and a married woman's in her fidelity, as well as her supposedly natural inclination toward wife and motherhood and her ability to keep a home for her family. This was hardly out of step with many other Americans at the time, but because Comstock held these beliefs rather rigidly, he was in for a rude awakening when he eventually moved to a rapidly industrializing—and openly sexual—New York City.[4]

Before his move to New York, Comstock served in the Civil War as an enlisted soldier in the Seventeenth Connecticut Infantry Regiment from 1863 to 1865. He did his level best throughout his time in the Union forces to attend church services as much as possible, even when his own regiment did not have a chaplain assigned to it. He found his comrades' profanity and drinking deeply distasteful, and it is clear from the diary he kept during his service that they found him as irritating as he found them sinful. In March of 1864, for instance, he records: "Heard some persons speaking against me. Do not know the reason. Tried hard to do my duty. Will not join with them in sin and wickedness; though loose [*sic*] all of their friendship." It may be apocryphal, but one account has it that when soldiers received their regular ration of whiskey, Comstock promptly poured his on the ground. It would certainly be in keeping with his attitudes toward sin and drink.[5]

Following his service, he was mustered out in 1865 and returned to New Canaan, where one of his brothers was trying to make ends meet on a now-failing Comstock farm. Anthony had a brief stint clerking at a store in nearby New Haven before finally gathering enough funds to relocate to New York City, where he again found work in a dry goods store in 1867. For three years he worked as a porter or as a shipping clerk in different stores, living in boardinghouses in Manhattan and Brooklyn, until he had managed to save enough money to buy himself a small home in Brooklyn, which was still an independent city at the time. In 1871, he married Maggie Hamilton, who was ten years his senior. Soon thereafter Maggie gave birth to a daughter, Lillie, who died in infancy. While Maggie never gave birth again, the Comstocks adopted a daughter, a one-year-old orphan called Adele, whom Comstock had discovered during a raid in search of obscenity. Her mother and brother had died and her father was incarcerated.[6]

From the year of his arrival in New York City in 1867, Comstock had been a member of the Young Men's Christian Association

(YMCA), whose goals were to provide wholesome entertainment and foster friendship among young men just like Comstock, men who were newly arrived in the city and at risk of falling into a life of sin and debauchery. The YMCA, which opened a new building in 1869, offered a lecture hall, a gymnasium, and a library, among other facilities, all designed to facilitate good Christian habits among its membership. These habits were seen as particularly threatened in the New York of the 1860s, not just because prostitution was rampant, contraception was available on a black market, and laws against abortion were mostly unenforced and unenforceable. New York was home to the nation's publishing industry, large swathes of which were dedicated to the production of obscene literature and images. In fact, Comstock's job at the dry goods store on Warren Street was located about a block away from such a publisher. In 1868 he visited and then returned with police officers intent on shutting down the business. Over the next four years, Comstock worked with police officers to raid purveyors of obscene materials, which had been criminalized in 1868 by the New York state legislature. While Comstock would come to target many types of illegality during his long career, he was perhaps most upset by "obscene publications," which he saw as fundamentally corrupting of the nation's youth:

> The effect of this cursed business on our youth and society, no pen can describe. It breeds lust. Lust defiles the body, debauches the imagination, deadens the will, destroys the memory, sears the conscience, hardens the heart, and damns the soul. It unnerves the arm, and steals away the elastic step. It robs the soul of manly virtues, and imprints upon the mind of the youth, visions that throughout life curse the man or woman. Like a panorama, the imagination seems to keep this hated thing before the mind, until it wears its way deeper and deeper, plunging the victim into practices that he loathes.

For Comstock, then, dirty pictures were not just bad, in and of themselves. The problem, he believed, was that they effectively ruined young men for the possibility of engaging in what he would have thought of as normal sexuality: marriage and family life.[7]

It should be noted that at this stage his crusade was entirely extra-curricular. He worked for no particular organization charged with in-vestigating vice; he had simply taken it on himself to root it out and then bring in the police to seal the deal. He was also enraged by saloons in his neighborhood in Brooklyn that refused to obey laws that man-dated closures on the Sabbath, which he found particularly vexing. The difficulty for Comstock was that the producers of smut, especially, were exceedingly difficult to pin down. Precisely because it was illegal, the literature was printed in one location, stored in another, and shipped and sold from yet a third location. He was convinced, prob-ably correctly, that police officers were being bribed by the publishers, and he was deeply frustrated that they seemed to evade punishment. No sooner did he bring police to one location than another popped up nearby. What was called for, he believed, was a much more systematic means of prosecuting and punishing the offenders.[8]

While Comstock had been trying in a relatively minor way to make a dent in what he saw as the glut of American pornography, officers within the YMCA were attempting to be more systematic both in their study of the problem and in their attempts to solve it. Following an exhaustive 1865 study, the YMCA had devoted funds toward the passage of the 1868 New York statute aimed at obscene literature and articles of indecent use. But even with its passage, the YMCA also found that police and district attorneys were reluctant to apprehend and prosecute the offenders. In 1872, Comstock wrote a letter to the leadership of the YMCA, which found its way into the hands of Morris Ketchum Jesup, chair of the board of the YMCA. He was so impressed with Comstock's entrepreneurial spirit when it came to apprehending pornographers that he immediately invited him to visit his home on Madison Avenue in April of 1872. There, the two men formed a part-nership that would have a lasting impact on sex and civil rights in the United States for almost a century to come.[9]

Beginning in 1872, Comstock worked under the aegis of the YMCA's Committee for the Suppression of Obscene Literature, largely doing work that was similar to what he had already been doing. In November of 1872, he also targeted the notorious publishing, stockbroking, and suffrage-advocating sisters Victoria Woodhull and Tennessee Claflin, in this case for publishing an exposé of the notorious Beecher-Tilton adultery scandal in their *Woodhull and Claflin's Weekly*. Comstock was particularly incensed that the sisters were targeting Henry Ward Beecher, among the most celebrated ministers of the day. Comstock had managed to secure the sisters' arrest by writing from his former home in Connecticut and asking for them to mail him a copy of the *Weekly*. Under a statute passed during the Civil War to regulate the sending of erotica through the mails, federal agents arrested Woodhull, Claflin, and Woodhull's husband, though the charges didn't stick. This partially led Comstock and his allies in the YMCA in search of a stricter federal statute. They turned their attention to Congress, seeking to pass federal legislation that would not only criminalize obscenity but perhaps more importantly ban its distribution through the mails. The legislation would also lead to a new position for Comstock—overseeing its enforcement.[10]

Working together, Comstock, his YMCA colleagues, a handful of senators, and Supreme Court justice William Strong crafted a bill that built on the New York statute, but was actually stricter, incorporating some categories of obscene material that Comstock had encountered in his various raids. On March 3, 1873, Congress passed An Act for the Suppression of Trade in, and Circulation of, Obscene Literature and Articles of Immoral Use. The act criminalized the giving, selling, lending, exhibiting, advertising, publishing, or having in one's possession

any obscene book, pamphlet, paper, writing, advertisement, circular, print, picture, drawing or other representation, figure, or image on or of paper or other material, or any asset, instrument, or other article of an immoral nature, or any drug or medicine, or any article whatever, for the prevention of conception, or for causing unlawful abortion,

in Washington, DC, and any federal territory, whose laws were controlled by Congress. It also criminalized using the mails—also controlled federally—to send any such object or literature. New York's 1868 obscenity statute had not included abortifacients and contraception, but Comstock believed they were intrinsically linked to literature and objects used to stimulate arousal and made sure they were included in the bill. The act also applied to sex toys and to any information that described sex, abortion, or contraception, meaning that even some medical literature and advice manuals could be subject to seizure if suspected of being obscene. The law also increased what New York State mandated as the minimum and maximum sentences for those prosecuted under the law: a term of hard labor between six months and five years or a fine between $100 and $2,000. While the law did not regulate the possession or sale of obscenity outside the mails at the state level, most states passed laws, so-called mini–Comstock laws, like the one in New York that would do so.[11]

The law allowed for anyone to petition a judge or marshal if they believed someone was in violation of the law; the judge would then issue a bench warrant, which would be served by a marshal. Whatever the marshal found would be kept as evidence at trial. In the wake of the successful passage of the law, the U.S. postmaster general, so impressed with Comstock's dedication to eradicating obscenity in the mail, appointed him to be a special agent to the Post Office Department. Comstock refused a salary on principle, but the job did enable him to travel free of charge on trains across the country as he pursued his duties of ridding the United States of obscenity. Finally, in May of 1873, Comstock and his colleagues at the YMCA founded the New York Society for the Suppression of Vice (NYSSV), which was designed to take over the activities Comstock had previously been engaging in under the aegis of the YMCA. The society then turned to the New York state legislature to make the NYSSV an official organ-

Anthony Comstock. His signature whiskers covered the scar he incurred when arresting a pornographer, who slashed him with a bowie knife. Photograph is from *Anthony Comstock, Fighter: Some Impressions of a Lifetime of Adventure in Conflict with the Powers of Evil* by Charles Gallaudet Trumbull (New York: Fleming H. Revell, 1913).

ization in the state. This act of incorporation was somewhat unusual in that the legislature granted the NYSSV the full cooperation of the police force of the city of New York (and any other town where police forces existed in the state). When called on by the NYSSV, police officers were duty bound to assist them in their work enforcing any law that regulated obscenity, abortion, or contraception. The law also awarded one-half of all fines collected through its work back to the agency itself. The year 1873 was a watershed for Comstock. As a postal inspector and the secretary of the newly formed NYSSV, Comstock was doubly empowered to seek out vice almost anywhere he might find it, and to arrest and prosecute those who traded in it.

Given that Comstock had been pursuing obscenity since 1868 and by 1873 had enhanced powers over the mails, which Madame Restell used with frequency to send her abortifacients and "female monthly pills," and now the powers of the New York police force on his side, one wonders why Comstock did not try to arrest Restell almost immediately. Any answer would, of course, be speculative, but there are a few possibilities. The first is that Comstock was already extremely busy. In his estimation, there was an awful lot of vice and obscenity to investigate. His 1880 compendium *Frauds Exposed; Or, How the People Are Deceived and Robbed, and Youth Corrupted* included thirty-three different chapters detailing all of the various frauds and criminals he had exposed or helped to bring down since 1873, which included bankers and brokers, bogus mining companies, bogus lotteries (he was somewhat obsessed with lotteries), watch and jewelry swindlers, sawdust swindlers, quacks, obscene publications, infidelity, and many more.[12]

The YMCA's report of their committee's work before 1873 noted that Comstock had worked to collect 134,000 pounds of books, 194,000 photographs, 60,300 rubber articles, and thousands more letters, newspapers, and circulars. And this was prior to the formation of the NYSSV. Comstock kept meticulous records, both when he was working on behalf of the YMCA's committee on vice and when for the NYSSV. The early years of that organization's work included many arrests for "mailing obscene books + advertisements of articles for abortion + prevention of contraception," but there were all kinds of other cases as well. In September of 1874, Comstock wrote of arresting a fifteen-year-old boy for exposing himself to women. Two years later, he arrested William A. Van Wagner for "indecently exposing himself entirely nude at window for an hour at a time." The vast majority of the arrested were men, at least in these early years, though women were sometimes arrested with their husbands. Women do occasionally appear singly in the records as well. In 1875, Comstock led police to arrest Sarah Heart for solicitation and Jane Beebe for "giving away pictures of her own nude person, to young men, on the street." That same year he arrested Sarah E. Sawyer for "mailing obscene circular, of

The Osborne Apartments, directly beside the Lohman residence, were built by the Lohmans in 1875 and fully equipped with two steam elevators, quite luxurious for the time. The photo dates from around 1880. Courtesy of the New York Public Library.

articles for abortion, prevention of conception, + indecent + immoral use." He explained in his always-extensive notes, "She came in when arrested with an elegant silk dress trimmed with lace + a camels hair shawl on her, said to be worth from $1000 to $1500. An old she-villain." His record indicates that she did one year's hard labor in the Dedham jail in Massachusetts. The extensive record keeping demonstrates that this was clearly a passion project for him.[13]

Madame Restell's very notoriety meant that there was no way Comstock was not aware of the person some called the wickedest woman in New York. He may have shied away from arresting her at first because he believed she was too powerful. Some thought the reason she operated with impunity was that she paid off the police and prosecutors. It is not beyond the realm of possibility. Whatever the reason, for most of the 1870s, Comstock left Restell to her own devices.

* * * *

Further changes were also occurring in the Lohman household. Restell's granddaughter, Caroline Purdy, who went by Carrie, had begun to court a young man named William P. Shannon. They were soon engaged to be married. The Lohmans had also become landlords. For years they had owned the lots on Fifth Avenue immediately north of their home and had been trying to sell them, but no one wanted to live next door to Madame Restell, at least no one who could afford lots on Fifth Avenue. In 1875, they built an apartment building there instead and began renting out apartments to earn income on what otherwise would have remained empty land. The building was called the Osborne.[14]

Tragedy struck the Lohmans when, on January 5, 1877, Charles R. Lohman died. He had been ill for six months and at the end slipped into a coma caused by uremia, itself a symptom of kidney failure. While newspapers at the time appeared not to have taken much notice of his passing, which was consistent with his general anonymity compared with the fame of his wife, the household was plunged into mourning. Lohman was sixty-seven years old at the time of his death. Ann and Charles had been married for more than forty years, and they had essentially invented themselves together. It was more than a marriage; it had been a partnership little understood by the public, who had paid so much more attention to Madame Restell than to her husband. Charles was buried under a tall obelisk in the Sleepy Hollow Cemetery, along the Hudson River. The Lohmans had purchased the plot and the memorial obelisk itself at the death of their granddaughter, who was buried there as well, planning for future interment at the time of their own deaths They had chosen this location for their burial because their son-in-law Isaac Purdy's family were all buried in the cemetery and their daughter and son-in-law had once lived nearby. The obelisk over Charles's grave is adorned with a marble carving of a sleeping baby. The inscription reads "Dedicated to the Memory of Frances Annie. The daughter of Isaac and Caroline S. Purdy. Born

Gravestone of Charles Lohman and Ann Lohman and Frances Purdy, Sleepy Hollow Cemetery. Photo by the author.

May 7th, 1856. Died February 1st, 1859." On the reverse are four lines of verse:

> *Hush! Tread light, our child is sleeping,*
> *Her life on earth is o'er;*
> *Vacant hearts at home are weeping,*
> *She sleeps to wake no more.*[15]

Lohman's will, which had been signed and dated in 1862, bequeathed the bulk of his estate to his wife, Ann. There were some individual bequests beyond that. To Joseph Trow he left the annual interest of 7 percent on a principal of $10,000 for the duration of Ann Lohman's life, the principal then passing to Trow upon her death. He also

Detail of gravestone of Charles and Ann Lohman. The carving of the sleeping baby, Frances Annie Purdy, was originally surrounded by plate glass. Photo by the author.

left a bequest of $1,000 annually to Caroline Purdy (as she still was named at the time of the writing of the will). He also separately bequeathed to Carrie Summers Purdy, his step-granddaughter, $1,500 per annum, as well as half his estate after the death of Ann Lohman. He also gave £40 sterling per annum to John Trow, his father-in-law, still resident of Painswick, in Gloucestershire. Finally, he declared the will's executors to be his brother-in-law Joseph Trow and his wife, Ann Lohman. The will was relatively straightforward, almost everything accruing to his wife but with bequests set aside for those who were also important to him: Joseph and John Trow, Caroline Farrell, and Carrie Purdy. The will, which aside from the individual bequests, did not name any sums, conveyed the home and apartment building on Fifth Avenue, the home they still owned on Chambers Street, all personal property, and all wealth to Ann Lohman.[16]

In April of 1877, Joseph Trow petitioned to have himself removed as an executor, which a judge granted. Trow was about to begin the arduous process of suing his own sister for the $10,000 in bonds that he claimed she had given to him in 1870 and that continued to be kept at the mansion on Fifth Avenue. He claimed his sister had transferred the bonds to her banker, then refused to give them to him when he asked for them in 1873 and subsequently sold them for $11,500 on January 1, 1874. Trow believed he was entitled to the bonds and the interest that had accrued to them since his sister had given them to him. Her new status as a widow, coupled with the increased acrimony with her brother, prompted her to cut Trow out of her own will entirely. She wrote a new will that gave the bulk of her estate to her two grandchildren, Carrie and Charles, and included an allowance for her estranged daughter, Caroline. At the same time, Trow continued to operate the office on Liberty Street as Dr. A.M. Mauriceau. It was no stretch for him to continue placing advertisements in New York newspapers.[17]

* * * *

If newspapers made little note of Charles Lohman's passing, such was not the case for their coverage of abortion and contraception in New York more broadly, which only increased during the 1870s. Joining the regular arrests, deaths, and trials were two new trends. The first was the greater number of formally trained doctors who were accused either of practicing abortion or of counseling women on birth control, breaking ranks with the dictates of the AMA either out of principle or in pursuit of profits. A Dr. Sara Blakeslee Chase, of the new generation of female doctors who had taken MDs, arrived in New York from Ohio in the early 1870s and immediately began advertising her services in the newspapers. She saw patients and gave lectures to women on "the Best Means of Having Healthy Bodies." She gave corresponding lectures to all-male audiences, one called "Man as a Father" or "Typical Manhood." On the side, Chase was selling contraception and douching syringes, to be used after intercourse to prevent pregnancy.[18]

Catharine Maxwell, once operating under the alias Madame Costello, perhaps the longest-standing of Restell's competition, had continued in practice, but by March of 1875, she had been arrested after a twenty-year-old Brooklyn woman named Antoinette Fenner had died after Maxwell had terminated her pregnancy. At this point, Maxwell was almost eighty years old, and when called before the coroner's jury "had to be carried on a litter, an object of loathing to the spectators who confronted her brazen face in the Coroner's office." Maxwell had originally been called to testify in Brooklyn, where Fenner lived. The coroner there, having determined that the crime had actually occurred in a different county, Manhattan, was forced to set Maxwell free. In Manhattan, the difficulty was that the only two witnesses to the crime were Maxwell herself and the now-deceased Fenner. The prosecutor dropped the charges and Maxwell was released. She was advertising again within the year. She died on April 28, 1876, at the age of eighty and was buried in Mount Auburn Cemetery in her native Cambridge, Massachusetts.[19]

These were by no means the only cases, as newspapers listed the names of many others alongside that of Madame Restell, who remained the most famous and paradigmatic of the female physicians. When James McCabe Jr. published his *Lights and Shadows of New York Life; Or, the Sights and Sensations of the Great City* in 1872, he included a long chapter on what he called "Child Murder." Of Madame Restell he explained,

> She is said to be worth fully a million of dollars. She has practiced her peculiar branch of medicine for many years, and with uniform success. Every one knows it, yet none can bring her to justice. She is too careful and too rich for that. Her immunity from punishment has been entirely owing to the fact that she only takes safe cases, never practicing on a woman who has been pregnant more than four months. Her charge is $500 a case. Need there be any better confirmation of the assertion that the rich are greater votaries of the crime of abortion than the poor? Yet every crime has its punishment.

Madame ——'s is her loneliness. She has made frantic efforts to get into some part of society better than the lowest.

These compendia of stories about New York City—or other metropolises—were not uncommon in this era and usually featured racy anecdotes about sex, prostitution, and other sorts of crimes. Restell featured in many of them. McCabe concurred with doctors that "it is fashionable here, as elsewhere, not to have more than one, two, or three children. . . . There is scarcely a physician in the city who is not applied to almost daily by persons of good position for advice as to the best means of preventing conception." While good men of honor refused these requests, women "seek the advice, and purchase the drugs, of the wretches whose trade is child murder. The evil grows greater every year. These wretches send their drugs all over the country and 'the American race is dying out.'" It was McCabe who referred to Restell as a "professor of infanticide."[20]

In a similar account, called *Thirty Years' Battle with Crime, Or the Crying Shame of New York, as Seen Under the Broad Glare of an Old Detective's Lantern* (1874), John H. Warren Jr. documented what he called the "three most diabolical trades that flourish in this city, to wit: Private lying-in hospitals, abortion hospitals, and the most recent outrage upon our civilization, the den of the 'baby-farmer.'" "Baby farming" was the name given to the practice of a woman taking in multiple infants and nursing them for a fee until their parents could retrieve them. The difficulties with baby farms were that some parents never came back and many babies died of malnutrition or starvation. Warren saw all three trades as the outcome of illicit sex. Indeed, he believed that their very existence *encouraged* illicit sex because those having it could be sure that there was a solution to pregnancy that did not involve taking responsibility for the child.[21]

The baby farms to which Warren refers were a much more recent development. The first mention of them in the U.S. press was via a case that broke in Scotland in 1867. Their presence in the United States, especially in major cities, was soon discovered by eager reporters and vice crusaders. By 1873, stories about American baby farmers were constantly appearing in the press: "Discovery of a Baby Farming Establishment" (Washington, DC, May 1873); "Starving to Death" (Long Island, August 1873); "Baby Farming Horrors" (New York City, September 1873); "Shocking Case of Baby Farming" (New York City, September 1873). Baby farms were essentially an outgrowth of wet-nursing, that is, the nursing of an infant not one's own by a lactating woman. But at a time when wet-nursing could be deadly, especially for poor babies whose wet nurses tended to multiple children, baby farming was even worse. The criticism of baby farming was twofold. Those who left their children with baby farmers sometimes did not return for them, leaving them to an almost certain death. And the baby farmers themselves were often accused of starving babies and pocketing the money they should have been using to purchase more milk. Baby farming had its origins in the desperate straits of poor, working women in cities, but there is no question that there were also baby farmers who sought to make a profit through intentionally allowing infants to starve to death.[22]

Warren referred to baby farming as a "wholesale slaughter of the innocents," "in plain English, baby destruction, by that gentlest of all remedies known as starvation, is the exclusive inheritance of the present age." Warren believed that of the 34,000 children born annually in New York City (his figures), 8,000 are

unaccounted for in accordance with the provisions and regulations of the Health Board. Two thousand five hundred of these are illegitimate, and about three thousand are abandoned or ordered to be got rid of by any means known to the modern art of infant destruction. Twenty-five hundred are adopted or sold at twenty-five dollars *per capita*, a sum a trifle more remunerative to their owner than that which calves bring to theirs in our markets. Those that fall (we mean the human babies) into the hands of the baby farming mid-wife, the modern butcher of our surplus infant population, never give their mothers, fathers, or anybody else, not even Coroner Woltman, any trouble.

Madame Restell was not a baby farmer—it was a decidedly more down-market trade—but she had certainly been accused of infanticide in the past. The problem with analyses like Warren's is that they equated all three practices together as "diabolical" trades, when they were really quite different from one another. While Warren was willing to admit that some of Restell's clients were "married women of supposed respectability," the women who tended to most upset the doctors, he primarily focused on single women who had become pregnant illegitimately. And by comparing baby farmers with female physicians who delivered babies and terminated pregnancies, he utterly elided the differences between the practices, further equating abortion with the murder of living children.[23]

Warren was not the only one to do this; newspapers also regularly linked the practices. In an 1873 story on "Baby Poisoning," the *Brooklyn Times Union* explained that "the baby-farmers manage to evade the gallows, while the abortionists receive new encouragement in the paucity of convictions of the members of their profession." In an article later the same year, the *Brooklyn Review* explored the issue of "how to get rid of babies, somehow, anyhow, so they are got rid of safely, is something of great interest at all times in large cities." While the article was primarily concerned with baby farming, it did note that "it is a large field to go over the whole story of abortionists' dens, foundling hospitals, children's homes, and other adjuncts of the profession," essentially linking them all together in the mind of a reader. In a society that by the 1870s had even more fully embraced a vision of childhood individuality and innocence, at least among the middle class, it became even more challenging to support abortion.[24]

* * * *

By the later 1870s then, Madame Restell was not doing well. Her husband had died, her brother had—at least in her eyes—forsaken her and was now suing her. Her grandchildren, Carrie and Charles Purdy, continued to live with her and bring her comfort, but she had not managed to bridge the estrangement with their mother, her only child,

Caroline Farrell. The laws regulating abortion were as strict as they had ever been, as were Anthony Comstock's newly passed statutes on obscenity that regulated almost anything she sold through the mails: medical advice, contraception, and abortifacients. Madame Restell must have thought that things could not possibly get worse. She was wrong.

12

A RECKONING

On January 28, 1878, at about a quarter to eleven in the morning, the door of Madame Restell's office rang. Restell answered and found a large man standing before her. He had very little hair on the top of his head and bushy whiskers on the sides of his face that led to a moustache above his lips. He asked if "Doctor or Madam Restell were in." Restell inquired if he wanted to see her professionally and when he affirmed that this was the case, she led him inside to a room farther back into the house. She asked what his business was, and the man explained that he had "seen her advertisements and had called to see if she had any article for the prevention of conception." Restell answered that she certainly did but that it would be of no use if the woman's courses had already stopped, that is, if she were pregnant. She explained that she did, however, have a medicine that the woman could take if the courses were stopped already. She inquired if the woman in question was married or single. The man, who did not give his name, explained that it was all a very delicate matter but that he wanted to make sure that whatever he got was reliable. Restell said that there was a reason she was inquiring about whether the woman was married or single. Depending on how far along in her pregnancy the woman was, the medicine would bring on "such severe flooding as would lead to exposure." In other words, if this man was married to the woman in question, there was nothing to hide. If he was not and if it was for a single woman who had little control over her privacy, the solution might be different. In the case of a single woman who might fear exposure, she would not give this medicine "after 60 days" following the last period.[1]

Restell briefly left the room and returned with a package, explaining, "There are two kinds and the directions are inside." According to the directions, one was to take a "teaspoonful of the extract every two hours during the day, two pills night and morning." Once again Restell emphasized how expeditiously the woman must begin the course of medicine. If the pregnancy were already more than sixty days along "the girl would be so exhausted that she would have to have someone with her, as she said she would stain the bedding and very likely lead to exposure." When the man asked her if it would really bring on a miscarriage, Restell replied, "It is not infallible, no medicine is infallible, but in nine cases out of ten, this does the work." The man then asked when he would know if it had worked, and she told him it should be done by Thursday night, three days later. Restell explained that if it had not worked by then, "you had better bring her right on to me, or is it a case of sufficient importance for me to go to the place[?]." Restell and the man went back and forth about the possibility of the woman coming to Restell's office for an operation if need be—he had claimed she lived out of the city—and Restell explained that the operation would cost $200. As they were talking, the bell rang again and Restell went out in the hallway to attend to another client. When she returned, she explained, "Poor little dear; her husband has been away for some two months and she has been indiscreet and got caught [become pregnant], and has come for relief." She said that she regularly served women who feared they had "got caught." Restell then explained that the next time the man was in town, she could provide an article that would prevent conception altogether, but that it was clearly too late for that right now. The man inquired about the safety of the medicine he was purchasing, and Restell said that she had "used it for years and that there was no danger if they could take it before the 60 days." "If used according to directions, it would bring on the menses." The man paid Restell $10 for the medicine and he left the office.[2]

It could be that Restell did not expect that she would ever see him again, though given the directions she gave him for what he should do if the medicine were not effective, perhaps it was not entirely unexpected when he reappeared the next week. Between 2:00 and 3:00 p.m. on February 7, the man again rang the bell. Upon opening it, Restell recognized him and said, "Oh, you were here last week." On this occasion, Restell led him into a room by the door, where he handed her a note. Having read it, she said, "Oh, she is an unmarried woman and she wants—I know what she wants, she wants a preventative." The man affirmed that this was the case, explaining that upon returning home with the abortifacient he had purchased last time, the woman's courses had already returned. He made a bit of a joke of it: "It had the desired effect without taking it; it must be a very powerful preparation." At that point Restell went to the sideboard in the room and came back with two boxes. She asked him whether he or the woman would hold on to the powders, and he explained that he wasn't sure. She told him to put them in a trunk or safe somewhere "and mark them tooth powders. . . . There is no name on them; it won't do to have any name or directions, because it is very dangerous to sell these."[3]

She then demonstrated how to dilute the powders in water and draw the liquid into a large syringe and explained that one should "place it up the parts—she had better stand up when she does it, because if she don't it might not get up under where the man was and this fluid kills the seed." Madame Restell was showing how to use a contraceptive douche, to be used immediately after sexual intercourse. She raised her right leg to show the proper placement to make sure it would be used effectively. She then told him about other customers' methods for keeping the powders with them and using them even in less-than-ideal circumstances, like "in the parlor, where they can't go upstairs, where the girl's parents are strict and he gives the bottle to this girl and she use[s] it. It must always be used within 10 or 15 minutes after connection; if it is not, it would be risky but the girl must never lay over night because this must be used immediately after the act."

The man asked a couple more questions about the reliability of the method and was reassured by Restell that it was infallible. He paid $20 and was told the powders would be good for three years. With the transaction completed, the man was once again on his way.[4]

Four days later, he was back, this time accompanied by four other men. It was Monday, February 11. Madame Restell ushered them into her office, observing, "You have brought quite a party with you. This is a friend with you?" At this point the man told her that he had a warrant for her arrest and a search warrant "to seize her articles for abortion and preventing conception." One of the other men, a police officer, told her that she was now in his custody and that he "would act in a civil manner towards her." At this point Madame Restell did what many in her situation might have done: she lied, claiming that no such articles were on the premises. The officers showed their identification and read the warrant aloud to Restell. The man who had visited before explained that she would "have to produce any medicine that she had for the purpose that she mentioned to him the day that he visited." At that point, Restell must have finally realized who this man was. "Is this Mr. Comstock?" she asked. It was indeed. Until that point she clearly had not recognized him and yet she obviously knew who he was. At least in the realm of sexuality and obscenity, the only person more famous than Anthony Comstock was Restell herself. She admitted, "I have heard a great deal about you and read about you." She asked him if he had "a severe cut in the face by an encounter with some person?" Comstock assented that he had, the result of an encounter with an angry pornographer who had cut Comstock with a bowie knife. His signature whiskers covered the wound. At this moment, Restell must have realized just how much trouble she was in. She had sold Comstock an abortifacient and a contraceptive douche, on two separate occasions, and she was likely well aware of just how much illegal material she had on hand. The search commenced. In total, Comstock and the officers found "10 doz. condoms, 15 bots. for abortion, 3 syringes, 2 qts. pills for abortion or about 100 boxes, 250 circulars, 500 powders for preventing conception." In his notes in the log he kept

This depiction of Restell's arrest was published on February 23, 1878, in the *New York Illustrated Times*. Note the woman in the background attempting to disguise her identity.

for the New York Society for the Suppression of Vice (NYSSV), Comstock noted, "At time of arrest, a prominent man's wife, a mother of 4 children was there to consult this woman professionally. She was very greatly excited, and pleaded I would not expose her, saying 'she would kill herself first.' I told her to sin no more, your secret shall be kept sacredly by me."[5]

The police officers, Comstock, and Restell all traveled downtown in a carriage to the police court of the Second District of New York, where Comstock swore out testimony before police justice James Kilbreth and identified the woman in custody as Ann Lohman, also known as Madame Restell. At the Jefferson Market police court, Justice Kilbreth set bail for Restell at $5,000 for each of the two crimes of which she was accused—selling an abortifacient and selling contraception. Restell offered to deposit the sum in cash, but Kilbreth refused and remanded her to the Tombs. The next day, February 12, Restell's counsel, Edward McKinley, petitioned to have her bailed and produced two people who could stand as her sureties. Justice Kilbreth once again refused and ordered "that Mme. Restell stand committed until Friday morning at 10 o'clock." According to the *New York Times*, this decision "astounded Mme. Restell's counsel" as well as all those who were assembled "waiting for the disposition of the case." It is possible that Restell's notoriety led Kilbreth to break with precedent and refuse to entertain the matter of bail as he would normally do. The *Times* also speculated that Restell's counsel would attempt to call as witnesses various "people who will resort to any means and go to any expense to prevent it as the only means of keeping their connection with Mme. Restell from the public." Remanded back to the Tombs, Restell then "had a long interview with her counsel, after which she was conducted to a cell near the entrance to the second tier of the female prison," that tier being the one reserved for the more well-to-do prisoners.[6]

Comstock was ecstatic, writing almost immediately to his supervisor in the U.S. Post Office about his triumph:

> Several months ago I detected her sending her vile article through the mails. I did not arrest her then as I could not get a real strong case + did not deem it wise, to move until I secured such a case. I tried repeatedly to get her, but failed, and so tried under the state laws. . . . Her business has been for years, that of abortion or selling medicines for that purpose and for preventing Conception. She is reputed as being worth $1,500,000, all made in this traffic.

He continued: "I think I have a good case. I am so advised by my counsel + the District Attorney to whom I submitted the case before arrest."[7]

On February 13, Restell's attorney petitioned in New York's supreme court for a writ of habeas corpus, in essence alleging that she was being held illegally because Justice Kilbreth was unwilling to grant her bail, even though she had sureties willing to serve and she herself had sufficient cash to pay the $10,000 he had demanded. Supreme court judge Donohue held a hearing on the writ and concluded that he was unable to overrule the decision of the police court, which left Restell in jail. Apparently influenced by the petition, however, and avowing some desire to be lenient toward women prisoners, Justice Kilbreth announced that afternoon that he was willing to admit Restell to bail. Restell's counsel indicated that present in the courtroom were a number of gentlemen he had assembled who were willing to serve as sureties for Restell, but they had one condition: that their names never be revealed to the public "for fear they will be compromised by association with her." When the judge expressed skepticism about doing so, Restell's lawyer asked if it would simply be possible to exclude the press from the courtroom during the period in which the bondsmen were interviewed about their property qualifications. The judge refused, explaining that even if he had allowed it, he would still have to file a record of their names, to which reporters would have access.[8]

It took Restell's counsel two days to find two men who were qualified as sureties—that is, they possessed enough real estate that they met the court's requirements—and were willing to have their names revealed. One bondsman was James Gonoude, who owned houses and lots on the northwest corner of Second Avenue and Eightieth Street. Even Gonoude asked the reporters to please print his name with mistakes so that he could not be identified. The second bondsman was Jacob Schwarz, a baker, who owned property at Third Avenue and 113th Street. Both men had been fully indemnified by Restell herself, so they faced no financial risk, only the risk to their reputations. Once the men had signed the bail bonds, Restell was free to go. She left the court "accompanied by her grandson, a handsome young man who has patiently and laboriously struggled for his grandmother's release, being the first one in court every day and the last one to leave," according to the *Times*.[9]

Friday, February 16, was the day Justice Kilbreth had originally set for Restell's examination, which would be necessary before a grand jury could choose whether to indict her, which itself was required before there could be a trial. A little after 10:00 a.m., "a plain dark green coach—drawn by a well-kept pair of bay horses, driven by a well-fed, red-faced coachman"—arrived at the Jefferson Market police court. Inside were Madame Restell, her grandson, and one of her lawyers, Edward McKinley. Waiting inside the courtroom were her other lawyer, Ambrose Purdy, and Samuel Colgate, president of the New York Society for the Suppression of Vice, along with Justice Kilbreth, Assistant District Attorney Leary, and all those who had assembled to watch the case unfold. Leary first explained that the people wished to postpone the examination because Comstock was unable to appear that day and would not be available for another week. Restell's counsel did not object, though he had an issue of his own. James Gonoude, who had agreed only yesterday to serve as bondsman, now wished to step down. Justice Kilbreth ordered Restell to wait in another room while her counsel and grandson secured for her another bondsman. In the meantime, a large crowd gathered outside the courtroom to gawk at Madame Restell's carriage and coachman.[10]

By noon, Restell's counsel had secured two more possible bondsmen. The first was a Samuel J. Blakley, who owned a good deal of real estate that he had inherited from his grandmother and father. John Lauritz was the second, a retired grocer turned liquor saloon owner who also possessed real estate sufficient to meet the court's terms. Reappearing was Jacob Schwarz, who had served as bondsman the previous day. He explained that while he did not know Restell and had contemplated withdrawing his name, Restell had deposited $10,000 in government bonds into his bank account and further, "I don't think she is quite as bad as some other people in this world. She has acted squarely with me in this business, and so far as I'm concerned I want her to have a fair show." The court opted to retain Schwarz and Lauritz as bondsmen. Restell returned from the adjoining room and was told that she was free until the day of the examination. She departed with her grandson at 4:30 p.m. and returned to her home. The *Times* reported that Restell had already spent as much as $3,000 attempting to retain bondsmen, and that did not include the $20,000 in bonds deposited in the two current sureties' bank accounts.[11]

All this back-and-forth had been covered by newspapers across the country, some of which gleefully reported on the bondsmen who were too embarrassed to have their names associated with her. Madame Restell was clearly a household name by 1878. In late February, the *Christian Union* heaped praise on Comstock, who it claimed "ought to be put at the head of the detective force in this city" for gaining admittance to Restell's home as well as for obtaining "a full account of her methods and medicines, with some specific prescriptions and drugs." It noted also that she was a "notorious woman, perfectly well known to the police, yet thus far successful in setting them at defiance." Thanks to Comstock, who had given "her so serious an admonition of the danger of her criminal craft," she might finally get her due.[12]

The long-awaited examination of witnesses commenced on Saturday, February 23. Madame Restell arrived that morning accompanied by her grandson in a carriage "drawn by a splendid pair of dun-colored horses." She was dressed in black silk "and wore a heavily beaded black velvet sacque and velvet hat trimmed with deep crimson. Her gait was rather slow and she seemed quite careworn," reported the *Brooklyn Daily Eagle* in a story titled "The Wages of Sin." The *New York Times* reported that "she seemed to be annoyed by the curiosity of the spectators." No doubt this arrest and possible trial were indeed weighing on her. She had not been arrested for more than twenty years, and the law had changed enough that the possibility of her conviction was much higher than it had been in the past, especially given the evidence against her and the celebrity of the source of that evidence, Comstock. She was now sixty-six years old, and her husband and longtime partner had died just the year before.[13]

The first witness was Comstock, who gave testimony about the first of the two charges, selling medicine for the purpose of terminating a pregnancy. Comstock attested to his visit to Restell's office and to what she had sold him: two bottles of a dark-colored liquid and two envelopes filled with pills, complete with directions. Some newspapers also delighted in recounting the story of the married woman who had been conducting an affair while her husband was out of town and now feared she would be caught. Restell's counsel, Ambrose Purdy, objected to various parts of the testimony, but the judge overruled most of his objections and Comstock's testimony continued. Officer Charles Sheldon was also examined, and he testified to the events of the day of Restell's arrest. His testimony was "mainly corroborative of Comstock's as to the finding of the medicines." Following the testimony by Comstock and Sheldon, the hearing was adjourned until the following Wednesday.[14]

That day, Purdy once again asked the justice to allow for a private examination of Restell so that it would not be "rehashed in the newspaper." Assistant District Attorney Herring objected and claimed that "in the fairest portion of our city this woman had built up a business so nefarious, so infamous, that all who walk in the shadow of the building in which she lives feel the taint of her crime." It was she, claimed Herring, who had already exposed New York to her crimes; there was no need to shield her from the press now. Justice Kilbreth ruled that no exception to the rule would be granted in this case; the examination would be public. Purdy then declared in that case he would call no witnesses and moved to dismiss the case on the grounds "that no offense had been proven." Kilbreth responded that if Purdy himself would not examine the defendant, it fell to him to do so. The exchange proved brief. Restell gave her name as Ann Lohman and stated her address. When asked her occupation, she said midwife. That concluded the examination on the first of two charges related to selling an abortifacient. The attorneys then turned to the charge related to selling articles for criminal purposes—the contraceptive douche. Comstock again testified, but this time about his second visit to Restell's office. He explained also that on the day of the arrest, in the carriage ride from Restell's home to the police court, Restell had admitted to him that "the articles seized by [Comstock] were similar to those sold to him at his two previous visits." This was key to establishing not only that she had these articles in her possession on the day of the arrest but that she had also sold them earlier. Once again, Officer Sheldon corroborated Comstock's account. Near the end of the day, Purdy asked that the "case should stand at least for a day to give time to call witnesses" and provide a summation of the defense, at which point the court adjourned until the next day.[15]

On March 1, Restell appeared in police court in "heavy black velvet and silk," as on the first day of the examination. The *Herald* claimed that she "affected the same composure and cool indifference to her surroundings." Her counsel, Purdy, explained to the court that while he had previously promised he would deliver a summation of Restell's defense, he believed this would not be beneficial for the case, instead choosing to "conduct the case as quietly as possible." He would simply move to dismiss the complaint. Justice Kilbreth denied the motion, as Purdy and Restell surely knew he would. Restell entered the plea "not guilty."[16]

Justice Kilbreth ruled at this time that Madame Restell would be tried in the court of general sessions, which meant that Restell was once again remanded into custody, her bail remaining at $10,000, as before. One of her bondsmen, John Lauritz, was in attendance at the examination, however, and had decided he no longer wished to serve as surety. Kilbreth relieved him of the responsibility, but this meant that Restell was once again in need of a second bondsman. In the interim, one of her counsel, McKinley, had gone to the supreme court and had once again procured a writ of habeas corpus, again claiming that Kilbreth was holding Restell illegally. McKinley was attempting to keep her out of the Tombs by having her delivered to the supreme court. Restell exited one courthouse in order to be taken to another. Reporters and eager spectators followed her there. Before Judge Donohue of New York's supreme court, Purdy argued that he "desired the discharge of the prisoner, against whom, he alleged, nothing had been shown proving her guilty of a violation of the law." Donohue explained that he was exhausted after a long day's work and would not hear the habeas petition. He said that the case could be heard the next Tuesday, four days later. Until that time, Restell would be in the custody of Deputy Sheriff McGonigal. According to the *New York Sun*, she then rode with him in her own carriage to her home, where she and the sheriff would stay under house arrest until Tuesday. Purdy had succeeded in keeping Restell out of the Tombs, but only barely. The *Sun* noted that Purdy had yet to reveal any of the defense's legal strategy and speculated that they would claim that her medications were "harmless and inefficacious."[17]

On Tuesday, a large crowd gathered at the court of Judge Lawrence, most curious to see Madame Restell. "She was elegantly dressed, as usual, and was speedily surrounded by several gentlemen, with whom she kept up an unceasing conversation until her case was called for argument," according to the *New York Herald*. Purdy made his argument before Judge Lawrence that Restell had committed no crime and should not be charged. He argued that no one had tested any of the so-called medicine that Comstock had bought from Restell, and so no one could positively say that the medicines were capable of the things that Comstock averred. The burden of proof, Purdy claimed, was on the prosecution. The assistant district attorney pointed to the directions that Restell had herself included as proof of the medicine's capabilities. Lawrence said he would have a ruling two days later, on Thursday. Restell remained in her own home in the custody of the sheriff.[18]

Madame Restell and "quite a coterie of personal friends" returned on Thursday. According to the *Herald*, "her toilet was as conspicuous for its elegance as on her recent appearance before the same tribunal." Judge Lawrence ruled that he found the evidence compelling enough to warrant a trial; he dismissed the writ and ordered that Restell be remanded to custody. Restell's counsel, McKinley, then asked to have the bail reduced from $10,000 ($5,000 for each offense) to $5,000 total. Lawrence said he would take it under advisement. In the meantime, Restell, her grandson, and two lawyers petitioned a different judge to have the bail reduced. That judge explained that, not knowing the facts of the case, he could not alter the bail that had been set by Kilbreth. Assistant District Attorney Lyon said he would consider accepting Restell as surety alongside one other bondsman. Restell would also be required to deposit an additional $10,000 with "the District Attorney as additional security for her appearance." The sheriff then surrendered her, and she was transferred to the custody of the court. She eventually became her own surety on both charges, "giving as security her house and lot on Fifth Avenue, which she values at $25,000." John Lauritz, who had previously served as bondsman, was once again entered in as surety. After a stop at the office of the district attorney, where Restell deposited $10,000 in bonds, she was bound for home, "a crowd of spectators" gazing curiously at her as her carriage headed north. Her attorneys had managed to win the battle of her bail—she was temporarily free—but the war was still to come. There was little doubt that the case would go to trial.[19]

Perhaps knowing that Restell's time as a free woman was limited, on March 10, her granddaughter was married to her fiancé, William Pickell Shannon. This way her beloved grandmother could be in attendance. They were twenty-three and twenty-four years old, respectively. No record survives to indicate where the ceremony took place and whether Restell's daughter, the mother of the bride, attended. In all likelihood, it was a small affair. Too much foreboding hung over the Lohman household on Fifth Avenue that March. On March 12, the grand jury began to hear testimony on the charges against Restell. The very next day they indicted her on the charges of selling contraception and abortifacients and of advertising pills and powders "for the prevention of conception." The indictment made headlines across the nation. Restell was ordered to appear for arraignment on March 29. On that day, the indictments were read aloud. Her new counsel, Orlando Stewart—who had assisted her in legal matters in earlier decades— argued that the indictments were flawed because Restell had sold the articles not to a woman but to a man, who himself admitted that he "did not intend to give them to any other person to use," in essence arguing that if Comstock or any supposed fictional woman did not intend to use the abortifacient or contraception, no crime had been committed. The difficulty with this argument was that New York state law criminalized the selling of both contraceptives and abortifacients, regardless of whether they were ever used. He also argued that the court should analyze the medicines to see if they were capable of contraception or abortion. He entered a plea of "not guilty" and reserved the right to again try to quash the indictments. The case was then moved from the court of general sessions to the court of oyer and terminer, essentially an indication of how serious the charges were, and on Saturday, Restell's attorney was told that he should be prepared to argue the motion to quash the indictment on the morning of April 1.[20]

Madame Restell was depressed. That Sunday, the day before her trial was due to start, she could be found walking from room to room in the mansion on Fifth Avenue, "wringing her hands and asking why she should be so persecuted as she had never done anybody any harm in her life." Her granddaughter and grandson-in-law attended an evening church service, and when they returned home, found that she had retired to bed early. They visited her there and spoke for a while. She was "greatly distressed" and reminded them to be up early in the morning for her appearance in court. "I feel better tonight," she said, "but oh! How I dread to-morrow; how shall I ever get through the trial." As they were leaving her room, she turned her head restlessly on her pillow, muttering "Oh, how I dread 2 o'clock," which they did not understand at the time. The trial was due to begin in the morning and the remark was curious, but their grandmother was under an extraordinary amount of pressure and had been behaving strangely all weekend. They thought little of it and went to bed.[21]

On the morning of April 1, a large crowd gathered at the courthouse to see Madame Restell brought to justice—or just to see the woman in the flesh. Comstock, as well as the police officers who had been present when she was arrested, were all there to give their evidence. The case was the first on the docket. But there was no sign of Madame Restell, nor were her lawyers there. Presently, a murmur spread through the courtroom, which eventually swelled to a crescendo, as the word was passed among the onlookers: Madame Restell was dead.

13

"End of an Infamous Life"

Early on the morning of April 1, Margaret McGrath, housemaid in the Lohman home, descended from her room at the top of the house and, as she passed by Mrs. Lohman's rooms on the way downstairs, noticed her "mistress's clothes lying on a chair in the bath-room on the second floor," where the door was slightly ajar. She thought this odd, as Mrs. Lohman was in the habit of bathing in the evenings. Knowing that she had chores to begin and that breakfast awaited, McGrath continued downstairs. About an hour later, as she was ascending back through the home, seeing that the clothing was in exactly the same position, she knocked on the door and called out her mistress's name. Hearing no response, she entered the bathroom. She could see no one there, but the doors surrounding the bathtub were partially closed. McGrath opened the doors and saw the body of Ann Lohman, clearly dead. She screamed and ran from the room, alerting the other residents of what she had found. Lohman was submerged in water, "with a gaping wound in her neck from ear to ear." The faucets were on, and the running water had removed most of the blood, "but there was a dark-red line about the neck, and a few splashes of blood appeared on the side of the tub." Lying near the body, at the bottom of the tub, was a large carving knife Madame Restell had used to slit her own throat.[1]

Resident in the Lohman home at the time, in addition to servants, were Lohman's grandchildren, Charles Purdy and Carrie Shannon, and Carrie's husband, William. When they had collected themselves following the shocking discovery, they summoned Lohman's attorney, Orlando Stewart. Upon arrival, he also examined the body and almost immediately hurried away in search of the coroner. From the coroner's office, he sent a note to District Attorney Phelps: "Mrs. Lohman is dead. I am at Coroner's office making arrangements for inquest." Word spread quickly across New York, though at first the news was "received with sceptical [sic] shakings of the head and shrugging of shoulders by those who fancied they saw in it an April fools 'sell' of large magnitude." Soon, however, people came to understand that it was true. In the court of oyer and terminer, where Restell was to have been tried that morning, Assistant District Attorney Herring at first seemed unwilling to believe the news. But when word came from the coroner and police officials, he, Judge Daniels, and the witnesses who had been called, including Anthony Comstock, all abandoned the trial. Soon thereafter, Comstock made a notation to the entry on Restell in his ledger at the New York Society for the Suppression of Vice: "Committed suicide by cutting her throat morning of trial. A Bloody ending to a bloody life."[2]

Coroner Woltman and Deputy Coroner Cushman both examined the body and conducted the inquest. Restell's grandson-in-law testified about her state of mind in the days leading up to her death, about the constant wringing of her hands and the belief that she was being persecuted. On several occasions he had heard her say, "If I could only get sick and die. I wish I was dead, as it would end all." His memory of her claiming the night before that she dreaded two o'clock now made more sense, as the coroner estimated the time of death to be very early that morning. She must already have planned her death when she spoke with William and Carrie. Henry Curran, a servant in the Lohman residence, testified that he had locked "all the doors at night as it was his custom to do," meaning that no outsider could have been responsible for Lohman's death. The coroner's jury found that Ann Lohman had died by "suicide by cutting her throat with a knife." The death certificate elaborated that the precise cause of death was "shock from hemorrhage from incised wound of the throat, severing the carotid (external) on right side and jugular veins on both sides." Death would have been close to instantaneous. The certificate listed her as Ann Lohman, widow, with thirty-five years residence in the United States. Under "Occupation," the word "tailoress" is written and then crossed out, replaced with "midwife." By the time of her death, Madame Restell had not been a tailoress for more than three decades.[3]

By the next day, Restell's death had made the front page of New York's newspapers. "End of a Criminal Life," proclaimed the *Times*, while the *Tribune* titled its article "End of an Infamous Life: Mme. Restell Cuts Her Throat." As the *Brooklyn Daily Eagle* explained, "The sensational features of the case, the notorious character of the woman, the frightful social rottenness which her immense wealth revealed, the manner of her detection, the various incidents of her career, her bearing in the police court, and the deliberate and ghastly manner of her death combined to attract public attention to her in an extraordinary degree." As newspapers nationwide reprinted stories detailing her death, her daughter and grandchildren prepared to bury her. At ten o'clock on the morning of April 2, a "handsome team and a single carriage" arrived at the door of the Lohman residence at 657 Fifth Avenue to retrieve the body. "The thick curtains of the reception room were closely drawn, and the throng outside could see nothing of the last farewell taken by the dead woman's family." Madame Restell's body lay in a rosewood casket with silver-plated handles, lined with white satin, "the lid bearing a small silver plate with the name and date of birth and death of the deceased." The Lohman servants, as well as her descendants, all paid their respects before the coffin was taken to the Grand Central Depot by Charles Purdy, William Shannon, William Farrell, and the undertaker who accompanied it on the 11:03 a.m. train for Tarrytown.[4]

When the train arrived at Tarrytown, a hearse was waiting to take Restell's body to the cemetery at Sleepy Hollow, about two miles from the village. The *New York Times* noted that "extraordinary precautions had been taken to conceal the time and place of the funeral," so even as spectators saw the hearse pass through Tarrytown and Sleepy

Gravestone of Ann Lohman, Sleepy Hollow Cemetery. Her daughter, grand-children, and some great-grandchildren are buried nearby. Photo by the author.

Hollow, they may not have known whose body the coffin contained. Gabriel Purdy of Tarrytown, the father of Isaac Purdy, Caroline Farrell's first husband, had dug a grave for Madame Restell immediately beside that of her husband, who had been buried there so recently, "in the shade of a great willow." "The coffin was hastefully but respectfully lowered into this grave, and after a few shovelfuls of earth had been thrown down, the friends withdrew." The carving on the obelisk lists Restell as "Ann, wife of Charles R. Lohman," as if her daughter and grandchildren were attempting to retroactively restore the Lohman marriage to some semblance of a proper gendered order that it had evaded during the Lohmans' lifetime.[5]

On April 4, Ann Lohman's will was offered for probate in the sur-rogate's office in Manhattan. She had written this revised version on

April 28, 1877, in the wake of her husband's death. Her grand-children, Carrie Purdy Shannon and Charles Robert Purdy, were the two primary beneficiaries and were also appointed as executors, though the latter was unable to serve as he had not yet achieved the age of majority, twenty-one. The will first set about equalizing the inheritances left behind by her late husband, who had devised that half of his estate should pass to Carrie Shannon at Ann Lohman's death. Lohman herself declared that the second half of Charles Lohman's estate should pass to Charles Purdy, making the two grandchildren equal inheritors of the estate of Charles Lohman. Ann Lohman next bequeathed a sizable number of pieces of jewelry to her granddaughter. These included a diamond necklace, diamond bracelet, one rich gold bracelet with opal and diamond settings, and one pair of pearl earrings, among others. She also left Carrie the parlor organ and Steinway piano, both "used by her," and the Bibles and Bible stand. She left also to her grand-daughter her entire "wardrobe and dresses and laces of every kind." As well as all her "horses, carriages, harnesses, accoutrements, robes, blankets, and other stable property to me belonging." Charles and Carrie would share equally in the rest of the estate, including all real estate, "furniture, paintings, silver and silver ware and all other . . . household furniture and property."[6]

Her daughter, Caroline, should receive "three thousand dollars per year for and during the term of her natural life," noting that the payments should be made "for her sole and separate use, free from the control of any husband." Her twelfth provision, just in case it had not been clear in her earlier dictate, was that "any bequest or devise herein made for the benefit of any female is intended to be for her own sole and separate use free from the control of any husband and in no event subject to his contracts, debts, or liabilities." Even in death, Ann Lohman wanted to ensure that her granddaughter would live her life on her own terms.[7]

Lohman was clear that Charles and Carrie were entitled to rent, sell, or invest the proceeds of their inheritance—which included the home on Fifth Avenue, the adjacent apartment building, the former home on Chambers Street, and government securities—in any way they saw fit. Newspapers estimated the overall value at anywhere from $600,000 to well over $1 million, which would be somewhere between $15 and $30 million today. Regardless of the precise value of the estate, there is no question that Ann Lohman had been a very wealthy woman, and now so were her grandchildren.[8]

* * * *

In the wake of his sister's death, Joseph Trow, still intent on regaining the $10,000 in savings bonds he believed Lohman had promised him, renewed his lawsuit in the court of common pleas, now against his great-niece, Carrie Purdy Shannon, who was the sole executrix of her grandmother's estate. Shannon chose to fight her great-uncle in court, continuing to insist that he had no right to the savings bonds. The case brought renewed attention to Madame Restell as multiple witnesses testified about the inner workings of the Lohman household and the squabble between the estranged siblings. As the *Herald* reported in December of 1878, "not even pelting rain and fierce winds which howled about the Court House yesterday could keep away the crowd thronging the entrance to Judge J. F. Daly's Court." On December 11, the jury sided with Trow and rendered a verdict in his favor in the amount of $15,127.45, which included the interest that the bonds would have accrued. Not content with the verdict, Shannon appealed and lost the case in New York's supreme court, which affirmed the lower court's judgment in late 1879. The next year, the U.S. census listed Trow as "Retail Medicine Manufacturer," and ads for various remedies under the name A.M. Mauriceau at 129 Liberty Street continued to appear in New York newspapers at least through 1884. Trow died in 1889, eleven years after his sister, and is buried with his wife in Greenport, on New York's Long Island. They did not have children.[9]

Caroline Summers Purdy Farrell lived only three years longer than her mother, dying at the age of fifty-seven on December 16, 1881. At the time of her death, she was living uptown on East 116th Street. Farrell bequeathed all her jewelry to her daughter, Carrie Shannon; a photo album and portrait of herself in childhood to her son, Charles Purdy; and the remainder of her estate to her husband, William B. Farrell.[10]

Following their grandmother's death, at least initially, Carrie and William Shannon and Charles Purdy all continued to live at 657 Fifth Avenue, along with a staff of five servants. In 1883, five years after her death, the Shannons and the Purdys converted both the mansion on Fifth Avenue and the neighboring Osborne Apartments, which they had also inherited from Restell, into a large hotel called the Langham, which they ran with a staff. They continued to reside in rooms in the hotel, renting out the others to paying guests. Carrie and her husband had five children. Of those children, only two survived into adulthood. Carrie herself died in 1891, when her eldest child was only twelve. She was buried near her grandmother in Sleepy Hollow Cemetery.[11]

Madame Restell's grandson, Charles Purdy, also married, in 1888 to Abbie Wilkinson, at the Presbyterian Church, in Bergen, New Jersey. The Purdys chose to move out of the Langham with their young son, and the family relocated to a town on the southern shore of Long Island. The Restell fortune supported the Shannons and Purdys, neither of them seeming to have worked for a living. Charles's occupation is listed as "gentleman" in the 1920 census. He died on January 29, 1922, at his home in Bayport. He is buried in a large mausoleum in the Sleepy Hollow Cemetery, around the corner from the resting place of his sister and her children. The mausoleum clearly has room for at least five other caskets, but Charles is its only occupant.[12]

As late as 1901, New York's city directory listed the Langham hotel at 657 Fifth Avenue, with Charles Purdy as the proprietor with a home in Bayport, Long Island. In 1902, some of the remaining heirs sold the Langham to the United States Realty and Construction Company for $1.3 million, though other reports had the price as low as $600,000. The final link between the Lohman/Purdy family and the large property at the corner of Fifty-Second Street and Fifth Avenue had been severed. A rumor at the time had it that the purchasing company was a front for the Vanderbilt family, who already owned houses on the same block. In June of 1903, the contents of the Langham were auctioned off over the course of four days. No doubt some of the "Brussels carpets" and "solid mahogany, Bird's-eye maple, and Oak bedroom Furniture" dated from the building's original occupants. In subsequent years, the corner lot had a number of different occupants, and Madame Restell's home was razed. It is today the New York flagship store of Ferragamo, the Italian luxury leather goods company.[13]

* * * *

Two years after Madame Restell's death, the state of New York once again revised a section of its law on abortion, to now stipulate that it was a crime to "advise or procure any such woman to submit to the use or employment of any instrument or other means whatever, with intent thereby to procure" a miscarriage. The prior statute, from 1872, had already criminalized the sale, manufacture, and prescription of abortifacients and those who advised women to take them, but lawmakers had neglected to include the advising of women who sought an abortion via instruments. In 1880, they closed that loophole. Thanks to male doctors and legislators, abortion remained illegal in New York State for the next ninety years, just as it was in the rest of the United States.[14]

Anthony Comstock also cast a long shadow over the twentieth century, especially in the realm of birth control and obscenity. It was under Comstock's legal regime that birth control crusaders like Margaret Sanger were prosecuted, for decades limiting women's access to the ability to control their reproductive lives. It was not until 1965 that the U.S. Supreme Court ruled that married couples had a constitutional right to use contraception. Single people were not guaranteed that right for another seven years, in 1972. Comstock's other great target—anything he deemed obscene—was not reevaluated by the highest court in the land until 1957. In *Roth v. United States*, the court widened First Amendment protections for materials that some might find sexually offensive. In 1973, in *Miller v. California*, the court further limited what could be censored by the government. At least some portion of the Comstock Act (or various mini–Comstock laws) had then been in effect for a full one hundred years. His influence lives on in calls to use the Comstock Act to ban the United States Postal Service from delivering drugs meant to induce abortion.[15]

Among the other lasting impacts of the nineteenth-century crusade against abortion, particularly that waged by doctors, was a thorough devaluation of women's knowledge of their own bodies and their ability to make decisions about them. Abortion, which had once been a safe and routine medical procedure that a woman herself could elect to undergo, had been removed from women's control. Recall the American Medical Association's statement in 1857: "We are the physical guardians of women; we, alone, thus far, of their offspring in utero." Even when *Roe v. Wade* was decided in 1973, it afforded a woman the right to terminate a pregnancy in its early stages with the "medical judgment of the pregnant woman's attending physician." Just as the natural process of childbirth had been thoroughly medicalized and wrested from the supervision of female midwives over the course of the nineteenth century, so too had abortion care been subsumed under doctors' domain.[16]

Just as in the age of Madame Restell, however, women continued to terminate their pregnancies in the years before *Roe*. The practice tended to come to light when women died following a botched abortion. Police and prosecutors often attempted to procure "dying declarations" from women, which could be used in court to prosecute those who had operated on them. For every abortion that came to light through tragedy, however, there were thousands more performed by skilled practitioners just like Madame Restell. Ruth Barnett operated a successful clinic in Portland, Oregon, between 1918 and 1968, illegally seeing thousands of patients over the course of her career. Inez Brown Burns ran a series of clinics in San Francisco between 1922 and 1946, when she was eventually convicted. She estimated that she and her staff performed more than 150,000 abortions in those twenty-four years. In 1969, near the tail end of the era of illegal abortion, and energized by the second wave of the women's movement, a group of feminists in Chicago taught themselves how to terminate pregnancies and formed a collective they called Jane, or the Abortion Counseling Service of Women's Liberation. The one-hundred-member collective helped some eleven thousand women end their pregnancies.[17]

Even after the 2022 Supreme Court ruling in *Dobbs v. Jackson Women's Health Organization*, women will not stop terminating their pregnancies. The issue, including during the period when it was mostly legal, remains access. Wealthy and white women living in more Democratic-leaning states have long enjoyed access to abortion and other reproductive health care that poor women of color, as well as those in Republican-controlled states, have been denied. In an era when abortion remained a constitutionally protected right nationwide, anti-choice activists worked to limit its access, either through passing more than 1,100 laws that are burdensome on clinics or that delay a woman's ability to access abortion care, or through outright intimidation of abortion providers and the people they serve. By 2017, five years before *Dobbs*, there were already six states that had only a single clinic. In anticipation of a post–*Dobbs* era, pro-choice activists have themselves worked tirelessly on behalf of abortion funds that transport women to states with abortion access and to publicize self-managed abortions, where women take misoprostol or a combination of mifepristone and misoprostol to terminate their own pregnancies. But just as in prior eras, there is no question that women of means will have greater access.[18]

The charged debates about abortion, laden with notions of life and death, gender, sexuality, and childhood, both were and were not about abortion itself. In the nineteenth century, abortion, as well as people like Madame Restell who provided it, became symbols for societal changes: the size of families, the authority of doctors, the origin of the nation's populace, women's autonomy. While the issues that animate today's debate about abortion are different in some ways from those of the nineteenth century, at their heart they can still be condensed down to whether we believe that a woman should be entrusted with making among the most important choices she can about her own body and livelihood. As the obstetrician-gynecologist Lisa H. Harris wrote in a 2019 op ed in the *New York Times*, "I know that for every woman whose abortion I perform, I stop a developing human from being born. And I also know that I can't turn my back on the people who ask for my care. Both things are true at the same time." We also know from the landmark 2020 *Turnaway Study* that women who are denied the right to an abortion are worse off ten years later, by almost every measure, than are those women who were able to terminate their pregnancies. From her earliest advertisement in 1839, Madame Restell demonstrated that she knew this as well. Her success owes as much to her skill as it does to her understanding of women's fundamental need to control their own bodies and their lives.[19]

ACKNOWLEDGMENTS

I wrote much of this book during the 2020/21 academic year at a time when most of us were locked away in our homes trying to avoid COVID-19. That I was not teaching, remotely or otherwise, is thanks to a fellowship from the American Council of Learned Societies, without which this book would not exist, at least not in its present form. I am very grateful for the time afforded by that fellowship. Thanks also to Pam Gordon, who stepped in as department chair for the year; little did she know what was in store for her when she first accepted the job in February of 2020. I am grateful that she remained willing even when the worst of the pandemic was upon us. Thanks also to Robin Bernstein, Mike Grossberg, and Wendy Kline, who wrote letters of recommendation to multiple fellowships, including the ACLS, and to Kathy Porsch, at the University of Kansas's Hall Center for the Humanities, who kept all of the applications in order and actually submitted them. Thanks to Marie Brown and Aimee Wilson, who read early drafts of those applications.

Thanks to the archivists at the Schlesinger Library at Radcliffe College; the New York City Municipal Archives; the New York State Archives in Albany; the American Antiquarian Society; the Library of Congress; the Countway Medical Library; the Museum of Contraception and Abortion in Vienna; and the National Archives and Records Administration in Washington, DC. For putting me up as I traveled to archives, thanks to Tom Meyers, Guillaume Normand, and Emily G. Ford. Thanks also to the University of Kansas for funds to pay for these trips. For research assistance, I am indebted to Emma Piazza and Brian Trump, who mined newspaper databases in the early stages of this project.

I was able to present early portions of this research, pre-pandemic and virtually at Duke University (thanks to an invitation from Frances Hasso), in the Gender Seminar at KU's Hall Center for the Humanities (thanks especially to Ann Schofield for questions), and at the annual meeting of the Organization of American Historians and the biannual meeting of the Society for the History of Children and Youth. I also received feedback from participants in the biographers' workshop at the annual meeting of the Society for Historians of the Early American Republic. Thanks to fellow panelists and participants for their comments and questions. Thanks also to Tom Meyers and Greg Young, who had me on an episode of *The Bowery Boys* podcast to talk about Madame Restell when I was just starting work on this project; and to Will Mackintosh and Elena Ryan for soliciting a short essay for *The Panorama*.

I am especially grateful to my agent, Deirdre Mullane, who responded within about half an hour when I first sent her a proposal. Her enthusiasm and publishing know-how and the continued alacrity of her responses made the publication of this book an enjoyable process. Thanks to Julie Enszer, formerly of The New Press, who signed up the book. And to Ben Woodward, who took over when Julie left. Ben's critical eye has sharpened my prose and made the book—especially the trial chapters—so much more readable. Many thanks to Emily Albarillo who saw the book through production and to Kat Thomas for her keen copyeditor's eye. Thanks also to my longtime friend Libby McCalden for the map of Madame Restell's New York.

I am lucky to have two workplaces at the University of Kansas and wonderful colleagues in both of them: the Department of Women, Gender, and Sexuality Studies and the Office of the Dean of the College of Liberal Arts and Sciences. As chair of our department, I especially enjoyed coordinating its doings with Katie Batza, Amara Simons, and Stacey Vanderhurst. In the dean's office, I am grateful to my colleagues Heather Anderson, Mercedes Bounthapanya, Margaret Brumberg, Amanda Burghart, John Colombo, Alesha Doan, Ben Eggleston, Arash Mafi, Jill Mignacca, Maria Orive, Mark Reynolds, and Melinda Robinson.

A number of scholars either answered my questions or took the time to contact me about sources they had found. Thanks to Patricia Cline Cohen, Nancy Cott, Holly Dugan, April Haynes, Marni Kessler, Julie Miller, and especially

Lisa H. Harris, who walked me through Madame Restell's likely medical practices and the logistics of self-managed abortion. My colleague and reproductive policy expert, Alesha E. Doan, read and discussed the conclusion with me. Novelist Glori Simmons and I exchanged drafts of our work; I learned much from her fictional portrayal of Restell's early days. Andy Denning and I walked through the Lawrence Mutt Run with our dogs many times when we couldn't meet inside, talking about the books we were both writing.

Marie Grace Brown, Patricia Cline Cohen, and Corinne T. Field read the whole manuscript. I am very grateful to them. Marie read the chapters as I wrote them and often provided the deadline I needed; she also pointed out what I couldn't see. Pat, though she may not know it, spurred me to start writing and read the whole manuscript when I was done, pointing out all kinds of silly errors and assumptions I was making. Cori read chapters as I wrote them and the whole thing once I was done, always urging me to pay attention to the bigger picture. The book is far better for all of their reading and suggestions; any errors that remain are my own. Thanks also to Tom Meyers, Pat Cohen, Debby Applegate, Rachel Louise Snyder, V, Ann Fabian, and Martha Hodes, who graciously read the manuscript and provided pre-publication blurbs.

I am an obsessive reader of acknowledgments and I have long believed that including one's pet is a foolish affectation, even though I am also a lover of dogs. Yes, it is true that Sadie Louise Poppleton Pahr-Syrett sat with me as I wrote almost every word of this book, but she'll never be able to read any of the words, including the ones in these acknowledgments. I changed my mind the day Sadie escaped our yard, probably chasing a rabbit, and disappeared for almost three bitterly cold days in December of 2022. On Christmas she reappeared, as blasé as can be, almost entirely unharmed. No matter what happened—and I feared the worst—I had already vowed that I would take every opportunity to document my devotion to her. Whoever bothers to read these words shall know that this book's author adores his dog beyond measure.

Thanks, finally, to my friends and my family: my mother, Katie Syrett; brother, Tim Syrett; sister-in-law, Angela Brooks; nephews, Alex and Zach Syrett; and my partner, Michael Pahr, for everything else.

NOTES

INTRODUCTION

1. The *New York Express* story is reprinted in "Madame Restell Repudiated," *New York Daily Tribune*, March 16, 1855, 7. My thanks to April Haynes for alerting me to this incident and sending me the article.
2. Descriptions of Restell in prior coverage are from "Restell, the Female Abortionist," *National Police Gazette*, March 13, 1847, 27; "The Case of Madame Restell," *New-York Tribune*, April 28, 1841, 2; "City Intelligence," *New York Evening Post*, February 4, 1846, 2.
3. "Madame Restell Repudiated."
4. "Shirt Sewers and Seamstresses' Union," *New York Times*, March 23, 1855, 6.
5. "Thin-Skinned, Questionable Morality," *New York Atlas*, March 18, 1855, 2. On other reporting, see coverage reprinted from the *New-York Tribune* in *Buffalo Courier*, March 24, 1855, 2.
6. Restell letter dated March 17, 1855 in "Thin-Skinned," March 18, 1855.
7. Restell letter in "Thin-Skinned."
8. "Madame Restell and Her Husband," *Wheeling Daily Intelligence*, August 28, 1856, 2; "Madame Restell and Her Husband," *Weekly Wisconsin*, October 15, 1856, 1.

1. ANN TROW SUMMERS LOHMAN

1. "To Married Women," *New York Sun*, March 27, 1839, quoted in Clifford Browder, *The Wickedest Woman in New York: Madame Restell, the Abortionist* (Hamden, CT: Archon, 1988), 9.
2. Birth date is on her headstone at Sleepy Hollow Cemetery in Sleepy Hollow, New York; baptism date and parents' names are at Gloucestershire, England, Church of England Baptisms, Marriages, and Burials, 1538–1813, ancestry.com. Marriage of John Trow and Anne Biddle in Gloucestershire Church of England Marriages and Banns, 1754–1938: December 19, 1802, ancestry.com. On Painswick, see "A Short History of Painswick," www.painswick users.org.uk/plhs/history/historyofpainswick.htm.
3. Baptism records for William Trow (December 4, 1803); James Trow (April 4, 1806); Thomas Trow (August 14, 1808); John Trow (October 31, 1813); Mary Trow (March 10, 1816); Stephen

Trow (October 10, 1818); Joseph Trow (October 7, 1821); and Edwin Trow (February 8, 1824), all in Gloucestershire, Church of England Baptisms, 1538–1813, ancestry.com.

4. Marriage record of Ann Trow and Henry Summers, March 26, 1829, Wootton Bassett, Wiltshire, England, ancestry.com; banns are found at Wiltshire, England, Church of England Marriages and Banns, 1754–1916, March 8, March 15, and March 22, ancestry.com; christening record for Henry Summers, son of Samuel and Anne, July 17, 1803, Wootton Bassett, Wiltshire, England, ancestry.com. R.B. Outhwaite, "Age at Marriage in England from the Late Seventeenth to the Nineteenth Century," *Transactions of the Royal Historical Society* 23 (January 1973): 55–70.

5. Baptism record for Caroline Summers, February 21, 1830, Wootton Bassett, Wiltshire, England, ancestry.com; Robert Ernst, *Immigrant Life in New York City, 1825–1863* (New York: King's Crown, 1949), 10.

6. "Aboard a Packet," National Museum of American History, americanhistory.si.edu/on-the-water/maritime-nation/enterprise-water/aboard-packet; Ernst, *Immigrant Life*, 11–13.

7. Ernst, *Immigrant Life*, 25–26.

8. Ernst, *Immigrant Life*, 27–29.

9. "Total and Foreign-Born Population New York City, 1790–2000," www1.nyc.gov/assets/planning/download/pdf/data-maps/nyc-population/historical-population/1790-2000_nyc_total_foreign_birth.pdf; Edwin G. Burrows and Mike Wallace, *Gotham: A History of New York City to 1898* (New York: Oxford University Press, 1999), 479; Leslie M. Harris, *In The Shadow of Slavery: African Americans in New York City, 1626–1863* (Chicago: University of Chicago Press, 2003), chap. 3.

10. Burrows and Wallace, *Gotham,* 456–59; de Tocqueville quoted on 459.

11. Burrows and Wallace, *Gotham,* 475–77.

12. For the address on William Street, see Browder, *The Wickedest Woman in New York,* 4; Joseph Trow, respondent, against Carrie S. Shannon, Ex'x, and c., appellant *New York Court of Appeals, Cases and Briefs,* Vol. 51, 1878, 21, New York State Library, Albany.

13. Record for Henry Summers, August 16, 1831, Manhattan Deaths, Vol. 7, 1829–32, New York Municipal Archives.

14. Timothy Gilfoyle, *City of Eros: New York City, Prostitution, and the Commercialization of Sex, 1790–1920* (New York: Norton, 1992), chap. 2.

15. Christine Stansell, *City of Women: Sex and Class in New York, 1789–1860* (New York: Knopf, 1982), 110–11.

16. Stansell, *City of Women,* 55–57.

17. Wedding announcement in *New York Spectator,* September 30, 1833, 1. Some historians have dated the marriage to 1836, but this announcement makes it clear it occurred three years earlier. Bob Greiner, "The Pastoral Records of Frederick W. Geissenhainer," September 26, 2012, www.nyhistory.org/blogs/the-pastoral-records-of-frederick-w-geissenhainer.

18. Katharina Neufeld, "The History of Russian-Germans," Museum fur RusslandDeutsche Kurturgeschichte, www.russlanddeutsche.de/en/russian-germans/history/the-history-of-russian-germans.html; "The American Library," *American,* September 13, 1834, 2; Harriet Martineau, *Retrospect of Western Travel,* vol. 1 (New York: Charles Lohman, 1838); *The Addresses and Messages of the Presidents of the United States to Congress: Comprising All the Inaugural, Annual, Special, and Farewell Addresses and Messages of Washington, Adams, Jefferson, Madison, Monroe, John Q. Adams, Jackson and Van Buren, Complete in One Volume* (New York: Charles Lohman, 1837); "Citizenship Declaration of Charles

Lohman, Marine Court of the City of New York," April 19, 1836, vol. 17, p. 310, ancestry
.com.

19. "List of Manifest of All the Passengers on Board the Ship *Ontario,* October 25, 1838, District of New York, Port of New York, Arriving Passenger and Crew Lists," ancestry.com.

20. The portrait is in the collection of the Museum of Contraception and Abortion in Vienna. The museum acquired the miniature at auction from Dr. Jeurgen Fischer, Heilbronner Auction House, GmbH and Co. KG. My thanks to art historian Marni Kessler for helping me to understand the miniature.

21. Judith Walzer Leavitt, *Brought to Bed: Child-Bearing in America, 1750–1950* (New York: Oxford University Press, 1986), 37–38; Laurel Thatcher Ulrich, *A Midwife's Tale: The Life of Martha Ballard, Based on Her Diary, 1785–1812* (New York: Vintage Books, 1991); Susan H. Brandt, *Women Healers: Gender, Authority, and Medicine in Early Philadelphia* (Philadelphia: University of Pennsylvania Press, 2022); Sharla Fett, *Working Cures: Healing, Health, and Power on Southern Slave Plantations* (Chapel Hill: University of North Carolina Press, 2002), esp. chap. 3.

22. Leavitt, *Brought to Bed;* Ulrich, *A Midwife's Tale;* Elizabeth Fee, "The First American Medical School: The Formative Years," *The Lancet* 385, no. 9981 (2015): 1940–41.

23. On Blackwell, see Janice P. Nimura, *The Doctors Blackwell: How Two Pioneering Sisters Brought Medicine to Women—and Women to Medicine* (New York: Norton, 2021). For examples of "female physician," see Mott: Thomas Longworth, Joline J. Butler, and George P. Scott and Co., *Longworth's American Almanac New-York Register and City Directory for the Sixty-Third Year of American Independence* (New York: Thomas Longworth, 1838), 462; *Longworth's American Almanac New-York Register and City Directory for the Sixty-Fourth Year of American Independence* (New York: Thomas Longworth, 1839), 478, 548; Welch: "Card to Ladies," *New York Daily Herald,* November 21, 1837, 4; Costello: "To Married Ladies," *New York Daily Herald,* March 3, 1843, 4; Bird: "Dr. Vandenburgh's Female Renovating Pills," *New York Daily Herald,* February 12, 1838, 3; "Physician, n.," OED Online. Oxford University Press, www-oed-com.www2.lib.ku.edu/view/Entry/143129?result=1&rskey =ByjQ3q&; Ruth Horowitz, *In the Public Interest: Medical Licensing and the Disciplinary Process* (New Brunswick, NJ: Rutgers University Press, 2013); Regina Markell Morantz-Sanchez, *Sympathy and Science: Women Physicians in American Medicine* (New York: Oxford University Press, 1985), 188–89.

24. "Indictment and Arrest of the Notorious Mrs. Restell," *Morning Courier and New-York Enquirer,* August 19, 1839, 1, lists Charles Lohman's address as 39 Catherine Street; advertisement in *New York Evening Post,* July 2, 1837, 1; "Medical Communication," *New York Evening Post,* January 2, 1838, 3; "Dr. Evans' Celebrated Medicines," *New York Morning Herald,* December 4, 1839, 3; advertisement in *New York Herald,* April 23, 1838, 4. On the "change of life," see John Edward Tilt, *The Change of Life in Health and Disease: A Practical Treatise on the Nervous and Other Affections Incidental to Women at the Decline of Life,* 3rd ed. (London: John Churchill and Sons, 1870).

25. On abortifacients, see John M. Riddle, *Eve's Herbs: A History of Contraception and Abortion in the West* (Cambridge, MA: Harvard University Press, 1997); Linda Gordon, *Woman's Body, Woman's Right: Birth Control in America* (New York: Penguin, 1974), 36–37; Andrea Tone, *Devices and Desires: A History of Contraceptives in America* (New York: Hill and Wang, 2001), 14.

26. "Coroner's Office," *New York Herald,* August 13, 1839, 3; "Death from Oil of Tanzy," *Morning Courier and New-York Enquirer,* August 13, 1839.

27. "Mysterious Case," *New York Evening Post*, March 19, 1840, 2; "Mysterious Death of Susan Skaats," *New York Evening Post*, April 17, 1840, 2; "Charge of Manslaughter," *Albany Argus*, May 25, 1840, 4.

28. Roger Thompson, *Sex in Middlesex: Popular Mores in a Massachusetts County, 1649–1699* (Amherst: University of Massachusetts Press, 1986), 25; Cornelia Hughes Dayton, "'Taking the Trade': Abortion and Gender Relations in an Eighteenth-Century New England Village," *William and Mary Quarterly* 48, no. 1 (January 1991): 19–49; James C. Mohr, *Abortion in America: The Origins and Evolution of National Policy* (New York: Oxford University Press, 1978), 3–6; William Blackstone, *Commentaries on the Laws of England* (Oxford: Clarendon, 1765), 1:125–26.

29. Mohr, *Abortion in America*, 21; *Report of the Trial of Ammi Rogers, for a High Crime and Misdemeanor, in a Brutal and High Handed Assault on the Body of Asenath Caroline Smith, of Griswold, Conn.* (New London, CT: Samuel Green, 1820).

30. *Revised Statutes of the State of New York* (Albany, NY: Packard and Van Benthuysen, 1829), 2:661, 663. § 9 was subsequently revised to make clear that the crime could only be manslaughter if either the fetus or mother died as a result of the abortion. In other words, an attempted abortion could not be manslaughter. See *Revised Statutes of the State of New York* (Albany, NY: Packard and Van Benthuysen, 1829), 3:158.

31. *1829 Statutes*, 2:694; Mohr, *Abortion in America*, 27.

32. Mohr, *Abortion in America*, 28–29; Cyril C. Means Jr., "The Law of New York Concerning Abortion and the Status of the Foetus, 1664–1968," *New York Law Forum* 14, no. 3 (Fall 1968): 411–515.

33. Entry for Charles Lohman, year: 1840; census place: New York Ward Three, New York, New York; roll 299; page 127; family history library film: 0017194, ancestry.com.

2. A LETTER TO MARRIED WOMEN

1. "Mrs. Restell, Alias, Mrs. Loman," *Sunday Morning News*, July 21, 1839, clipping attached to note from James R. Whiting of same date, Anna Dall folder, Madame Restell Papers, Schlesinger Library, Harvard University (hereafter Restell Papers).

2. On abortion in earlier eras, see James Mohr, *Abortion in America: The Origins and Evolution of National Policy, 1800–1900* (New York: Oxford University Press, 1979), chap. 1; Cornelia Hughes Dayton, "Taking the Trade: Abortion and Gender Relations in an Eighteenth-Century New England Village," *William and Mary Quarterly* 48, no. 1 (January 1991): 19–49. For the regulations as of 1829, see Title 2, § 9 and Title 6, § 21, *Revised Statutes of the State of New York* (Albany, NY: Packard and Van Benthuysen, 1829), 2: 661, 694; Mohr, *Abortion in America*, 26–28.

3. "Genuine English Patent Medicines," *New York Evening Post*, May 18, 1833, 3; "Female Complaints," *New York Daily Herald*, November 8, 1837, 3; "Midwifery," *New York Daily Herald*, October 27, 1837, 3; "Dr. Vandenburgh's Female Renovating Pills," *New York Daily Herald*, February 12, 1838, 3.

4. Martin Olasky, "Advertising Abortion During the 1830s and 1840s: Madame Restell Builds a Business," *Journalism History* 13, no. 2 (1986): 50. For more on advertising abortion in this era, see Mohr, *Abortion in America*, chap. 3; Helen Lefkowitz Horowitz, *Rereading Sex: Battles Over Sexual Knowledge in Nineteenth-Century America* (New York: Knopf,

2002), 198–200; Janet Farrell Brodie, *Abortion and Contraception in Nineteenth-Century America* (Ithaca, NY: Cornell University Press, 1994), 224–31.

5. "Madame Restell's Monthly Female Regulating Pills," *New York Morning Herald*, November 2, 1839, 3.

6. "To Married Women," *New York Morning Herald*, November 2, 1839, 3; "Madame Restell's Female Monthly Pills," *Public Ledger* (Philadelphia), November 12, 1839, 3; "Female Monthly Pills," *Boston Post*, November 10, 1840, 1; "Right and Proper," *New York Mechanic*, March 27, 1841, 2.

7. On maternal mortality rates, see Judith Walzer Leavitt, *Brought to Bed: Child-Bearing in America, 1750–1950* (New York: Oxford University Press, 1986), 25; Judith Walzer Leavitt, "Under the Shadow of Maternity: American Women's Responses to Death and Debility Fears in Nineteenth-Century Childbirth," *Feminist Studies* 12, no. 1 (Spring 1986): 136. Today the rate is about fifteen women per one hundred thousand pregnancies in the United States. See Laura Helmuth, "The Disturbing, Shameful History of Childbirth Deaths," *Slate*, September 10, 2013.

8. "Morals of the Rising Generation," *New York Herald*, March 27, 1839, 2.

9. James R. Whiting to grand jury, July 21, 1839, Dall folder, Restell Papers.

10. On the development of a paid police force as we know it today, which commenced in 1845 in New York, see Wilbur R. Miller, *Cops and Bobbies: Police Authority in New York and London, 1830–1870* (Chicago: University of Chicago Press, 1973), chap. 1; Amy Gilman Srebnick, *The Mysterious Death of Mary Rogers: Sex and Culture in Nineteenth-Century New York* (New York: Oxford University Press, 1997), 96–97.

11. Mark Kadish, "Behind the Locked Doors of an American Grand Jury: Its History, Its Secrecy, Its Purpose," *Florida State University Law Review* 24, no. 1 (1996): 19; Richard D. Younger, *The People's Panel: The Grand Jury in the United States, 1634–1941* (Providence, RI: American History Research Center, Brown University, 1963), 4.

12. Deposition of Pamela Palmer, August 20, 1839; deposition of Hester Wells, August 20, 1839, Dall folder, Restell Papers.

13. Palmer and Wells depositions.

14. Deposition of Anna Dall, August 6, 1839, Dall folder, Restell Papers.

15. Indictment in *People of the State of New York v. Madame Restell*, August 16, 1839, Dall folder, Restell Papers.

16. Indictment in *People v. Madame Restell*.

17. Indictment in *People v. Madame Restell*; "The Grand Inquest," *New York Daily Herald*, August 19, 1839, 2; "Indictment and Arrest of the Notorious Mrs. Restell," *Morning Courier and New-York Enquirer*, August 19, 1839, 1.

18. Indictment in *People v. Madame Restell*; "The Grand Inquest"; "Indictment and Arrest." On the Tombs, see Julie Miller, *Cry of Murder on Broadway: A Woman's Ruin and Revenge in Old New York* (Ithaca, NY: Three Hills, an imprint of Cornell University Press, 2020), 58–64.

19. "The Case of Mrs. Restell," *New York Daily Herald*, August 21, 1839, 3. On immigration and abortion, see also Nicola Beisel, *Imperiled Innocents: Anthony Comstock and Family Reproduction in Victorian America* (Princeton, NJ: Princeton University Press, 1997), 9; Nicola Beisel and Tamara Kay, "Abortion, Race, and Gender in Nineteenth-Century America," *American Sociological Review* 69 (2004): 498–518; Mohr, *Abortion in America*, 166–67; Carroll Smith-Rosenberg, "The Abortion Movement and the AMA, 1850–1880," in *Disorderly Conduct: Visions of Gender in Victorian America* (New York: Knopf, 1985), 217–44.

20. "General Sessions," *New York Daily Herald*, October 7, 1839, 3; "Madame Restell's New Issues," *New York Daily Herald*, November 2, 1839, 2.

21. Almshouse ledger confirms the admission of Anna "Dale," an eighteen-year-old from Germany on December 17, 1839; see "Bellevue Alms House Ledger, 1839–1841," Almshouse Ledger Collection, New York Municipal Archives Digital Collections; Statement of Dr. Fraché, July 22, 1840, in Dall folder, Restell Papers; Madame Restell, "Legal Injustice: Effects of Persecution!," *New York Daily Herald*, November 24, 1840, 5. On the almshouse as the only site for an impoverished and unmarried woman to give birth at that time, see Virginia A. Metaxas Quiroga, *Poor Mothers and Babies: A Social History of Childbirth and Child Care Hospitals in Nineteenth-Century New York City* (New York: Garland, 1991), 30–31.

22. "Legal Injustice: Effects of Persecution!," 5, and also in *New York Sun*, November 21, 1840, 1; "Court of Sessions," *New York Herald*, November 19, 1840, 1; "Court of Sessions—Yesterday," *New York Sun*, November 19, 1840; "Removal—Madame Restell," *New York Daily Herald*, April, 15, 1840, 3.

23. "Legal Injustice"; "Court of Sessions"; "Court of Sessions—Yesterday"; "Removal."

24. Dale Cockrell, *Demons of Disorder: Early Blackface Minstrels and Their World* (New York: Cambridge University Press, 1997), 49, 96–101; Patricia Cline Cohen, Timothy J. Gilfoyle, Helen Lefkowitz Horowitz, eds., in association with the American Antiquarian Society, *The Flash Press: Sporting Male Weeklies in 1840s New York* (Chicago: University of Chicago Press, 2008), 10, 18, 35, 38.

25. Cockrell, *Demons of Disorder*; Cohen, Gilfoyle, and Horowitz, *The Flash Press*.

26. "Keep It Before the People," *Dixon's Polyanthos*, February 16, 1841, 44.

27. "Keep It Before the People."

28. On Dixon's politics and that of the *Polyanthos*, see Cohen, Gilfoyle, and Horowitz, *The Flash Press*, 40; Nicole C. Livengood, "'Thus Did Restell Seal This Unfortunate Lady's Lips with a Lie': George Washington Dixon's *Polyanthos* and the Seduction Narrative," *American Journalism* 33, no. 3 (2016): 289–316.

29. "Madame Restell," *Dixon's Polyanthos*, March 6, 1841, 66; Tyler Anbinder, *Five Points: The 19th-Century New York City Neighborhood That Invented Tap Dance, Stole Elections, and Became the World's Most Notorious Slum* (New York: Free Press, 2001), esp. 207–19.

30. "Restell Caught at Last," *Dixon's Polyanthos*, March 20, 1841, 84–85; "General Sessions," *Morning Courier and New-York Enquirer*, March 17, 1841; *Newark Daily Advertiser*, March 18, 1841, 2; "Presentment," *Philadelphia Daily Chronicle*, March 22, 1841, 4.

31. "Restell Caught at Last," 85.

32. Restell, "Legal Injustice," 5.

33. Restell, "Legal Injustice," 5.

3. IN THE FAMILY WAY

1. Deposition of Ann Maria Purdy, March 22, 1841, Purdy folder, Restell Papers, Schlesinger Library, Harvard University. Much of Ann Maria Purdy's deposition was reproduced in newspapers throughout New York State, though the original is worth examining, because many of the papers' accounts either exaggerate or ignore certain statements made by Purdy. Bear in mind that depositions, though often written in the third person, were composed as if the deponent were simply speaking in a monologue about the events they had witnessed. What actually occurred was that someone interviewed the witness and the answers were strung together into a narrative, which the witness then affirmed by signing the deposition. What this means is that some of the answers Purdy gave, or the emphasis that certain events might be given in a deposition, could be a reflection of the questioner and not the deponent herself. Depositions were mediated documents, in other words, and those that did not include the answers *as well as* the questions, which this one does not, are often tailored to paint a particular picture. Many scholars have examined Restell's trial for Purdy's abortion, and while I learned much from their accounts, I also differ from some of them in my interpretation. For other accounts, see Amy Gilman Srebnick, *The Mysterious Death of Mary Rogers: Sex and Culture in Nineteenth-Century New York* (New York: Oxford University Press, 1995), esp. 97–107; Helen Lefkowitz Horowitz, *Rereading Sex: Battles over Sexual Knowledge in Nineteenth-Century America* (New York: Knopf, 2002), 200–201; A. Cheree Carlson, *The Crimes of Womanhood: Defining Femininity in a Court of Law* (Urbana: University of Illinois Press, 2009), 111–35; Eric Homberger, *Scenes from the Life of a City: Corruption and Conscience in Old New York* (New Haven: Yale University Press, 1994), 98–99, 110; Clifford Browder, *The Wickedest Woman in New York: Madame Restell, the Abortionist* (Hamden, CT: Archon, 1981), chap. 2; Nicole C. Livengood, "'Thus Did Restell Seal This Unfortunate Lady's Lips with a Lie': George Washington Dixon's *Polyanthos* and the Seduction Narrative," *American Journalism* 33, no. 3 (2016): 289–316.

2. Deposition of Ann Maria Purdy.

3. Deposition of Ann Maria Purdy.

4. Deposition of Ann Maria Purdy.

5. Deposition of Ann Maria Purdy.

6. My thanks to Dr. Lisa Harris, MD, PhD, for walking me through this method and its implications.

7. Title 2, § 9 and Title 6, § 21, *Revised Statutes of the State of New York* (Albany, NY: Packard and Van Benthuysen, 1829), 2: 661, 662–63, 694.

8. Deposition of Ann Maria Purdy.

9. "Police: Arrest of Madame Restell," *Brooklyn Daily Evening Star*, March 24, 1841, 2.

10. Deposition of Ann Maria Purdy; Bill of Exceptions, *Madame Restell v. the People*, May 10, 1842, Supreme Court of the Judicature Pleadings, 1838–1847, box 9, New York State Archives, Albany; opinion in *People v. Madam Restell, alias Ann Lohman*, 3 Hill 289 (1842 NY Lexis 208).

11. "Examination of Mrs. Restell," *New York Morning Express,* March 25, 1841, 2; "Madam Restell," *New York Herald*, March 29, 1841.

12. "Before Judge Inglis," *Brooklyn Daily Evening Star*, April 2, 1841, 2; "Madame Restell," *Morning Courier and New York Enquirer*, April 3, 1841; "Madame Restell," *Evening Post*, April 7, 1841, 2; "City Intelligence," *New-York Tribune*, April 28, 1841, 2; "The Case of Madame Restell," *New-York Tribune*, April 28, 1841, 2. On the death of Ann Maria Purdy, see "Death of Mrs. Purdy," *Dixon's Polyanthos*, May 1, 1841, 129; "Trial of Madame Restell," *Brooklyn Evening Standard*, July 15, 1841, 2.

13. "Madame Restell," *Dixon's Polyanthos*, March 27, 1841, 90.

14. "Madame Restell," 90; "The Infamous Restell!!!," *Dixon's Polyanthos*, March 27, 1841, 91; "The Case of Madame Restell," *New-York Tribune*, April 28, 1841, 2.

15. "Madame Restell," 90; "The Case of Madame Restell," 2; "A Chapter on Mystery, Blood, and Murder," *Morning Courier and New-York Enquirer*, March 24, 1841; "City Intelligence," *New York Herald*, March 24, 1841. On the representation of Rebecca, see also Livengood, "'Thus Did Restell,'" 310.

16. Indictment in *People v. Madame Restell,* April 21, 1841, Restell Papers; "Madame Restell," *New York Spectator,* March 27, 1841, 2; "Madame Restell," *New-York Tribune,* April 24, 1841.

17. "Confinement," *New-York Atlas,* March 28, 1841, 2; "A Visit to the Prison," *Advocate for Moral Reform,* May 1, 1841, 71.

18. "City Intelligence," *New-York Tribune,* April 28, 1841, 2; "Case of Madame Restell," *New York Evening Post,* May 3, 1841, 2. See also "Madame Restell," *Dixon's Polyanthos,* May 1, 1841, 130; "General Sessions," *New York Herald,* May 11, 1841.

19. "To the Public," *New York Herald,* May 3, 1841. The *Morning Courier and New-York Enquirer* had indeed reported that Restell had been indicted for manslaughter and later claimed she was charged with murder. See "Restell," *Morning Courier and New-York Enquirer,* April 27, 1841, 1; "Death of Mrs. Purdy," *Morning Courier and New-York Enquirer,* May 4, 1841, 1.

20. "Madame Restell," *New-York Tribune,* May 13, 1841, 3; "City Intelligence," *New York Herald,* May 13, 1841; *New-York American,* May 13, 1841; "City Intelligence," *New York Herald,* second edition, May 14, 1841; *Longworth's American Almanac, New York Register, and City Directory* (1840–41) (New York: Thomas Longworth, 1840), 112; advertisement for "Madame Restell," *New York Herald,* June 1, 1841.

21. "General Sessions," *New York Herald,* July 15, 1841; "City Intelligence," *New-York Tribune,* July 15, 1841, 2; *Brooklyn Evening Star,* "Trial of Madame Restell," July 15, 1841, 2; Anonymous [George Washington Dixon], *Trial of Madame Restell, alias Ann Lohman for Abortion and Causing the Death of Mrs. Purdy* (New York: privately printed, 1841), 8.

22. Dixon, *Trial of Madame Restell,* 9–11, 12.

23. Dixon, *Trial of Madame Restell,* 12–13.

24. Dixon, *Trial of Madame Restell,* 14–17, quotation on 15.

25. "Court of Sessions," *New-York Tribune,* July 20, 1841, 2; Dixon, *Trial of Madame Restell,* 17, 18.

26. "Court of Sessions," 2; Dixon, *Trial of Madame Restell,* 18.

27. Dixon, *Trial of Madame Restell,* 18.

28. Dixon, *Trial of Madame Restell,* 18.

29. Dixon, *Trial of Madame Restell,* 19–20.

30. Dixon, *Trial of Madame Restell,* 19–20.

31. Bill of Exceptions, lines 76–77; "City Intelligence," *New-York Tribune,* July 21, 1841, 2; "General Sessions," *New York Herald,* July 21, 1841, 1. The transcript of the trial in the bill of exceptions makes it seem as if Betts did not actually carry out his errand, but it is a transcription, and the word "not" could easily have been mistakenly introduced. Multiple news sources state the opposite and there seems no reason that the defense would call Betts as a witness if he had not actually followed through on the errand.

32. Dixon, *Trial of Madame Restell,* 20; Bill of Exceptions, lines 78–79.

33. Dixon, *Trial of Madame Restell,* 21; "Madame Restell," *Brooklyn Evening Star,* July 21, 1841, 2.

34. "To the Public," *New-York Tribune,* July 22, 1841, 2.

35. Srebnick, *Mysterious Death of Mary Rogers*; "Madame Restell," *Dixon's Polyanthos,* October 9, 1841, front page.

36. Bill of Exceptions, *Madame Restell v. the People,* May 10, 1842; "Supreme Court," *Brooklyn Evening Star,* May 28, 1842, 2; opinion in *People v. Madame Restell, alias Ann Lohman,* 3 Hill 289 (1842 NY Lexis 208).

37. "Case of Madame Restell," *New-York Tribune,* August 24, 1842, 1; "Case of Madame Restell," *New York Herald,* August 27, 1842, 1 (italics in the original).

38. "Case of Madame Restell," *New-York Tribune*, 1; "Case of Madame Restell," *New York Herald*, 1.

39. "Case of Madame Restell," *New-York Tribune*, 1; "Case of Madame Restell," *New York Herald*, 1.

4. MADAME RESTELL'S COMPETITION

1. "Midwifery," *New York Daily Herald*, October 27, 1837, 3. Albertina Kowing arrived in Baltimore on the *Schiller* from Bremen to visit her mother in October of 1842. See "Baltimore, Maryland, U.S., Passenger Lists, 1820–1964." A J.F. Kowing, who may or may not be the same as Francis Kowing, arrived in New Orleans in 1843, also having left from Bremen. See "New Orleans, Louisiana, U.S., Passenger Lists, 1813–1964." Both records are available on ancestry.com.

2. "Mrs. Bird's Celebrated Soothing Syrup," *New York Daily Herald*, October 27, 1837, 3; advertisement, *New York Daily Herald*, October 30, 1837, 4; "A Real Blessing to Mothers," *New York Atlas*, January 24, 1841, 4; "Dr. Vandenburgh's Female Renovating Pills," *New York Daily Herald*, February 12, 1838, 3; "Mrs. Bird," *New York Daily Herald*, May 9, 1838, 3; *Longworth's American Almanac, New York Register and City Directory, 1840–41* (New York: Thomas Longworth, 1840), 95; *Doggett's New-York City and Co-Partnership Directory, 1843–44* (New York: John Doggett Jr., 1843), 37.

3. *Log Cabin* (New York, NY), March 27, 1841, 3; Virginia A. Metaxas Quiroga, *Poor Mothers and Babies: A Social History of Childbirth and Child Care Hospitals in Nineteenth-Century New York City* (New York: Garland, 1989), chap. 2.

4. "Inquest," *New York Evening News*, March 24, 1841, 1; "Police," *New York Commercial Advertiser*, March 24, 1841, 2; "An Extraordinary Affair," *Hudson River Chronicle* (Ossining, NY), March 30, 1841, 3; Record of the Inquest of Maria E. Shaw, March 23, 1841, New York County Coroner Inquests, January 1841 to June 1841, roll 18, New York Municipal Archives.

5. Record of the Inquest of Maria E. Shaw.

6. "Case of Maria E. Shaw," *Dixon's Polyanthos*, March 27, 1841, 92 (italics in the original).

7. "Mrs. Bird," *Dixon's Polyanthos*, March 27, 1841, 92–93 (italics in the original).

8. "Mrs. Bird," 92–93.

9. "Mrs. Bird," 92–93.

10. *Dixon's Polyanthos*, April 3, 1841, 97.

11. "Flight of a Bird," *Dixon's Polyanthos*, April 11, 1841, 108; "Costello, Bird, and Restell," *Dixon's Polyanthos*, April 11, 1841, 108.

12. Catherine Cashdollar Maxwell, 1795–1876, at findagrave.com; Massachusetts death record for Jacob Weatherwax, January 18, 1831, ancestry.com; 1870 federal census record for Maxwell household, Ward Seventeen, District Ten, New York, New York, roll 593_998, page 423A, ancestry.com; "Manhattan Home of Black Abolitionist Among City's Forgotten Stops on Underground Railroad," *NY1 News*, February 24, 2016, spectrumlocalnews.com /nys/rochester/news/2016/02/22/david-ruggles-home-lower-manhattan; *Longworth's New York City Directory, 1839–40* (New York: Longworth, 1839), 184; *Longworth's New York City Directory, 1841–42* (New York: Longworth, 1841), 194; *Longworth's New York City Directory, 1842–43* (New York: Longworth, 1842), 173; "General Sessions," *New York Daily Herald*, March 22, 1844, 2; advertisements for Madame Costello, *New York Daily Herald*,

February 10, 1840, 2; "Mrs. Costello," *Dixon's Polyanthos*, May 9, 1841, 10; "Madame Costello, the 'Female Physician,'" *New York Sporting Whip*, February 11, 1843, reprinted in Patricia Cline Cohen, Timothy J. Gilfoyle, and Helen Lefkowitz Horowitz, eds., *The Flash Press: Sporting Male Weeklies in 1840s New York* (Chicago: University of Chicago Press, 2008), 185–86. On Costello, see also Clifford Browder, *The Wickedest Woman in New York: Madame Restell, the Abortionist* (Hamden, CT: Archon, 1988), 24.

13. Restell's advertisement appeared in the *New York Herald* on December 8, 1841, and is quoted in Martin Olasky, "Advertising Abortion in the 1830s and 1840s: Madame Restell Builds a Business," *Journalism History* 12, no. 2 (1986): 52.

14. "City Intelligence," *New York Daily Herald*, December 3, 1843, 5; "Memoir of Zulma Marache," *New York Daily Herald*, March 27, 1844, 6.

15. "Memoir of Zulma Marache"; "City Intelligence," *New York Daily Herald*, December 3, 1843, 5; "General Sessions," *New York Daily Herald*, March 24, 1844, 1.

16. "General Sessions," *New York Daily Herald*, March 22, 1844, 2; "Madame Costello's Card," *New York Daily Herald*, April 2, 1844, 2; "Sentence of an Abortionist," *New York Daily Herald*, April 13, 1844, 2; *People v. Costello*, 1 Denio 83 (May 1845).

17. "City News," *Evening Post* (New York), April 15, 1844, 2; "Coroner's Office," *New-York Tribune*, April 16, 1844, 3 (italics in the original).

18. "Case of Abortion," *New York Daily Herald*, April 17, 1844, 2.

19. "Case of Abortion," *New York Daily Herald*, April 18, 1844, 2.

20. "Case of Abortion," *New York Daily Herald*, April 18, 1844, 2.

21. "Abortion Case," *New York Daily Herald*, April 19, 1844, 2.

22. "Abortion Case," 2; "The Abortion Case in New York," *Brooklyn Evening Star*, April 20, 1844, 2.

23. "Mrs. Bird Bailed," *New York Daily Herald*, May 18, 1844, 2; "Trial of Madam Bird for Procuring an Abortion," *New York Daily Herald*, September 14, 1844, 1; "General Sessions," *New York Daily Herald*, September 17, 1844, 1; "General Sessions—Sentence," *Evening Post* (New York), October 16, 1844, 2; "Sentence," *Brooklyn Evening Star*, October 17, 1844, 2; "Sentences," *New-York Tribune*, October 17, 1844, 3; Indictment in *People v. Margaret Dawson, alias Bird, and Francis Kowing*, May 17, 1844, New York County DA Indictment Records, roll 226, New York Municipal Archives.

24. Gunning S. Bedford, MD, "Vaginal Hysterotomy," *New York Journal of Medicine and Collateral Sciences* 2 (March 1844): 199–203.

25. James C. Mohr, *Abortion in America: The Origins and Evolution of National Policy* (New York: Oxford University Press, 1978), 120–21.

26. Mohr, *Abortion in America*, 123–25; chapter 260, *Laws of the State of New York Passed at the Sixty-Eighth Session of the Legislature* (Albany, NY: C. Van Benthuysen, 1845), 285–86. The fourth and fifth sections of the law, which I will discuss in the next chapter, also criminalized the concealment of the birth of an illegitimate child, either alive or dead. On the revision of the first section of the statute, see "Abortion a Felony," *National Police Gazette*, March 14, 1846, 1.

27. "Most Horrible Discoveries," *New York Evening Post*, August 27, 1845, 2.

28. Indictment in *People v. Catharine Costello, alias Maxwell, and Charles Mason*, August 25, 1845, New York County DA Indictment Records, roll 233, New York Municipal Archives; "Madame Costello," *New York Daily Herald*, September 4, 1845, 2; *Evening Post*, September 5, 1845, 2; "Police Intelligence," *New York Daily Herald*, September 5, 1845, 3; "City

Intelligence," *Evening Post*, September 13, 1845, 2; *New York Evening Post*, September 19, 1845, 2; "Madame Costello," *New York Daily Herald*, October 3, 1845.
29. "General Sessions," *New York Daily Herald*, February 13, 1846, 1; "Madame Costello's Trial," *New-York Tribune*, February 14, 1846, 1; "Case of Costello," *Brooklyn Evening Star*, February 13, 1846, 1; Mohr, *Abortion in America*, 124.
30. *Brooklyn Daily Eagle*, February 14, 1846, 2; "Court of General Sessions," *New York Daily Herald*, February 14, 1846, 1.
31. "General Sessions," *National Police Gazette*, February 21, 1846, 1, 24.
32. "General Sessions," *National Police Gazette*, February 21, 1846, 1, 24.
33. "Madame Costello," *New York Daily Herald*, February 17, 1846, 2; "Costello," *Brooklyn Evening Star*, February 26, 1846, 2; *New York Evening Post*, April 1, 1846, 3; "Mad. Costello," *New-York Tribune*, April 9, 1846, 5 (italics in the original).
34. "Madame Costello," *New York Evening Express*, August 18, 1846, 2.
35. *Trow's New York City Directory, 1860–61* (New York: John F. Trow, 1860), 79, and *Trow's New York City Directory, 1860–61* (New York: John F. Trow, 1861), 78, both have her living at 242 Madison Street. Records of naturalization in the United States for Albertina Kowing (January 26, 1859) and Francis Kowing (June 9, 1848) are to be found on ancestry.com. Both declare the Kingdom of Hanover as their prior nationality.

5. ILLEGITIMACY AND INFANTICIDE

1. *New-York Tribune*, February 24, 1846, 2; "Restell in Danger," *Brooklyn Daily Eagle*, February 24, 1846, 2; "Anti-Restell Meeting," *New York Daily Herald*, February 24, 1846, 2. For others who have written on the case of Mary Applegate and this minor riot, see Eric Homberger, *Scenes from the Life of a City: Corruption and Conscience in Old New York* (New Haven, CT: Yale University Press, 1994), 105–8; Clifford Browder, *The Wickedest Woman in New York: Madame Restell, the Abortionist* (Hamden, CT: Archon, 1988), 58–66.
2. Deposition of Applegate is in "Police Intelligence," *New York Herald*, February 6, 1846, 1. It also appeared in the *Evening Post* and the *New-York Tribune*, among others. On Edwards as clerk, see "A Comparative Statement," *Boston Evening Transcript*, July 5, 1845, 2.
3. "Police Intelligence," 1.
4. Leonard L. Richards, *"Gentlemen of Property and Standing": Anti-Abolition Mobs in Jacksonian America* (New York: Oxford University Press, 1970); Timothy J. Gilfoyle, "Strumpets and Misogynists: Brothel 'Riots' and the Transformation of Prostitution in Antebellum New York City," *New York History* 68, no. 1 (January 1987): 44–65; Leslie Harris, *In the Shadow of Slavery: African Americans in New York City, 1626–1863* (Chicago: University of Chicago Press, 2003), 189–94.
5. For more on the connections between illegitimacy, abandonment, and abortion, see Virginia A. Metaxas Quiroga, *Poor Mothers and Babies: Childbirth and Child Care Hospitals in Nineteenth-Century New York City* (New York: Garland, 1989), chap. 3.
6. Susanna Rowson, *Charlotte Temple*, ed. Marion Rust (1791; repr., New York: Norton, 2000); Hannah Webster Foster, *The Coquette or, the History of Eliza Wharton* (1797; repr., New York: Dover, 2015). On domestic service, see Christine Stansell, *City of Women: Sex and Class in New York, 1789–1860* (New York: Knopf, 1982), 12–13 and chap. 8. On "ruin," see Stansell, *City of Women*, 175–76. On the rise in prostitution and reaction to it, see Stansell, *City*

of Women, chap. 9; Timothy J. Gilfoyle, *City of Eros: New York City, Prostitution, and the Commercialization of Sex, 1790–1920* (New York: Norton, 1992), chap. 3, p. 59 for the estimates.

7. On the Bowery, see Stansell, *City of Women*, 89–100.

8. On the evolution of seduction law, see Estelle B. Freedman, *Redefining Rape: Sexual Violence in the Era of Suffrage and Segregation* (Cambridge, MA: Harvard University Press, 2013), chap. 2; Michael Grossberg, *Governing the Hearth: Law and Family in Nineteenth-Century America* (Chapel Hill: University of North Carolina Press, 1985), 45–49.

9. "Have You a Daughter?"*Advocate of Moral Reform*, March 15, 1839; "Seduction, Murder, and Suicide," *Advocate of Moral Reform*, February 1, 1839; "Distressing Case of Seduction," *Advocate of Moral Reform*, January 15, 1840, 15; "Do Not Send Your Children to the City," *Advocate of Moral Reform*, May 15, 1844, 77; "Seduction, Murder, and Suicide," *Advocate of Moral Reform*, April 15, 1840, 59; Julie Miller, *Cry of Murder on Broadway: A Woman's Ruin and Revenge in Old New York* (Ithaca, NY: Three Hills, an imprint of Cornell University Press, 2020), 138–39, 143.

10. Miller, *Cry of Murder on Broadway*; "Acquittal of Amelia Norman," *Brooklyn Daily Eagle*, January 20, 1844, 2.

11. "Acquittal of Amelia Norman," 2.

12. "Awful Disclosures," *New York Daily Herald*, February 4, 1846, 2; "City Intelligence," *New York Evening Post*, February 4, 1846, 2.

13. "Police Intelligence," 1. On the history of informal adoption before its legal regulations, see Grossberg, *Governing the Hearth*, 268–78; Julie Miller, *Abandoned: Foundlings in Nineteenth-Century New York City* (New York: New York University Press, 2008), 55–56; Julie Berebitsky, *Like Our Very Own: Adoption and the Changing Culture of Motherhood, 1851–1950* (Lawrence: University Press of Kansas, 2000), 20–28. Adoption advertisement is "Mrs. Maxwell, M.D." (the former Madame Costello), *New York Times*, March 25, 1863, 7.

14. On the Nursery for the Children of Poor Women, see Miller, *Abandoned*, 110–12. On wet nurses in this era, see Janet Golden, *A Social History of Wet Nursing in America: From Breast to Bottle* (New York: Cambridge University Press, 1996), chaps. 2 and 3, and Lara Vapnek, "The Labor of Infant Feeding: Wet-Nursing at the Nursery and Child's Hospital, 1854–1910," *Journal of American History* 109, no. 1 (2022): 90–115.

15. "Police Intelligence," 1.

16. "Police Intelligence," 1.

17. "City and County of New York,"*Evening Post*, February 6, 1846, 2.

18. On survival rates with wet nurses, see Miller, *Abandoned*, 61–69; Vapnek, "Wet-Nursing."

19. "Another Chapter of Supposed Infant Murder," *National Police Gazette*, February 7, 1846, 1.

20. "Madame Restell and Some of Her Dupes," *New York Medical and Surgical Reporter* 1, no. 10 (February 21, 1846): 160–61.

21. "Some of Her Dupes," 160–61.

22. "The Child Murderess," *National Police Gazette*, February 28, 1846, 1.

23. "Arrest for Abandonment," *Advocate for Moral Reform*, January 1, 1839; Unknown Male Infant, December 25, 1840, New York County Coroner Inquests, roll 18, New York Municipal Archives; "City Intelligence," *New York Daily Herald*, February 13, 1845, 1; Thomas A. Crist, "Babies in the Privy: Prostitution, Infanticide, and Abortion in New York City's Five Points District," *Historical Archaeology* 39, no. 1 (2005): 19–46; Paul A. Gilje, "Infant Abandonment in Early Nineteenth-Century New York City: Three Cases," *Signs* 8, no. 3 (1983):

580–90; Marcela Micucci, "'Another Instance of That Fearful Crime': The Criminalization of Infanticide in Antebellum New York City," *New York History* 99, no. 1 (2018): 68–98; Chap. 1, Article 2nd, § 36, *Revised Statutes of the State of New York,* 3 vols. (Albany: Packard and Van Benthuysen, 1829), 2:665.

24. Miller, *Abandoned,* esp. 30–31, 41–42.

25. Miller, *Abandoned,* 17–18, 65; Quiroga, *Poor Mothers and Babies,* 55–56.

26. Julie Miller, "Transatlantic Anxieties: New York's Nineteenth-Century Foundling Asylums and the London Foundling Hospital," *Annales de Démographie Historique* 2 (2007): 37–58; "Curious View of the Value of Foundling Hospitals," *New York Daily Herald,* February 16, 1846, 1.

27. George Thompson, *City Crimes; Or Life in New York and Boston* (1849) in *Venus in Boston and Other Tales of Nineteenth-Century City Life,* ed. David S. Reynold and Kimberly R. Gladman (Amherst: University of Massachusetts Press, 2002), 124–126.

28. Miller, *Abandoned,* 18; Crist, "Babies in the Privy," 25–26; Peter C. Hoffer and N.E.H. Hull, *Murdering Mothers: Infanticide in England and New England, 1558–1803* (New York: New York University Press, 1984), epilogue; Micucci, "'Another Instance,'" 70, 77; Katie M. Hemphill, "'Driven to the Commission of this Crime': Women and Infanticide in Baltimore, 1835–1860," *Journal of the Early Republic* 32, no. 3 (2012): 437–61.

29. Quiroga, *Poor Mothers and Babies,* 54–56; Steven Mintz, *Huck's Raft: A History of American Childhood* (Cambridge, MA: Belknap, 2006), chap. 4; Viviana A. Zelizer, *Pricing the Priceless Child: The Changing Social Value of Children* (Princeton, NJ: Princeton University Press, 1994).

30. Hemphill, "'Driven.'" On premarital chastity and respectability in the middle class, see Nancy Cott, "Passionlessness: An Interpretation of Victorian Sexual Ideology, 1790–1850," *Signs* 4, no. 2 (1978): 219–36; Barbara Welter, "The Cult of True Womanhood, 1820–1860," *American Quarterly* 18, no. 2 (1966): 151–74. On working-class premarital sex, see Stansell, *City of Women,* 87–88. On contraception, see Andrea Tone, *Devices and Desires: A History of Contraceptives in America* (New York: Hill and Wang, 2001), 13–15.

31. Chap. 260, §§ 4 and 5, passed May 13, 1845, *Laws of the State of New York, Passed at the Sixty-Eighth Session of the Legislature* (Albany, NY: C. Van Benthuysen, 1845), 285–86.

32. "To the Public," *New-York Tribune,* February 25, 1846, 2.

33. "Things in Philadelphia," *New-York Tribune,* February 7, 1846, 10. Applegate in 1850 federal census for the New Market Ward of Philadelphia, p. 357, line 195, ancestry.com.

34. "Restell, the Female Abortionist," *National Police Gazette,* March 7, 1846, 1; "Abortionism a Felony," *National Police Gazette,* March 14, 1846, 1; *New York Daily Herald,* February 19, 1846, 4.

6. "A DISGRACE TO HER SEX"

1. Wonderful Trial of Caroline Lohman, Alias Restell, Reported in Full for the National Police Gazette (New York: Burgess and Stringer, 1847), 5, 6, 8. For other accounts of the Bodine trial, see Clifford Browder, *The Wickedest Woman in New York: Madame Restell, the Abortionist* (Hamden, CT: Archon, 1988), chap. 4; A. Cheree Carlson, *The Crimes of Womanhood: Defining Femininity in a Court of Law* (Urbana: University of Illinois Press, 2009), 122–28; Eric Homberger, *Scenes from the Life of a City: Corruption and Conscience in Old New York* (New Haven, CT: Yale University Press, 1994), 108–15.

2. Wonderful Trial, 6, 10.

3. Wonderful Trial, 7, 10; "Law Intelligence," *New York Daily Herald*, October 27, 1847, 1.

4. Wonderful Trial, 7, 10.

5. Wonderful Trial, 10–13.

6. "Restell, the Female Abortionist," *National Police Gazette*, March 13, 1847, 2.

7. "City Intelligence," *New York Evening Post*, September 8, 1847, 2; "Case of the Child-Killer, Restell," *Brooklyn Daily Eagle*, September 9, 1847, 2; "Mad. Restell," *Brooklyn Evening Star*, September 9, 1847, 2; "Police," *Commercial Advertiser*, September 9, 1847, 2; "The Case of Madame Restell," *Albany Evening Journal*, September 10, 1847, 2; "Arrest of the Wretch Restell," *National Police Gazette*, September 11, 1847, 2; "Arrest of a Fugitive," *New York Herald*, September 16, 1847, 3; "Another Arrest in the Restell Case," *National Police Gazette*, September 18, 1847, 2.

8. "Bailed," *New York Evening Post*, September 13, 1847, 2; "Arrest of the Wretch Restell," *National Police Gazette*, September 11, 1847, 2; "Madam Restell," *Maine Farmer*, September 16, 1847, 15; "The Woman Restell," *Brooklyn Evening Star*, September 18, 1847, 2; "Madame Restell Bailed," *New York Evening Post*, September 18, 1847, 2. For Benjamin Day, see *Doggett's New York Directory, 1846–1847* (New York: Doggetts, 1846), 107; "Madame Restell's Bail," *New York Daily Herald*, September 19, 1847, 2. Indictment in *People v. Caroline Lohman, alias Ann Lohman, alias Madame Restell*, September 7, 1847, New York Municipal Archives, New York City.

9. "The Woman Restell," *Brooklyn Evening Star*, September 23, 1847, 2; "Court of General Sessions," *New York Daily Herald*, October 9, 1847, 1; *Wonderful Trial*, 3–4; "Court of General Sessions," *New York Daily Herald*, October 22, 1847, 3.

10. "Death of Ex-Recorder Scott," *New York Times*, September 21, 1854, 3.

11. "John M'Keon's Work Done," *New York Times*, November 23, 1883, 8; *Wonderful Trial*, 5. For more on changes to the household order and working women in this era in cities, see Christine Stansell, *City of Women: Sex and Class in New York City, 1789–1860* (New York: Knopf, 1982), esp. chaps. 1 and 5; Jeanne Boydston, *Home and Work: Housework, Wages, and the Ideology of Labor in the Early Republic* (New York: Oxford University Press, 1994); Lori Ginzberg, *Women and the Work of Benevolence: Morality, Politics, and Class in the Nineteenth-Century United States* (New Haven, CT: Yale University Press, 1990).

12. Wonderful Trial, 5. On midwifery, see for instance, Laurel Thatcher Ulrich, *A Midwife's Tale: The Life of Martha Ballard, Based on Her Diary, 1785–1812* (New York: Knopf, 1990). On brothel madams and riots, see Timothy J. Gilfoyle, *City of Eros: New York City, Prostitution, and the Commercialization of Sex, 1790–1920* (New York: W.W. Norton, 1992), chap. 4.

13. Wonderful Trial, 5.

14. Wonderful Trial, 7–8.

15. "James T. Brady," in *The National Cyclopaedia of American Biography* (New York: James T. White, 1893), 3:387; David Graham Jr., *A Treatise on the Practice of the Supreme Court of the State of New-York* (New York: Gould Banks, 1836); David Graham Jr., *A Treatise on the Organization and Jurisdiction of the Courts of Law and Equity in the State of New York* (New York: Halsted and Voorhies, 1839); "Death of Hon. David Graham," *New York Times*, June 28, 1852, 1.

16. Wonderful Trial, 8, 9; "Law Intelligence," *New York Daily Herald*, October 27, 1847, 1.

17. Wonderful Trial, 10, 11.

18. Wonderful Trial, 12–13; "Law Intelligence," *New York Daily Herald*, October 29, 1847, 2.

19. Gunning S. Bedford, MD, "Vaginal Hysterotomy," *New York Journal of Medicine and Collateral Sciences* 2 (March 1844): 199–203; Bedford editorial in *New York Medical and Surgical Reporter* 1, no. 10 (February 21, 1846), reprinted in compiled version of same publication, ed. Clarkson T. Collins (New York: Piercy and Reed, 1846), 162–65; *Wonderful Trial*, 17–18.

20. *Wonderful Trial*, 17–18.

21. *Wonderful Trial*, 17–19.

22. *Wonderful Trial*, 19–20; "Law Intelligence," *New York Daily Herald*, October 30, 1847, 2.

23. "Trial of Madame Restell," *National Police Gazette*, October 30, 1847, 2.

24. *Wonderful Trial*, 21.

25. *Wonderful Trial*, 26–28.

26. *Wonderful Trial*, 26–28.

27. *Wonderful Trial*, 28; depositions of Delia Morgan and Maria Walden, November 4, 1847, in *People v. Madame Restell*, New York Municipal Archives.

28. *Wonderful Trial*, 28–29.

29. *Wonderful Trial*, 29–30.

30. *Wonderful Trial*, 31.

31. *Wonderful Trial*, 31.

32. *Wonderful Trial*, 32,

33. *Wonderful Trial*, 34–35.

34. *Wonderful Trial*, 35.

35. *Wonderful Trial*, 35–36.

36. *Wonderful Trial*, 36.

37. *Wonderful Trial*, 37.

38. *Wonderful Trial*, 37–38.

39. *Wonderful Trial*, 38.

40. *Wonderful Trial*, 38.

41. "Conviction of the Child-Murderess Restell," *Brooklyn Daily Eagle*, November 11, 1847, 2; "Trial of Madame Restell—State of Society," *New York Herald*, November 12, 1847, 3.

42. *Wonderful Trial*, 38; "Case of Madame Restell," *Brooklyn Daily Eagle*, November 12, 1847, 2; "Inefficiency of Certain Laws," *Brooklyn Evening Star*, November 12, 1847, 2; "An Outrage on Justice and On Public Decency," *Brooklyn Daily Eagle*, November 13, 1847, 2.

43. "Supreme Court—Chambers," *New York Daily Herald*, November 16, 1847, 3.

44. Advertisement for *Wonderful Trial*, *New-York Tribune*, November 16, 1847, 3; "A Physician of New York," *Madame Restell: An Account of Her Life and Horrible Practices, Together with Prostitution in New York, Its Extent—Causes—and Effects* (New York, 1847), 7.

45. *People v. Ann Lohman, Alias Madame Restell*, 2. Barb. 216; 1848 NY App. Div. Lexis 110 (January 1848); "Doings in the Law Courts this Morning," *New York Commercial Advertiser*, January 20, 1848, 2.

46. *People v. Ann Lohman, Alias Madam Restell*, 2 Barb. 450; 1848 NY App. Div. Lexis 127 (February 1848); "Madame Restell," *Baltimore Sun*, February 9, 1848, 1; "Wages of Sin," *Lancaster Examiner* (Pennsylvania), February 9, 1848, 1.

47. *People v. Ann Lohman, Alias Madame Restell*, 1 NY 379; 1848 NY Lexis 29 (June 1848); "Justice Slow but Sure," *New York Evening Express*, June 29, 1848, 2; "Madame Restell's Case Decided," *Daily Albany Argus*, June 29, 1848, 2.

48. "Before Rikers, Blackwell's Was DOC's First Home," *Correction News*, 1995, www.correctionhistory.org/html/chronicl/nycdoc/html/blakwel1.html; Stacy Horn, *Damnation Island: Poor, Sick, Mad and Criminal in 19th-Century New York* (Chapel Hill, NC: Algonquin Books, 2018), 196–99.

49. Charles Dickens, *American Notes for General Circulation*, 2 vols. (London: Chapman and Hall, 1842), 1:225–26.

50. "Madame Restell," *Trenton State Gazette*, July 21, 1848, 1. See also "Madame Restell," *Cincinnati Commercial Tribune*, November 29, 1848, 1, and *New York Evening Express*, July 18, 1848, 4; "Madame Restell and John Harrison," *Biblical Recorder* (Raleigh, NC), December 9, 1848, 2; "Blackwell's Island," *Brooklyn Evening Star*, January 10, 1849, 2.

51. "Madame Restell," *Brooklyn Daily Eagle*, November 17, 1848; *Middlebury Register* (Vermont), November 28, 1848, 3; "Release of Madame Restell," *Maine Cultivator and Hallowell Gazette* (Hallowell, ME), November 18, 1848, 2; "Audacious Parade of the 'Wages of Sin,'" *Times-Picayune* (New Orleans), June 27, 1848, 1.

52. Browder, *Wickedest Woman*, 93; "The Victim of Restell," *Brooklyn Evening Star*, July 3, 1848, 2; "The Board of Supervisors," *Evening Mirror* (New York), October 29, 1851, 3.

7. A.M. Mauriceau, Professor of Diseases of Women

1. Lohman and her daughter appear on the ship manifest for the *Great Western*, arriving in New York on September 10, 1845. An official, presumably in immigration, has noted "Madame Restell and daughter" in the ship manifest, a testament to their notoriety. See "New York, U.S., "Arriving Passenger and Crew Lists, 1820–1957," ancestry.com.

2. "Portuguese Female Pills," *New York Daily Herald*, February 10, 1840, 2.

3. "Female Monthly Pills," *New York Daily Herald*, October 17, 1843, 3. On Baudelocque, see P.M. Dunn, "Jean-Louis Baudelocque (1746–1810) of Paris and *l'art des accouchemens*," *Archives of Diseases in Childhood, Fetal, and Neonatal Edition* 89 (2004): F370–72.

4. "Important to Females," *New York Daily Herald*, May 21, 1843, 4; "To Those Without Children," *New York Daily Herald*, September 19, 1944, 4. On Desormeaux, see M. Chailly, *A Practical Treatise on Midwifery*, trans. Gunning S. Bedford (New York: Harper and Brothers, 1844), i.

5. "To Those Without Children"; "The Invisible Wig"; "A Strange, Blessed, Astounding and Supernatural Invention," all in *New York Daily Herald*, September 19, 1844, 4.

6. "Restell Case," *Brooklyn Evening Star*, September 15, 1847, 2.

7. Record for Charles Lohman and family in 1850 federal census,, roll 535, p. 401b, lines 31–39, family number 1115, living in Third Ward, New York, New York, ancestry.com.

8. Christening record for Joseph Trow, October 7, 1821, Stroud, Gloucestershire, England in "Church of England Baptisms, 1813–1913"; declarations of intent to become U.S. citizens of Joseph Trow and Caroline Summers, March 21, 1848, both resident of 148 Greenwich Street, New York, ancestry.com. Accounts of life in the Lohman household are found in testimony in *Joseph Trow s. Carrie S. Shannon, New York Court of Appeals, Cases and Briefs*, vol. 51, 1878, p. 8, New York State Library, Albany.

9. Record of Joseph Trow, head of household, Greenport, Suffolk, New York, roll 935, p. 528C, line 48, U.S. census of 1880, ancestry.com; testimony in *Trow v. Shannon*, 27–28, 31–32, 68. On Hegeman and Company, see advertisement from 1800 at the Library of Congress, www.loc.gov/resource/rbpe.13407000/, and in *Wall Street Daily News*, March 9, 1894, 3. The Hegeman and Company logo, which includes the date of establishment, was etched on many products, now available for sale on eBay.

10. Advertisement for *Married Woman's Private Medical Companion* in *New York Daily Herald*, March 14, 1847, 4; "Marriage: Why So Often Unhappy," *New-York Atlas*, November 16, 1856; advertisement in *New York Daily Herald*, December 29, 1848, 3; "Observations d'un médecin," *Courrier des États-Unis*, April 8, 1851, 6. On François Mauriceau, see Helen Lefkowitz Horowitz, *Rereading Sex: Battles over Sexual Knowledge and Suppression in Nineteenth-Century America* (New York: Knopf, 2002), 468n21.

11. A.M. Mauriceau, *The Married Woman's Private Medical Companion* (New York, 1847), v–viii.

12. Horowitz, *Rereading Sex*, 47, 75–83.

13. Mauriceau, *Married Woman's Private Medical Companion*, iii; see also advertisement in *New York Daily Herald*, March 14, 1847, 4.

14. Mauriceau, *Married Woman's Private Medical Companion*, 3–8, 15–16, 104, 142, 143, 177, 237. See also Horowitz, *Rereading Sex*, 208.

15. Mauriceau, *Married Woman's Private Medical Companion*, 48, 57–59.

16. Mauriceau, *Married Woman's Private Medical Companion*, 104–7, 123, 142.

17. Mauriceau, *Married Woman's Private Medical Companion*, 150, 154. For the substitution of prevention for withdrawal in Owen, see *Moral Physiology: Or, a Brief and Plain Treatise on the Population Question*, 5th ed. (London: J. Watson, 1841), 47 of appendix.

18. Mauriceau, *Married Woman's Private Medical Companion*, 215, 222, 223, 181, 188–89.

19. Mauriceau, *Married Woman's Private Medical Companion*, 192, 194, 195. On forceps and the rise of doctors attending births, see Judith Walzer Leavitt, *Brought to Bed: Childbearing in America, 1850–1950* (New York: Oxford University Press, 1986), chap. 2. On Wooster Beach, see Howard Kelly and Walter Burrage, eds., "Beach, Wooster (1794–1859)," in *American Medical Biographies* (Baltimore: Norman, Remington, 1920), 79–80.

20. Mauriceau, *Married Woman's Private Medical Companion*, 168–69.

21. Mauriceau, *Married Woman's Private Medical Companion*, 180–81; M. Chailly, *A Practical Treatise on Midwifery*, trans. Gunning S. Bedford (New York: Harper and Brothers, 1844), 134.

22. Advertisement in *New York Herald*, March 14, 1847, 4; advertisement in *New Orleans Times-Picayune*, April 16, 1847, 3; *Hartford Courant*, May 25, 1847, 3; *Augusta Daily Constitutionalist*, June 22, 1847, 3; *Poughkeepsie Journal*, July 3, 1847, 3; "Restell Case," *Brooklyn Evening Star*, September 15, 1847, 2; "Police Intelligence," *New York Daily Herald*, September 17, 1847, 2; "Arrest of Lohman, Alias Dr. Mauriceau," *Brooklyn Evening Star*, September 17, 1847, 2; "Bailed," *New York Daily Herald*, September 21, 1847, 3.

23. "Mauriceau's Married Woman's Medical Companion," *Louisville Courier*, September 27, 1847, 2.

24. "Mauriceau's Married Woman's Medical Companion," 2.

25. U.S. census for 1860, roll M653_789, page 135, line 340, family 446, Third Ward, New York City, ancestry.com.

8. Seduced and Abandoned

1. *New York Evening Post*, June 27, 1853; Marriage record for Caroline Summers and Isaac Lent Purdy, June 27, 1853, ancestry.com; "Official Canvas of Westchester County," *Hudson*

River Chronicle (Ossining, NY), November 21, 1843, 6; "New York and Albany Railroad," *Hudson River Chronicle*, September 9, 1845, 2; "Second Assembly District Convention," *Westchester Herald*, September 3, 1850, 2; "Greenburgh Town Officers—1847," *Westchester Herald*, April 13, 1847, 3; passenger records for Stephen, 35, Liberty, 8, and Elijah Trow, 10, August 18, 1853 (Stephen listed as laborer), "New York, U.S., Arriving Records and Crew Lists, 1820–1957," ancestry.com; Stephen, Elizabeth, Elijah, Anne, and Alice Trow in 1860 federal census for Barre, Orleans County, New York, roll M653_836, p. 1118, family number 1175, ancestry.com. The 1860 federal census has Isaac L. Purdy, Caroline Purdy, and children Caroline and Charles Purdy resident in Greenburgh, Westchester, New York. See 1860 federal census, roll: M653_881, p. 727, ancestry.com.

2. "Arrest of Madam Restell," *Brooklyn Daily Eagle*, February 13, 1854, 2; "Madame Restell Charged with Abortion," *New York Daily Herald*, February 14, 1854, 3.

3. On the workings of police courts, see Thomas Cragg, "Habitués of the Police Court: Criminal Justice and the Poor in Antebellum Detroit," *Michigan Historical Review* 35, no. 1 (Spring 2009): 1–28; James F. Richardson, *The New York Police, Colonial Times to 1901* (New York: Oxford University Press, 1970), 75; Carolyn B. Ramsey, "The Discretionary Power of 'Public' Prosecutors in Historical Perspective," *American Criminal Law Review* 1309 (2002): 1326–27, 1329; Wilbur R. Miller, *Cops and Bobbies: Police Authority in New York and London, 1830–1870* (Chicago: University of Chicago Press, 1973), 94. On blackmail in police courts, see Cragg, "Habitués of the Police Court," 17.

4. "George Shackford, the Seducer of Miss Grant—Eventful Life," *Weekly Wisconsin* (reprint from *National Police Gazette*), March 29, 1854, 3.

5. "George Shackford, the Seducer of Miss Grant," 3.

6. "George Shackford, the Seducer of Miss Grant," 3; "Police Intelligence," 2; birth record for George Shackford, August 6, 1818, Chester, New Hampshire, ancestry.com; marriage record for George R. Shackford and Margaret E. Robinson, May 14, 1841, Brentwood, New Hampshire, ancestry.com; *Saturday Courier* (Philadelphia), June 5, 1841, 3; "Mortuary Notice," *New York Commercial Advertiser*, January 24, 1845, 3; death record for Margaret E.R. Shackford of a kidney infection, January 24, 1845, resident at 136 Greenwich, in the Presbyterian Church records, Seventh Presbyterian Church, New York, ancestry.com; "Sudden Bereavement," *Boston Courier* (reprinted from *Portsmouth Journal*), April 10, 1848, 2.

7. On seduction under promise of marriage, see Estelle B. Freedman, *Redefining Rape: Sexual Violence in the Era of Suffrage and Segregation* (Cambridge, MA: Harvard University Press, 2013), 42–44.

8. Affidavit of Cordelia Grant is reprinted in full in "Police Intelligence," *New York Daily Herald*, February 14, 1854, 3.

9. Grant affidavit in "Police Intelligence," 2.

10. Grant affidavit in "Police Intelligence," 2.

11. Grant affidavit in "Police Intelligence," 2 (italics in the original).

12. "Police Intelligence: Madame Restell Charged with Causing an Abortion," *New York Daily Herald*, February 14, 1854, 3; "Marriages," *Boston Daily Bee*, April 16, 1853, 3; marriage record for Rutha Crosby and George Shackford, April 13, 1853, Boston, MA, "Massachusetts, U.S., Town and Vital Records, 1620–1988," ancestry.com; Massachusetts state census for 1855 shows the Shackfords living in Boston's second ward, ancestry.com.

13. *Daily Telegraph* (Jersey City, NJ), February 16, 1854, 2; "The Abortion Case," *New York Daily Herald*, February 23, 1854, 8.

14. "The Abortion Case," 8.

15. "The Abortion Case," 8; "The Restell Abortion Case—Mr. Busteed's Statement," *New York Daily Herald*, March 7, 1854, 7; *New London Daily Star* (Connecticut), February 28, 1854, 2.

16. "The Case of Madame Restell," *Brooklyn Daily Eagle*, March 3, 1854, 2; "Things in New York," *Baltimore Sun*, March 4, 1854, 1. On the ability to detain a material witness in New York State, see Wesley MacNeil Oliver, "The Rise and Fall of Material Witness Detention in Nineteenth Century New York," *NYU Journal of Law and Liberty* 1, no. 2 (2005): 733; James F. Richardson, *The New York Police, Colonial Times to 1901* (New York: Oxford University Press, 1970), 76.

17. *Philadelphia Sunday Dispatch*, February 19, 1854, 2. Thanks to Holly Dugan, Shakespearean extraordinaire, for help with this passage. Melville's *Moby Dick*, published just three years before this case in 1851, also makes reference to spermaceti in chapter 92: "Who would think, then, that such fine ladies and gentlemen should regale themselves with an essence found in the inglorious bowels of a sick whale!"

18. "Restelle [*sic*] Still at Large," *Daily National Era*, March 4, 1854, 2; "Madame Restell," *Jackson Standard* (Ohio), March 16, 1854, 2; "Police Intelligence," *New York Daily Herald*, March 11, 1854, 7; "The Restell Abortion Case," 7; "Things in New York," *Baltimore Sun*, March 14, 1854, 1; *Lancaster Examiner* (Pennsylvania), March 15, 1854, 2; "The Restell Abortion Case," *New York Herald*, March 9, 1854, 9.

19. "City Intelligence," *New York Daily Herald*, March 17, 1854, 8; "Brooklyn City Intelligence," *New York Daily Herald*, March 18, 1854, 3; "The Restell Case," *Brooklyn Daily Eagle*, March 18, 1854, 2. On Mary Rogers, see chapter 3 in this book and Amy Gilman Srebnick, *The Mysterious Death of Mary Rogers: Sex and Culture in Nineteenth-Century New York* (New York: Oxford University Press, 1995), 32, 96.

20. "Police Intelligence," *New York Daily Herald*, March 23, 1854, 1; "Miss Grant," *Brooklyn Daily Eagle*, March 24, 1854, 2.

21. "Police Intelligence," *New York Daily Herald*, March 23, 1854, 1; "Miss Grant," *Brooklyn Daily Eagle*, March 24, 1854, 2.

22. "New York Crime," *Buffalo Morning Express*, April 12, 1854, 2.

23. "Marriages," *Portland Weekly Advertiser*, March 6, 1855, 3; Marriage record for Samuel J. Noble and Cordelia A. Grant, February 25, 1855, Portland, Maine, "Maine, U.S., Marriage Records, 1713–1922," ancestry.com; "Cordelia Grant Again," *National Police Gazette*, March 28, 1857, 2.

24. 1870 federal census shows George, Rutha, George A., and Hannah Shackford in East Boston (roll M593_640, p. 226A), ancestry.com. The same census shows Samuel Noble, apothecary, with Cordelia, Blanch, Gertrude, and Mary Welch, Irish domestic servant, in the Eighth Ward (roll 593_645, p. 20A), ancestry.com.

9. IN THE PUBLIC EYE

1. This account draws on Madame Restell's testimony, December 31, 1861, Neidlinger case folder, Madame Restell Papers, Schlesinger Library, Harvard University (hereafter Restell Papers), and "Rearrest of Madame Restell," *New York Herald*, August 20, 1856, 1.

2. "Re-Arrest of Madame Restell—Attempted Abortion and Abduction," *New York Herald*, August 20, 1856, 1; "Madame Restell Again Arrested," *New York Evening Mirror*, August 20, 1856, 3; "Re-Arrest of Madame Restell—Attempted Abortion and Abduction," *Brooklyn*

Daily Eagle, August 20, 1856, 3; "Re-Arrest of Madame Restell," *Boston Herald*, August 21, 1856, 2; *Baltimore Sun*, August 21, 1856, 4; "Re-Arrest of Madame Restell," *Sacramento Daily Union*, September 22, 1856, 3. On Kaiser, see "Charge of Seduction and Abortion—Madame Restell Arrested," *New York Herald*, August 1, 1856, 1; "The Notorious Madame Restell Again Arrested," *Frank Leslie's Illustrated Newspaper*, August 16, 1856, 12; "The Morals of New York," *Buffalo Evening Post*, August 14, 1856, 2; "Horrible Depravity in New York," *Reynold's Newspaper* (London, England), September, 7, 1856, 7, reprinted from the *New York Police Gazette*.

3. "Re-Arrest of Madame Restell," *New York Herald*, August 20, 1856, 1.

4. Madame Restell, "Gross Unfairness," *New York Herald*, August 21, 1856, 6.

5. Restell, "Gross Unfairness," 6; *Baltimore Sun*, August 23, 1856, 4; *Lancaster Examiner* (Pennsylvania), August 27, 1856, 3.

6. "The Restell Abortion Case," *New-York Tribune*, August 29, 1856, 8 (italics in the original).

7. "Madame (Restell) Lohman and the Missing Child," *New York Times*, December 17, 1856, 3.

8. "Madame (Restell) Lohman and the Missing Child," 3.

9. "Madame Restell in Court," *New York Herald*, December 17, 1856, 5.

10. Report of Charles Edwards, October 16, 1857, Neidlinger case folder, Restell Papers.

11. "Supreme Court, Special Term, Before Hon. Judge Clarke, the People at the Relation of Frederica M. Neidlinger vs. Mary Lohman, Commonly Called Madame Restell," April 21, 1858; "New York Supreme Court, the People on Relation of Frederica W. Neidlinger Against Mary Lohman, Alias Madame Restell," April 21, 1858, both in Neidlinger case folder, 1857–61, Restell Papers. The court was quoting from chap. 9, title 1, article 2, §32, no. 1, *Revised Statutes of the State of New York* (New York: Packard and Van Benthuysen, 1829), 2:566.

12. Statement of Madame Restell, May 3, 1858, Frederica Neidlinger folder, 1857–61, Restell Papers.

13. Statement of Madame Restell, May 3, 1858.

14. Statement of Madame Restell, May 3, 1858.

15. Statement of Madame Restell, May 3, 1858 (emphasis in the original).

16. Statement of Madame Restell, May 3, 1858.

17. Statement of Madame Restell, May 3, 1858.

18. "Madame Restell," *Detroit Free Press*, February 24, 1860, 1. The story also appeared in the *Chicago Tribune*, *Daily Nashville Patriot*, and abbreviated versions in the *Baltimore Sun*, *Evansville Journal* (Indiana), *Boston Cultivator*, *New Hampshire Statesman*, among others. See "Rich," *Boston Investigator*, February 29, 1860, 7.

19. "Personal," *New York Herald*, April 13, 1861, 2. While Restell did not advertise for adoption with great regularity, such ads were not uncommon in nineteenth-century newspapers in New York.

20. See various motions in Neidlinger, 1857–61 file dated October and November 1861, Restell Papers; as well as the charge issued by Judge Leonard, December 9, 1861, Neidlinger folder, Restell Papers; "Madame Restell in Court Once More," *New York Evening Express*, December 10, 1861, 3; "A Mother Seeking an Illegitimate Child," *New York Times*, December 11, 1861, 7.

21. Restell testimony, December 31, 1861, pp. 1–2, Neidlinger folder, Restell Papers.

22. Restell testimony, December 31, 1861.

23. Restell testimony, December 31, 1861.

24. Restell testimony, December 31, 1861.

25. Restell testimony, December 31, 1861.

26. Paperwork in *People ex rel Frederica Neidlinger v. Ann Lohman*, July 20, 1862, Neidlinger folder, Restell Papers. One account of the verdict in the *New York Times* claimed that Restell's December testimony did not lead to a decision, but when Neidlinger again applied for an attachment in July 1862, offering Restell's advertisements as proof that she was an abortionist—unrelated to the issue of kidnaping, obviously—that was when a judge finally ruled in Restell's favor. In his judgment, however, he acknowledges reading Restell's testimony. See "Law Reports," *New York Times*, July 20, 1862, 6.

27. Enlistment record for Isaac L. Purdy, August 13, 1862, "New York, U.S., Civil War Muster Roll Abstracts, 1861–1900," ancestry.com. On the will and intemperance, see Clifford Browder, *The Wickedest Woman in New York: Madame Restell, the Abortionist* (Hamden, CT: Archon, 1988), 116–17; "7th Artillery Regiment" at New York State Military Museum and Veterans Research Center, museum.dmna.ny.gov/unit-history/artillery/7th-artillery -regiment; New York State, *Annual Report of the Adjutant General of the State of New York for the Year 1897: Registers of the Seventh and Eighth Artillery in the War of the Rebellion* (New York and Albany: Wynkoop Hallenbeck Crawford, 1899), 281.

28. Muster roll for Isaac Purdy notes death on November 15, 1864, "New York, U.S., Civil War Muster Roll Abstracts, 1861–1900," ancestry.com; ; National Park Service, "History of the Andersonville Prison," September 3, 2020, www.nps.gov/ande/learn/historyculture /camp_sumter_history.htm.

29. "The Lives of a Former Chambers Street Firehouse," Ephemeral New York, ephemeral-newyork.wordpress.com/2018/04/23/the-lives-of-a-former-chambers-street-firehouse; New York Landmarks Preservation Commission, "(Former) Firehouse, Engine Company 29, 160 Chambers Street," www.neighborhoodpreservationcenter.org/db/bb_files/2016----Former --Firehouse--Engine-Company-29.pdf; Browder, *Wickedest Woman*, 118.

30. Farrells and Charles Purdy are in the 1870 U.S. census, Eleventh District, Eighth Ward, New York County, New York state, family 174, NARA microfilm roll M593_981, ancestry .com; Browder, *Wickedest Woman*, 122–23.

31. Browder, *Wickedest Woman*, 122–23.

32. Estimates are in articles in the *Buffalo Commercial Advertiser*, May 24, 1865, 4; *Troy Daily Times*, May 24, 1865, 2; "The New Residence of Madame Restell," *Boston Traveler* (reprint of *New York News*), May 23, 1865, 6; "The Wages and the Work of Sin," *Indianapolis Star*, May 31, 1865, 4; "A Palace of Blood," *Patriot* (Harrisburg, Pennsylvania), June 8, 1865, 1.

33. "The New Residence of Madame Restell," *New York Evening Express*, May 19, 1865, 3.

34. George Ellington, *Women of New York, Or, Social Life in the Great City* (New York: New York Book Company, 1870), 406. James D. McCabe Jr., *Lights and Shadows of New York; Or, the Sights and Sensations of the Great City* (Philadelphia: National, 1872), plagiarizes almost the entirety of Ellington's description of Restell and her house.

35. Ellington, *Women of New York*, 408–9. The fourth floor is technically the fifth if one includes the basement as the first floor.

10. Doctors Against Doctors

1. Mrs. W.H. Maxwell, *A Female Physician to the Ladies of the United States: Being a Familiar and Practical Treatise on Matters of Utmost Importance Peculiar to Women* (New York: printed by author, 1860), 5–7. On women with MDs, see Regina Markell Morantz-Sanchez, *Sympathy*

and Science: Women Physicians in American Medicine (New York: Oxford University Press, 1985), 49.

2. No part of the abortion debate in nineteenth-century America has been studied more than the history discussed in this chapter. For important studies, some of which I cite herein, see James Mohr, *Abortion in America: The Origins and Evolution of National Policy* (New York: Oxford University Press, 1978); Carroll Smith-Rosenberg, "The Abortion Movement and the AMA, 1850–1880," in *Disorderly Conduct: Visions of Gender in Victorian America* (New York: Knopf, 1985), 217–44; Nicola Beisel and Tamara Kay, "Abortion, Race, and Gender in Nineteenth-Century America," *American Sociological Review* 69 (2004): 498–518; Janet Farrell Brodie, *Contraception and Abortion in 19th-Century America* (Ithaca, NY: Cornell University Press, 1994); Leslie J. Reagan, *When Abortion Was a Crime: Women, Medicine, and Law in the United States, 1867–1973* (Berkeley: University of California Press, 1997); J. Shoshanna Ehrlich and Alesha Doan, *Abortion Regret: The New Attack on Reproductive Freedom* (Santa Barbara, CA: Praeger, 2019), chap. 1.

3. Morantz-Sanchez, *Sympathy and Science*, 31.

4. Thomas Blatchford to Horatio Storer, March 23, 1857, and May 13, 1857, quoted in Mohr, *Abortion in America*, 151. The Storer papers were previously housed in the Countway Medical Library at Harvard, which was closed throughout the COVID-19 pandemic, during which I could not access them. Just as the Countway was opening for access to non–Harvard researchers in the summer of 2022, the Storer papers and other archives were transferred to the Boston Medical Library, which is processing the collections, meaning they are unavailable to researchers.

5. "Extracts from the Records of the Suffolk District Medical Society," *Boston Medical and Surgical Journal*, May 7, 1857, 282–83; "The Report upon Criminal Abortion," *Boston Medical and Surgical Journal*, May 28, 1857, 346.

6. *Transactions of the American Medical Association* (Philadelphia: printed for the association, 1857), 10:30.

7. "Report on Criminal Abortion," *Transactions of the American Medical Association* (Philadelphia: printed for the association, 1859), 12:75–76.

8. "Report on Criminal Abortion," 12:77–78.

9. "Report on Criminal Abortion," 12:76; Smith-Rosenberg, "Abortion Movement and the AMA, 1850–1880," 230–31.

10. Susan E. Klepp, *Revolutionary Conceptions: Women, Fertility, and Family Limitation in America, 1760–1820* (Chapel Hill: University of North Carolina Press, 2009), introduction; John D'Emilio and Estelle B. Freedman, *Intimate Matters: A History of Sexuality in America* (New York: Harper and Row, 1988), chap. 4.

11. Beisel and Kay, "Abortion, Race, and Gender in Nineteenth-Century America," 498–518; H.R. Storer, "On the Decrease of the Rate of Increase of Population Now Obtaining in Europe and America," *American Journal of Science and Arts* 43, no. 28 (March 1867), 45, 55 (the publication notes that the original lecture was delivered in 1858); J.T. Cook, *Woman's Great Crime!* (1868), quoted in Beisel and Kay, "Abortion, Race, and Gender," 509; Horatio Robinson Storer, *Why Not?: A Book For Every Woman* (1867; reprinted Boston: Lee and Shepard, 1871), 85.

12. Morse Stewart, "Criminal Abortion," *Detroit Review of Medicine and Pharmacy* 2, no. 1 (January 1867), 7.

13. Hugh L. Hodge, *On Criminal Abortion; A Lecture Introductory to the Course on Obstetrics; and Diseases of Women and Children* (Philadelphia: T.K. and P.G. Collins, 1854), 18;

"Editorial: Infantiphobia and Infanticide," *Medical and Surgical Reporter*, March 17, 1866, reprinted in S.W. Butler, ed., *The Medical and Surgical Reporter: A Weekly Journal* 14 (January 1866–July 1866) (Philadelphia: Alfred Martien, 1866), 212; John Todd, "Fashionable Murder," in *Serpents in the Dove's Nest* (Boston: Lee and Shepard, 1867), 9. See also O.C. Turner, "Criminal Abortion," *Boston Medical and Surgical Journal* (April 21, 1870): 300.

14. Andrew Nebinger quoted in "Medical Societies," *Medical and Surgical Reporter* 4, no. 26 (September 19, 1860): 542; Montrose A. Pallen, "Foeticide, or Criminal Abortion," *Medical Archives* 3, no. 4 (April 1869): 201.

15. Storer, *Why Not?*, 12, 37, 81; lunatic asylum director quoted in Ehrlich and Doan, *Abortion Regret*, 21.

16. Ruth Bloch, "American Feminine Ideals in Transition: The Rise of the Moral Mother, 1785–1815," *Feminist Studies* 4, no. 2 (1978): 100–126; Jeanne Boydston, *Home and Work: Housework, Wages, and the Ideology of Labor in the Early Republic* (New York: Oxford University Press, 1994); Steven Mintz, *Huck's Raft: A History of American Childhood* (Cambridge, MA: Belknap, 2004), chap. 4.

17. "Criminal Abortion," *Boston Medical and Surgical Reporter*, May 15, 1844, 302; "Obstetrical Clinic of Prof. Chas. A. Budd," December 18, 1865, *Medical and Surgical Reporter* 14, 46; Gunning S. Bedford, "Vaginal Hysterotomy," *New York Journal of Medical and Collateral Sciences* (March 1844): 199.

18. Horatio R. Storer, MD, *On Criminal Abortion in America* (Philadelphia: J.B. Lippincott, 1860), 54–56, quotation on 56; "Infanticide and Criminal Abortion," *Medical and Surgical Reporter* (April 7, 1866): 277; Pallen, "Foeticide," 204.

19. Chap. 430, *Laws of the State of New York Passed at the Ninety-First Session of the Legislature* (Albany: Van Benthuysen and Sons, 1868), 856–58.

20. Chap. 631, *Laws of the State of New York Passed at the Ninety-Second Session of the Legislature* (Albany: William Gould and Son, 1869), 2:1502–3.

21. Tanfer Emin Tunç, "Unlocking the Mysterious Trunk: Nineteenth-Century American Criminal Abortion Narratives," in *Transcending Borders: Abortion in the Past and Present*, ed. Shannon Stettner, Katrina Ackerman, Kristina Burnett, and Travis Hay (London: Palgrave Macmillan, 2017), 35–52.

22. Augustus St. Clair, "Evil of the Age: The Slaughter of the Innocents," *New York Times*, November 13, 1871, 4–5; "The Evans Abortion Case," *New York Herald*, May 17, 1871, 4; "Supreme Court-General Term," *New York Mercury*, December 14, 1871, 6; "'Dr.' Thomas Lookup Evans," *Brooklyn Daily Eagle*, August 29, 1879, 4; "The Evans Abortion Case," *New York Daily Herald*, May 13, 1871, 8; "The Evans Abortion Case," *New York Daily Herald*, May 19, 1871, 4.

23. Augustus St. Clair, "The Evil of the Age," *New York Times*, August 23, 1871, 6. See also Sahand K. Rahbar, "'The Evil of the Age': The Influence of the *New York Times* on Anti-Abortion Legislation, 1865–1873," *Penn History Review* 23, no. 1 (2016): 146–76.

24. "Abortionists in Court," *New York Commercial Advertiser*, September 1, 1871, 4; "The Van Buskirk Trial," *Brooklyn Daily Eagle*, October 4, 1871, 4; Augustus St. Clair, "The Evil of the Age," *New York Times*, September 1, 1871, 8.

25. New York Medico-Legal Society, "Report on Criminal Abortion," *New York Medical Journal* 15, no. 1 (January 1872): 77, 79 (italics in the original).

26. New York Medico-Legal Society, "Report on Criminal Abortion," 84–86.

27. Chap. 181, *Laws of the State of New York Passed at the Ninety-Fifth Session* (New York: Banks and Brothers, 1872), 1:509–10.

28. Faye E. Dudden, "Women's Rights Advocates and Abortion Law," *Journal of Women's History* 31, no. 3 (2019): 102–23, esp. 113.

11. NEMESIS

1. 1870 federal Census for Thirteenth District, Nineteenth Ward, roll M593_1004, p. 68B, ancestry.com; record in *Trow v. Shannon*, 1878, *New York Court of Appeals, Cases and Briefs*, vol. 51, pp. 51, 4, 22, 35, New York State Archives, Albany; Joseph Trow, November 10, 1859, arriving on the *Congress*, "Arriving Passenger and Crew Lists, 1820–1957," ancestry.com.
2. Marriage record of Joseph Trow and Marie Sherwood Clark, September 24, 1872, New York City marriage records, 1829–1940, familysearch.org; record in *Trow v. Shannon*, 4.
3. Trow v. Shannon, 69.
4. D.M. Bennett, *Anthony Comstock: His Career of Cruelty and Crime* (1878; reprint New York: Da Capo Press, 1971), 1012; Heywood Broun and Margaret Leech, *Anthony Comstock: Roundsman of the Lord* (New York: Albert and Charles Boni, 1927), 36–37 (diary entries are on p. 56). Comstock's historians are legion. See, in particular, Nicola Beisel, *Imperiled Innocents: Anthony Comstock and Family Reproduction in Victorian America* (Princeton, NJ: Princeton University Press, 1997); Amy Werbel, *Lust on Trial: Censorship and the Rise of American Obscenity in the Age of Anthony Comstock* (New York: Columbia University Press, 2018); Amy Sohn, *The Man Who Hated Women: Sex, Censorship, and Civil Liberties in the Gilded Age* (New York: Knopf, 2021); Helen Lefkowitz Horowitz, *Rereading Sex: Battles over Sexual Knowledge and Suppression in Nineteenth-Century America* (New York: Knopf, 2002), chap. 16.
5. Broun and Leech, *Anthony Comstock*, 45–47 (diary quoted on p. 45).
6. Broun and Leech, 59–61, 67; Werbel, *Lust on Trial*, 145–46, 147–48.
7. Werbel, *Lust on Trial*, 52; Anthony Comstock, *Frauds Exposed; Or, How the People Are Deceived and Robbed, and Youth Corrupted. Being a Full Exposure of Various Schemes Operated Through the Mails, and Unearthed by the Author in a Seven Years' Service as a Special Agent of the Post Office Department and Secretary Chief Agent of the New York Society for the Prevention of Vice* (1880; reprint Montclair, NJ: Patterson Smith, 1969), 416.
8. Broun and Leech, *Anthony Comstock*, 71–72.
9. Werbel, *Lust on Trial*, 54–57.
10. Broun and Leech, *Anthony Comstock*, 94 and chap. 7; Debby Applegate, *The Most Famous Man in America: The Biography of Henry Ward Beecher* (New York: Crown, 2007), 422.
11. "An Act for the Suppression of Trade in, and Circulation of, Obscene Literature and Articles of Immoral Use," Forty-Second Congress, Sess. 3, Chapter 258.
12. Comstock, *Frauds Exposed*, 9–12.
13. YMCA report is cited in Werbel, *Lust on Trial*, 90; John Gordon: September 2, 1874, p. 43; Van Wagner: January 17, 1876, p. 63; Beebe: December 1875; Sarah E. Sawyer: October 9, 1873, pp. 27–28, Volume 1, New York Society for the Suppression of Vice Records, 1871–1953, Library of Congress.
14. Christopher Gray, "Madame Restell's Other Profession," *New York Times*, October 10, 2013, RE section, 8.
15. Death record for Charles R. Lohman, January 5, 1877, New York City death records, 1795–1949, familysearch.org. Cause of death is detailed in Clifford R. Browder, *The Wicked-*

est Woman in New York: Madame Restell, the Abortionist (Hamden, CT: Archon, 1988), 154; "Ann Lohman's Burial," *New York Sun*, April 3, 1878, 1.

16. "Last Will and Testament of Charles R. Lohman, signed July 15, 1862," ancestry.com; *New York Times*, January 11, 1877, 2.

17. *Trow v. Shannon*; *New York Herald*, December 12, 1878, 11; "Restell's Money," *New York Herald*, December 10, 1878, 4.

18. "A Free Lecture to Ladies," *New York Herald*, May 16, 1875; "The Proper Care of Woman's Health," *New-York Tribune*, May 18, 1875, 10; "A Strange Lecture for a Woman," *New York Commercial Advertiser*, January 8, 1876, 4; "Anthony Comstock's Prisoner," *New York Herald*, May 10, 1878, 10; Andrea Tone, *Devices and Desires: A History of Contraceptives in America* (New York: Hill and Wang, 2001), 32–35.

19. "The Most Despicable Character," *Brooklyn Daily Eagle*, July 1, 1877.

20. James D. McCabe Jr., *Lights and Shadows of New York Life; Or, the Sights and Sensations of the Great City* (Philadelphia: National Publishing Company, 1872), 628, 629, 630, 624.

21. John H. Warren Jr., *Thirty Years' Battle with Crime, Or the Crying Shame of New York, as Seen Under the Broad Glare of an Old Detective's Lantern* (New York: A.J. White, 1874), 150.

22. "Discovery of a Baby Farming Establishment," *New York Daily Herald*, May 22, 1873, 10; "Starving to Death," *Brooklyn Daily Eagle*, August 20, 1873, 3; "Baby Farming Horrors," *New York Sun*, September 5, 1873, 2; "Shocking Case of Baby Farming," *New York Times*, September 24, 1873, 8; Sherri Broder, *Tramps, Unfit Mothers, and Neglected Children: Negotiating the Family in Late Nineteenth-Century Philadelphia* (Philadelphia: University of Pennsylvania Press, 2002), chap. 5, especially; Ruth Ellen Homrighaus, "Wolves in Women's Clothing: Baby-Farming and the *British Medical Journal*, 1860–1872," *Journal of Family History* 26, no. 3 (July 2001): 350–72. For early press coverage in the United States, see "Baby-Farming in Scotland," *Brooklyn Daily Eagle*, January 4, 1868, 4.

23. Warren, *Thirty Years' Battle with Crime*, 167, 153.

24. "Baby Poisoning," *Brooklyn Times Union*, October 29, 1873, 2; "Baby Farming," *Brooklyn Review*, November 23, 1873, 1.

12. A RECKONING

1. Testimony of Anthony Comstock in *The People on the Complaint of Anthony Comstock v. Ann Lohman*, February 23, 1878, 2–5, Comstock case folder, Madame Restell Papers, Schlesinger Library, Harvard University.

2. Comstock testimony, 5–7.

3. Comstock testimony, 32–33.

4. Comstock testimony, 35–37.

5. Testimony of Anthony Comstock and Charles O. Sheldon in *The People on the Complaint of Anthony Comstock*, February 23, 1878, pp. 11–13, 26–28, 13–14; listing of stock is in entry for February 11, 1878, p. 111, volume 1, New York Society for the Suppression of Vice Records, 1871–1953, Library of Congress.

6. "Mme. Restell's Arrest," *New York Times*, February 13, 1878, 8.

7. Anthony Comstock to David R. Parker, February 13, 1878, Ann Lohman folder, box 23, RG 28, Postal Inspection Service, 1832–1970, Records of the Post Office Department, National Archives, Washington, DC.

8. "Mme. Restell's Arrest," *New York Times*, February 14, 1878, 8.

9. "Mme. Restell's Arrest," *New York Times*, February 14, 1878, 8; "Mme. Restell Released on Bail," *New York Times*, February 15, 1878, 2. See also the bail bond forms for James Gonoude and Jacob Schwarz, February 14, 1878, in Comstock folder, Madame Restell Papers.

10. "The Case of Mme. Restell," *New York Times*, February 16, 1878, 3.

11. "The Case of Mme. Restell," 3.

12. *Christian Union*, February 20, 1878, 17, 8.

13. "The Wages of Sin," *Brooklyn Daily Eagle*, February 24, 1878, 4; "The Case of Mme. Restell," *New York Times*, February 24, 1878, 5.

14. "The Wages of Sin," 4.

15. "Madame Restell Again in Court," *New-York Tribune*, February 28, 1878, 8.

16. "Mme. Lohman-Restell," *New York Daily Herald,* March 2, 1878, 9; Records of Examination of Ann Lohman, February 27 and March 1, 1878, Comstock folder, Madame Restell Papers.

17. "Mme. Lohman-Restell"; "Madam Restell in Custody," *New York Sun*, March 2, 1878, 1.

18. "Madame Restell," *New York Evening Post*, March 5, 1878, 4; "Mme Restell," *New York Herald*, March 6, 1878, 4.

19. "Mme. Restell," *New York Herald*, March 8, 1878, 8.

20. Marriage record for Carrie Summers Purdy and William Pickell Shannon, March 10, 1878, ancestry.com; indictment of Ann Lohman, Comstock file, Madame Restell Papers; "Madame Restell Indicted," *New-York Tribune*, March 13, 1878, 3; "Madame Restell's Plea," *New-York Tribune*, March 30, 1878, 7; "Restell," *Brooklyn Daily Eagle*, April 2, 1878, 4.

21. "Restell"; "End of an Infamous Life," *New-York Tribune*, April 2, 1878, 1.

13. "END OF AN INFAMOUS LIFE"

1. "End of an Infamous Life," *New-York Tribune*, April 2, 1878, 1; "End of a Criminal Life," *New York Times*, April 2, 1878, 1.

2. Orlando Stewart to DA Phelps, April 1, 1878, folder marked "Death of Madame Restell, 1878," Madame Restell Papers, Schlesinger Library, Harvard University; "End of an Infamous Life," 1; entry for Ann Lohman, p. 111, vol. 1, New York Society for the Suppression of Vice Records, 1871–1953, Library of Congress.

3. "End of an Infamous Life," 1; "End of a Criminal Life," 1; death certificate of Ann Lohman, April 1, 1878, New York City Municipal Archives.

4. "End of an Infamous Life," 1; "End of a Criminal Life," 1; "The Woman Restell," *Brooklyn Daily Eagle*, April 2, 1878, 2; "A Hurried Funeral," *New York Times*, April 3, 1878, 5.

5. "A Hurried Funeral," 5; "Ann Lohman's Burial," *New York Sun*, April 3, 1878, 1.

6. "Madame Restell's Will," *New-York Tribune*, April 5, 1878, 3; "Last Will and Testament of Ann Lohman, April 28, 1877," ancestry.com.

7. "Last Will and Testament of Ann Lohman."

8. "Madame Restell's Will," 3.

9. *Trow v. Shannon*, 78. NY 446; 1879 NY Lexis 935; Record in *Trow v. Shannon*, *New York Court of Appeals, Cases and Briefs*, vol. 51, 1878, New York State Library, Albany; "Civil Notes," *New-York Tribune*, April 22, 1878, 2; "Restell's Money," *New York Daily Herald*, December 10, 1878, 3; "Law Reports," *New York Times*, December 10, 1878, 3; "Mrs. Restell's Heirs," *New York Daily Herald*, December 11, 1878, 8; *New York Times*, April 8, 1879; *New*

York Dispatch, March 2, 1884, 9. Trow's death date is available at www.findagrave.com /memorial/130095179/joseph-trow.

10. Caroline and William Farrell appear on East 116th Street in the 1880 U.S. federal census (roll 898, p. 51), ancestry.com. Caroline is listed as keeping house, while William has no occupation. Last will and testament of Caroline Farrell, 1881, "New York Wills and Probate Records, New York Surrogate Court, Wills, Volume 292, 1881–1882," ancestry.com. Caroline's death is listed at www.findagrave.com/memorial/200452299/caroline-farrell. William's death is at www.findagrave.com/memorial/200452266/william-b-farrell.

11. 1880 federal census for New York, New York; Roll: 895; Page: 323C; Enumeration District: 577; Shannon children are noted on gravestone at Sleepy Hollow Cemetery; Carrie S. Shannon death record, December 16, 1891, in New York, New York Extracted Death Index, 1862–1948, ancestry.com; www.findagrave.com/memorial/63161298/caroline-s-shannon; "Last Will and Testament of Carrie S. Shannon, July 8, 1891," ancestry.com; 1900 Census Place: Manhattan, New York, New York; Roll: 1113; Page: 5; Enumeration District: 0743; FHL microfilm: 1241114, ancestry.com.

12. Wedding: November 2, 1888, Presbyterian Historical Society; Philadelphia, Pennsylvania; U.S., Presbyterian Church Records, 1701–1907; Accession Number: 97 0415a 53a 2 Box 1, ancestry.com; 1910 census record for Charles R. Purdy: Year: 1910; Census Place: Islip, Suffolk, New York; Roll: T624_1082; Page: 5A; Enumeration District: 1373; FHL microfilm: 1375095, ancestry.com; 1920 census (including mention of "gentleman" as occupation): Year: 1920; Census Place: Islip, Suffolk, New York; Roll: T624_1082; Page: 5A; Enumeration District: 1373; FHL microfilm: 1375095, ancestry.com; "Purdy," Brooklyn *Daily Eagle*, January 30, 1922, 20.

13. *Trow's General Directory of the Boroughs of Manhattan and the Bronx, City of New York* (New York: Trow Directory Printing, 1901), 753, 1069; Christopher Gray, "Madame Restell's Other Profession," *New York Times*, October 10, 2013, 8; "The Langham Hotel Sold," *New York Times*, December 31, 1902, 1; *New York Times*, June 6, 1903, 1; "Glimpses from the Metropolis," *Democrat and Chronicle* (Rochester, New York), January 31, 1903; "Auction Sales," *Brooklyn Daily Eagle*, June 7, 1903, 5.

14. Chapter 383, passed May 13, 1880, *Laws of the State of New York Passed at the One Hundred and Third Session of the Legislature* (Albany, NY: Weed, Parsons, 1880), 419–20.

15. *Griswold v. Connecticut* 381 U.S. 479 (1965); *Eisenstadt v. Baird* 405 U.S. 438 (1972); *Roth v. United States* 354 U.S. 476 (1957); *Miller v. California* 413 U.S. 15 (1973); Mary Kekatos, "USPS Is Allowed to Continue Delivering Abortion Pills, Justice Department Says," *ABC News*, January 4, 2023, https://abcnews.go.com/Health/usps-allowed-continue -delivering-abortion-pills-justice-department/story?id=96177613.

16. "Report on Criminal Abortion," *Transactions of the American Medical Association* (Philadelphia: printed for the association, 1859), 12:75–76; *Roe v. Wade* 410 U.S. 113 (1973).

17. Leslie J. Reagan, *When Abortion Was a Crime: Women, Medicine, and Law in the United States, 1867–1973* (Berkeley: University of California Press, 1997); Rickie Solinger, *The Abortionist: A Woman Against the Law* (New York: Free Press, 1994); Lisa Riggin, *San Francisco's Queen of Vice: The Strange Career of Abortionist Inez Brown Burns* (Lincoln: University of Nebraska Press, 2017); Laura Kaplan, *The Story of Jane: The Legendary Underground Feminist Abortion Service* (New York: Pantheon, 1995).

18. Jessica Arons, "The Last Clinics Standing," American Civil Liberties Union, www.aclu .org/issues/reproductive-freedom/abortion/last-clinics-standing; Alesha E. Doan, *Opposition and Intimidation: The Abortion Wars and Strategies of Political Harassment* (Ann Arbor:

University of Michigan Press, 2007); Julia Tasset and Lisa H. Harris, "Harm Reduction for Abortion in the United States," *Obstetrics and Gynecology* 131, no. 4 (2018): 621–24; Lisa Harris and Daniel Grossman, "Complications of Unsafe and Self-Managed Abortion," *New England Journal of Medicine* 382, no. 11 (2020): 1029–40.

19. Lisa H. Harris, "My Day as an Abortion Provider," *New York Times*, October 22, 2019, A23; Diana Greene Foster, *The Turnaway Study: Ten Years, a Thousand Women, and the Consequences of Having—or Being Denied—an Abortion* (New York: Scribner, 2020).

INDEX

menopause, 25
Merritt, Henry W., 59–60, 64, 68–69
Meyers, George, 202, 217
middle-class reformers, 108, 124
middle-class women and families,
nineteenth-century, 45–46, 124–26;
abortion and married women, 36–39,
45–46, 125, 231–36; fewer children
and family limitation, 124, 231–32;
views of illegitimate pregnancies and
abortion, 107–8, 125–26; views of
the purpose and value of children,
124–25, 236
Middlesex County, Massachusetts, 28
midwifery, 10, 21–23, 142, 178, 226; Ann
Lohman's training in, 21–25; charges
for services, 22, 137–38; Mrs. Bird, 35,
80; rejection by male medical doctors,
22–23, 231, 237
mifepristone, 27, 288
Miller v. California (1973), 286
Millspaugh, Peter, 147
Millspaugh, Thomas, 147–50
mini-Comstock laws, so-called, 252,
286–87
miscarriages: Charles Lohman's (Mauriceau's) views on, 178–79; Madame
Restell and the Bodine case, 130–31;
Madame Restell and the Purdy case,
54–59, 67; Madame Restell's 1839
grand jury investigation, 42–43;
medical care following, 58–59;
through herbal abortifacients or
manual intervention, 6, 7, 10–11, 28,
57–58, 130–31
misoprostol, 27, 288
Missouri State Medical Association, 235
Mohr, James C., 29, 98
Moore, Dorothy, 121
Moral Physiology (Owen), 173, 176–77
Morand's Elixir, 175
Morgan, Delia, 147–48
*Morning Courier and New-York
Enquirer*, 64
Morrell, John, 60, 65, 67, 72

motherhood, and women's duty, 25–26,
37, 42, 49, 63, 136–37, 175–76, 209,
221, 228–29, 232, 234, 236, 244, 247
Mott, Elizabeth, 24
Mount Auburn Cemetery (Cambridge,
Massachusetts), 260
Munson, Eliza Ann, 92–96
"The Mystery of Marie Rogêt" (Poe), 74, 97

Napoleon Bonaparte, 166
National Police Gazette, 122, 182; Applegate story, 118–20, 134; Bodine trial
coverage, 133–34, 138–39, 140, 145,
157, 158; Cordelia Grant story, 187, 200
Native American women, 7, 15, 21–22, 28
nativism, 5, 45–46, 127, 232–33
Nebinger, Andrew, 235
Neidlinger, Frederica Wilhelmina
("Mina"), 202–18; affidavit on
Madame Restell's abduction of her
child, 202–6; extortion story, 206, 207,
215; Madame Restell and the adoption
of Neidlinger's child, 202–3, 206–14,
216–18; Madame Restell's letter to the
press rebutting the accusations, 205–6;
Madame Restell's refusal to name the
adoptive mother, 209–13; newspapers
on Madame Restell's arrest, 203–5;
stay at Madame Restell's lying-in
hospital, 202–7
New Canaan, Connecticut, 247, 248
New England Puritans, 247
New York Asylum for Lying-In Women,
81–82
New York Atlas, 3, 65
New York City Almshouse at Bellevue,
46, 115, 120–22
New York County Court of General
Sessions, 91–92, 186, 275–78; Bodine
trial, 136–57; Comstock's arrest of
Madame Restell, 275–78; Dall case,
44, 46–47; Purdy trial, 60, 67–74, 75,
76, 78
New York Daily Herald, 102, 165
New York Evening Express, 82, 102, 222

Primrose, Randolph L., 94

prostaglandins, 26–27, 43

prostitution in antebellum New York,
17–18, 51, 106–7, 108–11; the Bowery,
109; brothel riots, 106–7; brothels,
17–18, 106–7, 120, 138; and seduction
narratives, 108–11; wealth of brothel
madams, 138

publishing industry in antebellum New
York, 19

puerperal fever, 46, 239

Purdy, Ambrose, 272, 274–76

Purdy, Ann Maria, 54–78, 81, 83, 86,
130, 181, 191; death from tuberculosis, 61, 70; deposition, 59–60, 61, 65,
67–69, 74–75; home at 341 Broome
Street, 59–60, 68–69; services from
Madame Restell, 54–59. *See also* Purdy,
Ann Maria (trial of 1841)

Purdy, Ann Maria (trial of 1841), 54–78;
Madame Restell's appeal and overturned conviction, 72–76, 132;
Madame Restell's arrest and imprisonment, 59–60, 64–65, 67, 81; Madame
Restell's conviction, 72–73; Madame
Restell's defense witnesses, 70–72;
Madame Restell's public letters, 73,
75–78; newspaper coverage, 61–64, 72,
74, 75–76; prosecution witnesses,
67–70, 76; Purdy's deposition and its
admissibility, 59–60, 61, 65, 67–69,
74–75

Purdy, Caroline Summers. *See* Farrell,
Caroline Summers Purdy (daughter
of Madame Restell); Shannon, Carrie
Summers Purdy (granddaughter of
Madame Restell)

Purdy, Charles Robert (grandson of Madame Restell), 218, 221, 259, 263–64,
271–73, 278, 279–81, 283–84, 285–86;
death, 285; and Madame Restell's 1878
arrest and indictment, 271–72, 273,
278; and Madame Restell's suicide,
279–81; and Madame Restell's will
and bequests, 283–84

Purdy, Eleanor, 184

Purdy, Florence Annie, 218, 219

Purdy, Frances Annie, 218, 219, 256–57,
258

Purdy, Gabriel, 184, 282

Purdy, Isaac Lent, 184, 218–19, 256–57,
282

Purdy, William (husband of Ann Maria
Purdy), 59, 61, 67–68, 70, 71, 73, 76

quickening doctrine, 28–29, 144, 229–30,
231, 242; and abortion legislation,
28–29, 30, 58, 97–98, 101, 132, 144,
155, 242; Bodine's pregnancy timeline
and Madame Restell's 1847 trial, 132,
139–44, 146, 147, 151, 154, 155;
English common law, 28–29, 242;
Grant's abortion, 194–95; Lohman/
Mauriceau on, 175

"Report on Criminal Abortion" (1872
report of New York Medico-Legal
Society), 241–42

Restell, Madame: advertisements, 1–2, 10,
25–26, 32–33, 34–39, 46–47, 51, 63,
78, 89, 184; Applegate infant disappearance, 104–28, 158, 203; Bodine
trial, 129–63; competition of other
female physicians, 24, 35, 79, 89, 93,
260; Comstock's arrest of, 254, 255,
265–78; Dall case and first indictment,
43–47; death by suicide, 278, 280–82;
Dixon's *Polyanthos* on, 47–51, 61–63,
64, 67, 72, 74, 85–87; first grand jury
investigation (1839), 39–43; grand jury
presentment against (1841), 51–53;
Grant's allegations, 184–201; home at
162 Chambers Street, 1, 3, 163, 169,
183, 184, 189–91, 194, 196–97, 202,
204, 215, 219–20; home at 657 Fifth
Avenue, 6, 214–15, 220–23, 245–47,
256, 278, 279–81, 285–86; letter
"To Married Women" (1839), 36–39;
lying-in hospital, 6, 28, 81, 104–6, 115,
118–19, 190–91, 202–7; Munson case,

About the Author

Nicholas L. Syrett is an associate dean and professor of women, gender, and sexuality studies at the University of Kansas. He is the author of *The Company He Keeps: A History of White College Fraternities*, *American Child Bride: A History of Minors and Marriage in the United States*, and *An Open Secret: The Family Story of Robert and John Gregg Allerton*. He lives in Lawrence, Kansas.

PUBLISHING IN THE
PUBLIC INTEREST

Thank you for reading this book published by The New Press; we hope you enjoyed it. New Press books and authors play a crucial role in sparking conversations about the key political and social issues of our day.

We hope that you will stay in touch with us. Here are a few ways to keep up to date with our books, events, and the issues we cover:

- Sign up at www.thenewpress.com/subscribe to receive updates on New Press authors and issues and to be notified about local events

- www.facebook.com/newpressbooks

- www.twitter.com/thenewpress

- www.instagram.com/thenewpress

Please consider buying New Press books not only for yourself, but also for friends and family and to donate to schools, libraries, community centers, prison libraries, and other organizations involved with the issues our authors write about.

The New Press is a 501(c)(3) nonprofit organization; if you wish to support our work with a tax-deductible gift please visit www.thenewpress.com/donate or use the QR code below.